CRITICAL SURVEY OF POETRY
Asian Poets

Editor

Rosemary M. Canfield Reisman
Charleston Southern University

SALEM PRESS
A Division of EBSCO Publishing, Ipswich, Massachusetts

Cover photo:
Matsuo Bashō (© Tibor Bognar/Corbis)

Copyright © 2012, by Salem Press, A Division of EBSCO Publishing, Inc.
All rights in this book are reserved. No part of this work may be used or reproduced in any manner whatsoever or transmitted in any form or by any means, electronic or mechanical, including photocopy, recording, or any information storage and retrieval system, without written permission from the copyright owner except in the case of brief quotations embodied in critical articles and reviews or in the copying of images deemed to be freely licensed or in the public domain. For information address the publisher, Salem Press, at csr@salempress.com.

ISBN: 978-1-42983-667-8

CONTENTS

Contributors iv

Chinese Poetry 1
Tibetan Poetry 25
Du Fu 36
Li Bo 43
Li Qingzhao 53
Meng Haoran 61
Ruan Ji 66
Tao Qian 74
Wang Wei 83
Xie Lingyun 93

Indian English Poetry 100
Postcolonial Poetry 117
Agha Shahid Ali 129
Vikram Seth 134
Rabindranath Tagore 140
Vālmīki 152

Japanese Poetry to 1800 157
Japanese Poetry Since 1800 178
Issa 189
Matsuo Bashō 199
Kenji Miyazawa 207
Mitsuye Yamada 214
Yosano Akiko 221

Checklist for Explicating a Poem 229
Bibliography 232
Guide to Online Resources 241
Geographical Index 244
Category Index 245
Subject Index 247

CONTRIBUTORS

Richard P. Benton
Trinity College

Nicholas Birns
Eugene Lang College, The New School

Harold Branam
Savannah State University

Susan Butterworth
Salem State College

Paul A. Draghi
Indiana University

Desiree Dreeuws
Sunland, California

Cliff Edwards
Fort Hays State University

Lydia Forssander-Song
Trinity Western University

Keiko Matsui Gibson
Kanda University of International Studies

Morgan Gibson
Urbana, Illinois

Kenneth A. Howe
Michigan State University

Helen Jaskoski
California State University, Fullerton

Rebecca Kuzins
Pasadena, California

Jeanne Larsen
Hollins College

Robert W. Leutner
University of Iowa

Leon Lewis
Appalachian State University

R. C. Lutz
CII Group

John Marney
Oakland University

James O'Brien
University of Wisconsin

Makarand Paranjape
Indian Institute of Technology

Rosemary M. Canfield Reisman
Charleston Southern University

J. Thomas Rimer
University of Pittsburgh

James Whitlark
Texas Tech University

Pauline Yu
University of Minnesota

CHINESE POETRY

China has traditionally been a nation of poets. From ancient times through the first decade of the twentieth century, Chinese poetry held a position of importance unequaled by poetry in any other nation. By virtue of several important factors—linguistic, cultural, social, educational, and political—Chinese poetry, until the downfall of the monarchy in 1911, manifested certain unique characteristics.

Ancient Chinese writing

The earliest known examples of Chinese script were inscribed on tortoise shells and animal bones around 1300 B.C.E., the time of the Shang Dynasty (c. 1600-1066 B.C.E.). These objects are referred to as "oracle bones" because they were employed by shamans, or priests, to predict future events. Later in the Shang, inscriptions were made on bronze vessels. When the Zhou (Chou) Dynasty (1066-221 B.C.E.) succeeded the Shang, its bronzes were also inscribed. A series of hunting songs carved on boulders, erroneously termed "stone drums," dates to around 400 B.C.E. In 219 B.C.E., by order of Shi Huangdi (Shih Huang Ti), the first emperor of the Qin (Ch'in) Dynasty (221-206 B.C.E.), the Chinese script underwent a standardization process. Two new types of script were devised: One, to be used for formal and official purposes, was called *xiao juan* (*hsiao chüan*); the other, intended for general use, was called *li shu* (clerk's style). Because it was found that the speediest and most efficient way of writing *li shu* was with brush and ink, such writing soon developed into an art in itself, the art of calligraphy. By the time of the Han Dynasty (206 B.C.E.-220 C.E.), calligraphy had achieved equality as an art with painting and poetry. Calligraphy and painting not only were seen as twin arts of the brush but also were intimately associated with poetry. This attitude is shown in the famous remark made by Su Dongpo (Su Tung-p'o) about the great Wang Wei, who was outstanding as a calligrapher, a painter, and a poet: "In his poetry there is painting, and in his painting, poetry."

The distinctive visual properties of Chinese script that made its writing an art transcend its pictographic origins. Although Chinese writing began with pictographic word-signs, these word-signs were soon conventionalized into almost complete abstractions. Single characters were then combined to form not only compound but also complex characters, many simply with determinants of the broadest meaning and others with signs to indicate sound. The Chinese written language thereby expanded from around twenty-five hundred characters in early times to between forty thousand and fifty thousand by the Qing (Ch'ing) Dynasty, which was founded in the seventeenth century.

Writing such characters demands skill in drawing, a sense of form and proportion, and a sensitivity to the qualities of line, dot, and hook. Although a number of single

A fourteenth century wenrenhua, *or literati painting, featuring a poem inspired by the artwork.*

characters can be combined into one, the resulting character must occupy the same amount of space and have the same square appearance as that of any other character. Furthermore, calligraphers tended to view the strokes in their characters in terms of natural objects and forces. To them, a horizontal stroke was a mass of clouds; a hook, a bent bow; a dot, a falling rock; a turning stroke, a brass hook; a drawn-out line, an old dry vine; a free stroke, a runner on his mark; and so on. Painters considered calligraphy their training ground, and poets saw their art as a kind of word painting. The three arts of calligraphy, painting, and poetry can be seen woven together in that school of composite art known as *wenrenhua* (*wen-jen-hua*; literary "men's painting"). Here, the scholar-artist would display his calligraphy in the brushstrokes he used to fashion trees, rocks, or bamboo shoots. Then he would balance his picture with a poem inspired by his painting, written in his best calligraphy, as an integral part of his composition. Later, his friends or other connoisseurs might write additional poems or laudatory inscriptions on his painting that would add to its value.

Although the visual was preeminent in the development of Chinese poetry, it must not be thought that the musical quality of the words, even in silent reading, was ignored or considered unimportant. The sounds of spoken Chinese in its various dialects have their phonetic systems of vowels and consonants and also their distinctive tonal systems, which depend on the movement of or the holding of the pitch of the voice.

At the same time, however, classical Chinese written characters are independent of any particular pronunciation or dialect. The origins of this literary language can be traced to a period sometime after the establishment of the Zhou Dynasty, when a new class of men began to replace the Shang priesthood as magical religion gave way to a philosophy of history. This new class was the scholar class; only such men could memorize the large number of characters that their language then contained. These scholars, later called the literati, were responsible for the transmission of China's cultural heritage to future generations.

Classical Chinese

By the fall of the Han Dynasty in 220 C.E., the literati had so monopolized the Chinese script that it had broken away from the vernacular language and gone its separate way. Soon, it was recognized that writing need not be restricted to utilitarian purposes—that it was capable of producing aesthetic pleasure. This view elevated the status of belles lettres to a high position for the first time in Chinese history. In this way, *wenli* (*wen-li*; classical Chinese), or *wenyan* (*wen-yan*; literary Chinese), became the only form of the written language used everywhere for all serious purposes, quite divorced from the spoken language. Such written Chinese has no pronunciation of its own but is pronounced in as many different ways as there are dialects. All Chinese poetry considered as literature has been written in *wenli*, or classical Chinese, from its formulation until the advent of the Chinese literary renaissance in 1917, when it was almost entirely replaced by bai hua (*pai hua*), or the living language of the people, used for literary as well as practical purposes.

Regardless of the independence of *wenli* with respect to the sounds that are attached to it, Chinese poetry has its own peculiar sound structure, which includes metrical forms as well as rhyme and other auditory effects. In short, there is a "music" of Chinese poetry that has its own rules of versification relative to genre and purpose. Indeed, this sound structure of Chinese poetry is so peculiar to itself that it is impossible to render in translation.

Chinese Versification

Chinese versification is based on two principal auditory qualities that may be attached to the Chinese word-signs. Every character is monosyllabic when sounded, and each monosyllable has a fixed pitch, called a "tone," which is semantic—that is, gives a clue to its meaning. Hence, generally speaking, the number of syllables in a poetic line is equivalent to the number of characters in that line. The number of characters and their monosyllables, however, is not invariably equal to the number of "words" in a given line, because there are some characters that never appear alone and make up "words" of two or more characters. The regularity or the variation of the number of characters (or syllables) and the regularity or the variation of their fixed tones are the basis of Chinese poetic meter and play the major role in Chinese versification, together with some incidence of rhyme.

During the Tang (T'ang) Dynasty (618-907), classical Chinese had eight tones, which could be reduced to four pairs. By the Yuan (Yüan) Dynasty (1279-1368), the eight tones had been reduced to four. These pitches were distinguished, ranging from one to four, as level (*ping*, or *p'ing*), rising (*shang*), falling (*qu*, or *ch'ü*), and entering (*ze*, or *tse*). These four tones, however, were arbitrarily reduced for poetic purposes to two, the first being regarded as level while all the rest were simply considered as deflected. For example, in the demanding form of the *lüshi* (*lü-shih*; regulated poem), the requirement was that a poem be made up of eight lines of equal length with each line comprising either five or seven characters. The poet had various tone patterns from which he or she could choose, depending on whether five or seven characters was selected for the line length. The first full line might call for the following tone pattern: deflected (but level permitted), deflected, level, level, deflected. Each of the rest of the lines would have its specific tone pattern. Such regulated verse also required a particular rhyme scheme. In addition to varieties of pitch, the poet could use contrasts in the length or quantity of syllables, because the tones differ in length and movement. All this sound variation gives the recitation of a Chinese poem a singsong quality.

Music and Folksongs

From the beginning, Chinese poetry has been intimately connected with music. The folk poems collected in the earliest anthology, *Shijing* (traditionally fifth century B.C.E.; *The Book of Songs*, 1937), were originally songs meant to be chanted or sung. Some were popular songs, others courtly songs or sacrificial and temple songs. The popular songs were intended to be sung to the accompaniment of music with group dancing. Early commentators on the *The Book of Songs* were musicians as well as literary critics.

The history of Chinese poetry shows the marked influence of folk songs. *The Book of Songs* established a poetic tradition that was to be followed by serious poets until the twentieth century. Its typical four-line character poem became an esteemed and standard form. Its tone of refined emotional restraint, its sympathy with human nature, and its general lack of malice toward others became a poetic ideal followed by many later poets. A number of other standard Chinese poetic forms were derived from folk songs, such as the Han *yuefu* (*yüeh-fu*), the Tang *ci* (*tz'u*), and the Yuan *qu* (*ch'ü*). All these standard forms were derived from the songs of the people, but once they became the standard fare of the literati, the words and music were divorced from each other, and the poetry was written to be read rather than sung, with little or no regard for its musical potential. The history of Chinese poetry also shows that once a form became too refined and overly artificial—too far removed from normal reality—poets would return to folk traditions for new inspiration.

The politics of poetry

Certain cultural factors peculiar to China, quite apart from the nature of its language and the relation of that language to the other arts, have also shaped Chinese poetry. Although philosophy and religion have played important roles (particularly Confucianism, but also Daoism and Buddhism), perhaps the major role has been played by government. From the time of the early Zhou Dynasty, the Chinese state took a decided interest in poetry. The government realized that the popular songs of the people could serve as an index to the ways in which the people felt about the government and their lives under it. Rulers or their emissaries would travel over the feudal states collecting popular songs and their musical scores. A department of music called the Yuefu (Yüeh-fu; "music bureau") was established for this purpose. Although it languished for a time, it was revived by Wudi, the emperor, in 125 B.C.E. Thus, folk poems were written down and preserved, inspiring sophisticated poets to imitate them in their own work.

Because the difficulty of the Chinese written script had led to the formation of a scholar class from whose ranks the government was obliged to select its officials, teachers such as the great Confucius (551-479 B.C.E.) were engaged primarily in educating and training students as prospective government servants. Confucius believed that the study of poetry had an important role in the development of moral character, a prerequisite of just and efficient government. For this reason, he selected from the government collections of the feudal states the poems that make up *The Book of Songs*, which he edited and used as a textbook in his seminars. After his death and the official sanction of the Confucian doctrine during the Han Dynasty, *The Book of Songs* became one of the five official classics, which, together with the four books, made up the nine official classics considered indispensable to the education of the scholar-official.

During the Han Dynasty, the government decided that the best way to discover "men of talent" suitable for public service was on the basis of merit, and a merit system based on competitive examinations was established. The government began to employ the Confucian-trained graduates of the National University. This practice indissolubly linked an education in the Confucian classics with an official career, and by the time of the Tang Dynasty, a nationwide system of public competitive examinations to recruit officials on the basis of merit had been established. Theoretically, these competitive examinations were open to all Chinese citizens except those who followed certain occupations classified as base or common. The subsequent major Chinese dynasties relied on these public examinations to obtain the best possible government officials until as late as 1905, when the system was abandoned as obsolete. Thus, for many centuries, the civil-service examination system provided the ruling class with an influx of new talent that had undergone intensive intellectual and artistic training, including skill in the writing of poetry.

The system required a candidate to acquire three successive degrees—taken, respectively, at the county, province, and national capital levels—before being eligible for official appointment. The first degree, that of *shengyuan* (*sheng-yüan*; "government student"), and the second degree, that of *xiucai* (*hsiu-ts-ai*; "budding talent"), were simply preparatory for the third and highest, that of *jinshi* (*chin-shih*; "metropolitan graduate"), the acquisition of which entitled the graduate to be appointed to some official post in the government. The *jinshi* degree required a thorough knowledge of the Confucian classics, skill in calligraphy, and the ability to write poems as well as essays. The standards were high, and only a few of the many candidates were passed by the examiners.

The prevalence of this system of competitive examinations had a profound effect not only on Chinese society, education, and politics but also on literature. Apart from its role in perpetuating poetic conventions from generation to generation, the civil-service experience furnished themes that are common to Chinese poetry as a whole. Indeed the vast majority of Chinese poets were government officials.

Grammar and syntax

The grammar and syntax of Chinese have also played their part in the shaping of China's poetry. Some writers have declared that the Chinese language has no grammar and that its words may serve as any part of speech. Neither of these allegations is correct. Although Chinese has no inflection of number, case, person, tense, or gender—and more words in Chinese than in English have multiple functions—Chinese verbs do have aspects, and some words are normally nouns, whereas others are normally verbs. Although the basic pattern of the Chinese sentence is subject followed by predicate, the Chinese "subject" is the topic of the sentence, not necessarily the agent that performs the action of the verb. In addition, the subject or the verb of the Chinese sentence is often omitted, and coordinate constructions frequently lack conjunctions.

The Chinese language is, therefore, more compact and concise than English. In economy of expression, it resembles a telegram in English, and *wenli*, or classical Chinese, is even more abbreviated than *bai hua*, or everyday speech. If Chinese is more sparing in its words than English, however, it is also less precise. If this feature is a disadvantage in prose concerned with the particular, it is a distinct advantage in Chinese poetry, which is concerned essentially with the universal. Chinese poetry can therefore exploit its compactness and economy of expression in conjunction with its grammatical and syntactic fluidity to enhance its power to mean far more than it says.

Zhou Dynasty (1066-221 b.c.e.)

The earliest great monument of Chinese poetry is *The Book of Songs*, an anthology of folk poems selected and edited by Confucius. The poems themselves come from the earlier period of the Zhou Dynasty, from between 1000 and 700 b.c.e. Their collection and preservation by Confucius, China's greatest teacher, shows the importance he attached to the study of poetry, which he believed was essential to the proper moral development of man, and since his time, *The Book of Songs* has been regarded as one of the great classics of Chinese literature.

The Book of Songs not only possesses great aesthetic value but also is an important historical document that strongly influenced all subsequent Chinese poetry. Revealing the minds and hearts of the Chinese people during the ancient Zhou times, it established a poetic tradition that was followed by later Chinese poets down to modern times. Throughout the history and development of Chinese poetry, *The Book of Songs* has served as a model of poetic eloquence, a storehouse of words, images, themes, and poetic forms (its typical four-character line became a standard form), and a continual source of inspiration to later poets.

By the beginning of the fifth century b.c.e., the power of the feudal state of Zhou had begun to wane, and new national states emerged whose rulers appropriated the title *wang* ("king"). Of these new states, two emerged as the most powerful—Chu in the south and Qin in the northwest. Chu had become a prosperous and beautiful state with a high degree of refined culture. The leisurely cultivation resulting from its economic prosperity eventually produced a series of popular religious songs that were collected under the title *Jiuge* (*Chiu Ko*; nine songs). These elegant songs dating from the fifth century b.c.e. became the model for an irregular and flexible type of elegy that was to inspire sophisticated poets to create a new poetic genre, the *Chu ci* (*Ch'u tz'u*; "Chu elegy").

By the next century, an identifiable person emerged from the anonymity of collective authorship to become China's first known poet. This was Qu Yuan (Ch'ü Yüan; 343?-290? b.c.e.), author of the distinctive masterpiece "Li sao" (*The Li Sao, an Elegy on Encountering Sorrows*, 1929). A son of the nobility, he had served his king as second in rank to the prime minister. Having for some reason lost his political office, however, Qu Yuan was exiled to wander throughout the land. Deciding to devote his life to poetry, he eventually composed *The Li Sao*, a poem that significantly influenced the course of Chinese poetry. Qu Yuan's work conferred distinction on the new genre of the *Chu ci* and inspired a school of poetry responsible for the establishment of a Chinese elegiac tradition that continued to exist until modern times. This tradition eventually led directly to the creation of another new genre, the Han *fu*.

QIN AND HAN DYNASTIES (221 B.C.E.-220 C.E.)

A struggle for power went on among the feudal states during what is called the Warring States Period (475-221 B.C.E.). This struggle was concluded when the state of Qin succeeded in crushing all opponents to form the first unified empire in Chinese history. Prince Zheng of Qin, who ascended the throne in 221 B.C.E. as Shi Huangdi, was a man of authoritarian mold: During his reign, all literature of which he disapproved was burned, and the Chinese script was standardized.

The earliest examples of Qin poems appear in *The Book of Songs*, but they do not differ significantly from the rest of the poetry in the collection. Other specimens of Qin poetry appear in the hunting songs carved on the so-called stone drums. The most important Qin scholar and poet was Li Si (Li Ssu; 280-208 B.C.E.), who was the scholar the emperor assigned to standardize the Chinese script and who initated a new poetic genre—the *song ci* (*sung tz'u*), or panegyric. When the emperor toured the country, large stone tablets were erected on which were carved panegyrics to commemorate his visits to various places. These imperial panegyrics were composed and inscribed by Li Si.

The Qin Dynasty did not last long. When Shi Huangdi died in 210 B.C.E., rebellions broke out, resulting in internal warfare. This anarchy was resolved with the establishment of the Han Dynasty in 207 B.C.E. During the Han Dynasty, two new poetic genres made their appearance—the *fu* and the *yuefu*. Generally, the word *fu* means "to display," and specifically, it means "to chant or to narrate." As a poem, the *fu* originally was one to be chanted rather than sung—that is, performed without musical accompaniment. Under the Han, the *fu* became a poem of social criticism, but later this motive was replaced by the desire to treat its subject in an elegant or refined manner. This later motive eventually resulted in cutting the poem off from the real world, and even some of the best writers of such *fu* considered them frivolous exercises, worthless as literature. Nevertheless, the *fu* dominated the Han period.

At its best, the *fu* is characterized by flowing rhythm, pleasant rhyme, and splendid imagery. An offshoot of the *Chu ci*, the form came to prominence when Wudi (r. 140-87 B.C.E.) became fascinated by the work of the great Han *fu* writer, Sima Xiangru (Ssu-ma Hsiang-ju; c. 180-117 B.C.E.). Author of such *fu* as "Zi xu fu" ("Master Nil"), "Shang lin fu" ("Supreme Park"), "Meiren fu" ("The Beautiful Lady"), and "Chang men fu" ("Long Doors"), Sima Xiangru was rewarded for his skill by appointments to important government posts.

The Han *yuefu* emerged from the popular folk songs collected by the government's music bureau. This sophisticated type came to maturity about 200 C.E., by which time it had been discovered that the form was particularly suited to narration. Perhaps the most famous writer of the narrative type was a woman, Cai Yan (Ts'ai Yen, fl. 206 C.E.), who composed two "Songs of Distress," which became famous. Taken captive by the Huns and forced to become the consort of a Hun chieftain for twelve years before she was ransomed, she tells of her life during her captivity and reflects on her experiences. Another Han narrative *yuefu*, titled "Kong jue dongnan fei" (author unknown; "Southwest the Peacock Flies"), is generally considered a masterpiece and is the longest medieval poem of China at 353 lines. Later, poems of this type based on the folk style and rendered in five- or seven-character lines became known as *gushi* ("ancient verse").

SIX DYNASTIES AND SUI DYNASTY (220-618 C.E.)

With the end of the Han Dynasty, China again lapsed into disunity. Three independent kingdoms struggled with one another for power. Wei had retained much of the power it had usurped from Han, but soon it was challenged by Shu and Wu. This period of political contention is known as the Three Kingdoms period (220-265). The powerful house of Jin then arose and eliminated both Shu and Wu to found the Jin (Chin) Dynasty (265-419). By 420, China had divided itself into the South and North Dynasties; this division lasted until 589. Finally, the Sui Dynasty took over and ruled China until 618.

Despite the political confusion and social unrest resulting from the power struggles of the Six Dynasties period (220-588 C.E.), it was an age of rapid development in poetry, in both form and content. Beginning in the third century, a profound change took place in the intellectual climate of China, the positivism of Han Confucianism being replaced by mystical Confucianism supported by the *yin-yang* cosmology. With this change, a new attitude toward poetry as an art emerged. *The Book of Songs* was interpreted in terms of mystical philosophy, the *Lunyu* (*Lun yü*; later sixth-early fifth centuries B.C.E.; *The Analects*, 1861) of Confucius was interpreted on Daoist principles, and the *Yijing* (*I Ching*; eighth to third century B.C.E.; English translation, 1876; also known as *Book of Changes*, 1986), the classic of spiritual or psychological transformation, became the dominating Confucian text. In short, a fusion was effected between Confucianism and Daoism, and Indian Buddhism was integrated into Chinese intellectual life. Buddhists and Daoists came to the fore, and a number of poets were predominantly one or the other.

During the time of the last Han emperor, the five- or seven-character poetic line had replaced the old four-character pattern of *The Book of Songs*. Although the irregular verse form of the popular folk song had been rejected, the poets had not entirely lost contact with the spontaneity of these songs. A master of this new type, called *shi* (later *gushi*; *ku-shih*), was Cao Zhi (Ts'ao Chih; 192-232), perhaps the most important member of the group called the Seven Masters of Jian An (Chien An). Another significant group, the Seven Worthies of the Bamboo Grove, was composed of poets who had abandoned the city for the country to escape the political confusion of the time. Ruan Ji (Juan Chi; 210-263) was the most outstanding member of this group; his eighty-two *yonghuai shi* (*yung-huai shih*; "poems expressing feelings") express the new attitude that poetry should be an honest disclosure of the poet's feelings and emotions. Poets termed this attitude *tou*, and *tou qing qing* (*t'ou ch'ing ch'ing*) means "to call up and expose one's inmost feelings."

In accord with the mysticism of the time, this attitude was linked to *tong* (*t'ung*), the ability to see into the nature of things—literally, "to go through things." At the same time, a number of poets rejected the orthodox Confucian idea that the main purpose of poetry was didactic and moralistic, a view that emphasized content over form. The poet and critic Lu Chi (261-303), for example, in his *wen fu* (literary *fu*), adamantly declared that form is as important as content and insisted that poetry has an intrinsic aesthetic value.

In addition to the five- or seven-character *shi*, another genre was developed during the Six Dynasties period: a new kind of *fu*, a shorter version that omitted dialogue and tried to capture the lyric quality of the *Chu ci*. It also employed the rhetoric of *pian wen* (*p'ien wen*; "balanced prose"). Lu Chi as well as Zuo Si (Tso Ssu, fl. 265-305) were both great masters of this new kind of *fu*. Later came the literary giant Tao Qian (T'ao Ch'ien; 365-427), also known as Tao Yuanming (T'ao Yüan-ming), a many-sided man. The scion of a great official family, he joined the civil service, but loving his freedom and independence more than official rewards, he resigned at the age of thirty-three and never returned to public life. His poem on retirement, "Homeward Bound," has been much admired, but he is most famous for his *fu* "The Scholar of Five Willows" and "Peach Blossom Spring." He is the greatest of the recluse poets of the Six Dynasties period.

Although China was unified once again under the Sui Dynasty (581-618), little need be said about that dynasty's poetry. No significant developments took place, and no great poets emerged. The two best poets were Yang Guang (Yan Kuang, 580-618), who succeeded his father on the throne in 605, and the Lady Hou, one of Yang Guang's concubines.

TANG AND FIVE DYNASTIES (618-960)

The Tang Dynasty, founded by Li Yuan (Li Yüan) after he crushed the Sui regime, was the golden age of Chinese poetry. Li Yuan reigned as Gaozu (Kao Tsu), then voluntarily stepped down in 626 in favor of his second son, Li Shimin (Li Shih-min), who reigned as Taizong (T'ai Tsung) and was a great patron of literature. Under these rulers and their successors, a new system of land tenure was put into effect, and the competitive trade that developed on a wide scale produced a new social class, the urban bourgeoisie. Changes also took place in the realms of philosophy, religion, the arts, and literature. Orthodox Confucianism was modified by the inclusion of mystical elements, new religions such as Nestorian Christianity came on the scene, and two new forms of *shi* made their appearance and became very popular: *jueju* (*chüeh-chü*, literally "cut short") and *lushi* (*lü-shih*, literally "ruled verse"). Until the Rebellion of An Lushan in 755, during the reign of Xuanzong (Hsüan Tsung; reigned 712-756), the nation enjoyed unprecedented peace, prosperity, and cultural development. The Tang Dynasty produced China's two greatest poets, Li Bo (Li Po; 701-762) and Du Fu (Tu Fu; 712-770), as well as a host of other major poets: Wang Wei (701-761), Han Yu (Han Yü; 768-824), Bo

Juyi (Po Chü-yi; 772-846), Yuan Zhen (Yüan Chen; 779-831), Du Mu (Tu Mu; 803-852), and Li Shangyin (Li Shang-yin; 813-858). Although poetry flourished at the court of the early Tang, it was mostly of the occasional type, inspired by festivals and sumptuous banquets. With the appearance of the *jueju* and the *lushi* forms, poetry was taken more seriously. The *jueju* was a poem of four lines of equal length, with either five or seven characters to the line, a set tone pattern, and a rhyme scheme. The *lushi* was a poem of eight lines of equal length, again with either five or seven characters to the line, contrasting intonations in each pair of lines, and a rhyme scheme. Parallel construction was required in the four middle lines of the eight-line poem, rhyme was required in the even-numbered lines, and a set tonal sequence was required in all eight lines. Two masters of court poetry, Shen Juanqi (Shen Chüan-ch'i; c. 650-713) and Song Zhiwen (Sung Chih-wen; c. 660-712), are credited with crystallizing the *lushi* form.

Xuanzong was a lover of beauty and the arts, and he succeeded in bringing the best poetic talent of China to his court. Two of the poets he employed turned out to be the two greatest poets China has produced: Li Bo and Du Fu.

Li Bo

As a boy, Li Bo developed two consuming interests—poetry and swordsmanship. At the age of ten, he was writing poetry and studying fencing. He apparently never entertained any political ambitions and did not study the Confucian classics in preparation for taking the examinations. Rather, he was a dabbler in Daoism and alchemy. He left home at the age of nineteen to seek adventure and wandered from place to place. Occasionally he sought employment as a bodyguard, and it is said that he thrust his sword through a number of opponents; otherwise, he indulged his passion for writing poetry. He eventually arrived at Changan, where his poetic talent was brought to the attention of the emperor, who employed him as a court poet for a brief period (742-744).

Xuanzong found that Li Bo was as fond of drinking wine as he was of writing poetry, and the two activities frequently went hand in hand. Independent in spirit and incapable of sycophancy, Li Bo soon lost his position and resumed his wandering. According to legend, he drowned while boating on a lake; having grown intoxicated from drinking wine, he tumbled out of his boat into the water in an effort to embrace the moon's reflection. True or false, this legend accurately reflects the spirit of Li Bo, a lover of nature and beauty who continually sought to plunge into the unknown.

A poetic genius in the romantic mold, Li Bo was intent on being himself, yet he sought to transcend the self as well. A visionary poet, he never lost his humanity. If he ascended the mountain to touch the stars, he descended to enjoy a bowl of rice and the welcoming pillow of a farmer friend. He relished listening to a Buddhist monk playing his lute as much as he did fencing or drinking wine. Poetry was always foremost in his mind.

Du Fu

China's other great poet, Du Fu, was a man and a poet of a character quite different from that of Li Bo. A native of Gongxian, in what is now Henan Province, he was descended from a family of scholars and writers. He studied the Confucian classics with the object of qualifying himself for an official career, and at the age of twenty-five, he journeyed from his home to the capital to take the *jinshi* examinations. Failing to receive his degree, however, he decided to take up the career of poet and journeyed about the country riding on a donkey. At the age of thirty-eight, he submitted three *fu* compositions to Xuanzong. Impressed, the monarch rewarded him with an official appointment. Soon, however, the An Lushan Rebellion drove Xuanzong from power and Du Fu into exile. The shock of the rebellion had a pronounced effect on him and on his subsequent poetry.

Following the accession of Suzong (Su Tsung), Du Fu returned to the capital to accept the dangerous office of imperial censor. His critical memorials to the throne, however, displeased the emperor, who, in effect, banished him by appointing him governor of a small town. Consequently, Du Fu resigned and retired to the country. Called out of retirement to serve on the board of works, Du Fu resigned again after six years and retired to the country, this time permanently. Dedicating his life to poetry, he grew old before his time and died in poverty at the age of fifty-eight.

Li Bo was a romantic, "a heavenly immortal in temporary exile on earth." His poetry tends to move away from the real toward the unreal; he sought not to reform the society of his time but to escape from it. Du Fu was a classicist, an earth-rooted man, a mortal with a social consciousness, a serious man with a heart full of sorrow and passionate indignation. His poetry tends to concentrate on the real and to avoid the unreal. He faced up to the hard facts of life: the suffering of the masses, social injustice, corruption in government, the extravagances of the rich, the horrors of war, the ravages of time, and the desires and fears of living people in the everyday world. He was a critical realist with a tragic sense of life. However, despite the sorrow he carried in his heart, he had his light side and never lost his sense of humor.

Du Fu's poetry can be divided into an early, a middle, and a late period. His early period (c. 750-755), that prior to the An Lushan Rebellion, is characterized by such poems as "The Eight Immortals of the Wine Cup," a clever piece of lighthearted satire, and the glittering satirical ballads "The Ballad of the Beauties" and "The Ballad of the War Chariots." The middle period (755-765), that of the rebellion and its aftermath, is characterized by such poems as "Lament of the River Bank" and "Lamenting of the Imperial Heir," both of which feature nostalgia, sadness, and cynicism. The late period (766-770) is characterized by poems such as "My Thatched Roof Whirled Away by an Autumn Gale," a vivid picture of the hardships of poverty and old age. Du Fu called Li Bo the "unrivaled poet," yet Du Fu surpasses his friend in intellectual power and emotional range. No Chinese poet has displayed more mastery of the regulated form.

Other Tang Poets

Of the other major Tang poets, Bo Juyi stands above the rest. A very successful government official, he rose to high rank under Xuanzong. He was a leader in the development of the long narrative poem called the *xin yuefu* (*hsin yüeh-fu*; "new lyric ballad"). Despite their length, his two poems "Song of Everlasting Sorrow" and "Song of the Lute" were in their day extremely popular with both commoner and aristocrat. Wang Wei, poet, painter, calligrapher, and musician, followed a political career. His devotion to the Chan (Japanese Zen) school of Buddhism is evident in both his painting and his poetry. He was noted for his mastery of the *jueju* form. Han Yu was a highly successful government official and a noted essayist and writer of short romances as well as a poet. He was the leader of a reform movement that sought to free literature from its artificialities. His poems "Mountain Stones" and "Poem on the Stone Drums" were particularly admired.

Yuan Zhen is as famous for his thirty-year friendship with Bo Juyi as for his own poetry. A government official, his career was not very successful, but he is known for the poems and letters that passed between him and Bo Juyi. Du Mu (Tu Mu) had a moderately successful official career. He is regarded as a transitional figure between the middle and late Tang periods and was a sharp critic of both Li Bo and Du Fu. He is noted for the descriptive talent displayed in his "Traveling in the Mountains."

Li Shangyin also pursued a moderately successful political career while achieving a considerable literary reputation. In his poetry, he makes much use of myth, symbolism, and classical allusions, and his work is regarded by some as obscure. He is noted especially for his love poems and funeral elegies.

After the Tang restoration, which followed the suppression of the An Lushan Rebellion in 757, the imperial administration experienced increasing difficulties in maintaining control over the empire. Finally, in 907, a local military commander murdered the Tang emperor and proclaimed himself the founder of a new dynasty, the Liang. This dynasty, however, was short-lived and was followed by four others before China was reunited with the establishment of the Song (Sung) Dynasty in 960. This period between 907 and 960, known as the Five Dynasties period, did not produce distinguished poetry.

Song Dynasty (960-1279)

Under Emperor Tai Zu (T'ai Tsu), China became an empire again, with its capital at Kaifeng (K'ai-feng, then called Pien-ching, or Bianjing), just south of the Yellow River in East Central China. In 1126, the Jin Empire invaded the North China Plain, captured Kaifeng, and held the emperor prisoner. The Chinese court fled southward to establish a new capital at Hang (present Hangchow) on the lower Yanzi Plain, not far from the East China Sea. Hence, the Song is divisible into the Northern Song (960-1127) and the Southern Song (1127-1279).

Although the Song was a period of turmoil, warfare, and chaos, in many ways it was also an age of great culture and refinement. The dynasty is noted for its landscape painters as well as for its writers. Indeed, in the arts and literature, the Song nearly equaled the accomplishments of the Tang. The chief poets of the Song Dynasty were Ouyang Xiu (Ou-yang Hsiu; 1007-1072), Wang Anshi (Wang An-shih; 1021-1086), Su Dongpo (Su Tung-p'o; pen name of Su Shi; 1036-1101), Li Qingzhao (Li Ch'ing-chao; 1084-c. 1151), and Lu You (Lu Yu; 1125-1210).

Ouyang Xiu

Ouyang Xiu was both a major political figure—he was president of the board of war—and the acknowledged leader of the literary world of his time. A great prose master and a major poet, he was a reformer and innovator. His position of influence and his own exemplary prose style were largely responsible for the success of the *guwen* (*ku-wen*) prose movement, which had originated with Han Yu several hundred years earlier. As for *shi* (*shih*), or regulated poetry, he was a master of the *jueju*, or quatrain. This can be seen in his "The Pavilion of Abounding Joy" and "Returning Home in the Rain," which are direct, simple, and fluent. Although he closely followed tradition in these works, his individual voice is apparent. His *ci*, or poems based on musical scores, are short but produce a distinctive musical effect. His most outstanding *fu* is "Qiu shenfu" ("Sounds of Autumn"). Ouyang Xiu was a painstaking writer and a tireless reviser of his work.

Wang Anshi

Wang Anshi was a powerful political figure and a controversial social reformer. As prime minister under Shenzong, who ascended the throne in 1068, Wang instituted a reform program that caused great controversy and resulted in his resignation. He became the governor of what is now Nanjing and received many subsequent honors, but he never regained his former political power. He was an outstanding prose writer as well as a superb poet and was particularly famous for his direct and clear-cut memorials to the throne and for his funeral inscriptions. He invented the "five-legged essay," the precursor of the famous "eight-legged essay" later required in the public examinations. In poetry, his *jueju* were much admired. Poems such as "Night Duty" and "Early Summer" present concrete images in swift sequence with vivid realism.

Su Dongpo

The most original poet of the Song was Su Dongpo, an important public official and an outstanding calligrapher and painter as well as a major poet. He opposed Wang Anshi's reforms and was therefore banished. Su Dongpo returned to the capital in 1085, after Wang's fall. From 1089 to 1091, Su Dongpo was the governor of Hang. He returned to the capital but was soon banished again, first to Huizhou in Guangdong Province and then to Hainan Island. As a poet, he was a keen student of such previous literary greats as Tao Qian, Du Fu, and Han Yu. He was also a great admirer of his contemporary, Ouyang Xiu. He deliberately strove to break out of the limitations of Tang poetry and succeeded more spectacularly than his contemporary Wang Anshi. With a view toward perpetuating his technique, he drew around him some of the outstanding poets of his time. His school succeeded in dominating *shi* poetry for the remainder of the Song period.

Su Dongpo liked to write regulated poetry of the kind that allowed him maximum freedom—long, freewheeling *fu* or short, seven-character *jueju*. His twin *fu* on the "Red Cliff" are memorable descriptions and meditations on history. His quatrain "Mid-Autumn Moon" shows his disciplined economy of expression. He broke away entirely from the conventions of the *ci* and wrote a meditative kind of poetry without much regard for its musical possibilities. Whatever kind of poems he wrote, he was always original. His poetry is noted for its range of vision, its inclusion of vernacular language, and its organic form.

LI QINGZHAO

Li Qingzhao and Lu You are perhaps the two most interesting poets of this group because of their unusual personalities and the peculiar circumstances of their lives. Li Qingzhao has been called the greatest woman poet of China. She was a native of Shandong Province, and her father was the renowned scholar and writer Li Gefei (Li Kei-fei). Having married scholar and antiquarian Zhao Mingcheng (Chao Mingch'eng), Li Qingzhao apparently had found an ideal relationship. When the Jin invasion forced the Chinese court to flee southward, she and her husband did likewise, but her husband died on the way, and she was obliged to continue her flight alone. This tragic loss profoundly affected Li Qingzhao for the rest of her life. After a few years in Hang, she removed herself to Zhejiang, where she spent the rest of her days. Li Qingzhao wrote both prose and verse, but the vast majority of her writings have been lost. She enjoyed a high reputation in her time, particularly for her *ci*. Her poetry displays a sensibility that is distinctively feminine. Many of her *ci* express her feelings regarding her widowhood and increasing age. Her images are precisely selected and her poems show a capacity for deep feeling.

LU YOU

Lu You, a native of Zhejiang Province, has been regarded as the greatest poet of the Southern Song. At the age of twelve, he wrote prose and verse sufficiently distinguished to attract the attention of the highest officials in the government, including the emperor himself. Lu You began a career in public life, but he soon encountered difficulties. His independent spirit and pronounced talent excited the envy of many, who spread malicious gossip about him; furthermore, he found great difficulty in conforming to the expectations of others. An ardent patriot who felt deeply dishonored by China's loss of its former territory, he consequently took a strong interest in the military. He served on the staff of Fan Chenda when that renowned poet was the military commander of Sichuan Province. He wrote a large body of nature poetry, but despite its high quality, the keys to his work are his patriotism and his respect for the art of war. He saw a special dignity in the profession of soldier and held that warfare was indispensable to national defense. He yearned to be a man of action but never could find the proper context in which to act. The most prolific poet in the history of Chinese literature, Lu You lived to the advanced age of eighty-five.

Although the Song Dynasty is noted for the production of some great *shi* and *fu*, the dominant poetic genre of the period was the *ci*. The *ci* was the most popular form of the age, despite the fact that it was rated below the *shi* and *fu* in terms of literary merit.

YUAN DYNASTY (1279-1368)

The ruling class of the Southern Song had believed in negotiation, appeasement, and opportunistic alliances rather than an aggressive foreign policy and a strong national defense. Militarily weak, its treasury exhausted by the payment of exorbitant tribute, the government sought an alliance with the Mongols against their common enemy, the Jin Tartars. This policy backfired when Kublai Khan, the grandson of Genghis Khan, suddenly grown powerful, blatantly annexed China to the Mongol Empire. The Chinese people awakened from their long dream to find themselves under the heel of a foreign conqueror.

To the imperialistic Mongols, China was simply a colony for exploitation. Ignoring Chinese tradition and customs, they did whatever they thought necessary to maintain control over the country. In place of the traditional Chinese class hierarchy of scholars, farmers, merchants, and soldiers, the Mongols instituted a hierarchy based on race: Mongols, useful foreigners, Northern Chinese, and Southern Chinese. At first, the Chinese as a whole were excluded from participating in the government, but soon realizing the enormity of its mission, the Mongol regime decided that such a policy might have dire results. Accordingly, the regime began depending heavily on the Chinese official class. Many Chinese scholars, however, refused to cooperate with the Mongols and retreated to the country to become recluses and wanderers.

Thus, energies that might have been exerted in governmental administration were channeled into the arts, particularly into painting and musical drama. The Yuan Dynasty was a great age of *wenrenhua*, the art that combined painting, calligraphy, and poetry into a single unit and produced the Four Great Masters of the Yuan Dynasty: Huang Gongwang (Huang Kung-wang), Ni Zan (Ni Tsan), Wang Men, and Wu Zhen (Wu Chen). It was also the golden age of the Chinese opera, the Mongols being particularly fond of this theatrical form, and it produced four great masters of the Northern school: Guan Hanqing (Kuan Han-ch'ing; c. 1220-1307), Wang Shifu (Wang Shih-fu; c. 1250-1337), Ji Junxiang (Chi Chün-hsiang; fl. 1260-1280), and Ma Zhiyuan (Ma Chih-yüan;

c. 1265-1325). Although the Northern style of drama predominated during the Yuan period, a Southern style had developed under the leadership of Gao Ming (Kao Ming; fl. 1345-1375).

In the realm of nondramatic poetry, the most important Yuan form was a new kind of lyric that developed from the *qu* (*ch'ü*), or dramatic verse, and was known as the *sanqu* (*san-ch'ü*), or "unattached song." Poets who were not dramatists began to write these "unattached songs" based on the style of dramatic verse but not intended to be part of any play. This new type of lyric was looser in its requirements than *shi* with respect to rhythm, diction, and treatment of subject matter. The most prominent author of *sanqu* after the year 1300 was Zhang Kejiu (Chang K'o-chiu; fl. 1275-1325). A songwriter who occupied various civil-service posts under the Mongols, he wrote mainly about his disappointments in life and his efforts to console himself.

Ming Dynasty (1368-1644)

The last years of the Yuan Dynasty were plagued by rebellions, the work of military adventurers and quasi-religious leaders; behind the scenes were the wealthy gentry, ambitious for political power. A Buddhist monk named Zhu Yuanzhang (Chu Yüanchang), crafty and ruthless, was able to best all opponents and oust the Mongols at the same time. He became the founder of the Ming Dynasty and reigned as Hongwu (Hung Wu) from 1368 to 1399. An absolute monarch, he tightened the hold of the government on the everyday life of the nation.

Free of Mongol domination, the Chinese people welcomed native rule and reacted strongly against foreign practices. The emperor himself led this pro-Chinese movement by reviving ancient Chinese customs and ceremonies and emphasizing agricultural pursuits. He revised the civil-service examinations and introduced the very rigid format of the eight-legged essay, which was required of all degree candidates. As a consequence, candidates were driven away from poetry, which previously had been their main preoccupation, to concentrate on this rigid essay format. Indeed, the spirit of originality and innovation was suppressed altogether in favor of maintaining tradition and observing established conventions.

Although for a time the Ming experienced considerable trouble in keeping the Mongols at bay, the third emperor of the Ming Dynasty, Yongluo (Yung Lo; r. 1402-1424), succeeded in frustrating all their efforts, reestablishing the empire in most of the northwest. With peace restored, interest in art and literature increased. The technique of block printing was perfected, publishing flourished, and scholars were put to work selecting the best literature of the past and present for preservation and circulation. Illustrated encyclopedias, dictionaries, collections of stories, plays, and poems; treatises and monographs on the arts and sciences; and critical studies of art and literature were prepared and printed. It was an age of *tongshu* (*t'ung-shu*), or "collectanea." There was great activity in the writing and production of drama and in the writing of vernacular fiction. Much nondramatic poetry was written in the *shi* and *ci* forms, but it was the Southern *sanqu* that became a universal fad. Although superb craftsmen, the nondramatic poets were generally imitative and bound by tradition and conventions.

QING (OR MANCHU) DYNASTY (1644-1911)

In 1644, China was invaded by the Manchus, a nomadic Mongolian people. Unlike the Mongols, the Manchus were interested in China for its own sake, not merely as a colony to be exploited. They admired Chinese culture and gradually became completely assimilated, losing their own cultural distinctiveness. The second Qing emperor, Kangxi (Ka'ang Hsi), was not only a strong military leader and an able administrator but also a scholar and a lover of the arts and literature. From an early age, he had loved the Chinese language, Chinese literature, and Confucian philosophy. He encouraged Chinese scholarship to such a degree that scholarship became the dominating force of his time. Because of him, a great dictionary of more than forty thousand Chinese characters was compiled.

Massive compendia such as the *Gujin tushu jicheng* (1726; collection of pictures and writing) and the *Siku quanshu* (1773-1782; *The Emperor's Four Treasures: Scholars and the State in the Late Ch'ien-lung Era*, 1987) came into being. The former classified all the significant writings of the empire; the latter reedited all the major writings of the empire for inclusion and was so voluminous that it was never printed, although seven copies were made by hand. Interest in classical literature flourished, and vigorous creative efforts were made in drama and fiction. In poetry, all previous literary types were revived: the Tang *shi*, the Song *ci*, the Yuan dramatic and lyric *Chu ci*, and the Han *fu*. A similar revival took place in classical prose, with interest directed at the *guwen* of the Tang and Song Dynasties. Vernacular prose produced perhaps the greatest Chinese novel, *Hongloumeng* (1792; *Dream of the Red Chamber*, 1958), by Cao Xueqin (Ts'ao Hsueh-ch'in).

Most of the Qing poets were fine technicians, but few were able to free themselves from the old masters such as Li Bo, Du Fu, Bo Juyi, and Su Dongpo. Nevertheless, there were some poets whose independence of spirit penetrated their imitations so that they spoke in their own voice. The most outstanding of them were Qian Qianyi (Ch'ien Ch'ien-yi; 1582-1664), Wu Weiye (Wu Wei-yeh; 1609-1671), Wang Shizhen (Wang Shih-chen; 1634-1711), and Yuan Mei (Yüan Mei; 1715-1797). Important but less-skilled poets were Chen Zulong (Ch'en Tsu-lung; 1608-1647), Chen Weisong (Ch'en Wei-sung; 1626-1682), and Nara Singde, a Manchu (1655-1685), all of whom were noted for their *ci* during the early Qing. Among the noteworthy writers of *ci* during the late Qing were playwright Jiang Shiquan (Chiang Shih-ch'üan; 1725-1785), Wang Pengyun (Wang P'eng-yün; 1848-1904), and Huang Xing (Huang Hsing; 1874-1916).

By the end of the nineteenth century, Western ideas and the aggressive dynamics of Western power and technology had brought fear, dismay, turmoil, violence, and shame to the people of China. Despite pleas from its wise men for reforms that would enable China to survive as a nation and a civilization, the Dragon Throne and the power around it blindly opposed all change as capitulation to Western ideas and methods. Such intransigence brought about the revolt of the people in 1911, when, led by the revolutionary firebrand Sun Yat-sen, they overthrew the old autocratic system and established the Chinese Republic the following year.

Post-Qing Period (1911-1949)

In 1905, the civil-service examination system was abolished, and modern education along Western lines was introduced into China. Large numbers of students went abroad to study—to Japan, to North America, and to Europe. Depending on where they studied, they absorbed the influences of various foreign authors. They returned to their homeland with all sorts of Western ideas. In 1917, Hu Shi (Hu Shih), a philosopher trained in the United States, and Chen Duxiu (Ch'en Tu-hsiu) launched a radical literary movement advocating that literature be written exclusively in *bai hua*, the vernacular, and no longer in *wenli*, or classical Chinese. Furthermore, old genres, diction, and themes were to be abandoned, and a new value was to be placed on those novels, plays, and folk poems of the past that had been written in the everyday language of the people.

With the acceptance of this doctrine and the historical circumstances surrounding Chinese poets from 1917 to 1927, Chinese literature fell into turmoil. In 1923, a group of young writers gathered around Xu Zhimo (Hsü Chih-mo; 1895-1931) to form the Crescent Society. The aesthetic theoretician of this group was Wen Yiduo (Wen I-to; 1899-1946), who, under the influence of the French writer Théophile Gautier, championed the use of measured prosodic units to achieve a musical effect in the vernacular similar to that of the best classical poetry. Wen Yiduo believed in art free of politics, an orientation for which he was attacked by some. His volume *Sishui* (the dead water), published in 1928, has been admired as one of the finest volumes of poetry produced anywhere in the 1920's. Wen Yiduo may be the greatest Chinese poet of the twentieth century.

Another group, interested in expressing the relationship of humans to the universe, is represented by such poets as Feng Zhi (Feng Chih; 1905-1993) and Bian Zhilin (Pien Chih-lin; 1910-2000) advocating the use of metaphor to express metaphysical ideas.

Under the influence of French Symbolists such as Paul Verlaine and Stéphane Mallarmé, a group led by Li Jinfa (1901-1976) and Dai Wangshu (Tai Wang-shu, 1905-1950?) attempted to suggest through symbols that only humanity's impressions of the world have substantial reality. In this period of ferment and experimentation, the theme common to all was freedom from the old classical restraints.

From 1927 to 1932, revolutionary ideas were in the air, and social protest became the watchword behind the slogan "From literary revolution to revolutionary literature." Many radical writers were imprisoned and executed as a result of their overt protests.

Around 1932, revolutionary writing began to be replaced by what was called the New Realism; the sufferings of the masses were realistically described without recommendations for revolutionary action. The poetry of Zang Kejia (Tsang K'o chia; 1905-2004), Ai Qing (Ai Ch'ing; pen name of Chiang Hai-ch'eng, or Jiang Haicheng; 1910-1996), and Ren Jun (Jen Chün; born 1909) is typical of this period.

From 1937 to 1947, China was at war. In 1942, the Communist leader and poet Mao Zedong (Mao Tse-tung, 1893-1976) issued his famous dictum from Yenan calling for "Social Realism" in literature. By 1947, most writers had purged themselves entirely of classical ornament as well as of the conventions of Western literature, and the new vernacular medium had assumed its own Chinese shape. With the establishment of the People's Republic of China in 1949, however, Chinese literature became shackled in another manner: by communist ideology. It assumed the stereotyped role of supporting the new communist society in ways approved by the party leaders.

The Maoist Era (1949-1976)

Though his regime was harshly repressive of poetic creativity, Mao himself fancied his own poetic abilities and took a general interest in the state of Chinese poetry. The delicacy, precision, and suggestiveness of traditional Chinese poetry made an uneasy fit with the sloganeering and propaganda of the Maoist belief system, but Mao nonetheless produced many fervid poems that inevitably received much comment from Chinese literary organs. In Maoist ideology, the cultural sphere was an important vehicle for disseminating the ideology of the state. However, the modernist poets of the Guomindang era were not entirely silenced under Mao. Guo Moruo (1892-1978), who wrote in free verse, bridged several generations and was a living link between past and present. Although he served as a functionary in the communist government (he was head of the Chinese academy of science), Guo's poetic integrity was never compromised; he continued to range widely over aesthetic, historical, and philosophical concerns. Even the harsh repression of the Cultural Revolution of the 1960's failed to extinguish the spark of poetic imagination totally. The underground poetry of this era erupted, ironically, as an enthusiastic echo of government-sponsored frenzy; the initiative and spirit that was generated, however, was felt to be threatening by the leadership despite its apparent ideological conformity. Poets such as Huang Xiang and Quo Lusheng suffered terribly for their independence during this era. Though poetry did not entirely grind to a halt, creativity was trammeled.

The Post-Mao Era

The literary generation immediately following the Cultural Revolution produced what is known as scar literature (*shanghen wenxue*), whose main purpose was to provide a testimony to the ravages of the immediate past. Scar literature emerged particularly after the death of Mao in 1976 and after the April 5, 1976, protests occasioned by the death of Mao's colleague Zhou Enlai. Although, as far as politically possible, it excoriated the crimes of the government, scar literature was still overwhelmingly public in orientation, and it continued, if perhaps only in the mode of trauma, the idea that literature is a rendition of external reality.

Around 1978, several poets decided to go a step further than scar literature. *Meng long* ("misty" or "obscure") poetry that sprang up in this era went in tandem with the Democracy Wall movement of 1978-1979, yet paradoxically turned away from public expression into a more indirect and introspective mode, concentrating on the self in natural surroundings. Misty poetry in this way seemed to resemble traditional landscape poetry, but it often contained hidden symbols of ideological dissent from the communist government. Misty poetry produced the major names that dominated Chinese poetry into the twenty-first century: Bei Dao, Gu Cheng, Shu Ting, Yang Lian, and Mang Ke. Bei Dao (Zhao Zhenkai; born 1949) was the first of the misty poets to come to public light with his poem "The Answer" (1979); still the most famous living Chinese poet at the end of the century, Bei Dao and his work made new demands of the reader, not remaining within the customary conventions of Chinese lyric, although its influence by Western models did not at all equate to mere imitation. Gu Cheng (1856-1993) is contemporary Chinese poetry's *poète maudit*; his psychological turmoil eventually led him to kill both himself and his wife in exile in New Zealand in 1993. Simpler and more confrontational in his language than Bei Dao, Gu Cheng wrote poems whose final meaning is nonetheless elusive. Shu Ting (born 1952) was the only major woman poet in the misty group; her signature poem "To the Oak Tree" reveals more rhythmical and musical tendencies than do the poems of her contemporaries. The poetry of Yang Lian (born 1955) is often rhapsodic and dense with natural images, yet replete with an underlying cynicism; he has tended to write about Tibet and the western portions of China itself. In later years, he became more interested in the roots of Chinese identity. Mang Ke (born 1950), with Bei Dao, was coeditor of *Jintian* (today), the leading magazine of misty poetry. Mang was one of the first of his generation to publish serious poetry, and his images, most famously that of the sunflower, are vivid and bridge the gap between objectivity and subjectivity, nature and human desire.

The government began to react against misty poetry in the "anti-spiritual pollution" campaign of 1983, and some of the poets went underground or into exile. The misty poets nevertheless were still the most prominent group at the beginning of the twenty-first century, drawing increasing international attention. Their stature sometimes led to resentment on the part of less-well-known poets, many of whom began to adopt a more discursive and colloquial approach, one focusing less on the individual ego than on the intermittently intolerable conditions of human existence itself. Others, though, went in the opposite direction and introduced spiritual, sometimes explicitly Christian themes into their verse.

Chinese poetry in the 1990's was affected by a specific event and a long-term process: the Tiananmen Square massacre of June, 1989, and the onslaught of globalization that led Shanghai to be changed virtually overnight into a gleaming postmodern megalopolis. Although the communists adamantly retained control, Chinese writers were much more in touch with their counterparts abroad, especially in the Chinese diaspora. The government allowed freedom of expression in strictly literary matters, no longer aspiring to intervene in the cultural sphere or codifying a prescribed aesthetic, as in the Mao era. At the start of the twenty-first century, the main tension in Chinese poetry was between "vulgar," or *minjian* poets, who used the banalities of everyday life to express a pulse of authenticity, and more intellectual poets who sought to plug into advanced Western philosophical debates. The underground journal *Shi Cankao*, edited by Zhong Dao, tended to promote the *minjian* poets, especially Yi Sha (born 1966), who in "My Ancestors" took a completely anti-idealistic and antinostalgic view of his own relation to tradition. The *minjian* poets espoused an aesthetic that would have been out of fashion in the West, had they been Western, and thus provided a counterpoise to the inevitable cross-fertilization between Chinese and Western aesthetics. This cross-fertilization was expedited by the number of Chinese writers who, whether for political or for economic reasons, emigrated to Western countries.

Ouyang Yu (born 1955), for example, not only moved to Australia but also (in volumes such as *Songs of the Last Chinese Poet*, 1997) saw himself as much as an Australian as a Chinese poet and founded a bilingual journal, *Yuanxiang* (otherland). The translator Mabel Lee, also based in Australia, translated both Chinese poetry and fiction into English, making it more visible internationally. Other overseas poets, such as Bei Ling (born 1959), continued to be active in calling attention to human rights concerns within China. Bei Ling, with fellow exile Meng Lang (born 1961), in 1993 founded the literary periodical *Qing Xiang* (tendency), the most spirited and imaginatively comprehensive Chinese literary journal of its era. Bei Ling, who first left China in the late 1980's, returned to China and was arrested there in the summer of 2000 for his literary activities and was liberated only after international pressure. Bei Ling's poetry, praised by Western luminaries such as Joseph Brodsky, Seamus Heaney, and Susan Sontag, is measured in its diction and stance, yet is written with considerable emotion—one example of the many available new syntheses in the age-old tradition of Chinese poetry.

Bibliography

Barnstone, Tony, and Chou Ping, eds. *The Anchor Book of Chinese Poetry: From Ancient to Contemporary, The Full 3,000-Year Tradition*. New York: Anchor Books, 2004. This massive anthology is an excellent source for the study of Chinese poetry, collecting more than six hundred poems written over the past three thousand years.

Birrell, Anne, trans. *Chinese Love Poetry: New Songs from a Jade Terrace, a Medieval Anthology*. 2d ed. London: Penguin, 1995. Collects poems from the Chinese medieval period; Birrell adds an introduction, notes, and a map.

Cai, Zong-qi, ed. *How to Read Chinese Poetry: A Guided Anthology*. Bilingual ed. New York: Columbia University Press, 2007. A historical and literary guide through Chinese poetry, featuring more than 140 poems, some with close readings. The book is organized chronologically, with each chapter written by an expert in the area, but has an alternative thematic table of contents. Include helpful explanations of such matters as sound, rhythm, and syntax. Glossary-index.

Cao, Zuoya. *The Asian Thought and Culture: The Internal and the External, a Comparison of the Artistic Use of Natural Imagery in English Romantic and Chinese Classic Poetry*. New York: Peter Lang, 1998. An examination of the different ways that the English Romantic poets and the classic Chinese poets connected the inner and outer worlds, as well as their different poetics—correcting previous wrong notions about Chinese nature poetry. Close readings of more than thirty poems. Notes, bibliography.

Chang, Kang-i Sun, and Huan Saussy, eds. *Women Writers of Traditional China: An Anthology of Poetry and Criticism*. Stanford, Calif.: Stanford University Press, 1999. Women have long played a role in Chinese literature; this massive (nearly nine-hundred-page) work is important to literary, Chinese, and women's studies. Bibliography, index, maps.

Hamill, Sam, trans. *Crossing the Yellow River: Three Hundred Poems from the Chinese*. Rochester, N.Y.: BOA Editions, 2000. Hamill's introduction and a preface by poet W. S. Merwin make this a valuable compendium.

Hightower, James Robert, and Florence Chia-ying Yeh. *Studies in Chinese Poetry*. Cambridge, Mass.: Harvard University Press, 1998. This monograph of more than six hundred pages covers the history of Chinese poetry and poetics into the twentieth century. Bibliography, index.

Lin, Julia C., trans. and ed. *Twentieth-Century Chinese Women's Poetry: An Anthology*. Armonk, N.Y.: M. E. Sharpe, 2009. Contains 245 poems by women poets, both from the Chinese mainland and from Taiwan. Introduction traces the history of contemporary Chinese women's poetry. Biographical headnotes.

Lupke, Christopher, ed. *New Perspectives on Contemporary Chinese Poetry*. New York: Palgrave Macmillan, 2008. An impressive collection of scholarly articles, reflecting a variety of theoretical viewpoints. The arguments advanced are illustrated and supported by close readings. Bibliography and index.

Owen, Stephen. *The End of the Chinese "Middle Ages": Essays in Mid-Tang Literary Culture*. Stanford, Calif.: Stanford University Press, 1996. An examination of Chinese literary and intellectual life during the Tang Dynasty. Bibliographical references, index.

_____. *The Making of Early Chinese Classical Poetry*. Cambridge, Mass.: Harvard University Asia Center, 2006. A study of poems written between the end of the first century B.C.E. and the third century C.E., demonstrating that despite differences in author and genre, they were remarkably similar. The writer argues that later classical poetry evolved out of this tradition. Introductory overview, seven appendixes, bibliography, and index.

Seaton, Jerome P., ed. *The Shambhala Anthology of Chinese Poetry*. Boston: Shambhala, 2006. This book compiles 380 poems by China's great poets, representing three thousand years of Chinese literature. The poems Seaton chose for this volume are representative of the poets' works, and all were translated by Seaton himself. He makes the poems easily accessible by grouping them into historical periods and writing an informative introduction to each group, lending to their historical, cultural, and literary significance.

Sze, Arthur, trans. *The Silk Dragon: Translations from the Chinese*. Port Townsend, Wash.: Copper Canyon Press, 2001. Translations into English of Chinese poems from the fourth through the twentieth centuries.

Weinberger, Eliot, ed. *The New Directions Anthology of Classical Chinese Poetry*. New York: New Directions, 2003. Contains 250 poems, some of them in translations crafted by Ezra Pound, William Carlos Williams, Kenneth Rexroth, and Gary Snyder, and others by the esteemed poet, scholar, and translator David Hinton. Includes essays by the translators and comments by the Chinese poets themselves. In his introduction, Weinberg discusses how American poets have been influenced by their Chinese counterparts. Biographical notes.

Wu, Fusheng. *The Poetics of Decadence: Chinese Poetry of the Southern Dynasties and Late Tang Periods*. Albany: State University of New York Press, 1998. Includes examination of Li Shangyin and other poets of the fourth to tenth centuries. Bibliographical references, index.

Yeh, Michelle, and N. G. D. Malmqvist, eds. *Frontier Taiwan: An Anthology of Modern Chinese Poetry*. New York: Columbia University Press, 2001. A substantial (nearly five-hundred-page) anthology of Taiwanese poetry. Bibliography and a map.

Yip, Wai-lim, ed. and trans. *Chinese Poetry: An Anthology of Major Modes and Genres*. 2d ed. Durham, N.C.: Duke University Press, 1997. A classic anthology, containing 150 poems in every major genre. Poems are printed both in calligraphic form, with word-for-word annotations, and in English translation. In an introductory essay, the editor explains Chinese aesthetics, and each section of the volume is preceded by a short commentary and followed by a bibliography.

Richard P. Benton
Updated by Nicholas Birns

TIBETAN POETRY

Tibetans refer to their country as the "Land of Snows," and this name accurately conveys the remoteness, mystery, and beauty of the land that contains the world's highest mountain, Everest (or "Goddess Mother of the Snows" in Tibetan). Tibet continues to be, even in the twenty-first century, nearly geographically and politically isolated. Tibet, an autonomous region of the People's Republic of China, covers an area of approximately 500,000 square miles. By contrast, historical Tibet—the region over which the cultural, religious, and frequently political influence of Tibet extended—encompassed roughly double that area and included all the highland plateaus between the Himalayan mountain range in the south and the Altyn Tagh and Kunlun ranges in the north.

The Tibetan Empire was established prior to the seventh century C.E., and recorded Tibetan history begins with the reign of Srong-brtsan sgam-po, who ruled Tibet from 620 to 649. Through its military campaigns, Tibet came into contact with a number of civilizations which had an immediate and profound influence on Tibetan culture. The religions and cultures of Iran, Gilgit, Kashmir, Turfan, Khotan, China, and, perhaps most important, the Buddhist kingdoms of northern India, all had an impact on the development of Tibetan civilization.

Tibetans attribute the invention of their alphabet to Thonmi Sambhota, a minister of Srong-brtsan sgam-po. The king first sent a group of Tibetans to India to study Indian alphabets to develop an alphabet suited to the Tibetan language, but this group met with failure. Srong-brtsan sgam-po then sent Thonmi to India. Thonmi's success is attested by the epithet "Sam-bho-ta" ("Excellent Tibetan"), given him by his Indian teachers, and by the attribution to his authorship of eight books, only two of which are extant, on the subject of Tibetan grammar and scripts.

The Tibetan language, part of the Sino-Tibetan language family, is a monosyllabic language with no inflection of verbs or nouns. The alphabet that Thonmi devised for Tibetan includes thirty consonants and four vowels and is written from left to right. Thonmi adapted his alphabet from a Kashmiri model and fashioned two styles of script: The *dbu-can* (literally, "having a head") script is most frequently used in printed books, while the cursive script, *dbu-med* (literally, "without a head"), is used in documents, letters, and some books. Later, a more stylized cursive called *khyug-yig* (literally, "running script"), was developed and used for correspondence as well as for official documents.

The format of Tibetan books also followed an Indian model, the *pothi*: Tibetan books were printed on oblong pages and kept unbound between two wooden covers, which were frequently decorated with carvings or with polychrome paintings. Tibetan manuscripts were frequently adorned with illuminations of the Buddha or of various religious teachers, done in gouache; these manuscripts were often written in an ink made of ground gold or silver. Tibetan printed books were produced by means of hand-carved printing blocks or, less frequently, metal plates. Because an individual block or plate was required for each page of a work, the expense of producing a Tibetan book was considerable, and vast warehouses were required for the storage of printing blocks. The religious nature of Tibetan literature, however, transformed the labor and expense of book printing into an act of religious devotion. The colophons of Tibetan books customarily record the names of carvers, artists, editors, and patrons whose dedicated labor and financial support made the production of such books possible and gained spiritual merit for the participating individuals.

The actual printing of Tibetan books was supervised by the monasteries which owned the appropriate printing blocks, and it was customary for books to be printed only on demand. The customer generally was responsible for providing the necessary paper and was naturally expected to compensate the monastery for the labor involved in printing and, just as important, checking the finished edition for completeness and legibility. The paper of Tibetan books is frequently toxic, a result of the use of poisonous plants, notably several species of daphne, in its production, and of the practice of adding arsenic to the paper to discourage its destruction by insects. Extant catalogs (*kar-chag*) of many monastic printing houses are of enormous value in the study of Tibetan literary history. Manuscripts, particularly those with ornamental writing and illuminations, were produced up to the present century and were particularly favored by wealthy, if only marginally literate, patrons. Such manuscripts were most frequently copies of various editions of well-known Buddhist works, such as the *Prajnyaparamita* (perfection of wisdom), and were usually consigned to the altar of a wealthy individual to serve as an object of veneration, to be read only when a visiting monk was commissioned to read or chant the text.

Religion and Tibetan literature

Although Tibet enjoys a rich tradition of folk literature, the bulk of Tibetan literature is religious, representing the country's two major religions, Buddhism and Bonpo, the latter a pre-Buddhist Tibetan religion incorporating some elements of indigenous folk beliefs as well as influences from the religions of other countries, such as Iran. A significant amount of Buddhist literature consists of translations from the Indian Buddhist canon. The Tibetan *bKa'-'gyur* (also known as *Kanjur*), which is considered to contain the actual teachings of the Buddha, consists of 108 volumes, while the *bsTan-'gyur* (also known as *Tanjur*), which contains the orthodox textual exegesis of the *bKa'-'gyur*, contains 225 volumes.

The indigenous religious literature of Tibet is immeasurably vast and rich, including works which deal not only with religion and philosophy but also with history, medicine, science, grammar, astrology, divination, and the techniques of crafts, such as painting and the casting of bronze images. The collected works (*gsung-'bum*) of many important Tibetan religious figures are, in fact, encyclopedic in their contents and contain, in addition to learned discourses on the topics mentioned, a wealth of information in the form of correspondence and private biographical writings.

Tibetan literature abounds with a variety of minor religious genres that parallel those of medieval Europe, such as the hagiography, the pilgrimage guide, the exemplum, and the mystical visionary account. The *'das-log* genre, which deals specifically with visionary accounts of the journey to the underworld, is particularly rich in its correspondences, not only to similar visionary literature in the writings of medieval Christian saints but also to similar themes in many epic and folk traditions throughout the world.

The influence of earlier literary and oral traditions is often evident in Tibetan literature, particularly in the hagiographic literature. In addition to containing motifs and themes which clearly derive from a folk tradition, such works sometimes alternate passages of prose and verse, in which religious teachings are presented in the form of didactic poetry. The *Hundred-Thousand Songs* of the Tibetan poet and saint Milarepa (1040-1123) is the best-known example of such a work.

The provenance of many early Tibetan religious works, particularly those of the Buddhist *rNying-ma* (old ones) school and many works in the Bonpo tradition, is obscure. An entire genre called *gTer-ma* ("treasure") is purported to be the work of various historical (and sometimes mythical) religious personages and to have been unearthed by later religious masters called *gTer-bston* ("revealers of treasure"). The *Bar-do thos-sgrol* (book that grants liberation in the place between death and rebirth merely by its hearing, commonly called *The Tibetan Book of the Dead* in Western translations) is such a work and is attributed to the eighth century Indian Tantric master Padmasambhava, who is venerated as one of the two major founders of Tibetan Buddhism.

The Tibetan Book of the Dead is perhaps the best-known Tibetan work in the West, although it is far from representative of the many genres and schools of Tibetan literature. The book contains teachings that guide the deceased person through the transitory illusions that appear after death. These illusions serve to confirm the individual's belief in the existence of his or her individual ego, binding the individual to the cycle of death, rebirth, and suffering, which, in the Buddhist view, prevents one's entry into the state of nirvana. In *The Tibetan Book of the Dead*, poetic prayers alternate with admonitions and instructions in prose, both couched in an archaic style. Despite the book's title, which seems to guarantee its efficacy if it is simply read to the deceased, most Tibetan religious teachers insist that its contents must be internalized over years of serious study, so that one's responses to the illusions of *The Tibetan Book of the Dead* are both spontaneous and deliberate.

Since *The Tibetan Book of the Dead* contains several references to deities that may be of Bonpo origin, it is frequently supposed that much early Tibetan Buddhist literature, particularly of the rNying-ma sect, is suffused with non-Buddhist (that is, Bonpo, animist, or even shamanistic) ideas. This view does little justice to the seriousness with which the Tibetans translated Indian Buddhist works and ignores the system through which teams of highly educated monks proofread editions of religious works prior to their publication. Although Buddhist teachers were willing to accommodate the indigenous Tibetan deities, who were converted to the status of "Protectors of the [Buddhist] Religion" by Padmasambhava and other religious masters, the correct doctrinal content of Buddhist literary works was scrupulously maintained. Thus, the view that Tibetan Buddhism represents an unorthodox version of Buddhism (often labeled "Lamaism") is inaccurate and misleading.

It is evident that many of the similarities of Bonpo and Buddhist literature derive from a Bonpo imitation of the script, style, and genres of Buddhist literature brought to Tibet from India. Although the Bonpo religion had a rich tradition of its own, the existence of a Bonpo literature before the advent of Buddhism in Tibet is doubtful. The Bonpo possess several of their own specialized scripts, but the majority of these scripts clearly derive from the cursive Tibetan alphabet. The language of these texts is exceedingly complex, partly because of the custom of writing in an abbreviated form (in which several letters of certain words may be omitted) and partly because the vocabulary of Bonpo writings contains words of Zhang-zhung, rather than Tibetan, origin. Zhang-zhung was an area that lay to the west of Tibet in the Himalayas; it was at one time an independent country with its own language, and it was there that gShen-rab, the founder of the Bonpo religion, is believed to have lived. When the area was incorporated into the Tibetan state in the late eighth century, the language and script of the Tibetan Empire were adopted. The writings of the Bonpo religion, which flourished in Zhang-zhung, were thus translated into Tibetan and naturally followed the stylistic pattern of Buddhist writings. The Bonpo possess an extensive literature, including their own versions of the *bKa'-'gyur* and *bsTan-'gyur*.

The first period of Buddhist development in Tibet, initiated by its establishment as the state religion in 779, lasted until the reign of Glang-dar-ma, who ruled Tibet from 838 to 842 and who restored Bonpo as the official state religion. This period signaled the decline of Tibet as an imperial power in Inner Asia and witnessed the persecution of Buddhists and the return to a state of feudal anarchy. The establishment of the state of Gu-ge in western Tibet in the late ninth century marked a return to both political stability and Buddhism. This period is known as the "second introduction" of Buddhism to Tibet, and the vital link with Indian Buddhist teachers and monasteries played a central role. Countless Tibetans made the rigorous and expensive journey to India to learn Buddhist doctrine directly from eminent Indian Buddhist masters, and on their return to Tibet, many of these individuals naturally attracted their own disciples. The groups that formed in this manner developed their own particular literatures and liturgies. Each was Buddhist, but each had a peculiar identity shaped by the characteristics of its founder.

In this fashion, a number of Buddhist schools developed in Tibet: The bKa'-rgyud-pa school was founded by Mar-pa (1012-1096); the Sa-skya-pa school was founded by 'Khon-dkon-mchog rGyal-po in 1073; and so on. Several of these schools played a major role in both the internal and the external politics of Tibet. In the thirteenth century, the Sa-skya-pa school had a central role in Tibet's relations with the Mongol Empire, and in 1642, the control of secular power in the Tibetan state was transferred to a religious leader, the Dalai Lama (a Mongolian epithet meaning "Religious Teacher [whose knowledge is as vast as the] Ocean"). Thereafter, ecclesiastical rule (often, and inexactly, called a "theocracy") was to continue in Tibet until the Fourteenth Dalai Lama's flight from Tibet to India during the Chinese annexation of Tibet in 1959.

PRE-BUDDHIST FOLK LITERATURE

Both the Tibetan Buddhists and the Bonpo distinguish the period preceding the Tibetan imperial period as the time in which the *mi-chos* (religion of humans) flourished, in contrast to the later period in which Buddhism and Bonpo, which share the common label of *lha-chos* (divine religion), came to Tibet. The literature of this period consisted mainly of two genres: the *lde'u*, or riddle and the *sgrung* (sometimes called *sgrung-gtam*), a narrative legend or fable.

These early works dealt chiefly with creation legends and traditional codes of behavior. The *lde'u* are essentially proverbs that carry a moral message, while the *sgrung* are tales composed by storytellers and based on the earliest myths and legends of the Tibetan people. The language of these works is frequently complex, and the abundance of often obscure metaphors increases the difficulty of understanding such texts. Nevertheless, these texts are of great interest, since they represent an archaic body of writings which obviously had a basis in an oral tradition.

Some of the most striking examples of such literature are found in the ancient literary fragments unearthed at Dunhuang, an oasis city in the western part of the Chinese province of Gansu. Here, an ancient library was sealed up in the early part of the eleventh century, escaping discovery until the early part of the twentieth century. A collection of approximately eight hundred manuscripts was obtained from this site by the famous explorer Sir Marc Aurel Stein, and a selection of these manuscripts is available in English translation with extensive introductions and notes in F. W. Thomas's *Ancient Folk-Literature from North-Eastern Tibet* (1957).

The collection edited by Thomas includes writings in both prose and verse, the latter generally favoring dactylic meter. These texts include several tales of a mythical nature. One tale tells of humankind's fall from an earlier golden age to an "Age of Debts and Taxes," which was brought on by the return to the sky of a lineage of divine kings. Another tale repeats the theme of the decline of a golden age, during which all creatures lived in harmony, and the subsequent dark age, brought on by the influences of evil demons and ill luck, during which the horse became separated from its wild relative, the *kiang* (a species of wild ass) and fell under the subjugation of humans. Other texts contain long lists of proverbs or manuals devoted to the methods of *mo* divination. These writings display a vigorous style with frequent repetitions and parallelism, derivative of earlier oral sources, and extensive onomatopoeia. The overall tone of these works is decidedly pessimistic, and the theme of social decline that pervades them is reminiscent of similar complaints found in the authors of classical antiquity in the West.

THE GE-SAR EPIC

The Ge-sar epic is the most important epic cycle in Inner Asia, and versions of it are found in all the major areas of Tibet and Mongolia, as well as in areas occupied by various Turkic tribes and in areas bordering the Himalayas, such as Sikkim and Hunza. The epic alternates brief prose passages with longer poetic sections, which are sung by an epic bard in a variety of melodies; each melody implies a particular mood or tone and is selected by the bard to suit each poetic passage. The first written version of the Ge-sar epic dates from approximately the fifteenth century, but the earlier existence of the epic cycle is attested by references in eleventh century texts, and it is certain that portions of the epic existed in the oral literature of Inner Asia for centuries before that date.

Ge-sar's name derives from the Byzantine word for emperor, *kaisar*, a cognate of the Latin *caesar* and the German *Kaiser*, and early texts connect his name with the place-name Phrom (Rome, meaning, in this context, Byzantium). Despite this unexplained connection with Byzantium, the hero of the Tibetan epic is identified as the ruler of a land called Gling, a kingdom which once existed in an area of Tibet that later became part of the provinces of Kham and Amdo. It has been pointed out by Rolf A. Stein in *Tibetan Civilization* (1972), however, that the term *Gling* is to be considered an abbreviation for the phrase *'dzam-bu-gling*, a Tibetan term referring to the world continent of Jambudvipa; thus, the epithet *Gling* may be taken to mean that Ge-sar is the ruler of the entire world, not merely of a particular Tibetan kingdom.

There are many versions of the Ge-sar epic in Tibet, with many episodes devoted to his conquest of various countries, including China, Iran, Kashmir, and the Na-khi region of Yunnan. Several versions of the epic even include an episode in which Ge-sar descends to Hell and conquers the Lord of the Underworld; this episode is of particular interest to the comparative study of the epic in Asia and the West, since a majority of epics, including *The Epic of Gilgamesh* (c. 2000 B.C.E., *Gilgamesh Epic*, 1917), Homer's *Odyssey* (c. 725 B.C.E.; English translation, 1614), and several versions of the romances of Alexander the Great, feature an underworld journey. The Ge-sar epic invariably begins in a heavenly realm. There, a group of gods decide that it is necessary to send a divine leader to humankind, and they convince one of their number to be born as a man. After a miraculous birth and several attempts on his life by his uncle, the child who is to become Ge-sar retreats with his mother to a desert. By the use of magically produced illusions, Ge-sar convinces the tribal leaders—particularly his uncle—to take part in a horse race that will determine the leadership of the empire. Ge-sar naturally triumphs and goes on to lead his people to victory over all the countries of the world.

The religion of the Ge-sar epic belongs to the *mi-chos* tradition, although the epic has exerted an influence on later Bonpo and Buddhist works. The Ge-sar epic is still sung by epic bards and may take days or weeks to complete. The propagation of the Ge-sar epic is generally not encouraged by Tibetan Buddhist schools, although some versions of the epic have been recast in the Buddhist mold and maintain that Ge-sar was sent to Earth to protect the Buddhist religion from its enemies. Ge-sar is nevertheless an important popular hero in Tibet, and, like many folk heroes such as King Arthur in Britain and Frederick I in Germany, is connected with an apocalyptic *cultus* which maintains that Ge-sar will one day lead his people in a final battle against the evil forces of the world.

Tibetan folk poetry

Several distinct genres of folk poetry and songs exist in Tibet and are still performed at special times of the year, such as at the time of planting or harvesting crops, at the celebration of the new year, and at marriages and other special occasions. Popular songs and poems are generally termed *glu* or *glu-bzhas* and are distinguished from poems found in religious writings, which are most often called *mgur* or *dbyangs*.

Gral-glu (row songs) are chanted by groups of singers arranged in rows; their texts consist mainly of sayings whose recitation brings good luck, and they are therefore most frequently sung at weddings or at new year's festivals. *Chang-glu* (beer songs) are poems composed during drinking parties, while *sgor-bzhas* (circle songs) are sung by groups of men and women who hold hands in a circle and move to the left and right as they chant. *Bzhas-chen* (great songs) are long poems chanted at harvest celebrations.

Poetry in indigenous Buddhist literature

When Tibetan Buddhists engaged in an organized and meticulous campaign of translating the corpus of Indian Buddhist literature, the sophisticated metrical patterns of Indian literature became the models for Tibetan Buddhist poetry; the Tantric songs, called *doha*, of Indian Buddhist mystic poets such as Kanha and Saraha also exerted an influence on Tibetan poetry. The dactyl, which had been the dominant meter in the early Tibetan poetry of the Dunhuang documents, was supplanted by the trochee, which became the dominant form not only in most religious poetry but also in many varieties of secular songs.

Poems containing maxims and proverbs, which have been found in the earliest Tibetan documents excavated at Dunhuang, also found popularity in the writings of Tibetan Buddhist authors. The *Subhasitaratnanidhi*, composed by the eminent Tibetan master Sa-skya Pandita (1182-1251), is an excellent example. The work contains more than 450 four-line poems of an aphoristic nature; its popularity was so great that it was widely circulated in Mongolia as well as in Tibet.

Tibetan exegeses of Tantric Buddhist texts often contain verses which exactly duplicate the Indian *doha*. In a treatise dealing with the *Cakrasamvaratantra*, the Tibetan Sa-skya-pa master Sa-chen Kun-dga'-snying-po relates the legendary biography of the Indian teacher Kanha, a renowned master of the *doha*, by interweaving the narrative of his hagiography with Tibetan *doha* verses composed by Kun-dga'-snying-po. The alternation of prose and verse is a characteristic of much Tibetan literature; perhaps the finest example of this alternating structure of prose and verse is found in the *Biography* and *Hundred-Thousand Songs* composed by the Tibetan poet and Buddhist saint Milarepa.

Milarepa

Milarepa's *Biography* and *Hundred-Thousand Songs* (here, "hundred-thousand" is to be construed as meaning "many" and is not to be taken literally) are perhaps the most widely read books among literate Tibetan laymen and monks alike. Although Milarepa is venerated as one of the founders of the bKa'-rgyud-pa school in Tibet, his works are read by members of all Tibetan religious schools, and literary references to his writings are to be found in the literature of all Tibetan Buddhist sects. The best-known editions of the *Biography* and *Hundred-Thousand Songs* are those compiled by gTsang-smyon He-ru-ka (literally, the mad yogin of gTsang) in 1488, but other editions are known to exist; an especially important edition of the *Hundred-Thousand Songs*, compiled by Rang-byung rDo-rje (1284-1339), the Third Black Hat Karmapa, contains nearly twice as much material as is found in the gTsang-smyon version and was reprinted in 1978.

Milarepa's *Biography* begins with the story of the hero's childhood; in the manner of many Inner Asian folktales and epics, such as the Ge-sar epic and the *Secret History of the Mongols*, the death of Milarepa's father precipitates a period of degradation and poverty for his family that must be avenged by the son. Milarepa's aunt and uncle, who are named as custodians of the father's legacy, treat Mi-la, his mother, and his sister as virtual slaves, and the mother urges Mi-la to learn black magic to effect vengeance. Mi-la travels to study with several sorcerers, and his personal qualities of perseverance and obedience become evident. After acquiring the necessary magical powers, Mi-la avenges the greed of his aunt and uncle by sending a powerful magical assault on their eldest son's wedding feast, destroying his relatives' property and killing all of their guests. His mother is momentarily satisfied but soon informs her son that the villagers are planning to punish her for this destruction. Mi-la responds by sending a hailstorm to devastate the village's crops and thus complete his campaign of vengeance.

Far from resulting in satisfaction, these deeds trouble Milarepa's conscience and lead to an awareness of the karmic consequences that will follow Mi-la for countless future lives. Mi-la then decides to follow the Buddhist path of salvation with the same dedication he showed in his previous studies of black magic. He eventually encounters his religious teacher (*bla-ma* or lama), Mar-pa, whose rigorous and often brutal treatment of Mi-la fills the next section of the *Biography*. Milarepa's determination is rewarded when Mar-pa initiates him as his foremost disciple, and the final third of the *Biography* is an account of Milarepa's experiences as a Buddhist master who leads his own disciples toward the path of enlightenment.

The *Biography* and the *Hundred-Thousand Songs* both consist of prose passages interwoven with Milarepa's religious poems, fashioned after the mystic poems of the Indian *doha* tradition. Milarepa's works achieve a unique beauty, combining the clarity of Buddhist teachings with a distinctly Tibetan appreciation for the beauty of nature (generally perceived as an illusion in conventional Buddhist literature) and for the customs, occupations, and tastes of the Tibetan people. For this reason, Mi-la occupies a central position in Tibetan literature and especially Tibetan poetry; his influence and popularity have been both pervasive and constant in the history of Tibetan literature, art, and drama.

The sixth Dalai Lama

"The Love Songs of the Sixth Dalai Lama" (Tsangyang Gyatso; 1683-1706), translated in 1930 in the *Academia Sinica Monograph*, are a collection of four-line poems that resemble the most common form of the Tibetan folk poem, the *gtang-thung bzhad* ("short song"). This collection contains approximately sixty songs, written in a deceptively simple language. The Sixth Dalai Lama was reputed to be a libertine who frequently left the cloister of his palace, the Potala, in disguise to visit a variety of lovers in Lhasa and to enjoy the local taverns. Such behavior was contrary to the vows of all Buddhist monks, and the Dalai Lama's reputation became the pretext for an invasion of Lhasa by the Khoshot Mongols, who sought to gain control of Tibet. The Dalai Lama was replaced by a monk chosen by the Khoshot leader Lha-bzang and died in captivity.

Despite the seemingly unorthodox behavior of the Sixth Dalai Lama, Tibetans refused to recognize the Khoshot pretender and even today consider Tsangyang Gyatso to have been the legitimate Dalai Lama. It has been suggested that his poetry is, in fact, metaphorical and that the poems should be viewed within the context of Tantric Buddhism rather than as evidence of actual romantic adventures. The question of whether the Sixth Dalai Lama remained true to his monastic vows, however, remains secondary to the beauty of his poems, which may be appreciated for their imagery and language in any case. Several of his poems are remarkably similar to a medieval European form, the aubade, in which lovers are parted by the calls of a town watchman which signal the coming of a new day.

Modern secular poetry

In addition to the *gtang-thung bzhad*, which is the most frequent model for secular poetry, a poetic form favored by educated Tibetans in the past several centuries is the *ka-bzhas*. This poetic form derives its name from the letter *ka*, the first letter of the Tibetan alphabet, and uses the thirty consonants of the Tibetan alphabet as the initial letters, in alphabetical order, of a thirty-line poem. The *ka-bzhas* is often employed in love poems and is also used as an elegant form for correspondence.

WRITERS IN EXILE

During the early years, most of the Tibetan exiles producing literary works were monastic scholars, and if they wrote poetry, it was incorporated in religious texts. The generations that followed were unlikely to know the Tibetan language, for whether they lived in India, in the United States, or elsewhere, they used English in daily life. However, in the 1980's, after the Chinese government relaxed its policy on border crossings, young Tibetans began to arrive in India. Among them were a few who were both fluent in their native language and passionate about literature. In 1990, four of them founded the magazine *Ljang gzhon* (young shoots), whose purpose was to publish literary works written in Tibetan. Other similar publications followed, making it possible for an international literary community to develop. In 1995, the first conference of Tibetan writers was held, with some sixty people in attendance, some of them from as far away as Switzerland and the United States. That same year, several Tibetan anthologies were published.

When four volumes of poems by Hortsang Jigme appeared in 1994, it was the first time in Tibetan history that such a collection had been produced by a layperson, instead of a religious figure, such as a lama. Almost immediately, a number of other collections by lay poets were published, several of them by women writers who had recently escaped from Tibet. Thus literary works by women were accepted into the Tibetan canon. By the beginning of the twenty-first century, though each generation of Tibetans living under Chinese rule was becoming less Tibetan and more Chinese, Tibetans in exile were preserving their language and their culture, and many of the heroes and heroines of this effort were the writers who fled from their native country in order to live in freedom.

BIBLIOGRAPHY

Bosson, James E. *A Treasury of Aphoristic Jewels: The Subhasitaratnanidhi of Sa Skya Pandita in Tibetan and Mongolian*. London: Routledge Curzon, 1997. A collection of 457 quatrains, divided into three sections, Tibetan texts, Mongolian texts, and translations. Excellent introduction, notes, glossary, and bibliography.

Cabezon, Jose I., and Roger R. Jackson. *Tibetan Literature: Studies in Genre*. Ithaca, N.Y.: Snow Lion, 1995. Survey of poetry, novels, biographies, histories, and other writings that span thirteen hundred years.

Coleman, Graham, ed., with Thupten Jinpa. *The Tibetan Book of the Dead*. Composed by Padmasambhava. Translated by Gyurme Dorje. London: Penguin Books, 2005. The great Buddhist work about after-death experiences. Includes an introductory commentary by His Holiness the Dalai Lama. Illustrated. Appendixes, glossary, notes, bibliographical references, and index.

David-Neel, Alexandra, and the Lama Yongden. *The Superhuman Life of Gesar of Ling*. Reprint. Whitefish, Mont.: Kessinger, 2004. A version of the famous Central Asian epic, based on notes the author took at oral recitations.

Evans-Wentz, W. Y. *Tibet's Great Yogi Milarepa*. 3d ed. New York: Oxford University Press, 2000. A new edition of a classic biography of Milarepa, with the original annotations by Evans-Wentz and a new foreword by Donald S. Lopez, Jr.

Hartley, Lauran R., and Patricia Schiaffini-Vedani, eds. *Modern Tibetan Literature and Social Change*. Durham, N.C.: Duke University Press, 2008. Foreword by Matthew T. Kapstein. A volume of essays that has been acclaimed as the first systematic overview of modern Tibetan literature. Appendixes include glossaries of Tibetan spellings and of Chinese terms and a list of contemporary Tibetan literary works in translation. Index.

Jinpa, Thupten, and Jas Elsner. *Songs of Spiritual Experience: Tibetan Buddhist Poems of Insight and Awakening*. Boston: Shambhala, 2000. Fifty-two newly translated works ranging from the eleventh to the twentieth century. Includes helpful introduction and glossary-commentary.

Milarepa, Jetsun. *Drinking the Mountain Stream: Songs of Tibet's Beloved Saint, Milarepa*. Rev. ed. Translated by Lama Kunga Rinpoche and Brian Cutilla. Boston: Wisdom, 1995. Buddhist songs about meditation and liberation. Introductory material explains Buddhist theory and practice, describes Milarepa's world, and comments on his style. Illustrated. Notes and glossary.

Schaeffer, Kurtis R. *The Culture of the Book in Tibet*. New York: Columbia University Press, 2009. Traces the influence of printed works on Tibetan history and culture from the fourteenth century to the eighteenth. Bibliography and index.

_____. *Dreaming the Great Brahmin: Tibetan Traditions of the Buddhist Poet-Saint Saraha*. New York: Oxford University Press, 2005. Explains how such figures as the legendary, mystical poet Saraha were transformed over time and places him and the songs attributed to him within the context of Tibetan literature.

Tucci, Giuseppe. *Tibetan Folk Songs from Gyantse and Western Tibet*. 2d ed. Ascona, Switzerland: Artibus Asiae, 1966. Includes two appendixes by Namkhai Norbu and biographical footnotes.

Zeitlin, Ida. *Gessar Khan: The Legend of Tibet*. 1927. Reprint. Varanasi, India: Pilgrims Publishing, 1998. Chiefly based on the German version of the Mongolian text, edited by Isaac Jakob Schmidt and published in St. Petersburg, Russia, 1839, under the title *Die Thaten Bogda Gesser Chans*. Illustrated by Theodore Nadejen.

Paul A. Draghi
Updated by Rosemary M. Canfield Reisman

DU FU

Born: Gongxian, China; 712
Died: Tanzhou (now Changsha), Hunan Province, China; 770
Also known as: Tu Fu

PRINCIPAL POETRY
Quan Tang shi, 1706
Tang shi san bai shou, 1763 (*The Jade Mountain: A Chinese Anthology*, 1929)
Tu Fu: Selected Poems, 1962 (Zhi Feng, editor; Rewi Alley, translator)
The Selected Poems of Du Fu, 2002 (Burton Watson, translator)
Du Fu: A Life in Poetry, 2008
Spring in the Ruined City: Selected Poems, 2008

OTHER LITERARY FORMS

Du Fu (dew few) is known primarily for his poetry. The 1,450 poems he wrote have been collected through the years in frequently revised and reprinted anthologies and collections such as *Quan Tang shi* and *The Jade Mountain*.

ACHIEVEMENTS

Born during the Tang Dynasty (618-907), the classical period in Chinese literary history, Du Fu was one of four poets whose greatness marked the era. Some fifty thousand poems from that period have survived, the large number resulting primarily from the talents of Du Fu; Wang Wei, basically a nature poet; Bo Juyi, a government official whose poetry often reflected official concerns; and Li Bo, probably the best known of all Chinese poets, a poet of the otherworldly or the sublime.

Du Fu sums up the work of all these poets with the wide range of topics and concerns that appear in his poems. Known variously as "poet-historian," "poet-sage," and "the Master," Du Fu may be China's greatest poet. His "Yue ye" ("Moonlit Night") is perhaps the most famous poem in Chinese literature. His more than fourteen hundred extant poems testify to his productivity; the range of topics in his poetry and the variety of verse that he employed constitute Du Fu's main contribution to Chinese literature.

One of Du Fu's major contributions to Chinese literature was his extensive occasional verse—poems inspired by a journey or by a mundane experience such as building a house. Many of Du Fu's occasional poems were addressed to friends or relatives at some special time in their lives. Distant relatives who held official positions and achieved distinction would receive a laudatory poem. These poems could also be addressed to special friends. Du Fu traveled much in his life, both by choice and involuntarily, relying on friends to shelter and support him, because, for the majority of his life, he was without an official governmental position and salary. His poems would therefore be addressed to these persons as expressions of gratitude and friendship on the occasion of his visit.

Poems about nature abounded during the Tang period, and Du Fu contributed extensively to this genre as well. In contrast to Li Bo, who followed the Daoist philosophy of withdrawal from the world, Du Fu was very much a poet of everyday life, both in his response to nature and the physical world and in his active engagement in the social and political life of his times. Indeed, it has been said that Du Fu's poetry provides a running history of the Chinese state during his era.

Finally, Du Fu was a master of poetic form; his verse forms were as varied as his content. During the Tang period, the *gutishi* (old forms) in Chinese poetry coexisted with the *lushi* (new forms). The old, or "unregulated," forms placed no restrictions on the word tones used in the verse, did not limit the number of lines in a poem, and did not require verbal parallelism. The new forms, or "regulated verse," however, were much more demanding. They mandated certain tonal patterns, especially in rhyme words, a requirement which markedly affected word choice. They also usually restricted the total number of lines in a poem and utilized verbal parallelism. Each of these two major categories of Chinese poetry was also divided into subcategories depending on the meter, which in Chinese poetry depends on the number of words in each line rather than on stressed and unstressed syllables, as in Western poetry. Du Fu adeptly used both old and new forms in his verse, justifying in this respect as in every other his reputation as "the Master."

Biography

Du Fu's life could best be described as one of frustration. Although his mother's family was related to the imperial clan, and both his father and grandfather held official positions in the government, much of Du Fu's life was spent in poverty. Unable to pass the examination for entrance into official service, Du Fu remained, more often than not, a "plain-robed" man, a man without official position and salary. His poems from the mid-730's allude to "the hovel" in which he lived on the outskirts of the capital while the court members resided in the splendor of the palace. One of Du Fu's sons died from starvation in 755 because of the family's poverty, and the poet's sadness and anguish caused by his son's death is reflected in several of Du Fu's poems.

Du Fu was born in Gongxian, Henan Province, in 712. His natural mother died at an early age, and Du Fu's father remarried, eventually adding three brothers and a sister to the family. Du Fu was apparently a very precocious child. In his autobiography, he states unabashedly that at the age of seven he pondered "only high matters" and wrote verses about beautiful birds, while other children his age were dealing with puerile subjects such as dogs and cats. At an early age, Du Fu also mastered a great number of the characters which make up written Chinese. He was writing so extensively by the age of nine, he claims, that his output could easily have filled several large bags. Not much else is known about Du Fu's early years. As would be expected, he was schooled in literary matters in preparation for entrance into official service. A firsthand knowledge of the many facets of Chinese life and the geography of the country also became a part of Du Fu's education: He traveled for about three years before taking the official examination for public service. His poetry of this period reflects the experiences and sights he encountered while traversing the countryside.

In 735, at the age of twenty-three, Du Fu finally took the test to enter government service and failed. Apparently there was something in Du Fu's writing style, in the way he handled the Chinese characters, which did not suit the examiners. This setback in Du Fu's plans ushered in the first of several important phases in his life. Since the poet had failed the examination and was without a position, he resumed his travels. During these travel years, several significant changes occurred in his life. His father died in 740, which prompted a series of poems on the theme of life's impermanence. This event was followed by Du Fu's marriage to a woman from the Cui clan, a marriage which ultimately produced two sons and four daughters for the poet. Finally, and probably most important in terms of his literary work, Du Fu met Li Bo in 744.

Following the Daoist tradition, Li Bo, who was ten years Du Fu's senior, had become a "withdrawn" poet after his banishment from the court. As such, he represented a viewpoint opposite to that of Du Fu concerning a literate man's obligations to Chinese society at that time. Du Fu's poetry exhibits his grappling with these contending views. He was sometimes attracted to the simple lifestyle of Li Bo, but the Confucian ethic under which Du Fu had been reared persevered, and he returned to the capital in 746, eleven years after his first attempt, to repeat the test for an official position. He failed again; this time, according to the historians, one of the emperor's officials was afraid that new appointees to the bureaucracy would weaken the latter's power in the court, so he saw to it that everyone who took the examination failed. The frustration and humiliation resulting from this second failure to pass the examination, perhaps heightened by the fact that his younger brother had passed the examination earlier, did not seem to deter Du Fu from his goal of securing an official post. Although he was forced to move outside the capital with his family and to rely on support from friends and relatives to survive, Du Fu seemingly resolved to gain an official position through another route, this time by ingratiating himself with important people who could aid his quest.

Wei Ji was one such person. As an adviser to the emperor, he was in a position to help Du Fu when the occasion arose. Du Fu was also well acquainted with Prince Li Jin, a pleasure-loving, undisciplined figure who was an embarrassment to the court. The prince had a great appreciation for literature, however, and after Du Fu wrote several poems dealing with "The Eight Immortals of the Wine Cup," as the prince and his coterie were called, the prince took a special liking to the poet. Because of these friendships, Du Fu's name was heard around the court, and when he wrote the "Three Great Ceremonies" poems, their excellence and their laudatory treatment of the emperor engendered imperial recognition and favor. A third examination for an official position ensued as a result. Whether Du Fu passed or failed this one was of little consequence; finally, at the age of forty-four, he was given an official position by imperial decree. (Li Bo's position with the court had also been established by imperial decree because he had refused to take the civil-service exam as a matter of principle.) Ironically, Du Fu refused the position. It apparently involved moving to a distant western district, and because the position required him to be a part of the police administration, it would also have involved beating people for infractions of the law, something Du Fu was not inclined to do. The poet's refusal found some sympathy in the court, and he was appointed instead to the heir apparent's household. Thus, the years 755 and 756 stand as pivotal ones in Du Fu's life: He received his first official position in the government after many years of struggle, and strangely enough, he gave up that position because he rapidly grew to dislike the servile aspects of the job. Amid all this, the An Lushan Rebellion began.

For the remainder of his life, Du Fu was one of the many who endured the misfortunes of this war. When the rebellion began in 756, the emperor was forced to flee the capital, as did Du Fu. The latter's poems from that period depict the many defeats of the imperial army. Once he had established his family in the relative safety of Fuzhou in the north, Du Fu set out to join the Traveling Palace of the displaced emperor, but he was captured by rebel forces and taken back to the capital, which they occupied. Held by the rebels for several months, he finally escaped and joined the Traveling Palace as a censor, an official responsible for reminding the emperor of matters which required his attention. During this period, Du Fu did not hear from his family for more than a year, and he wrote possibly the most famous poem in Chinese literature, a love poem to his wife and children entitled "Moonlit Night."

The capital was retaken the next year, 757, and Du Fu was reunited with his family. His "Journey North" describes the effects of the war on the Chinese people and countryside, as well as his homecoming to his family. With the government reestablished in the capital, Du Fu returned there with his family for official service. This period of service was also short-lived; he once again grew tired of the bureaucratic life and its constraints. Floods and the war had devastated the countryside around the capital, so Du Fu took his family west to flee the war and to find food. The war, however, also spread to the west, and as a result, Du Fu once again shifted his family, this time southward to Zhengdu, five hundred miles from the fighting.

The time he spent in the south has been labeled Du Fu's "thatched hut" period. This was something of a pastoral period in his life, during which he seemed to emulate Li Bo and the Daoist ethic to some degree. The war, however, persisted both in the countryside and in Du Fu's poems. The rebellion finally spread even to the south, and Du Fu was forced to leave his thatched hut in 765. He spent the remaining five years of his life in restless travel, cataloging in poetry his journeys and the events he witnessed. Du Fu, "the Master," died in 770, at the age of fifty-eight, as he traveled the Xiang River looking for a haven from the ill health and ill times which had beset him.

Analysis

Du Fu's poetry deals with a multitude of concerns and events. His verses express the moments of self-doubt and frustration which plagued the poet, such as when he failed the civil-service examinations or when he became increasingly afflicted by physical ailments later in life, referring to himself in one verse as an "emaciated horse." Du Fu's poems also deal with painting and the other arts, and they often employ allusions to outstanding figures in China's literary and political past to comment on contemporary conditions. It is, however, in his poems addressed to family and friends and in his nature poems that the substance and depth of his verse can be most clearly seen.

Among Du Fu's finest poems are those which express his love for friends and family. Poems addressed to friends constituted both a literary and a social convention in China during the Tang period. In literate society, men sought one another for friendship and intellectual companionship, and poems of the "address and answer" variety were often composed by the poet. Several examples occur in the poems which Du Fu wrote either to or about Li Bo, his fellow poet. After the two met in 744, they traveled together extensively, and a firm bond, both personal and scholarly, was established between them. In one poem commemorating the two poets' excursion to visit a fellow writer, Du Fu explained his feeling toward Li Bo: "I love my Lord as young brother loves elder brother/ . . . Hand in hand we daily walk together." In "A Winter Day," Du Fu writes that "Since early dawn I have thought only of you [Li Bo]," thoughts which may have been both pleasant and painful for Du Fu as he grappled with the question of whether he wanted to continue his quest for a governmental position or follow Li Bo's example and become a "withdrawn" poet. Du Fu also highly praised Li Bo's verses. In a later poem, "the Master" laments the fact that Li Bo has become unstable, but he also rejoices in the gift of Li Bo's talent: "My thoughts are only of love for his talent./ Brilliant are his thousand poems."

The concern and admiration which Du Fu felt and expressed poetically were not directed solely to other poets. Many of his poems of this type were addressed to longtime friends. "Zeng Wei ba chu shi" ("For Wei Ba, in Retirement") is one example which not only expresses Du Fu's friendship for Wei Ba but also describes the life stages the two have passed through together. The poet comments on how briefly their youth lasted, observing that "Though in those days you were not married/ Suddenly sons and daughters troop in." The two friends have not seen each other for twenty years, "both our heads have become grizzled," and Du Fu knows that the next day will separate them again. He is elated, however, by the "sense of acquaintance" his friend revives in him, and the poet captures that sense in his verse.

"Moonlit Night"

Du Fu was separated from his family several times, sometimes by the war, sometimes by economic conditions. His most famous poem, "Moonlit Night," expresses his deep concern for his wife as "In her chamber she alone looks out/ . . . In the sweet night her cloud-like tresses are damp/ In the clear moonlight her jade-like arms are cold." The poet wonders how long it will be before ". . . we two nestle against those unfilled curtains/ With the moon displaying the dried tear-stains of us both?" Essentially a love poem for the poet's wife, "Moonlit Night" was an unconventional work in its time. Wives in ancient China were seen primarily as pieces of reproductive machinery, with no intellectual capabilities. A poet might lavish great sentiment in verse on a male companion, but tender thoughts concerning a wife were rarely expressed in poetry.

"The River by Our Village"

In true classical fashion, Du Fu was also a nature poet. He could portray nature in an idyllic vein, as in "The River by Our Village," in which the poet describes how "Clear waters wind around our village/ With long summer days full of loveliness/ Fluttering in and out from the house beams the swallows play/ Waterfowl disport together as everlasting lovers." These lines reflect the contentment of Du Fu's pastoral or "thatched hut" period; he ends the poem by asking: "What more could I wish for?"

"The Winding River"

While many of Du Fu's nature poems are distinguished by their vivid evocation of landscapes and wildlife for their own sake, he also treats nature symbolically. In "The Winding River," falling blossoms signify the changing of the seasons and cause the poet to ". . . grieve to see petals flying/ Away in the wind. . . ." This evidence of mutability engenders further reflection; as the poet watches "Butterflies going deeper and deeper/ In amongst the flowers, dragon-flies/ Skimming and flicking over the water," he is reminded that "Wind, light, and time ever revolve," that the only constant factor in life is change. In turn, the poet is led to reflect on the inconsequential and often futile nature of his and other men's ambitions: ". . . why should I be lured/ By transient rank and honours?" Nature instructs him ". . . to live/ Along with her" in a rich and full harmony rather than existing in the pale semblance of living which men have created for themselves.

Because of the range of his sympathy, Du Fu has been compared to William Shakespeare: Both were able to encompass in their works the whole teeming life of their times. Although Du Fu's declaration "In poetry I have exhausted human topics" may seem an overstatement, his many poems and their varied concerns seem almost to justify such a claim.

Bibliography

Chou, Eva Shan. *Reconsidering Tu Fu*. 1995. Reprint. New York: Cambridge University Press, 2006. Chou examines the styles and techniques of Du Fu's poetry as well as his literary legacy. Contains some translations of poems. Bibliography and index.

Davis, A. R. *Tu Fu*. New York: Twayne, 1971. General and concise, addressing simply the often complicated problems of form and theme.

Du Fu. *The Selected Poems of Du Fu*. Translated by Burton Watson. New York: Columbia University Press, 2002. A collection of Du Fu's poems, translated into English by a noted specialist on China. The introduction provides a great deal of biological and background information.

_____. *The Selected Poems of Tu Fu*. Translated by David Hinton. New York: New Directions, 1989. A collection of Du Fu's poetic works, translated into English.

Hawkes, David. *A Little Primer of Tu Fu*. Oxford, England: Clarendon Press, 1967. Written for readers who know little Chinese. The volume contains the texts of thirty-five of Du Fu's poems in Chinese characters and Pinyin romanization, with descriptions in English of titles, subjects, and poetic forms followed by exegeses and translations. Can be employed as a very useful textbook.

Hung, William. *Tu Fu: China's Greatest Poet*. New York: Russell and Russell, 1969. The most valuable study in English. Clear and highly readable, it includes a volume of notes and incorporates translations of 374 poems.

McCraw, David R. *Du Fu's Laments from the South*. Honolulu: University of Hawaii Press, 1992. An examination of Du Fu's travels in Sichuan and his poetic output. Bibliography and indexes.

Pine, Red, trans. *Poems of the Masters: China's Classic Anthology of T'ang and Sung Dynasty Verse*. Port Townsend, Wash.: Copper Canyon Press, 2003. A collection of poetry from the Tang and Song Dynasties that includes the work of Du Fu. Indexes.

Seaton, J. P., and James Cryer, trans. *Bright Moon, Perching Bird: Poems by Li Po and Tu Fu*. Scranton, Pa.: Harper & Row, 1987. This work, part of the Wesleyan Poetry in Translation series, features the works of Li Bo and Du Fu, two Tang poets. Provides some information on Tang Dynasty poetry.

Seth, Vikram, trans. *Three Chinese Poets: Translations of Poems by Wang Wei, Li Bai, and Du Fu*. Boston: Faber and Faber, 1992. A collection of poems by Du Fu, Li Bo, and Wang Wei. Commentary provides useful information.

Kenneth A. Howe

LI BO

Born: Xinjiang Uygur, China (now in Chinese Turkistan); 701
Died: Dangtu, Anhwei Province, China; December, 762
Also known as: Li Bai; Li Pai; Li Po; Li Taibo; Li T'ai-pai; Li T'ai-po

PRINCIPAL POETRY
"Ballad of Chang-an," n.d. (as "The River Merchant's Wife: A Letter"; Ezra Pound, translator, 1915)
The Poetry and Career of Li Po, 1950 (Arthur Waley, editor)
Li Po and Tu Fu, 1973 (Arthur Cooper, editor)

OTHER LITERARY FORMS

Some of the letters and other prose writings of Li Bo (lee boh) survive, but his reputation rests entirely on his poetry.

ACHIEVEMENTS

Li Bo and his younger contemporary Du Fu (Tu Fu) rank as the two greatest poets in the three thousand years of Chinese literary history. Each has the reputation, and the merit, of William Shakespeare in the English tradition.

By the age of forty, Li Bo was a popular poet, well known for the audacity of his poetry and his personality, but he was not widely considered an outstanding poet in his own lifetime. Contemporaries who liked his work despite its unconventional extravagance were highly enthusiastic about it. His friend Zui Zongzhi praised it as "incomparable," and for several years Li Bo held a special position as a favored writer in the court of the emperor. In the last few years of his life, however, Li Bo's influence waned.

Interest in Li Bo's work began to revive several decades after his death, and the acclaim he received from the leading poets and critics early in the next century established him in the position of high regard that he has held ever since. His works were read, and memorized, by educated people throughout East Asia. Many later poets reveal debts to his compelling language, his gift for visualizing imagined scenes, and his intensely personal way of viewing the world. Li Bo's ability to produce a unique twist in image, language, or perspective set his poems apart, even those on traditional topics.

In many ways, Li Bo's playfulness, his individualism, and his visionary flamboyance make him the most accessible of all traditional Chinese poets for the modern Western reader. One measure of Li Bo's effect on modern-day readers of English is the number of translations available. Some of the strongest of Ezra Pound's poems after Chinese originals in *Cathay: Translations by Ezra Pound for the Most Part from the Chinese of Rihaku, from the Notes of the Late Ernest Fenollosa and the Decipherings of the Profes-*

sors Mori and Ariga (1915) are those attributed to "Rihaku," which is the Japanese pronunciation of the Chinese "Li Bo." Shigeyoshi Obata's free renditions will appeal to some readers, though others will find the English old-fashioned and too ornate. Arthur Waley's brief book on Li Bo's life and poetry at times reflects Waley's lack of affinity with his subject. The layers of meaning in the poems are sometimes overlooked and the slippery facts of Li Bo's life get muddled, but Waley's skill in Chinese and in English gives the book value. Extensive notes to individual poems are only one of the strengths of Arthur Cooper's translations.

Among the many excellent translations are the lucid, striking renditions by the poet David Young, and the more scholarly—but highly readable—work of Eiling Eide and Stephen Owen. In addition, most anthologies of translated Chinese poetry include works by Li Bo. *Sunflower Splendor* (1975) makes an excellent starting place; it contains a bibliography of anthologies for further reading. Li Bo's daring and robust spirit, his vivid sense of the sublime and the supernatural, and his profound understanding of the creative power of the poetic mind have as much to say to the modern Westerner as they have said to Asian readers for more than a millennium.

Biography

Li Bo lived at the height of one of China's richest eras of cultural and political greatness. The Tang Empire stretched in some places beyond the borders of China today, and trade flourished, ranging to India, Japan, the Middle East, and even Greece. The poets of Li Bo's generation rode the crests of twin waves of innovation and the consolidation of earlier achievements. Despite the political instability that marred the final period of Li Bo's life, he lived for forty-four of his sixty-odd years under an emperor whose reign is rightly called a golden age.

It is difficult to pin down the facts of Li Bo's life. So colorful a figure naturally has inspired a number of legends. The poet evidently encouraged such legend making in his own lifetime, the more extravagant the better, such as the story that he was fathered by the spirit of the planet known in the West as Venus.

While the great majority of the people under the Tang Empire, especially the people in power, were Han Chinese, Li Bo himself was probably at least partly of Turkish or Iranian descent. Li Bo claimed that an ancestor of his had been exiled from China and that his family had lived for about a century in various settlements along trade routes in and around what is now Afghanistan. A good bit of evidence suggests the family's non-Chinese cultural orientation: Li Bo's ability to write poetry in "a foreign language," several family members' names (including those of Li Bo's two sons), the affinity for Central Asian culture shown in the content and form of many of his poems, and such stereotypically "foreign" personality traits as Li Bo's love of drinking. None of this evidence is conclusive, but it is the first of several indications that Li Bo's life was shaped by his position as an outsider in the empire. The Tang taste for the exotic and the

Turkish connections of the imperial family meant that the work of a "foreigner" would have had a special appeal (many poets of the era were influenced by Central Asian themes and music), but Han Chinese ethnocentricity meant that the "foreigner" himself would always have been regarded as exactly that.

Li Bo's family moved to Sichuan Province, in southwest China, when he was about five years old. They were probably traders. Family wealth would explain how Li Bo managed to live without a job in the government, which was the occupation of most male poets and scholars in traditional China, but the low status of merchants would have made his family background another strike against Li Bo in the eyes of the establishment. Even to have grown up in Sichuan would have given him a markedly regional air. Owen points out the impact the particular traditions of the area may have had on Li Bo in defining himself as a nonconformist, a bold and impulsive person, and a writer not of mainstream aristocratic verse, but of a poetry that returns to the greatness of the past.

Stories of Li Bo's youth suggest the intelligence and the interest in occult learning revealed in his poems. The biographies of most poets of Li Bo's era routinely claim that their subjects were brilliant students in childhood and that they could compose verse at an early age; the reports on Li Bo are the same, but there is no reason not to believe them, if taken with a grain of salt. Poems written when he was about fifteen show Li Bo's great talent and his already distinctive violation of contemporary ideas of "proper" restraint in poetry. Li Bo apparently also lived and studied as a mountain recluse for some time before leaving Sichuan.

In his early twenties, Li Bo began a period of wandering in the great valley of the Yangzi River in central China. The role he adopted, that of a daring and noble-hearted knight errant who righted wrongs with his sword, again shows his energy and his taste for an unconventional lifestyle.

At the time of Li Bo's first marriage, in the early 730's, he was living in what is now Hubei Province, in the north-central Yangzi Basin. He made exaggerated claims for the ancestry of his wife, whose family name was Xu, as he did for his own. It was to her that his daughter Pingyang and his elder son Boquin were born. His younger son's name was Poli. The poet probably had one other formal wife and two concubines, but the facts are unclear.

Li Bo then moved north and east to Shandong Province, where he continued writing and enjoying the company of friends, and from where he traveled to the scenic regions of southeast China. He enjoyed poem exchanges, banquets in the entertainment district, and poeticizing excursions to sites famous for their natural beauty. The constant succession of occasions calling for a poem had good results; like that of so many Chinese poets, Li Bo's work developed greatly in his middle years.

It was during this period that Li Bo met the Daoist religious teacher who finally arranged for his long-awaited introduction to the imperial court in 742. In that year or the next, the poet was granted a position in the Hanlin Academy, a prestigious group of scholars, holy men, and poets who enjoyed imperial favor.

The outsider had penetrated the inner sanctum of Emperor Xuanzong himself. Perhaps Li Bo never took the civil service exams that were the more usual route of upward mobility because he disdained orthodox learning and officialdom, as he claimed, or perhaps he never took them because he lacked the well-rounded education and influential connections that were necessary to obtain a post. Not all the famous male writers of the Tang era managed to pass the test, but, except for Li Bo, they all tried. Nevertheless, for nearly three years, Li Bo was an eccentric and admired figure in a brilliant court, carousing, composing poems and song lyrics for the emperor and the women of the imperial household, and dashing off imperial decrees on command.

Things changed. The boastful, impetuous Li Bo was no courtier. In 744, evidently as the result of an intrigue, he lost the emperor's favor and was given "permission" to "return to the hills." This banishment began another period of wandering and visiting whomever might take interest in the company of this colorful and brilliant poet. Li Bo and Du Fu met when Li Bo was in his early forties and Du Fu in his early thirties; Du Fu's many admiring poems addressed to Li Bo suggest the force of the older poet's personality.

A decade later, a rebellion forced the emperor to abdicate. Li Bo, who was then in the southeast, joined the court of a secretly disloyal prince. It is not clear whether Li Bo was naïve, coerced, or a willing participant in the treason, but when the prince was defeated in 757, Li Bo was imprisoned and condemned to death. The poet's reputation saved him: His sentence was reduced to banishment to the far southwest frontier lands. Li Bo dawdled on the long journey, was finally granted amnesty in 759, and returned to his life of travel and visiting. Late in 762, the official and calligrapher with whom he was staying published the first collection of Li Bo's works. The preface records that the poet was at the time seriously ill; this illness was evidently his last. There are, however, legends of his death by drowning, in a drunken attempt to embrace the moon's reflection on a river, and of the spirits who came on dolphin-back to summon him to heaven.

Analysis

Li Bo acquired—and liked—the nickname Exiled Immortal. Its implication of a rule breaker who transcends conventional limitations describes his poetry as well as his life. He could use the standard devices and postures of his rich literary heritage, but he usually did so in his own original manner. He wrote many kinds of poems, in many moods and wearing many masks, but behind them all is the unique quality of the poet himself.

Among the poems by Li Bo that have the greatest immediate appeal for the modern Western reader are those that suggest that the poetic mind operates on the level of the universe itself. This theme often appears in Li Bo's poems about famous mountains, those nodes—in the traditional Chinese worldview—of cosmic spiritual energy. For example, in the poem "Climbing Mount Emei," the speaker of the poem ascends the best known of Sichuan's "faerie mountains," entering a realm of weird beauty that calls into question normal evaluations of both perception and ambition. At the summit, he proclaims, his aesthetic and his supernatural abilities are released, as he finally grasps esoteric Daoist teachings and the secrets of making poetry and music. Li Bo closes the poem with a characteristically grand movement up and out: He is loosed from earthly ties ("All at once I lose the world's dust"), meets a youthful sprite, and hand in hand they move across the sky to the sun. This is not the only place where the poet sets himself in moments of inspiration on a par with the great forces of nature.

"Climbing the Peak of Mount Taibo"

Still, Li Bo acknowledges, the human mind cannot always achieve this sublime state. Sometimes the power dwelling within the mountains is elusive, or the response to it is uncertain. In "Climbing the Peak of Mount Taibo," the mountain is again a jumping-off point for heavenly realms, but here the poet adopts a persona that imagines a transcendent journey of the spirit—straddling the wind and raising a hand that could almost touch the moon—only to hesitate at the end and ask, "Once I've left Wugong county/ When could I come back again?" This undercutting of the traditional spirit-journey motif is prepared for by a typical bit of linguistic playfulness. There is a multiple pun in the poem's third line: "Then Taibo speaks to me." "Taibo" is, first, the mountain itself, a peak in modern Shensi Province that was thought to be especially magical because one of the fantastic Daoist "cave-heavens" was said to be located within its summit. "Taibo" is also both the evening star (the ascent is made at sunset) and the very planetary spirit said to have been Li Bo's true father. Finally, "Taibo" is Li Bo's pen name; for an instant, at least, the reader is invited to wonder if the poet is talking only to himself.

"Wandering About Mount Tai"

One of the best examples of the multiplicity of stances and personas Li Bo could adopt when considering the relationship of the individual to the supra-human is a poem cycle titled "Wandering About Mount Tai: Six Poems." In this description of travel around the easternmost of China's cosmos-ordering "Five Sacred Peaks," the poet achieves a mythic fusion of various traditional paradises: the ancient utopias located far away, across the sea or sky; the cave-heavens that riddle sacred ground; and the spiritually charged natural world itself. He also manages an emotional fusion of the various responses of a single persona to manifestations of the divine, ranging from frustration and embarrassment, through ecstasy and awe, to a final confident accommodation with the world and its spiritual force.

In the first poem of the group, despite the speaker's appreciation of the mountain's beauty, the stone gate of a cave-heaven is closed to him and the gold and silver pavilions of the Faerie Isles can be imagined but remain distant. Moreover, the beautiful "Jade Women" who come in response to the poet's magic, spirit-summoning whistle tease him, laughing and giving him nothing more than a cup of "Liquid Sunrise," the immortals' wine. He can only bow to them, ashamed of his mundane nature. Here as elsewhere, though he sorrows, he never lapses into self-pity. The second and third poems underline the theme of human limitations: The speaker meets a strange man who has achieved immortality through Daoist training, but the figure vanishes and the antique writing of the text he leaves behind cannot be deciphered; then, the wanderer has a moment of vision, only to chance on a youthful divinity who laughs at him for trying to achieve immortality so late, "when I've lost my grip, rosy cheeks faded." The exuberant fourth poem records a moment of hard-won spiritual achievement gained through Daoist study, fasting, and chanting. This otherworldly goal is replaced in the following poem by an awareness of the power in the natural landscape itself.

The resolution appears in the last poem of the sequence, as the poet's persona travels through sublime scenery alive with spirits. Although he is cut off from that sacred force of the Dao in which nature and spirits participate so freely, the poet presents himself as capable of actively making contact with the transcendent: He imagines a wedding dance of spirits; he reaches up to grope among the constellations. It is precisely the force of his own capacity for vision that wins that vision. Even though he acknowledges the evanescence of this magical night, he closes by stating that he will still be able to see the variegated clouds of dawn, clouds that are traditionally vehicles for immortals and that remind the reader of the Liquid Sunrise wine that was his gift from the divinities in the first poem of the group. The ability for imaginative action on the world's phenomena remains even when the moment of inspiration passes—as do the poems that have been created with it.

"In the Mountains"

The theme of the "spirit journey" noted above, and other symbols found in China's ancient shamanistic tradition, appear in many of Li Bo's works. Not all of his "mystical" poems, however, are so grandiose. In the famous "In the Mountains: Question and Answer," he quietly (and slightly smugly) strikes the pose of the reclusive sage who lives in the mountains for reasons that only a fool would ask to have put into words; behind this persona is the perhaps even more smug poet who has just done exactly that:

>You ask me for the reason
>I roost among emerald hills.
>I smile and yet do not reply,
>heart at its natural ease.
>Peach-blossom petals on Paradise Creek
>flow on their mysterious way.
>There is another heaven and earth
>that's not the human world.

"Gazing at Yellow Crane Mountain"

Parallel to Li Bo's interest in the strange chemistry of poetic creation was his interest in alchemy. In China, this arcane science developed as part of the Daoist search for elixirs that could give long life or even immortality. Li Bo used terms found in a textual tradition running back to the ancient holy book, the *Yijing* (eighth to third century B.C.E.; English translation, 1876; also known as *Book of Changes*, 1986). Such language was popular in the poetry of the era; whether Li Bo actually conducted experiments, alchemy served him well as a source of metaphors.

For example, in the poem "Gazing at Yellow Crane Mountain," alchemical imagery describes the catalytic moment in which mutability and human limitations are accepted. The mountain's cosmic power is forcefully described in the opening lines. The peak is "bold and virile, thrusting up in mid-air"; it "gives birth to clouds"; as an *axis mundi*, it links earth and sky. It is famous, moreover, for the hermit living there who—unlike the poet—achieved transformation into an immortal long ago and left his stone cell for the Faerie Isles. At this point, the poem pivots. An alchemical reaction is described: "The Golden Crucible gives birth to a haze of dust." The concluding passage focuses on images of sustenance amid aging and physical frailty. Finally, the poet presents himself as making peace with the gap between mortal flesh and transcendental power: "I'll knot my heart's pledge, to lodge under blue pines,/ Awakened forever, my wanderlust done with!"

"Drinking Alone in the Moonlight"

Natural wonders, such as mountains, and mysteries, such as alchemy, are only two of the sources of recurring metaphors by means of which Li Bo examines the multifaceted relationship of the self with the great forces outside it. The most famous of his metaphors are those concerning wine. In reading Li Bo's many deservedly famous poems on wine, it is important to remember the traditional Chinese view of intoxication as exhilaration and release. Li Bo the gregarious man enjoyed drinking; Li Bo the lover of life's pleasures found in that enjoyment a solace for their brevity; Li Bo the eccentric and spontaneous poet could hardly not have had a reputation for enjoying it—that was a hallmark of the type; finally, Li Bo the seeker after actualization of his original unrestricted nature used the drug—as others had before him—as an instrument of that search. Poems such as the four on "Drinking Alone in the Moonlight" are the first to come to mind when this poet's name is mentioned. In this witty sequence, nature, personalized through the imaginative inspiration of wine, recognizes Li Bo's particularity. The loneliness of individuality is eased by communion with the universal order, made possible through alcohol. In "Drinking Alone in the Moonlight" (titled "Drinking Alone by Moonlight" in Owen's translation), Li Bo, drinking alone, raises his glass to the moon and his shadow, so that they drink together: "When still sober we share friendship and pleasure,/ then, utterly drunk, each goes his own way—/ Let us join to roam beyond human cares/ and plan to meet far in the river of stars."

"THE ROAD TO SHU IS HARD"

In stressing Li Bo's individualism, it is important not to overlook his adept use of Chinese tradition. Well-known poems such as "The Road to Shu Is Hard" show the unique qualities of his work: the bold language of the opening line ("Ee-hoo-hee! Steep, whoo! High, phew!"); the irregular and musical outpouring of the wildly varied lines and stanzas; the powerful evocation of the natural scene and of the visions it inspires in the imagination; and the insistence on his own panting, persistent voice ("With dangers, yes! like these,/ ahh, man from afar,/ why oh why come, eh?"). At the same time, the poem's title is that of an old folk song that for centuries had been used by educated poets as a point of departure, stressing the difficulties of the rugged mountain road just as Li Bo does. Moreover, Li Bo weaves into the poem evocative legends of the early history of the region; allusions to historical events and to classical literature are characteristic of his work. It is his revitalizing variations, in form and content, on familiar themes that make this and other such poems so rich.

Li Bo, like many Chinese poets, sought to restore to the verse of his own era the greatness of the past, or his idealized version of the past. Throughout his oeuvre, there are reflections of his intimate knowledge of earlier poets, though the effect is never that of a mere imitation. One of his many "Ancient Airs," translated by Joseph J. Lee in *Sunflower Splendor*, proclaims, "I desire to select and transmit the old,/ So that its splendor will last a thousand ages."

Poems in this mode frequently combine the spare language and unadorned technique of earlier times with a strong moral statement. Another ancient air (translated by Pound as "Lament of the Frontier Guard") takes the traditional stance against the waste of human life and the cost to society when men serve as soldiers in the frontier lands. Such poems, with their serious messages and generally simple presentation, stood in conscious opposition to the decorative poetry associated with courtly writers of the preceding era.

FEMALE PERSONAS

Another group of poems in which Li Bo approaches a traditional subject in his own way includes those written with female personas. (Many men in traditional China wrote poems in which the speaker was a winsome chartreuse or a lonely wife.) In works such as "Poem Written on Behalf of My Wife" and "Song of Changgan" (in Pound's translation, "The River Merchant's Wife: A Letter"), the poet expresses longings common to all people through the figure of a woman addressing her husband. The vivid pictorial presentation of scenes from such women's lives reminds the reader of the skill of the man behind the mask.

TECHNIQUE AND FORM

It may be that the very force of Li Bo's images contributed to the traditional slighting of his technical skill as a poet. His was an era when many poets were directing their talents to the relatively recent "regulated verse," in which certain patterns of word pitch were to be created, somewhat like the stressed and unstressed syllables in English meter. Li Bo, however, usually preferred the freer form of old-style verse, though like a good writer of free verse in English, he still used the sounds of his language. He played with alliteration, assonance, and off rhyme. He varied line length to suit content or rhythmic need. He created striking patterns of word pitch, for example, in his powerful description of the thunderstorm in "In a Dream, I Wander Tianmu Mountain: A Chant of Farewell."

One trait of inferior Chinese poetry is a tendency to break down into a string of neat two-line units; as Owen points out, Li Bo's exuberant outpourings avoid this trap, though his effects are sometimes too easy or too loose. Eide's discussion of Li Bo's use of allusion and "revived" clichés to enrich his poems and to tighten the links between lines suggests how well crafted the poet's apparently spontaneous verse could be at its best.

In looking to the past for form, as he looked there for his poetic lineage, Li Bo found a fertile base for his own distinctive way of writing. He wrote in a variety of genres, from the old rhapsodic "rhyme-prose," or *fu*, to pseudofolk songs, *yuefu*. A high proportion of his poems have words such as "song," "ode," or "melody" in their titles, and many were actually written to be accompanied by music. Li Bo could write skillful, regulated verse when he chose or when the occasion (a formal farewell, for example) called for it. In addition, it may be that he was one of the first of the educated elite to write poems, called *ci* (lyrics), that were written to tunes of irregular line length; if he really wrote certain of these poems attributed to him, Li Bo made an important contribution to the development of a verse form that was to dominate the subsequent poetic era. In form, then, as in mood and theme, Li Bo's verse is marked by the skilled diversity often associated with greatness.

In all this wealth of poems, there is much for those who read Li Bo more than twelve hundred years after the poet's death. Even in translation, the power of his images and of his poetic personality comes through. Without knowledge of Li Bo's literary, political, or philosophical background, one can still experience his intense, expansive way of knowing the world. Indeed, Li Bo's skill is such that the reader is moved to put on the masks that the poet fashioned and walk into the landscapes he painted. For the duration of such moments, one shivers in the Gobi wind, eyes a tipsy, lisping exotic dancer, or rakes one's fingers through the Milky Way.

BIBLIOGRAPHY

Kroll, Paul. *Studies in Medieval Taoism and the Poetry of Li Po*. Burlington, Vt.: Ashgate, 2009. Focuses on Li Bo's poetry as it expresses Daoist concepts.

Li Bo. *Li Po and Tu Fu: Poems Selected and Translated with an Introduction and Notes*. Translated by Arthur Cooper. Harmondsworth, England: Penguin Books, 1973. The translations are generally excellent, and the extensive background material on the history of Chinese poetry and literature is helpful. Li Bo's connection with Du Fu is usefully discussed.

_____. *The Selected Poems of Li Po*. Translated by David Hinton. New York: New Directions, 1996. Includes commentary and background information as well as translations.

Owen, Stephen. *An Anthology of Chinese Literature: Beginnings to 1911*. New York: W. W. Norton, 1996. Contains background information and commentary on Li Bo as well as a selection of his poetry.

_____. *The Great Age of Chinese Poetry: The High T'ang*. New Haven, Conn.: Yale University Press, 1981. Provides information on Li Bo in the political and cultural milieu of the Tang Dynasty.

Pine, Red, trans. *Poems of the Masters: China's Classic Anthology of T'ang and Sung Dynasty Verse*. Port Townsend, Wash.: Copper Canyon Press, 2003. A collection of poetry from the Tang and Song Dynasties that includes the work of Li Bo. Indexes.

Varsano, Paula M. *Tracking the Banished Immortal: The Poetry of Li Bo and its Critical Reception*. Honolulu: University of Hawaii Press, 2003. Examines the critical reception of Li Bo's poetry, from early Chinese scholars to later Western ones. Besides being noted as worthy of praise, his poetry has been termed "all fruits and flowers" and morally decadent. Also provides analysis of the poetry.

Waley, Arthur. *The Poetry and Career of Li Po*. 1950. Reprint. London: G. Allen & Unwin, 1979. A still-useful introduction, although Waley's obsession with what he considers the immoral aspects of Li Bo's character sometimes prejudices his judgment of the poetry. Includes many translations.

Weinberger, Eliot, ed. *The New Directions Anthology of Classical Chinese Poetry*. New York: New Directions, 2003. Contains an informative commentary on the evolution of translations of classical Chinese poetry. Information on Chinese poetry and translators is provided as well as translations of the poetry of many Chinese poems. Includes translations of Li Bo's poetry by Ezra Pound, William Carlos Williams, and David Hinton.

Jeanne Larsen

LI QINGZHAO

Born: Jinan, Shandong Province, China; 1084
Died: Hangzhou, Zhejiang Province(?), China; c. 1155
Also known as: Li Ch'ing-chao

PRINCIPAL POETRY
Li Ch'ing-chao chi, 1962 (collected works)
The Complete Ci-Poems of Li Qingzhao, 1989

OTHER LITERARY FORMS

Li Qingzhao (lee chihng-JOW) was a serious scholar of antiquities and objets d'art and compiled book annotations and catalogs of antiques with her husband Zhao Mingcheng. An essay appended to one of the catalogs, *Jinshilu houxi* (c. 1135; epilogue to a catalog of inscriptions on bronze and stone), is a major source of biographical information. She also wrote a brief critical essay on *ci* poetry. A number of other prose pieces were collected posthumously, but nearly all of them are now lost.

ACHIEVEMENTS

Li Qingzhao's gender has certainly affected critical response to her work and has given her the mixed blessing of being regarded as "China's greatest poetess," but the high quality of her work is beyond question. It is impossible to know to what extent the preservation and transmission of those of her texts that have survived were influenced by traditional ideas of what kinds of poems were appropriate for women to write. Clearly, she understood and used the voices and the literary gestures of China's rich heritage of female persona poetry. Equally clearly, she could and did write on themes—politics and mysticism among them—outside the range found in the extant work of most Chinese literary women before the modern era.

One strength of Li Qingzhao's work, then, is its emotional variety. There are love poems ranging from the melancholy to the erotic. There are poems of despair at old age or at the defeat of the Northern Song Dynasty. Some poems exhort those in power to moral rectitude; others suggest with transcendental imagery the glories of spiritual transport to a world beyond this one.

Equally important are Li Qingzhao's contributions to the *ci* verse form. Her critical comments on the work of other *ci* poets suggest the seriousness with which she approached her art, as well as her capacity for innovation. At a time when the *shi* form—which had dominated Chinese poetry for nearly a millennium—was in danger of stagnation, she helped develop the newer kind of poetry, broadening its scope in theme and language.

The word *ci* is often translated as "lyrics"; indeed, the form had its origins in the lyrics to popular songs. Consequently, although *ci* were often beautiful to hear, they tended to focus on such lightweight topics as the pleasures of drinking and the appreciation of female beauty. Li Qingzhao, like her father's famous friend Su Shih (Su Dongbo) before her, wrote on more complex subjects and moods; her work retains the emotional delicacy associated with the *ci* while giving it more serious applications. Moreover, the wide range of levels of diction in her poems—from the elegant to the conversational—opened up new potential for self-expression and broadened options for later poets. One contemporary critic commented on her use of colloquialisms: "The fantastically vulgar expressions of the back alleys and streets, whatever suited her mood, she would write down in her poetry" (translation by Gaiyou Xu). Even after the old melodies were lost, *ci* were composed to set patterns of line length, word pitch, and rhyme; Li Qingzhao's variations on these patterns were so euphonious that they sometimes became the preferred versions. Finally, her skillful use of alliteration and assonance in this extremely difficult form has served as a benchmark of musicality that has seldom been equaled.

Ultimately, though, it is the effect of the individual poems that has earned for Li Qingzhao widespread critical regard. Her poetry retains a strongly personal vision without lapsing into self-absorption or self-pity; her sensuous descriptions of scenes come alive for the reader as they subtly express complicated moods through actions and objects in the external world. The poet used allusion to the literary tradition, as well as the repetitive phrases (for example, "chill, chill, clear, clear") that are a traditional ornament of Chinese verse. Both qualities show that her innovations were grounded in a sensitive understanding of the work of those before her.

Biography

Li Qingzhao's early life was one of privilege and happiness, but that happiness did not last. Political infighting resulted in her father's temporary exile and her father-in-law's disgrace. Her beloved husband's official duties caused repeated separations, and he died in his late forties. The conquest of North China by the Tartars meant the loss of her extensive art collection and difficult years as a widowed refugee. Despite the nostalgic and sorrowful tone of many of her poems, however, her work suggests the personal strength that enabled her to survive in such difficult times.

Li Qingzhao was born to a family that placed a high value on literature and education. Her father, Li Kefei, was an important figure in the national government and was well known for such prose writings as his essay on the famous gardens of the city of Luoyang. Her mother, whose family name was Wang, was a poet who had been educated at home by her grandfather, an outstanding scholar and former prime minister. Family friends of talent, influence, and learning filled the household. The lively, intelligent girl's abilities were encouraged by this literary atmosphere and by the approval of the adults around her, despite the strictures concerning education for women that were prevalent in her time. Her reputation for poems in the respected *shi* form was established while she was still in her teens, and she developed her talents for painting and calligraphy as well.

By most accounts, Li Qingzhao was eighteen when she married Zhao Mingcheng, a young student from another important family. The two were well-matched. In two years, her husband entered the civil service, and the couple developed their collection of books, antique bronzes, and other art objects. In 1134, she wrote a charming retrospective description of how the couple had enjoyed each other's company as they compiled information on their acquisitions. The marriage has attracted much interest. There is the story of her husband's prophetic childhood dream, signifying that he would marry a poet, and another in which he attempts unsuccessfully to outdo his wife's poem "Zui huayin" ("Tune: Tipsy in the Flower's Shade"). A portrait of Li Qingzhao at age thirty-one depicts a woman of beauty and refined sensibilities.

The factional politics that caused her father's exile early in this period of Li Qingzhao's life also sent her father-in-law into disfavor. He died shortly after, in 1107. The two men belonged to opposing political groups, which must have made her position as a daughter-in-law difficult. Perhaps it also gave her a clearer perspective on governmental folly; her political poems suggest that this was so.

Li Qingzhao's husband's career was affected by his father's fall, but the following years, while her husband was out of office, were perhaps the zenith of their happiness. In the early 1120's, he returned to government service; poems written while he was traveling on official business or in search of items for their art collection suggest her unhappiness during his absence, for upper-class women were not allowed to travel as men did.

Li Qingzhao was in her early forties when North China fell to the Tartars in 1127. She fled Shandong for the South, where her husband was serving as a magistrate. Much of their valuable collection of books, paintings, and antiques was left behind and burned. After a brief time of reunion, her husband was posted to another city, fell ill with malaria, and died.

Civil disorder increased as the Tartars pressed southward and the Chinese emperor retreated before them. Most of Li Qingzhao's remaining artworks were lost as she, too, repeatedly made her way to safety. Two unsubstantiated stories suggest further pressures on the poet. She was accused of attempting a treasonous bribery, and she is said by some sources to have had a brief and unhappy marriage. The cruelty of Zhang Ruzhou, the minor government official she reportedly married and divorced, was no more shocking to biographers of later centuries than the poet's defiance of social expectations by remarrying.

Li Qingzhao's last years were evidently spent in the household of her younger brother, Li Hang, in Zhejiang Province in southeastern China, but little else is known, except that she did continue writing. Most estimates of the year of her death put it around 1155.

Analysis

Li Qingzhao's work combines affective force with the aesthetic appeal of refined, well-crafted expression. The emotions behind her poems were powerful, but they are never simply self-indulgent. The exquisite sound effects of the originals are lost in English versions, yet the images, and the textures of joy or contemplation or loss that they generate, convey the poet's emotions to Western readers.

"Tune: Tipsy in the Flower's Shade"

One of the best-known and most frequently translated of Li Qingzhao's poems, "Tune: Tipsy in the Flower's Shade," shows her ability to develop such a texture, revealing feeling through ambiguous language and the accretion of sensations of vision, smell, and touch. The first line of the poem offers several possible readings. The "Thin mists—thick clouds" at the line's beginning are appropriate to the autumn festival day on which the poem is set, for the festival is associated with the uprising of the cloudy *yin* principle that, according to traditional Chinese cosmology, controls the autumn and winter months. It is the second half of the line that offers multiple levels of meaning. Are the mists and clouds themselves "sad all day long," or, as is often the case in Chinese poetry, is the subject of "sadness" an unstated "I," or is the line best understood as "Thin mists and thick clouds: sorrow makes the day endless"?

The poem's subsequent images build a tone of suppressed sexuality and murky melancholy: The reader catches the dull metallic gleam of an ornamental burner through streamers of incense smoke and feels the chill that works its way past the translucent gauze of the bed curtains. The poem is said to have been sent to her husband, and the subtle eroticism of the boudoir setting is underlined by "midnight" and "jade pillow." The bedroom trappings conjure up the traditional figure of the attractive woman alone and longing for her absent beloved. "Jade" is a common ornamental epithet, and the pillow was probably not literally made of jade. To the poet's audience, however, the word would have suggested the cool whiteness of the speaker's skin. This suits the tone established at the poem's start, inasmuch as the *yin* principle is further associated with women and with sexuality.

In the second stanza, the poet intensifies the mood of painfully stifled passion with mention of "dusk," "furtive fragrances," and the force of a wind that pushes the blinds aside. Moreover, she uses the standard imagery linked to the festival in her own way, increasing the complexity of the mood established in stanza 1. The fourth century poet Tao Qian, whom Li Qingzhao admired greatly, invariably came to mind on the day of the mid-autumn festival. Her allusion to the "eastern hedge" mentioned in one of his most famous poems immediately recalls other images associated with Tao Qian's work: Wine, a sad nobility in the face of the season's change, and the yellow chrysanthemums that endure when all the other flowers have yielded to the cold. The chrysanthemums of the last line also had been linked poetically with feminine beauty long before Tao Qian's time; Li Qingzhao uses all this in her much-praised closing assertion that she is "more fragile than the yellow chrysanthemum."

"TO THE TUNE: SOUND UPON SOUND, ADAGIO"

A similar nexus of coldness, wine, dark, and the wasted beauty of the late-blooming flowers appears in the famous poem "To the Tune: Sound upon Sound, Adagio." *Ci* were not required to fit their content to the old melodies' titles, but they sometimes did. Just as Li Qingzhao made use of the intoxication, the flowers, and the shadiness (literally, *yin*) indicated by the previous poem's title, here she creates a musical tour de force through repeated words and sounds and careful attention to the effect of word pitch. This dazzling focus on language—syllables falling one by one, like the fine rain she pictures drizzling drop after drop on the autumnal trees—prepares the reader for the poem's final twist. The poet denies the adequacy of words to relieve, or even to express, her grief. "How," she asks, "can the one word 'sorrow' finish off all this?"

MELANCHOLY THEMES

Some of Li Qingzhao's other poems, especially those written in the final period of her life, explore this theme of melancholy. In "Qingping yue" ("Tune: Pure Serene Music"), images of whiteness and purity—snow, plum blossoms, clear tears—set the scene for her description of graying hair that, to overtranslate the Chinese idiom, "engenders flowery patterns." The reference to intoxication, despite the ambiguous intimation that it is as if the plum blossoms themselves were exhilarating, is a reminder of the remarkable number of references to wine in Li Qingzhao's work. A great many Chinese writers in the nonconformist mode—including Tao Qian and the eighth century poet Li Bo—expressed their liberation from conventionality through praise of the effects of alcohol; it may be that the particularly bold stance necessarily taken, in traditional China, by the woman who claimed the role of artist made such references to the untrammeled state of inebriation especially apt. Just as characteristic is the closure, a depiction of nature that describes by implication the speaker's condition: The cutting evening wind suggests the force of aging as it scatters the pale flowers of spring.

AMATORY POEMS

Li Qingzhao's husband's death naturally figures in many of her poems of depression. The title of one well-known example is "Wuling chun" ("Tune: Spring at Wuling"). In an atmosphere that blends emotional stasis with a sense of time's inevitable passing ("The wind subsides—a fragrance/ of petals freshly fallen;/ it's late in the day . . ."), the speaker—like bereft women in poems written for centuries—neglects her grooming and broods on her man's absence. The poem's famous final image refers ironically to a place in the region where the poet lived out her widowhood: "I hear at Twin Creek spring it's still lovely." She, no longer part of a happy couple, says she would like to go pleasure-boating there, but she fears that "at Twin Creek my frail boat/ could not carry this load of grief."

Earlier poems on temporary separations from her husband range from loneliness to a teasing reminder of the pleasures of reunion. "Xiaochongshan" ("Tune: Manifold Little Hills"), for example, exploits the conventional association of spring with burgeoning sexuality. The grass is green, the swollen plum-blossom buds are ready to open, and "Azure clouds gather, grind out jade into dust" as the trees burst into jade-white bloom. The speaker's sensuous enjoyment of the springtime ends in a plea to her absent beloved to return so that they might more fully enjoy the season.

The attribution to Li Qingzhao of some other openly amatory poems is questionable. Some editors were doubtless quick to assign any free-floating, female-persona poem to the woman poet who stood foremost in their minds; others must have been shocked at the thought that a married woman of good family might have written on such a topic. However, there are poems that are certainly hers and are certainly sexual. The analysis by William H. Nienhauser, Jr., in an article published in *T'oung Pao* in 1978, of Li Qingzhao's poem "Ru mengling" ("Tune: As in a Dream a Song") shows how she used the technique of accreted implications to develop a fabric of delicately suggestive language, rhythm, images, and action. The poem has enjoyed long-lasting popularity; as Nienhauser observes, it is not pornography but a work of aesthetically pleasing subtlety, requiring considerable poetic skill.

POLITICAL POEMS

If Li Qingzhao's poems of joy and nostalgia reflect the events of her private life, there are others that show her concern for the disordered state of her nation. Some of these poems remain in the personal mode. This is true of her poem "Caisang ci" ("Tune: Song of Picking Mulberry") (another poem written to the same tune is among the frankly erotic poems attributed to her). Here, the huge exotic leaves of banana trees exemplify the strange new landscape of South China, to which the poet and others from the fallen heartland of the empire have fled before the Tartar onslaught. In her mind, the leaves, opening and furling, evoke human hearts pulsing with emotion. Here, too, the closely woven repetitions of sounds and words suggests the brooding, monotonous dripping of "rain at the midnight watch." The sentiments of grief and restless obsession voiced by this northerner are those of a generation in exile.

More strongly in a public voice are the admonitory poems that Li Qingzhao, like most of China's greatest poets, wrote on political themes. They display, in their form and their language, her understanding of the literary decorum so important in her culture. These poems are not *ci* but the older, loftier *shi*. (Some are written according to the rules of versification called "tonal regulation"; others are in the freer "old style.") Most of the poet's contemporaries would have considered *ci* no more appropriate to her public subject matter than a limerick would be. Moreover, the poems' diction suits the exalted positions of those to whom many of them were sent.

The message of these verses is that of the Confucian moralist, calling for righteousness on the part of the ruler and abstention from greed on the part of government officials. The poet reminds her readers of the value of learning and the consolations of study. She warns the emperor of the defeated dynasty against the reckless enjoyment of immediate pleasures and criticizes the nation-weakening dangers of political infighting. Through references, often satirical ones, to a variety of historical figures, the poet reveals her own knowledge of the classics. She also uses these allusions to cast her admonitions into a safer form. Indirectly, she censures the failure of the dynasty to stand up to the invaders and the subsequent appeasement of the Tartars.

TRANSCENDENTAL POEMS

Li Qingzhao was not the first woman to write on transcendental themes. In the eighth and ninth centuries, for example, Xue Tao, Li Ye, and Yu Xuangji all drew in their own ways on the rich stream of Daoist visionary imagery. Still, it was not usual for women to write such poems. Unconventional or not, Li Qingzhao is successful in her evocation of spiritual longing. She describes the lure of the contemplative life and reminds her readers of the value of the ascetic's pursuit of ritual purity and immortality. In "Tune: A Fisherman's Honor," the speaker sails through the sky to the paradise of the distant Faerie Isles in a spirit journey that has its origins in the shamanistic cults of centuries before. A *shi* poem, "Dream at Daybreak," relates a journey through dawn clouds to the marvelous realm of the immortals. The speaker awakens, however, asking ruefully, "Since human life can be like this,/ Why must I return to my old home?" Finally, she sits in meditation, covering her ears against the clamor of this world, thinking deeply on what she will not meet with again, and sighing. The poem expresses such yearnings with ethereal grace.

What remains of Li Qingzhao's work both tantalizes and satisfies. The various *ci* and *shi* poems just discussed, the few remaining essays, and at least one long rhyme-prose (*fu*) believed to be her work, provide a frustrating glimpse of the much larger corpus of her poetry and prose that was once in circulation. Nevertheless, what has survived is enough to stand on its own merits. The evocative, sometimes surprising imagery, lively and musical language, sensitive depiction of emotional nuance, and range of mood and tone ensure that her poetry will continue to be read a thousand years after her death.

BIBLIOGRAPHY

Chang, Kang-i Sun, and Haun Saussy, eds. *Women Writers of Traditional China: An Anthology of Poetry and Criticism.* Stanford, Calif.: Stanford University Press, 1999. Part 1 of this anthology contains the poets' works, divided by dynasty, and part 2 contains criticism. Biographies of the poets, including Li Qingzhao, are included. Bibliography and index.

Djao, Wei. *A Blossom like No Other: Li Qingzhao*. Toronto, Ont.: Ginger Post, 2010. A biography of the Chinese poet, with analysis of her works.

Hansen, Valerie. "Li Qingzhao." *Calliope* 13, no. 4 (December, 2002): 24. A brief profile of the poet and her works.

Hu, P'ing-ch'ing. *Li Ch'ing-chao*. New York: Twayne, 1966. This critical study on Li Qingzhao treats both her life and her works in great detail and provides one with a clear sense of her achievements. Most of her famous poems are translated in a lucid, though sometimes prosaic, style.

Idema, W. L., and Beata Grant. *The Red Brush: Writing Women of Imperial China*. Cambridge, Mass.: Harvard University Asia Center, Harvard University Press, 2004. This work on women writers in China includes a chapter on Li Qingzhao and her writing. Other chapters shed light on the culture in which she wrote.

Li Qingzhao. *The Complete Ci-Poems of Li Qingzhao*. Translated by Jizosheng Wang. Philadelphia: Department of Oriental Studies, University of Pennsylvania, 1989. A translation that strives to be accurate to the Chinese texts. Bilingual text.

_____. *Li Ch'ing-chao: Complete Poems*. Translated and edited by Kenneth Rexroth and Ling Chung. New York: New Directions, 1979. A collection of Li Qingzhao's poetry, with critical notes and a biography.

Rexroth, Kenneth, and Ling Chung, eds. *Women Poets of China*. Rev. ed. New York: New Directions, 1990. This collection of works by women poets of China, which first was published in 1972, contains works by Li Qingzhao and other notable poets.

Yang, Vincent. "Vision of Reconciliation: A Textual Reading of Some Lines of Li Qing-zhao." *Journal of the Chinese Language Teachers Association* 19 (1984): 10-32. This essay is a close reading of four representative poems by Li Qingzhao. Focusing on the imagery and structure of the poems, the author attempts to show the poet's art of lyricism. At the end, the particular nature of her imagination is illustrated through her use of poetic techniques. The analysis is an application of Western literary criticism to Chinese poetry.

Jeanne Larsen

MENG HAORAN

Born: Xianyang, China; 689
Died: Xianyang, China; 740
Also known as: Meng Hao-jan

PRINCIPAL POETRY
Meng Haoran shi ji, 745-750 (collected poems)
Meng Hao-jan, 1981 (Paul Kroll, translator)
The Mountain Poems of Meng Hao-jan, 2004 (David Hinton, translator)

OTHER LITERARY FORMS

Meng Haoran (muhng how-rahn) is known only for his poetry; no other literary works by him are known to exist.

ACHIEVEMENTS

Meng Haoran is considered the first great poet of the Tang Dynasty (618-907) in China. His poetry influenced later writers and affected Chinese poetic sensibilities for centuries to come, securing Meng lasting literary fame in China. Meng's contemporaries and later Chinese poets have admired his keen eye for specific features of the natural landscape, particularly mountains and rivers, and the personal emotion infused in his poems, which are rich in literary allusions. These allusions are not surprising; a classical Chinese poet would be expected to demonstrate mastery of earlier literary traditions.

Meng has been credited with invigorating Chinese poetry by bringing a carefully shaped measure of originality to the conventions of Chinese lyrics established in the fourth and fifth centuries. His poetry inspired his friends and subsequent Tang poets to attempt more innovative work and launched a great flowering of Chinese poetry. Even though only 270 of his poems have survived, in part because he destroyed many poems he deemed faulty, Meng's poems were widely anthologized in various collections after his death. His most famous poems were continuously read, appreciated, and studied by subsequent generations of Chinese poets and scholars.

BIOGRAPHY

Meng Haoran was born in 689 during the Tang Dynasty. His birthplace was his parent's family estate, South Garden, just outside the Chinese city of Xianyang in what is now Hubei province. His parents were small landowners, and he had two or three younger brothers and a sister. Meng's family claimed to be the descendants of the fourth century B.C.E. philosopher Mencius (also known as Mengzi or Meng-tzu), and his parents named the boy Haoran, meaning vast, boundless, or great, after a famous passage written by Mencius.

As landowners, Meng's parents could afford a classical education, stressing philosophy and literature, for the boy. This gave Meng the tools to create his poetry. In the fashion of the day, Meng exchanged his poems with fellow literate men. Meng married and had at least two sons.

At around the age of thirty, Meng started to write poetry to Tang Dynasty officials asking for an official appointment, as was usual for a young educated man. A surviving poem of that time makes reference to Meng's aging mother, for whom the son cannot provide enough food. Scholars doubt that Meng's mother really suffered from hunger and view this passage as a conventional way to justify Meng's request for a job out of filial duty.

At this time, Meng started to travel. First, he visited Luoyang, the eastern capital of the Tang Dynasty, where he made many literary friends but failed to gain employment. His many further travels in China inspired Meng to write poems to his appreciative friends about his impressions of the natural sights he encountered. At the age of thirty-nine, in 728, Meng finally tried to pass the *jinshi* exam for an imperial appointment. He failed.

Returning to Xianyang, Meng fashioned himself as a poet recluse who renounced the bustle of the world, and he took up temporary residence at famous Lumen Shan (Deer Gate Mountain), outside his estate. Meng's poetry impressed friends such as Zhang Jiuling, who secured for Meng the only position he ever held, as assistant investigator supporting Zhang. Friends commented that while Meng was employed, from late 737 until his resignation in the summer of 738, he and Zhang wrote poetry together while traveling on official business.

In 740, in Xianyang, Meng's back became infected. He died either from the infection or from eating spoiled raw fish after recovering from the infection. After Meng's death, from 745 to 750, Wang Shiyuan (Wang Shih-yüan), a local Daoist from nearby Icheng (I-ch'eng) shrine, and Meng's younger brother Meng Xiran (Meng Hsi-jan) collected, edited, and published 218 of Meng's poems. Later additions brought Meng's surviving poems to 270. The oldest known surviving copy of Meng's poetry is preserved through a 1935 facsimile of a Song Dynasty (960-1279) woodblock edition.

Analysis

A key characteristic of Meng Haoran's poetry is his attention to the nuances of natural landscapes together with his concrete images of the animals, plants, and people and buildings inhabiting these geographic regions. Critics have praised Meng for the variety of terms he uses for specific mountain features and his detailed descriptions of flora and fauna. His mountain poems are never generic but tied to very specific scenes.

Scholars have noted that Meng's poetry describes nature as perceived by the specific consciousness of the poet, thereby adding an individual vigor to his poems that distinguishes them. Meng's poems balance successfully the evocation of the persona's feelings, such as longing for home and friends or celebrating friendship, with the natural setting in which they take place. There is a social context to Meng's poems even when set in remote places.

Religion and spirituality enter Meng's poems whenever their setting encompasses a temple, shrine, or monastery. When this is a Buddhist place, Meng's poems show a keen perception of Buddhist teachings and history and successfully allude to them, tying a concrete location to a spiritual theme. When Meng's poems address Daoist themes, they tend to become less concrete. This more general reflection corresponds to Daoism's concern with the transcendent, extraterrestrial aspects of human consciousness.

A reader of Meng's poems in English translation should remember that, as with any translation, particularly of poetry, the translator has had to make difficult decisions as to how to render Meng's verse in accessible English. In the original Chinese, 254 of Meng's poems have only five characters (and therefore five syllables) per line. This means that any English translation cannot be both literal and poetic because English requires more than five syllables to capture the meaning that Meng's five syllables per line created for a Chinese reader. This means that translations of Meng's poems will vary depending on the translator.

MENG HAO-JAN

In his accessible 1981 book-length study of Meng's poetry, Paul Kroll offers his translations of many of Meng's most important poems. Kroll's translation uses a traditional, elevated diction to render the mood evoked by Meng's original Chinese syllables into poetic lines in English. As a result, Meng's poems sound somewhat like late nineteenth century English poetry, yet Kroll still manages to capture the central themes and concerns of Meng's poetry very well. For example, "I Pass the Night at My Teacher's Mountain Dwelling, Expecting Lord Ting Who Does Not Arrive," opens thus: "Evening's sunglow has crossed the west ridge;/ The serried straths suddenly, now, are darkcast." Meng's attention to the effects of the light of early evening, as well as his detailed rendition of the natural features observed, emerges very well in this translation.

A key concern of Kroll's selection is to show how Meng's poetry goes beyond closely observed natural landscapes and covers a wide range of subjects. "Springtime Complaint" features a young woman worrying about whom she may love, a query symbolized by her uncertainty over to whom she may give a blossom she has plucked by a pond reflecting her made-up features. "Drinking at the Official Residence in Hsiangyang" celebrates the occasion of an official banquet in Meng's hometown of Xianyang (Hsiang-yang) and ends with the persona exclaiming exuberantly, "Pleasure and joy, we should preserve together."

Kroll groups his translations and analyses of Meng's poems by theme. He begins with the poems set around Meng's hometown, then those inspired by his travels and his interactions with his friends. Kroll convincingly challenges the traditional view of

Meng as a mountain recluse, demonstrating that this image is more a poetic fabrication than historical reality. Meng's poems with a Buddhist theme are compared with those with a Daoist theme. Buddhist poems focus on concrete images, whereas Daoist ones favor the abstract. "Inscribed at the Aranya of Lord Jung," referring to the Buddhist teacher's dwelling, describes in detail how "A flowing fountain wraps around its steps./ Caltrop and waterlily scent your teaching mat." In contrast, "The Water Pavilion of the Taoist Adept Mei," comments on the presence of the master, even in his absence: "Dwelling hidden, he is not to be seen;/ His lofty discourse no one is able to requite." Kroll closes his book with an evaluation of the lasting power of Meng's poems.

The Mountain Poems of Meng Hao-jan

The Mountain Poems of Meng Hao-jan, translated and edited by David Hinton, presents sixty-six of Meng's poems centering on mountain landscapes. Some of Meng's best and most widely admired poems are captured in this work. Hinton's translation emphasizes Meng's interest in Zen Buddhism and Daoist cosmology and tends to evoke the voice of a meditative persona rendering keen perceptions of the world around him. For example, in "Spring Dawn," one of Meng's most famous and widely anthologized poems, the persona appears surprised by the advent of dawn: "In spring sleep, dawn arrives unnoticed." He ends up wondering who can really know what happened during the night, in particular, how "few or many" blossoms were torn down by the night's storm. This demonstrates the persona's observant nature, which is nevertheless limited by the bounds of human perception and knowledge about natural and cosmic events.

Hinton captures well the atmosphere suffusing Meng's key poem, "Year's End, on Returning to Southern Mountains," which helped make the poet known as a mountain recluse. Written most likely after Meng failed the imperial exam at age thirty-nine, the first couplet establishes the persona's decision to quit trying for imperial employment:

> No more hope of advising high ministers,
> I return to my hut in southern mountains

There is a sense of pain and regret as the persona states that he is unworthy of imperial employment, but he does not say if his failure to gain employment is because of an objective reason or a capricious judgment by the authorities. He also laments sickness, the absence of friends, and the advent of white hair before reaching some sort of comfort in the light of the moon through the pines at his home.

Overall, Hinton's selection of poems gives the reader a fine sense of how Meng combines a detailed rendition of natural landscapes with the persona's various feelings. The social quality of Meng's poetry becomes apparent as so many of his poems are addressed to friends and acquaintances or describe visits to them. At times, Meng's poetry also contains wonderful renditions of the emotions of the traveler. In "Overnight on Abiding-Integrity River," the second line spells it out explicitly: "It's dusk, time a traveler's loneliness returns"; dusk is a favorite time of day in Meng's poetry. Hinton's translation gives the reader a good sense of the key themes and the beauty of Meng's mountain poems.

BIBLIOGRAPHY

Hinton, David, trans. and ed. *Mountain Home: The Wilderness Poetry of Ancient China*. New York: New Directions, 2005. This collection of poetry contains an introduction to Meng's poetry and a representative selection in translation. Places Meng in the context of Tang and Song Dynasty poets with similar poetic interests. Map, introduction, notes, and bibliography.

Kroll, Paul W. *Meng Hao-jan*. Boston: Twayne, 1981. Full-length study of the poet and his works; offers translations of many of Meng's most famous poems. Relates Meng's poetry to his native place, his friends, culture, society, and religion, and illustrates his wide range of subjects. Illustrations, notes, bibliography, and index.

Levy, Andre. *Chinese Literature, Ancient and Classical*. Translated by William H. Nienhauser, Jr. Bloomington: Indiana University Press, 2000. Chapter 3, "Poetry," briefly discusses the achievement of Meng and indicates his place within the poetry of the Tang Dynasty, an era that had a lasting effect on Chinese poetry. Index.

Meng Haoran. *The Mountain Poems of Meng Hao-jan*. Translated and edited by David Hinton. New York: Archipelago Books, 2004. Contains a translation of sixty-six poems by Meng. Hinton's introduction places the poet in the context of Tang Dynasty culture and poetry, focusing on Meng's association with Zen Buddhism and explaining how this and Daoism inform the content and form of his poetry. Map, notes, and bibliography.

R. C. Lutz

RUAN JI

Born: Weishi, China; 210
Died: China; 263
Also known as: Juan Chi

PRINCIPAL POETRY

Poetry and Politics: The Life and Works of Juan Chi, A.D. 210-263, 1976 (includes translations of his *yonghuai* verses, *fu* rhyme-prose, and essays; Donald Holzman, translator)
Ruan Ji shi xuan = *The Poems of Ruan Ji*, 2006 (Wu Fusheng and Graham Hartill, translators)

OTHER LITERARY FORMS

Several of the rhyme-prose works—quasi-poetic compositions incorporating rhyme and rhythm—of Ruan Ji (ron jee) are lengthy effusions, extending to many hundreds of lines, and are celebrated for their novel profundity of thought in their treatment of such themes as "The Doves," "The Monkey," "Biography of the Great Man," and "Essay on Music." Other essays discuss philosophical issues in the Daoist tradition—critical interpretations of Laozi, Zhuangzi, and the *Yijing* (eighth to third century B.C.E.; English translation, 1876; also known as *Book of Changes*, 1986).

ACHIEVEMENTS

Together with his senior, Cao Zhi, Ruan Ji stands at the head of a new era in Chinese poetics. His verse provides a link between the earlier epoch of Han and pre-Han forms, and the post-Han tradition of lyric poetry. His diction and imagery often recall the canonic odes (1000-600 B.C.E.), the mid- to late-Zhou (600-221 B.C.E.) philosophical writings, and the rhetoric of the southern *Sao* anthology; in his hands, the new pentameter form becomes an acceptable and established vehicle for the expression of political and social anguish. Furthermore, in the long tradition in which courtly pomposities too frequently usurped genuine thought, Ruan Ji's poetry is admired to this day for its complexity of Confucian and Daoist ideals, its passionate concern for contemporaneous worldly ills, and the poet's own moral dilemmas, all expressed in a deceptively artless diction (characteristics for which the poetry of Tao Qian is also greatly admired). Indeed, so perplexing and perilous was Ruan Ji's political situation that his necessarily allusive satire became enigmatic, and his contemporaries, as much as later scholars, admitted difficulty in penetrating his precise import. Nevertheless, his quasi-religious mysticism has exerted a perennial fascination upon scholar-poets, and Ruan Ji's verse is among the most commonly cited and imitated in the Chinese literary heritage.

Biography

Ruan Ji, a member of the Daoist-inspired Seven Sages of the Bamboo Grove, was the son of Ruan Yu, himself a member of the celebrated coterie of poets known as the Seven Masters of the Jienan Era (the terminal period of the Han Dynasty, 196-220). Ruan Ji was ten years old at the time of the Caowei usurpation of the Han throne, and the latter half of his life was dominated by the decline of the Cao monarchs and the eventual usurpation of their power by the Sima clan.

Cao Cao overthrew the Han, and in 220, his son Cao Pei acceded to the throne as the emperor of the Caowei regime. He was succeeded at his death in 226 by Cao Rui, who squandered his patronage and oppressed the people. No direct offspring survived his death in 239, and a child successor was enthroned under the regency of Cao Shuang and an elderly general, Sima Yi. At first outmaneuvered by Cao Shuang, Sima Yi engineered a coup in 249 during which Cao Shuang, his relatives, and his supporters were massacred, so that the "number of famous men in the empire was reduced by half." Sima Yi himself died in 251 and was succeeded by his son Sima Shi, who executed still more of the Cao and their clique and in 254 deposed the twenty-year-old Cao Fang in favor of Cao Mao, seven years Fang's junior. Cao Mao was assassinated by the Sima in 260; Ruan Ji died in 263; and in 265 the Sima extinguished the Caowei and established the Jin Dynasty.

Ruan Ji's personal and political dilemma lay in his sense of obligation to serve in public office, his distaste for the degeneracy of his liege lords, the Cao rulers, to whom he was bound in loyalty, and his antipathy toward the cruel ambition of the Sima usurpers, into whose service he had become trapped. Actually a devout Confucianist, he turned to Daoist mysticism—the quasi religion available to third century Chinese—and the unconventional *ziran* (unrestrained spontaneity in behavior) and *qingtan* (pure discussion—that is, metaphysical speculation, rather than practical, political affairs) much in vogue among the politically disappointed and disillusioned intellectuals of his time. Such pursuits were typified by the activities of his coterie, the Seven Sages of the Bamboo Grove, among whom Ruan Ji gained a reputation for his skill as a cittern player.

Ruan Ji seems from his youth to have tried to avoid involvement in public affairs, however much this may have tormented his conscience. An anecdote relates how, at an interview with a provincial governor, the young Ruan Ji remained silent throughout—to the admiration of the officer, who deemed him extraordinary and "unfathomable." He must have resisted other summons, because it was not until 239, after the death of Cao Rui, that he was finally drafted, and he joined the entourage of regent Sima Yi. Ruan Ji was never thereafter able to retire from Sima employ and could only watch with dismay and passive resistance while the Sima furthered their own fortunes against the legitimate Cao, whom they ostensibly served.

In 242, Ruan Ji reluctantly accepted another post in the central government, but only after the composition of a now-celebrated letter to his patron, begging to be relieved. In any case, he later pleaded illness and returned home. In the late 240's, Cao Shuang's faction enlisted him, but again he soon resigned on the pretext of illness. He refused yet another post with Cao Shuang on the same pretense and retired to the countryside. When Cao Shuang was killed by Sima Yi in 249, Ruan Ji's reputation for political foresight was much enhanced.

With Sima Yi's death in 251, Ruan Ji was retained by Sima Shi, while all those who had been associated with Cao Shuang were executed. Three years later, upon the accession of Cao Mao, Ruan Ji was awarded an honorary knighthood, an official sinecure, and a substantive administrative position in the imperial secretariat—by then dominated by the Sima. Sima Shi died soon after Cao Mao's installation, and his son and successor, Sima Zhao, drafted Ruan Ji into his military headquarters.

The following year, in 256, Ruan Ji was promoted to the office from which he derived his sobriquet, *bubingxiaowei* (colonel of infantry, hence "Infantry Ruan"). The reason traditionally given for his acceptance of the post may be apocryphal: He is supposed to have been attracted by the skillful brewing and the quantity of fine wine boasted by the official kitchens. Tradition further relates that he became deeply intoxicated while on the job and abandoned his official duties. Greatly favoring him, nevertheless, Sima Zhao attempted to wed his own daughter to him, but Ruan Ji again remained drunk (for two months) so that no arrangements could be made. Stories are also told of how, in a grotesque sign of his displeasure, he would roll his eyes so that only the whites showed. He was finally granted a post in the countryside, away from the intrigues and perils of the capital; his descriptions of his new environment indicate his disgust with the general poverty of body and spirit among the population there.

The assassination of the puppet emperor Cao Mao in 260 brought Ruan Ji back into the center of politics, writing apparently in support of the Sima. Confucianist commentators, however, have taken pains to explain away his change of heart: It was his official responsibility to write such commendations, he was deliberately drunk at the time of writing, and other, satirical compositions from his pen at the time represent his true desire for noninvolvement. He died in office at the age of fifty-three.

Analysis

The works of Ruan Ji were mentioned in a sixth century imperial catalog that mentions Ruan Ji's collected works in fourteen folios (including a table of contents in one folio). A century later, they are listed as ten folios, and by the eleventh century, they are reduced to five. In the fourteenth century, however, they appear again as ten folios. Extant editions of his works include considerably fewer: about twenty essays and *fu* rhyme-prose, official letters, and poetry.

Ruan Ji eschewed the traditional *yuefu* (music bureau songs—that is, new lyrics set to old tunes and titles) that were in great vogue before, during, and after his time, but he espoused the pentameter verse form established during the preceding Han era (207

B.C.E.-220 C.E.). Indeed, his eighty-two enigmatic verses under the general designation *yonghuai shi* (poems singing of my emotions) are among the most assiduously studied and imitated poems in this genre. They vary from eight to twenty lines, the majority being of ten or twelve lines, in the traditional *abcbdb* rhyme scheme.

In view of the dominating political influences upon Ruan Ji and the oblique style in which he expressed his moral conflicts, commentaries on his work have, reasonably, followed two interests: line-by-line interpretation, whereby political targets are identified and his satiric references and allusions are explicated, and appreciation of the genuine personal torment he expressed in attractive poetic form. Near-contemporaneous texts reflect these attitudes. For example, the fifth century court poet Yan Yazhi says: "During the administration of Sima Zhao, Ruan Ji was ever fearful of catastrophe, and thus composed his verses." Yan Yazhi notes, again:

> Ruan Ji personally served in a chaotic regime and was ever fearful of being slandered and encountering disaster. Thus he composed his verses; and so, whenever he sighed, saddened for his life, although his situation lay in satire and ridicule, yet his writings contain enigma and obscurity. A hundred generations hence it will be difficult to fathom his sentiments. Thus I roughly clarify the overall meaning and outline the remote resonances.

During the sixth century, Zhong Hong completed one of the first and greatest canons of Chinese literary theory and criticism, the *Shipin* (classification of poets). Herein, Ruan Ji is included in the top rank of three classifications, Zhong Hong saying that his poetic heritage was the minor odes (a section of the Confucian *Canon of Poetry*, 1000-600 B.C.E., traditionally associated with political satire) and commenting:

> He made no effort at worm-whittling [that is, intricate, superfluous embellishment], yet his poems on expressing his emotions shape one's spirit, and inspire one's innermost thoughts. His words lie within ordinary sight and sound, but his sentiments lodge beyond universal bounds.

The necessity for obscure allegory and the obscurity itself are undisputed. In setting a scene, Ruan Ji typically makes reference, itself disguised, to a similar situation in ancient history, his allusions cleverly enhanced by synonymous location or other nomenclature. For example, he will "hitch up a carriage and go forth from the Wei capital." Here he exploits the fortuitous existence of an ancient state of Wei during the Zhou Dynasty (1066-221 B.C.E.), synonymous with his own regime. The "Wei capital" may then refer either to the ancient Daliang or to the Caowei metropolis at Loyang. Elsewhere, he will say, "In the past I wandered in Ta-liang" and, again, "I gaze back toward Ta-liang" for the same effect. Other references, revealing Ruan Ji's exceptional scholarship in a milieu in which vast erudition was a mere *modus vivendi*, recall in similarly recognizable and pertinent allegory scenes of splendor long since turned to dust, sounding the familiar theme of the transience of mortal glory and warning against the excesses of current rulers.

"The Doves"

The decline of society and political morality also features prominently in Ruan Ji's satire. Political aspirations, he suggests, were the cause of the pollution of original innocence. Ruan Ji's principal villains are not identified directly, but commentators have been in general agreement in their speculations. For example, the lines "Reckless extravagance bringing decline to worldly custom./ How could one say he'd make eternal his years!" refer to Cao Rui, while in "The Doves" (traditional symbols of honest government), Sima Yi is lampooned as a "ravening dog" which in a rage destroyed the "doves"—that is, Cao Shuang and his brother Cao Xi.

Court officers as a class are also pilloried for their hypocritical Confucianism. They are "perfumed herbs" that exist "East of Liang," blooming twice or thrice in a single morn ("morning" being an ancient pun on "court"—held in the early morn); their doubtful "achievements" and influence will disappear with the moment. In other complex imagery, the lush decay of a southern scene is to be understood as representing the decline of Cao Fang and his clique. At the conclusion of yet another tirade against the hypocrisies of court life—courtesies, frugality, and virtue in public, but venal petty-mindedness in private—Ruan Ji flatly avows that the posturing of his colleagues sickens him to the heart.

As much as such plaints fill the pages of Ruan Ji's verse, it is his own toil and suffering that attract the sympathy of the reader. His ideal was honorable public administration in the service of a legitimate, stable, and righteous sovereign—that is to say, the ideal of the sincere Confucian who sought to combine literary and scholarly pursuits with a career of public service. Ruan Ji was to live out his life, however, in fear of slander, entrapment, and disaster. Unable to achieve his Confucian ideal, he turned to an uneasy and conscience-stricken espousal of Daoist retreat, abandoning his public career for the safety and nourishment of his inner, eternal spirit.

"Monkey"

Much of the rhetoric of this plaint derives from the *Chu ci* (*Ch'u tz'u: The Songs of the South, an Ancient Chinese Anthology*, 1959), an anthology ranging from the fourth to the first century B.C.E., in which the lengthy poem "Li sao" (*The Li Sao, an Elegy on Encountering Sorrows*, 1929) mourns a career destroyed by sycophantic court rivals. Such slander had brought about the demise of many of Ruan Ji's more illustrious colleagues, whom he mourns, and thus he writes that he fears not the naked sword, but rather the words of some insinuating tongue. Like Qu Yuan (343?-290? B.C.E.) of *The Li Sao*, Ruan Ji feels that his sincerity, probity, and steadfastness—"a tall pine that does not wither in the bitter adversity of winter"—are not appreciated, but indeed are the source of jealousy and backbiting. In his "Monkey" rhyme-prose, he sees himself as an amusing pet, in captive service; at the same time, the animal may represent the empty ritual, the monkey tricks, of the lesser courtiers. In famous Daoist parlance, the poet recognizes that it is the useful who perish while the useless live out their vain lives.

Mount Shouyang

Under such circumstances, even traditional Confucianism sanctioned retreat. Ruan Ji's lines frequently summon forth the spirit of Mount Shouyang; indeed, he composed a forty-six-line rhyme-prose on the subject at the time of Cao Fang's removal in November, 254. This location was associated with the brothers Bo Yi and Shu Qi, who secluded themselves and died of hunger rather than serve the new Zhou Dynasty at the fall of the Shang (twelfth century B.C.E.).

One may give credence to Ruan Ji's own indifference to wealth and glory acquired during shameful times as he "northward gazed toward Shouyang's peak, below which those men gathered brambles." In Ruan Ji's mind, the argument of even this celebrated precedent was attenuated by his own very real potential, amply demonstrated by the favor shown to him by both the Cao and the Sima rulers.

Life in retreat

Even when a long-sought posting to the countryside offered Ruan Ji relief from metropolitan involvements, he found nothing of the bucolic idyll for which he yearned. Rather, his works describing his observations there became veritable models for misanthropic rhetoric. His rhyme-proses on the locations Kangfu and Dongping (in a marshy region of the modern northeastern province of Shandong), a total of three hundred lines, report that only inedible vegetables grow in the cold, wet climate there, and the peasantry are dull clods, for whom no civilization is possible.

Thus, neither circumstances nor venue permitted Ruan Ji the opportunity for either Confucian loyal service or the innocent simplicity of Daoist eremitism. Within this failure lie the tensions and paradoxes of Ruan Ji's thought, which have continued to intrigue Chinese intellectuals. Ruan Ji reveals contempt and shame for the corrupted Confucianism of his day, and he pines for settled times when moral virtue such as his can shine forth in worthy employment. Turning to Daoist principles, he despises himself for his fearful retreat. In his works, there appears only justification for temporary retirement, and none of the ridicule for Confucian precepts that marks the committed Daoist. The swift passage of time enters as a motif, defeating, says Ruan Ji, any strategy for patiently waiting out current alarms.

Daoist mysticism

In the end, Ruan Ji's philosophical preoccupations led him into a profound, if quasi-religious, Daoist mysticism—quasi-religious because the concept of divinity was foreign to the Chinese at that time. True freedom, writes Ruan Ji in some of the most difficult and obscure poetry in Chinese literature, lies in abandoning attachment to the world and its values, to the emotions which trap mortals in the snares of passion, and eventually to the self, at which point utter tranquillity is attained. This mystical rapture had been expressed in the fourth century B.C.E. by the Daoist Zhuangzi and would reappear centuries later in the Chinese Buddhist ethic. In the third century, however, Ruan Ji's sincerity of belief, born of his disillusionment with the social world, led him to strikingly original formulations. His search for a transcendent immortal, again made ambiguous by his rational Confucian disbelief in immortality, led him to what amounted to a concept of a deity, described in a vast effusion about a "Great Man" who would exemplify the ideal of sage-like aloofness from the dusty world while yet being of the world, and of service to it.

In summary, Ruan Ji favored the pentameter lyric poetry and rhyme-prose genres of his time, and while he added nothing to the development of these forms, he endowed them with a distinctive political, social, philosophical, and religious content, whose complexity of scholarship, allusion, and allegory has by turns bewildered and awed his audiences. He enlivened poems of dark political enigma and unfathomable mystical experience with profoundly sincere personal concern, and to the present day he remains one of the most admired and beloved of Chinese poets.

BIBLIOGRAPHY

Cai, Zong-qi. *The Matrix of Lyric Transformation: Poetic Modes and Self-Presentation in Early Chinese Pentasyllabic Poetry*. Ann Arbor: Center for Chinese Studies, University of Michigan, 1996. Includes an insightful study of Ruan Ji in the course of lyric genre transformation and poetic expression of the self and cultural identity.

Criddle, Reed Andrew. "Rectifying Lasciviousness Through Mystical Learning: An Exposition and Translation of Ruan Ji's Essay on Music." *Asian Music* 38, no. 2 (Summer, 2007): 44-72. While this article focuses on an essay on music written by Ruan Ji, it also provides background information and a context for understanding Ruan Ji's poetry.

Holzman, Donald. *Chinese Literature in Transition from Antiquity to the Middle Ages*. Brookfield, Vt.: Ashgate, 1998. Covers roughly the period from 221 B.C.E. through 960 C.E., placing Ruan Ji in context. Generous bibliographic references.

_____. *Immortals, Festivals, and Poetry in Medieval China: Studies in Social and Intellectual History*. Brookfield, Vt.: Ashgate, 1998. Excellent for understanding Ruan Ji's poetry in context. Includes bibliographical references and index.

_____. *Poetry and Politics: The Life and Works of Juan Chi, A.D. 210-263*. New York: Cambridge University Press, 1976. A full-length critical study of Ruan Ji's life and literary achievements. An extension of his 1953 publication on Ruan Ji.

Watson, Burton, ed. *The Columbia Book of Chinese Poetry*. New York: Columbia University Press, 1984. An excellent anthology. As no special collections of Ruan Ji's poems in English translation are available, this is a good place to locate his poems in English and discussions of the Chinese poetry of retreat.

Yu, Pauline. "The Poetry of Retreat." In *Masterworks of Asian Literature in Comparative Perspective*, edited by Barbara Stoler Miller. Armonk, N.Y.: M. E. Sharpe,

1994. A thoughtful discussion of Ruan Ji in the Chinese poetic tradition of the recluse, along with other poets such as Tao Qian and Xie Lingyun. Includes provocative comments on Ruan Ji's eighty-two "Poems Singing My Thoughts" and the conflict between his fidelity to Confucian principles of service and his interest in Daoist mysticism.

John Marney

TAO QIAN

Born: Xinyang (now in Henan), China; 365
Died: Xinyang (now in Henan), China; 427
Also known as: T'ao Ch'ien; T'ao Yüan-ming; Tao Yuanming

PRINCIPAL POETRY

T'ao the Hermit: Sixty Poems by T'ao Ch'ien (365-427), 1952 (William Acker, translator)
The Poems of T'ao Ch'ien, 1953 (Lily Pao-hu Chang and Marjorie Sinclair, translators)
The Poetry of T'ao Ch'ien, 1970 (James Robert Hightower, translator)
Complete Works of Tao Yuanming, 1992
Selected Poems, 1993

OTHER LITERARY FORMS

Tao Qian (tow chee-EHN) is known primarily as a poet. Among his extant works are two *fu* rhyme-prose compositions (that is, rhythmic and occasionally rhymed prose), the renowned "Return" in *ci* form (another quasi-poetic genre), a letter to an acquaintance, prefaces, seven *can* collophons (*envois*), a biographical note on an official colleague, several essays, obituaries, and the celebrated "Record of the Peach Grove."

ACHIEVEMENTS

Probably more has been written about Tao Qian, in whatever language, than about any other Chinese poet. Studies by Japanese scholars alone, to whom Tao Qian most strongly appealed, run into many hundreds of titles. Tao Qian is primarily associated with the foundations of the *tianyuan*, or "pastoral" (literally, "cultivated fields and orchards") school of poetry (as opposed to the rugged *shanshui* "mountains and waters" landscapes of his contemporary, the celebrated nobleman Xie Lingyun, 385-433). The unadorned directness of his poetic diction and the innocent, touching sentiment of his anchorite forbearance have perennially appealed to the oversophisticated Chinese bureaucrat-litterateur. Writing in the prevailing pentameter line of his day, Tao Qian was the first to exploit the *shi* lyric form extensively for such topics as wine (which he tirelessly celebrated) and the idiosyncrasies of his own children. These eventually became favorite themes in Tang and later poetry. As James Robert Hightower has observed in *The Poetry of T'ao Ch'ien*, "even the shortest and most selective list of famous Chinese poets would have to find a place for Tao Qian," and his poetry above that of all others appears the most frequently in anthologies of Chinese verse.

Biography

Biographies in the Chinese dynastic histories are principally concerned with their subject's official career and influence on national politics. Since Tao Qian's service career was minimal, and grudging at that, little contemporaneous record was kept, and the few remarks about him were included in the section on hermits, rather than in the "literati" category. His various sobriquets, too, reflect his preference for eremitic life. Later efforts to construct, or contrive, a respectable account befitting the life of a universally beloved poet relied largely on anecdote and on Tao Qian's autobiographical self-evaluations, such as "Biography of Mr. Five Willows" (a nom de plume describing his rustic environment). By his own account, Tao Qian was a quiet, unassuming man. He enjoyed scholarship but took no pleasure in pedantic obscurities. He would have his readers believe that he was a great drunkard, and indeed the greater part of the official record consists of stories illustrating his love of tippling, noting, for example, his insistence on cultivating brewing grain rather than food, however destitute his family. Even the memoir bringing him into friendly association with the then-ascendant court poet Yan Yazhi focuses on wine, relating how Tao Qian had deposited a large sum of money given him by Yen in a local wine shop.

Tao Qian lived during the decline of the Eastern Jin regime (317-420) of the Sima clan on a small farm south of the Yangzi River. His forebears had once been eminent officials, but the family had fallen on hard times, and Tao Qian lacked the all-important connections at court that would have secured for him, at the outset, an entrée into higher echelons of the administration. He was assigned various minor provincial posts, but he became disgusted with the pervasive corruption of the regime and with the petty drudgery of local officers and resigned rather than "crook his back for a five-peck salary." Thus, for most of his life he was a sort of gentleman farmer, living in relative poverty but wryly content with his wife and children, wine, chrysanthemums, friends, stringless lute, and poetry.

Analysis

Scholars of Chinese literature and literati throughout the ages have unanimously admired Tao Qian's poetry. Some eighty-eight of his poems survive. These are of varying length and in tetrasyllabic or pentasyllabic lines. Many are prefaced by an introduction explaining the circumstances under which they were composed. Tao Qian found no place for the artificial *yuefu* ("music bureau") compositions popular in his time—lyrics written to ancient tunes and titles which dictated theme, mood, and style. He did, however, on his own terms produce a set of poems "imitating" or "in the style of" earlier compositions.

Typical rhetoric describes Tao Qian's moral sentiments as "far-reaching waves, and lofty soaring clouds." Other famous poet-critics were drawn to imitate Tao Qian's style, notably the eleventh century poet Su Dongpo (also known as Su Shi), who wrote a set of

120 matching verses. A focus of controversy to this day is the dissenting judgment of the sixth century Zhong Hong, who, in his *Shipin* ("classification of poets"), placed Tao Qian in the second of three categories of poets because, in an age of florid ornamentation, Tao Qian's work disdained empty embellishments.

In the development of Chinese literature, Tao Qian is most securely associated with the flourishing of the *dianyuan* ("pastoral") genre, the embryonic origins of which stem from the tetrasyllabic odes of the great eleventh to seventh century B.C.E. canon. Poetry, thereafter, particularly during the Tang (618-907) and the Song (960-1279) dynasties, was imbued with his influence.

Although unwilling to compromise his principles for a corrupt regime, Tao Qian was acutely aware of the Confucian moral obligation of the literate gentleman to make his abilities available to the state. A number of his poems recall this duty, and they laud members of his own clan and other eminent bureaucrats who contributed their energies to public administration: "In hearing lawsuits he is just/ A hundred miles enjoy his help." He had had no taste for office as a youth, he says, but he too had tried to be of service, "fallen by mischance into the dusty net/ And thirteen years away from home." Such occupation was intolerable for him "in a time of decadence, when one longs for the ancient kings." Far too long, he had been a "caged prisoner." In the end, he was "not one to volunteer his services" and would "not be bound by love of rank," "scorning the role of opportunist." On the topic of posthumous fame, he was ambivalent. He asks, Daoist-like, what is the use of an honored name if it costs a lifetime of deprivation, yet he also suggests that fame may endure as an inspiration for a thousand years. Seeking solace for what he considered his own lifetime of failure, however, he stresses the transience of fame rather than its inspirational legacy.

DESTITUTION

In versifying the destitution to which he was reduced, Tao Qian indulged in no bleak self-pity. Virtually all his poems and many of his famous prose works mention his poverty, but he counts his blessings—and by Chinese standards, then and now, he must have been relatively self-sufficient. He owned a few acres of land and an ill-thatched cottage with "four or five" rooms (sometimes interpreted "as four plus five" rooms), shaded by elms and willows at the back, and with peaches and plums stretching out in front. He cultivated (or, more likely, oversaw the farming of) hemp, mulberry, and beans, and daily extended the area under his plow, delighting in the pleasures of the woods and fields.

Occasionally resorting to hyperbole, he claims in his poems that when his crops did badly, hunger drove him to begging, knocking on doors and fumbling for words. His house burned down several times, pests decimated his stock of grain, and even in winter, his family slept without covers, longing for the dawn. On a more cheerful note, his hut is repaired; plowing and spinning supply his needs; and if he is diligent in the fields, he will not be cheated. In fact, two poems specifically praise the farmer's lot, describing how new shoots enfold new life, and how labor, too, gives joy. Another dozen or so verses laud the "impoverished gentleman" along with other humble but principled men of ancient days. A long lament mourns "gentlemen born out of their times," who relinquished glory and took pleasure in poverty and low condition.

WINE

One consolation in Tao Qian's rustic plight was wine. A major part of his official biography and of his autobiographical comments focuses on his tippling, and some critics complain that his poetry revolves around little else. Certainly, no other poet before him had ever sung the praises of alcohol so prolifically and insistently, and in this, Tao Qian set a precedent for a subgenre that was to catch the imagination of later poets, notably Li Bo in the eighth century and Su Dongpo in the eleventh. Like poverty, wine is mentioned in virtually every one of Tai Qian's poems: Twenty poems were written "after drinking wine"; another describes "drinking alone in the rainy season"; yet another long poem gives "an account of wine"; and there is a rather pathetic poem in which Tao Qian confides that he wishes he could stop drinking—though the pathos of this admission is attenuated by the form of the verse, a game wherein the word "stop" appears in each of the twenty lines.

However undesirable Tao Qian's apparent alcoholism may seem to the modern Western reader, no odium attached itself to the poet in his time. The Chinese heritage better appreciated the spiritual liberation achieved by mild inebriation and credited much of the innocent genius of Tao Qian's poetry to this condition. Later critics, too, have defended Tao Qian by arguing that such drunkenness was a timeworn ploy in China (the antics of the poet Ruan Ji in the third century constitute a formidable example), to a large extent feigned to avoid the jeopardy of involvement in political machinations.

CHRYSANTHEMUMS

Almost as much as with wine, Tao Qian was fascinated by the chrysanthemum, a flower that has come to be associated with his poetry. The chrysanthemum bloom survives the blight of autumn; as the last flower of the year, it represented for Tao Qian his own fortitude in adversity. So too appear in his lines the cypress and the pine—evergreens that symbolize Confucian moral steadfastness.

Tao Qian found great comfort in his family. He was the first Chinese poet to record his feelings about his children so freely, and in doing so he left to posterity some of the most appealing lines in the Chinese literary heritage. In "Finding Fault with My Sons," the poet complains about the laziness and self-indulgence of his five boys: The nine-year-old, for example, wants only pears and chestnuts, and the thirteen-year-olds cannot even count to their age. It is Tao Qian's ability to capture casual moments from childhood, however—the toddler peeking through a crack in the door, anticipating his father's return from the fields—that has given his poems on children a timeless appeal.

RURAL DELIGHTS

Tao Qian's pastoral poetry typified the *dianyuan* genre. Rather than tramping in climbing boots among the wooded peaks and precipices of a Jiangsu-Zhejiang estate, as did Xie Lingyun, Tao Qian would sit quietly at his casement window in his tumbledown thatched cottage and contemplate the passing scene, sip his wine, think of old and absent friends, and muse on his approaching old age. Gentle delight in the rural community fills his verse, rather than the wonder of nature's vast power and magnificence that erupts from Xie Lingyun's nature poetry. Noteworthy, too, is the absence from Tao Qian's diction of the color, glitter, mysticism, classical obscurantism, and pedantic reference and allusion of the overrefined, overembellished poetry then in vogue—in particular the unctuous congratulatory court verse of his friend, Yan Yanzhi.

In the most simple, natural language, Tao Qian writes about the dense, hovering clouds, and the fine rain at dusk that settles on the road, making it impassable. These, typically, are static images, reinforced by the absence of boat or carriage that might bring visiting friends. Movement lies more in the new blossoms springing forth, eliciting the emotions of a sensitive observer. Still-life landscapes depict new grains and the waters of a wide lake stretching endlessly into the distance. Herbs and flowers grow in rows, over which trees and bamboo cast their shade. "Interior" scenes show a cittern (stringed instrument) across a bench and a jug half-filled with muddy wine.

Time passes in the pell-mell revolution of the seasons. Blossoms are dead by morning; the cicada's mournful chirp heralds the fading of summer's heat; plum and peach of springtime give way to autumn's chrysanthemum; one sees migrating geese and notes the morning cockcrow. Frosts wither the crops, and evening dew soaks the poet's gown. His years slip away, his hair turns gray, and his children mature. As the sun sets, a torch serves in place of a costly candle, and if the company is congenial, dawn arrives too soon. Thousand-year cares may be forgotten; tomorrow need not concern a person in his or her enjoyment of the moment.

Tao Qian's poems further adumbrate a kind of farmer's almanac, detailing the activities of his daily life. There is habitual drinking, but the poet also writes of hitching up his wagon at early dawn and starting along the road to his plowing and weeding. He discusses with the locals the prospects for the harvest of mulberry and hemp. Tired, staff in hand, he returns home by a path twisting through the bushes, pausing to bathe his feet in a mountain stream. He digs a well for water, and plucks a wild chrysanthemum by a bank. For leisure, there are books wherein to discover heroic models from the past who may inspire him in his adversity. As a series of thirteen poems reveals, he especially delights in the fantasies and adventures of the imaginative *Shan hai jing* (date unknown; *The Classic of Mountains and Seas*, 2000) and the magic and marvels of *Mu Tianzi zhuan* (c. fourth century B.C.E.; travels of King Mu). Always he sings of his contentment, however poor: how neat his garden is, and how glad he is to have relinquished worldly affairs.

CLASSICAL PHILOSOPHICAL VIEWS

The philosophical views that Tao Qian espoused were entirely classical. Although he lived within the shadow of Mount Lu, the great monastic seat of Hui Yuan's White Lotus sect of Buddhism, to which Xie Lingyun and other intellectual literati had been massively attracted, Tao Qian's works exhibit no interest in the newly introduced faith—celibacy and abstention were hardly characteristic of him. The popular Daoism of the time, too, with its mysticism and dilettante metaphysical speculation and searches for elixirs of immortality seems to have touched him but little, and he both doubts and eschews the labors and regimens recommended for the attainment of transcendent sagehood.

DEATH

In addition, death itself did not seem to frighten Tao Qian. He concludes his long discourse on "Substance, Shadow, and Spirit" with the simple attitude, "When it is time to go, then we shall simply go—there is nothing, after all, that we can do about it." Life, he explains, is nothing but a shadow play, which in the end reverts to nothingness: There is no immortality, no afterlife, no rebirth. Indeed, the primitive concepts he expresses smack most strongly of the early Daoism of Laozi (sixth century B.C.E.) and Zhuangzi (third century B.C.E.).

If frequency of citation is a criterion, then Tao Qian's favorite source of classical philosophical reference were the Confucian *Lunyu* (later sixth-early fifth centuries B.C.E.; *The Analects*, 1861) a collection of aphorisms attributed to Confucius and compiled some two centuries after his death. Tao Qian was especially observant of passages wherein the Master sanctioned retirement from officialdom during the administration of a corrupt and unworthy regime, doubtless to assuage his own pangs of conscience. The heroes who appear in his "Impoverished Gentlemen," drawn from philosophies and histories through the third century Han Dynasty, also exemplify the person of pure principle, who, like himself, would rather eke out an existence in humble obscurity than strive for empty glories in sycophantic court service.

One often anthologized verse exemplifies these various elements of Tao Qian's work and thought. The poem is dated in the ninth month of the year 410, after the rice harvest, and located in some "western field":

> Man's life may conform to the Way,
> But clothing and food are indeed fundamental.
> If no provision be made for them,

> How can one seek peace?
> At the opening of springtime, I took care of
> the ordinary jobs,
> And the harvest has turned out considerable.
> . . . .
> My four limbs in truth so weary,
> . . . .
> Far, far though the mind of Chü and Ni be,
> A thousand years I still sense affinity with them.
> Would that things be forever thus:
> It is not plowing the fields that I complain of!

Tao Qian affirms that mortal life is bound by morality, but, echoing the Confucian rationalist, Mencius, he realizes that the basis of ethical behavior is material sustenance. The life of the producer of these essential commodities is not an easy one, subject as it is to wearisome toil and the exigencies of the natural world. Well enough he appreciates the attitudes of the plowmen Zhangzhu and Jie, who rejected the overtures of Confucius and his disciple Zilu to engage them in discourse (a clever closure balancing the Confucian sentiments of the opening). Indeed, it is not the productive plowing of which Tao Qian complains. Rather, he implies, he grieves over the political situation, for the men of power and status have reneged on their mandate of moral leadership.

Utopia

Tao Qian describes his vision of utopia in his renowned "Peach Blossom Spring," the story of a fisherman who loses his way, enters a flowering peach grove, and comes upon a lost society—refugees from the rapacious Qin regime (221-206 B.C.E.). He remains there for several days, entertained by the inhabitants, and although enjoined to secrecy, upon his return home he reports his experience to the authorities. Searches, however, fail to rediscover the location of the peach grove.

As described in the narrative, Tao Qian's perfect society enjoys broad plains of rich fields and ponds and substantial dwellings. Well-tended paths traverse the fields, where mulberry and bamboo grow. Courtyards are stocked with domestic animals; the people dress unpretentiously and are happy and carefree. They till the soil in mutual contract, and at sunset cease from their toil. No taxes are extorted for imperial indulgences; roads remain untraveled by the king's officers. No calendar regulates the natural progression of the seasons; artful machines are not needed.

Such is the nature of Tao Qian's views as presented in his poetry. His wistful forbearance in the adversity of humble poverty—when riches and honor, however tainted by dishonorable service, could have been his—his cheerful self-consolation and his sincere attachment to the life of farmer and peasant that he intimately chronicled, his love of family, his high morality tempered by human failings, his doubts as to the rectitude of his retirement from admittedly evil times, and his refuge in quiet inebriation have endeared him and his work to Asian and Western readers irrespective of era, class, or aspiration.

BIBLIOGRAPHY

Davis, A. R. *T'ao Yüan-ming: His Works and Their Meaning*. 1983. Reprint. 2 vols. New York: Cambridge University Press, 2009. This thorough study consists of a volume of translation and commentary, and a second volume of commentary, notes, and a biography of the poet.

Field, Stephen L. "The Poetry of Tao Yuanming." In *Great Literature of the Eastern World*, edited by Ian P. McGreal. New York: HarperCollins, 1996. A brief teaching guide with an analysis of Tao Qian's three poems "A Returning to Live in the Country," "Return Home!" and "Peach Blossom Found."

Kwong, Charles Yim-tze. *Tao Qian and the Chinese Poetic Tradition: The Quest for Cultural Identity*. Ann Arbor, Mich.: Center for Chinese Studies, 1994. One of the few English-language literary studies of Tao Qian's work. Discusses the poet in his cultural and literary contexts, comparing his work to that of both Chinese and Western poets.

Lin, Pauline. "Rediscovering Ying Qu and His Poetic Relationship to Tao Qian." *Harvard Journal of Asiatic Studies* 69, no. 1 (June, 2009): 31. Lin argues that Tao Qian was influenced by the earlier poet Ying Qu. She compares their poetry, finding similarities, and discusses why Ying Qu is not as famous.

Rusk, Bruce. "An Interpolation in Zhong Hong's *Shipin*." *Journal of the American Oriental Society* 128, no. 3 (July-September, 2008): 553-558. Examines the part of *Shipin* in which the author assigns a "middle" grade to Tao Qian as a poet and argues that the text may be corrupt.

Swartz, Wendy. *Reading Tao Yuanming: Shifting Paradigms of Historical Reception (427-1900)*. Cambridge, Mass.: Asia Center, Harvard University, 2008. This critical analysis of Tao Qian's work looks at how his poetry was received in various time periods. Dismissed as a minor poet after his death, his reputation later grew to the point where he is considered one of China's major poets.

Tao Qian. *The Poetry of T'ao Ch'ien*. Translated and edited by James Robert Hightower. Oxford, England: Clarendon Press, 1970. The standard edition in English. The translations themselves are not noticeably superior to those of his predecessors, but Hightower's notes make the book an essential reference for anyone doing serious work on Tao Qian. It is by far the best guide to its subject's use of traditional elements of the Chinese literary tradition.

Tian, Xiaofei. *Tao Yuanming and Manuscript Culture: The Record of a Dusty Table*. Seattle: University of Washington Press, 2006. This analysis of Tao Qian's works examines how transmission of manuscripts has affected the poems. Editors and scholars along the way made changes to many of the poems. The author discusses the reliability of the texts used by Chinese scholars.

Yu, Pauline. "The Poetry of Retreat." In *Masterworks of Asian Literature in Comparative Perspective*, edited by Barbara Stoler Miller. Armonk, N.Y.: M. E. Sharpe, 1994. A thoughtful discussion of Tao Qian in the Chinese poetic tradition of the recluse, along with other poets such as Ruan Ji and Xie Lingyun.

John Marney

WANG WEI

Born: District of Qi, Taiyuan Prefecture, Shanxi Province, China; 701
Died: Changan (now Xian), Jingzhao Prefecture, China; 761
Also known as: Wang Mojie; Wang Youcheng; Wang Yu-ch'eng

PRINCIPAL POETRY
Wang Wei: New Translations and Commentary, 1980 (Pauline Yu, translator)
Laughing Lost in the Mountains: The Poems of Wang Wei, 1991 (Willis Barnstone, Tony Barnstone, and Shu Haixin translators)
The Selected Poems of Wang Wei, 2006 (David Hinton, translator)

OTHER LITERARY FORMS

Although known primarily for his poetry, Wang Wei (wong way) was also the author of several important writings pertaining to various traditions in Tang Dynasty Buddhism, in particular his funeral inscription for the *stēlē* of the Sixth Chan (Zen) Patriarch, Huineng. In addition, Wang was an accomplished musician and painter, acquiring considerable renown for the latter talent after his death. No painting authentically attributable to him is extant, but numerous copies of several of his works were executed over a period of centuries. One of the best known of these is the long scroll depicting his country estate on the Wang River. From the Song Dynasty onward, when only copies of his works survived, he became glorified as the preeminent Chinese landscape painter, with his work honored as the prototype of *wen ren hua* (literati painting)—amateur rather than academic, intuitive and spontaneous rather than formalistic and literal.

ACHIEVEMENTS

Wang Wei is generally acknowledged to be one of the major poets of the Tang Dynasty (618-907), the most brilliant period in the long history of Chinese poetry; he was probably the most respected poet of his own time. In one of the many classificatory schemes of which traditional Chinese critics were particularly fond, he was labeled the "Poet Buddha," ranked with the two poets of the era who were to exceed him in fame, Li Bo, the "Poet Immortal," and Du Fu, the "Poet Sage." This appellation reflects Wang's association with Buddhism, which flourished in eighth century China, but it is important to note that very few of his poems are overtly doctrinal or identifiable solely with any one of the many traditions or lineages of Buddhism active during the Tang.

Like those of most men of letters of the time, Wang's life and works reflect a typically syncretic mentality, integrating yet exploring the conflicts among the goals and ideals of Confucian scholarship and commitment to public service, Daoist retreat and equanimity, and Buddhist devotion. Such issues, however, are not dealt with directly or at length in his works. His poetry relies on suggestion rather than direct statement, presenting apparently simple and precise visual imagery drawn from nature which proves elusive and evocative at the same time. He eschews definitive closure for open-endedness and irresolution, leaving the reader to attempt to resolve the unanswered questions of a poem. His best poems rarely include any direct expression of emotion and frequently suppress the poet's own subjective presence, yet this seeming impersonality has become the hallmark of a very personal style.

Because Wang's poems embody what Stephen Owen has called the artifice of simplicity, they were frequently imitated, both by the coterie of court contemporaries at whose center he stood and by later poets, followers of the "Wang Wei school." Although many of the imitators were able to replicate the witty understatement, the stark imagery, and the enigmatic closure of Wang's work, none—by general critical agreement—succeeded in probing to the same extent depths of emotion and meaning beneath a deceptively artless surface.

Biography

Wang Wei (also known by his cognomen, Wang Mojie, and his courtesy name, Wang Youcheng) was the eldest child of a prominent family in Shanxi Province. He became known for his precocious poetic, musical, and artistic talents and was well received by aristocratic patrons of the arts in the two capital cities of the empire. After placing first in his provincial examinations at the age of nineteen, Wang went on to pass the most literary of the three main types of imperial civil-service examinations in 721, one of the thirty-eight successful candidates that year. (Typically, only 1-2 percent of the thousands of candidates recommended each year for this highly competitive examination would pass.) He received the *jinshi* (presented scholar) degree and began his slow but steady rise through government ranks.

Like all Chinese scholar-bureaucrats, Wang moved from post to post and to various parts of the empire, most of which appear in his poetry. From his position as a court secretary of music in the western capital of Changan, he was sent to the east in Shandong (720's), back to the capital (734), to the northwest frontier (737), south to the Yangzi River area (740), and back to the capital (742). His career was interrupted at intervals by temporary losses of favor, factional intrigues, and various infractions, the most serious of which was his collaboration—though forced—in the puppet government of the rebel general An Lushan, whose armies overran the capitals and forced Emperor Xuanzong into exile from 755 to 757. Only the intercession of Wang's younger brother, Wang Jin, who had fought valorously with the loyalist forces, secured a pardon for the poet in 758. The next year, he attained the high-ranking sinecure of *shangshu youcheng* (undersecretary of state) and is thus frequently referred to as Wang Youcheng. In this respect, his career differed markedly from that of his two most famous poet contemporaries, Li Bo and Du Fu, neither of whom passed the imperial examinations or enjoyed Wang's considerable family connections. Unlike them, Wang never suffered severe financial hardship (despite the posing of some of his poems), maintaining a relatively secure position in the social and cultural center of what was later to be perceived as the golden age of the Tang Dynasty itself, the reign of Emperor Xuanzong (713-755).

The date of Wang's marriage has not been recorded, nor the number and names of any children he may have had. His wife died around 730, however, and Wang remained celibate thereafter—somewhat unusual for the times and an index of his devotion to Buddhist principles. It was in fact around the time of his wife's death that he began a serious study of Buddhism. In addition to the several essays and inscriptions connected with issues and figures in Tang Buddhism that are included in Wang's collected works, the most illuminating evidence of his religious commitment is his choice of cognomen, Mojie. Combined with his given name, Wei, these syllables form the Chinese transliteration (Weimojie) of one of the Buddha's best-known contemporaries, Vimalakīrti, said to have preached a sutra that became especially popular in China, not only for its doctrines but also because he himself remained a layman throughout his life. Vimalakīrti also espoused such central Confucian social ideals as filial piety and loyalty to the ruler and demonstrated to the Chinese that the good Buddhist did not necessarily have to leave his family and retreat to a monastery.

This example was an important one for Wang, for his religious beliefs never led him to abjure totally his political and social relationships. Popular legend has long held Wang to have been but a reluctant bureaucrat, and his poetry speaks frequently of a desire for reclusion. Wang did spend much of his time on retreat in various locations, particularly at his country estate at Lantian on the Wang River, which he acquired around 750 and where he eventually built a monastery. All the same, he remained officially in office until his death.

Analysis

The poems of Wang Wei were first collected by his brother, Wang Jin, at imperial request and presented to the throne in 763. The number of poems that can be attributed definitively to him is small—371, compared with the thousand or more each of Li Bo and Du Fu. The official dynastic history records his brother as telling the emperor that there were once ten times that many, the rest having been lost during the turmoil of the An Lushan Rebellion.

Whatever the case, the poems for which Wang is best remembered have fostered an image of him as a private, contemplative, self-effacing observer of the natural scene. In fact, however, despite references in several poems to his solitude behind his "closed gate" at home, many of his poems were inspired by social occasions—visits from or to friends, journeys of fellow bureaucrats to distant posts, his own departures to new offices—and by official occasions as well. Wang was a highly successful court poet, the master of a graceful, formally regulated style whose patterns had been perfected during the seventh century.

The ability to write poetry on any occasion was expected of all government officials and was in fact tested on the civil-service examination. Several of Wang's poems bear witness by their titles to having been written "to imperial command" on some formal court occasion—an outing to the country, an important birthday, the construction of a new building, the presentation of some gift—and often "harmonize respectfully" with the rhymes of a model poem composed by the emperor himself. Most of these poems were written in a heptasyllabic eight-line form with rigidly regulated rules of tone, parallelism, and rhyme. Poets in attendance would vie with one another to complete their poems first, and there was often some official evaluation of literary quality. Other poems in Wang's corpus arose out of less formally decorous contexts but reveal nevertheless the demands on the Tang poet to be able to respond to the stimulus of an occasion in an apparently spontaneous and sincere, appropriate, economical, and witty manner.

"LADY XI"

A good example of Wang's mastery of the literary and contextual demands of the poem written on command is his early work "Xi furen" ("Lady Xi"). He is said to have composed this poem at the age of twenty (nineteen by Western reckoning), when he was preparing for the imperial examination and in residence at the court of the emperor's half brother, Li Xian, prince of Ning. It is one of several poems in Wang's collection for which was noted his supposed age at composition—unverifiable, but attesting the recognition of his early prowess. An anecdote recorded in a collection of stories attached to poems compiled in the ninth century provides the necessary explanation of the background of the poem. The prince, it seems, had been attracted by the wife of a pastry vendor and had purchased her as his concubine. After a year had passed, he asked her if she still thought of her husband, but she did not reply. The prince then summoned the vendor, and when his wife saw him, her eyes filled with tears. Ten or so people were present at the time, including Wang, and their patron commanded them to write a poem on the subject. Wang's quatrain was the first completed, and everyone else agreed that none better could be written. The prince then returned the pastry vendor's wife to her husband.

In the poem itself, there are, surprisingly, no overt references to the couple in question. The first two lines express a simple and general denial—that loves of the past can be forgotten because of present affections. The last two lines conclude with an allusion, but not to the pastry vendor and his wife; they refer to a text, a story in the Zuo commentary on the "Spring and Autumn Annals" (722-481 B.C.E.) of the *Chunqiu* (sixth to fifth century B.C.E.), one of the Confucian classics. There it is recorded that the king of Chu defeated the ruler of Xi and took the latter's wife as his own. Though she bore him children, Lady Xi never spoke to her new spouse, and when finally asked why, she is said to have answered: "I am but one woman, yet it has been my fate to serve two husbands. Although I have been unable to die, how should I dare to speak?"

This poem illustrates concisely Wang's typical "artifice of simplicity," his ability to charge the briefest of poems—twenty syllables in all—with a considerable burden. Typically, denials open and close the poem, revealing Wang's penchant for the open-ended quality of negation as opposed to assertion. What could have been a merely sentimental episode becomes dignified here through the link made to the moral dilemma of a historical ruler's wife and by the poet's choice not to mention the contemporary protagonists at all. Typically effective, also, is the poet's refusal to make any direct comment. Understatement and allusion work hand in hand here to make a point that is no less clear for not being stated explicitly.

The Wang River collection

These same methods of indirection and evocation, of using objects and events to suggest something lying beneath the surface, distinguish Wang's most famous poems, his limpid and apparently selfless depictions of natural scenes. These works are not, as a rule, devoid of people, and much of their impersonal quality derives simply from the general tendency of the classical Chinese language to avoid the use of subjective pronouns and to remain uninflected for person, tense, number, gender, and case. Wang does, however, exploit the inherent potential of the language to create indeterminate or multiple meanings more than do most other traditional poets. This is true, for example, of several poems in his well-known sequence, the Wang River collection. As Wang's preface explains, this group of twenty pentasyllabic quatrains, each of which names a site on Wang's country estate, was written in the company of one of his closest friends, a minor official named Pei Di (born 716). Pei wrote twenty poems to match those of his host, and these are also included in standard collections of Wang's poetry.

As Owen has noted in his history of poetry in the High Tang, Wang's quatrains as a whole probably represent his most significant contribution to generic development, particularly because of his substitution of enigmatic understatement for the epigrammatic closure more common at the time. The Wang River collection is informed by some of the key modes of consciousness of the poet's entire oeuvre: an emphasis on perceptual and cognitive limitations, a transcendence of temporal and spatial distinctions, and a sense of the harmony of the individual and nature. This is especially true of the fifth and probably most famous poem in the sequence, "Lu zhai" ("Deer Park").

"Deer Park"

This poem exemplifies typical quatrain form, narrowing its focus from the massiveness of a mountain to a ray of the setting sun entering a mossy grove. Each line presents a perception that is qualified or amplified by the next. What is given in the first line as an "empty mountain," where no people are seen, reverberates with echoes of human voices in the second line. Whether these echoes signify that other people are actually present on the mountain at some distance or are intended metaphorically, to suggest the poet's memories of friends in an altogether different location, however, remains unspecified. The third line places the plot in a specific place and time—toward sunset, when "returning" (*fan*) light sends a "reflected" (also *fan*) glow through an opening into a glade. The fourth line suggests that the poet has been in the grove that same morning, or perhaps all day, and thus knows that the light is shining on the blue-green moss "again."

More than a brief nature poem, "Deer Park" links keenly observed and deceptively simple perceptions with far-ranging Buddhist implications. Scholar Marsha L. Wagner has made some important observations about the title: that "Deer Park" was the name of the site near Benares where the Buddha preached his first sermon after becoming enlightened, that it was an alternate name for the monastery Wang built on his Wang River estate, and that the deer not caught in a trap was a conventional Buddhist symbol for the recluse. Within the poem itself, the crucial word is *kong* (empty), on which hinges more than the question about the unpopulated state of the mountain. *Kong* is also the translation of the Sanskrit word *śūnyatā*, which was a key term in the Buddhist traditions with which Wang was familiar, denoting the illusory or "empty" nature of all reality and the ultimate reality, therefore, of "emptiness." *Kong* is one of the most frequently recurring words in Wang's poetic vocabulary—translated sometimes as "empty," at other times meaning "merely" or "in vain," in each case with the same powerful resonance. Moreover, the vision of the light entering the grove, the counterpart of beams of moonlight in other poems, provides a concrete image of the experience of enlightenment itself. The poem as a whole, then, encapsulates key Buddhist notions about the nature of reality and human perception of it.

"Deer Park" provides a good example of how Wang suggests religious and philosophical doctrines and attitudes in an indirect manner. Even in poems that treat Buddhist subjects more directly, doctrinal elements are generally merely implicit. Many of his accounts of journeys to monasteries, for example, are by convention metaphorical from the outset: Since temples were frequently located high in the mountains, visiting them required an effort that represented the physical counterpart to the progress toward enlightenment. Several of Wang's poems on this topic emphasize the spiritual implications of the physical ascent, among which "Guo Xiangji si" ("Visiting the Temple of Gathered Fragrance") is particularly well known.

"Visiting the Temple of Gathered Fragrance"

Wang opens "Visiting the Temple of Gathered Fragrance" with a profession of ignorance. He does not "know" the temple, and this at once suggests several possibilities: He does not know of its existence, of its location, or of its significance—or perhaps he has discarded a rational, cognitive kind of "knowing" for an intuitive, nondifferentiating awareness more conducive to true spiritual knowledge. In any event, this special kind of ignorance sets the tone for the description of the journey up the mountain, each stage of which contains images of extreme ambiguity and vagueness. The second line speaks of "entering cloudy peaks," but the verb can refer either to the action of the speaker or to the location of the monastery, thus deliberately blurring the distinction between the traveler and his destination, or subject and object. The obscurity of these cloudy peaks is frequently associated in Wang's poetry with temples and transcendent realms and suggests the inadequacy of merely sensuous perception on such a journey of the spirit.

The poem continues to reinforce this sense of linguistic and perceptual ambiguity. The phrase "paths without people" in the third line can also be read as "no paths for people," thus further suggesting the speaker's venture into unknown territory, untraveled by others; this experience must be undertaken in absolute solitude. This sense of mystery is evoked again in the question of the following line: "Where is the bell?" As in the opening couplet, Wang reveals here a distrust of visual perception and purely intellectual cognition. Presumably the sound of a bell from somewhere deep in the mountains confirms the existence of the monastery, at least, if not its precise location. Has he heard the bell himself, though? He does not say. Thus, he must continue his ascent without the comforting knowledge of where he is or where he is going.

In the third couplet, the images appear to be more concrete than those in the preceding lines, but they are in fact equally ambiguous. In each line of the third couplet, the verb can be read either actively or passively, suggesting that the processes occurring cannot be subjected to rational analysis; they can be apprehended only intuitively as one total experience in which subject and object are indistinguishable. Furthermore, Wang's diction also undermines the sensuous precision of the couplet. Rather than focusing on the concreteness of the nouns—"stream" and "sun"—he speaks of the former's "sound" and the latter's "color," so that in each case he is describing an abstraction rather than a concrete object.

The final couplet of the poem in no way diminishes the mysterious quality of the journey. Wang has reached a pond—perhaps at the monastery, though he does not say—whose bends and curves continue to recall the winding paths of other spiritual journeys. What does it mean for the pond to be "empty"? Is it dried up, deserted, illusory, or an image of ultimate reality? In the last line, Wang simply presents a process without specifying the subject or the precise nature of the object. The "peaceful meditation" may be that of a monk from the temple or the poet himself, or it may not refer to an individual at all but rather to an intangible atmosphere of the place. The "poison dragons" tamed by the meditation are traditionally interpreted as passions or illusions that may stand in the way of enlightenment, and many possible sources in Buddhist texts have been suggested. They are controlled and not eliminated, present by virtue of their very mention, thus suggesting Wang's awareness, in this poem, at least, of the effort required to attain the tranquil and selfless union with the world that, in so many of his poems, he seems to possess.

This harmony is one that transcends boundaries between subject and object and those of language as well; hence Wang's reliance on understatement and what he does not say. One well-known poem, however, flirts briefly with the possibility that perhaps words are not inadequate after all. "Chou Chang shaofu" ("In Response to Vice-Magistrate Chang") opens quite discursively with an observation that occurs frequently in Wang's poetry on the contrast between past and present priorities. The profession that only age has enabled him wisely to reject worldly involvement is familiar also to readers of the poetry of Tao Qian, the poet of the past with whom Wang most strongly identified and in whose eighth century revival he played an instrumental role. Like Tao Qian, who left office early on matters of principle, Wang claims also to be rejecting the "long-range plans" associated with governmental policy. He now "only" (or "emptily"—*kong* again) knows "to return to the old forest," and the word "return" recalls the importance of the same word for Tao Qian, who employed it frequently for the implications it possessed in early Daoist literature of getting back to one's original nature, uncorrupted by civilization and its trappings.

The third couplet of "Visiting the Temple of Gathered Fragrance" provides images of Wang's newfound freedom. Pine winds blow loose the belt of his robe, and the moon provides congenial companionship as he plays the zither, the instrument traditionally associated with scholar-recluses. The penultimate line turns to a question posed by the addressee of the poem and suggests that Wang will finally put into words the wisdom he has gained, the "reasons for success and failure" or the "principles of universal change." His response in the last line, however, provides no easy answer, only an enigmatic image of a fisherman's song that can be read in a number of ways.

In the first place, the last line in the third couplet may be regarded as a nonanswer in the tradition of the Chan or Zen koan, by means of which a Buddhist master attempts to bring a student to enlightenment by answering a rational question with a non sequitur, thus jolting the latter out of conventional, logical, categorical modes of thinking, and liberating his mind to facilitate a sudden, intuitive realization of truth. Wang's answer, then, would deliberately bear no relationship to Chang's query, seeking instead to reject such cognitive concerns or indeed denying the validity of his question.

There is a second possibility. Because the fisherman, along with the woodcutter, was a favorite Daoist figure representing the rustic, unselfconscious life in harmony with nature, this final line may be read as a simple suggestion to change to follow the example of such recluses and escape from official life to the freedom and serenity of country living. This is a realm, moreover, where the vicissitudes of the world and such distinctions as failure and success will have no meaning.

A third interpretation of the line hinges on a possible reference to a specific fisherman's song, the "Yufu" ("Fisherman"), included in the southern anthology, the *Chu ci* (songs of Chu), compiled during the Han Dynasty. In the earlier poem, a wise fisherman converses with the fourth century B.C.E. poet Qu Yuan, who had been a loyal minister to the king of Chu and committed to the Confucian ideal of service but who was slandered by others at court and banished. He remained self-righteous about his inflexible moral purity and later chose suicide rather than compromise his principles. In this song, when Qu Yuan meets the fisherman, he explains the reasons behind his exile; the fisherman suggests that it might have been more circumspect to adapt to the circumstances, but Qu Yuan insists that he would rather drown than do so. The fisherman departs with a gentle mocking reply, singing that if the waters are clean, he will wash his hat-strings in them, and if they are dirty, he will wash his feet. Unlike the self-righteous Qu Yuan, the fisherman can adjust to the conditions he finds and paradoxically remains freer of their influence. Ultimately, perhaps, he realizes that, when seen from a higher perspective, the waters are all the same.

If Wang's use of this allusion is to be granted, then he is certainly affirming the kind of unifying vision and transcendence of distinctions that underlies his poetry as a whole. Perhaps the more important point, however, is Wang's failure to allow a definitive resolution to the question at all. The conclusion to this poem, as to so many of his poems, is purposely inconclusive and open-ended, leaving the reader to puzzle out what answers there may be.

BIBLIOGRAPHY

Chou, Shan. "Beginning with Images in the Nature Poetry of Wang Wei." *Harvard Journal of Asiatic Studies* 42 (June, 1982): 117-137. Chou proposes that the solution to the problem of meaning in Wang's nature poetry is to be found in understanding the Buddhist influence.

Owen, Stephen. "Wang Wei: The Artifice of Simplicity." In *The Great Age of Chinese Poetry: The High T'ang*. New Haven, Conn.: Yale University Press, 1981. Owen supplies an excellent short overview of Wang as poetic technician and relates the poet's work to his life and historical context.

Wagner, Marsha L. *Wang Wei*. Boston: Twayne, 1982. Part of the Twayne World Authors series, this scholarly, well-written account of Wang's life provides a balanced, perceptive appraisal of his contributions as poet, painter, and government official. Includes fine translations.

Wang Wei. *Laughing Lost in the Mountains: Poems of Wang Wei*. Translated by Tony Barnstone, Willis Barnstone, and Xu Haixin. Hanover, N.H.: University Press of New England, 1991. Excellent translation of 171 poems. The critical introduction, "The Ecstasy of Stillness," by the Barnstones provides insights into these poems.

_____. *The Poetry of Wang Wei: New Translations and Commentary*. Translated by Pauline Yu. Bloomington: Indiana University Press, 1980. This study provides excellent, scholarly translations and notes as well as knowing critical appraisals of Wang's poems.

_____. *The Selected Poems of Wang Wei*. Translated by David Hinton. New York: New Directions, 2006. A translation of Wang's poems, with an introduction providing critical analysis and a biography.

Wang Wei, Li Bo, and Du Fu. *Three Chinese Poets: Translations of Poems by Wang Wei, Li Bai, and Du Fu*. Translated by Vikram Seth. Boston: Faber and Faber, 1992. A collection of poems by Wang, Du Fu, and Li Bo. Commentary by translator Seth provides useful information.

Weinberger, Eliot. *Nineteen Ways of Looking at Wang Wei*. Mount Kisco, N.Y.: Moyer Bell, 1987. This short book offers insights into the art of translating Chinese poems. Includes commentary by both Weinberger and writer Octavio Paz.

Yang, Jingqing. *The Chan Interpretations of Wang Wei's Poetry: A Critical Review*. Hong Kong: Chinese University Press, 2007. Looks at Chan (Zen) Buddhism and how it relates to Wang's poetry.

Young, David, trans. *Five T'ang Poets: Wang Wei, Li Po, Tu Fu, Li Ho, Li Shang-yin*. Oberlin, Ohio: Oberlin College Press, 1990. Provides an opportunity for appreciating Wang along with contemporary poets during the Tang Dynasty.

Pauline Yu

XIE LINGYUN

Born: Zhejiang Province, China; 385
Died: Canton, Nanhai, China; June 26, 433
Also known as: Hsieh K'ang-lo; Hsieh Ling-Yün; Xie Kanglo

PRINCIPAL POETRY
The Murmuring Stream: The Life and Works of Hsieh Ling-yün, 1967 (2 volumes; J. D. Frodsham, editor)

OTHER LITERARY FORMS

The official biography of Xie Lingyun (sheh lihng-YUHN), compiled during the early sixth century, records his collected works in twenty folios and notes that Xie compiled a history of the Jin Dynasty, elements of which still survive. Also extant are fourteen *fu* rhyme-prose compositions (that is, prose poetry, with rhythm and occasional rhyme) and twenty-eight items of official prose, letters, prefaces, eulogies, *in memoriams*, and Buddhist essays totaling four folios.

ACHIEVEMENTS

Important critics from the sixth century to the eighteenth century have been unanimous in attributing to Xie Lingyun both the founding of the *shanshui* (literally "mountains and waters") or "nature" poetry, popular in his own day, and its highest development. His travels in mountain retreats, for which he invented special climbing boots with reversible studs, and which inspired his tumultuous landscape descriptions, further brought him into contact with newly introduced Buddhist ideals, and his profound philosophical speculations added dimensions to the religious debates of his time and to the evolution of Buddhist sectarian thought. A member of the most aristocratic of the Southern Dynasties' families, his great intellectual abilities and skill as a calligrapher and painter attracted the notice of emperors of two regimes, and he was involved—fatally, as it was to transpire—in the most serious matters of state. Locations in his native Jiangsu and Zhejiang provinces are still named after him.

BIOGRAPHY

Following the flight of the Jin aristocracy in 317, south across the Yangzi River to escape the invading Topa tribes from central Asia, the Xie clan came to prominence among the handful of cultured land barons who dominated the ensuing Southern Dynasties era (317-589). Their eminence stemmed from successive generations of extraordinary political and intellectual brilliance. Xie Lingyun's own direct forebears included the distinguished poet Xie Kun (280-322) and the statesman Xie An (320-385). On

Xie's mother's side, he was descended from the great calligraphers Wang Xizhi (321-379) and his son Wang Xianzchi (344-388).

The young Xie Lingyun was intellectually precocious and, presuming on his wealthy estate as a duke of the realm (the duke of Kangle), became notorious for his personal excesses and extravagances (even for the times) and for his sharp, critical wit. These tendencies and his later consort with rebellious peasantry and ruffians eventually brought about his downfall.

Near-contemporaneous records mention that as a child, Xie Lingyun was sent for safety to live with the Du family, esoteric Daoists associated with fine calligraphy, in Hangzhou (hence his sobriquet Little Guest Xie). These philosophical and artistic influences were ever to remain with Xie. Then, in 399-400, when Xie was fifteen, an uprising brought the Daoist-inspired rebel Sun En into Xie territories in Zhejiang and Jiangsu, and many of their clan, and the related Wang, were killed, including Xie Lingyun's father. The boy was transferred to the capital at Jiankang (modern Nanking) and lodged with his uncle, Xie Hun (who was married into the Sima royal family). Here, he acquired his first official appointment, in the service of a Sima prince, but in 406, with great political consequences, Xie was transferred into the entourage of a rival faction of the ascendant Liu clan.

At that time, Xie Lingyun's new patron, Liu Yi, headed the dominant clique at court, and he enjoyed the backing of the powerful Xie. By 410, however, the general Liu Yu had outmaneuvered supporters and contenders alike, so that Liu Yi, with Xie Lingyun in tow, found himself rusticated to a posting in Hubei. This chance circumstance brought about Xie Lingyun's first contact with the great Buddhist institution at Mount Lu, founded by the epoch-creating cleric Huiyuan (334-416). Here emerged the White Lotus sect of Buddhism, which, appealing as it did to the educated aristocratic laity, quickly attracted a coterie of extraordinary minds. The combination of religious intellectualism, the breathtaking mountain scenery, and release from court intrigue and official drudgery exerted incalculable affect on Xie Lingyun's literary endeavors.

The idyll, however, did not last long. In the provinces, Liu Yi attempted a coup but was suppressed by Liu Yu's forces. Xie Lingyun was captured; Liu Yi hanged himself. Luckily, Liu Yu appreciated Xie Lingyun's talents, bringing him back to the capital and installing him in an administrative post. For the next half-decade, Xie Lingyun was in and out of trouble, including a charge of murder; larger events, however, were to shape his future: In January, 419, Liu Yu strangled the idiot Emperor An and replaced him with Sima Dewen. In the spring of 420, Dewen was deposed and later assassinated. Liu Yu then ascended to the throne as the first emperor of the Liu Song regime (420-479).

The Xie clan found favor with the new emperor, but in the intrigues over the succession, Xie Lingyun was again caught on the wrong side. Liu Yu died on June 26, 422, and Xie Lingyun's clique was exiled to Yongjia (modern Wenzhou, in Zhejiang Province). The way was long and perilous, and Xie Lingyun had become ill from tuberculosis and leg ulcers. He made a detour via the family estates at Shining (modern Shangyu) and finally arrived in Yongjia in October that year. He remained bedridden for the winter months, contemplating Daoist and Buddhist thought; during this time, he produced a major contribution to the Buddhist tradition in China ("Discussion of Essentials"). Well enough by the spring of 423 to resume his duties, he nevertheless neglected official affairs and passed his time wandering in the hills until 424, when he resigned altogether, departed from Yongjia, and retired to an anchorite life at Shining. He devoted himself to costly repairs of the estate, damaged during the Sun En incursions; his monumental rhyme-prose "Dwelling in the Mountains" describes his labors and the wondrous beauties of the wilderness scene. His understanding of Buddhism, too, deepened at Shining, as witnessed by the four dozen or so poems he wrote there.

Another political upheaval occurred in August, 424, with the assassination of the emperor and the accession of Emperor Wen (reigned 424-453). Xie Lingyun was moved to write of his sorrows, and again he fell ill, but soon he was recalled to "illumine" an undistinguished court. He declined twice on account of problems with his legs but eventually accepted. His was the classic dilemma facing a Chinese bureaucrat: His duty was to serve, but he was disillusioned by the frustrations of public life. A scion of the highest aristocracy, he was yet denied consummate power by the upstart Sima and Liu monarchs and their minions. Nevertheless, he was assigned a congenial occupation—the compilation of an official history of the preceding Jin Dynasty, and an imperial bibliography. His verse and calligraphy had earned the royal epithet "twin gems," but his erratic behavior and unauthorized absences brought impeachment and disgrace. On April 1, 428, he found himself packed off once more to Shining, ostensibly on sick leave.

There, Xie Lingyun found his beloved cousin, the poet Xie Huilian, also in disgrace, and their mutual inspiration produced some of the most celebrated verse in the Chinese literary heritage. Dismissed from all offices in November of 428, he retired to his Daoist and Buddhist preoccupations, improvements to his estate, mountain climbing, and the assembling of a vast library. Some eighteen months later, Xie Huilian was pardoned; his departure for the capital occasioned yet more perennially admired verse.

Xie Lingyun's intellectual and literary brilliance and his high-born status and wealth had thus far protected him from greater harm than mere rustication, but his arrogance and lack of political acumen had provoked serious enmities. Slander, deriving from friction over the mutual encroachments of public and private lands at Shining, intensified, and to defend himself, Xie Lingyun presented an eloquent appeal at the imperial court. Meanwhile, the emperor's forces returned from a disastrous defeat in the North, in 431, and a bitter controversy over Buddhist doctrine was resolved in Xie Lingyun's favor. Xie Lingyun was found innocent of the charges against him, but was granted office-in-exile in distant Kiangsi, where, still contemptuous of his duties, he was arrested by local officials. Driven to the limits of his uncertain patience, he seized the arresting officers and declared an uprising for the restoration of the Jin. His unpremeditated coup was easily put down, but even then, the emperor overlooked his indiscretions, and instead of being sentenced to death, Xie Lingyun was merely reduced to the status of a commoner and was banished to the malarial southlands of Canton. There, his influence gone, and the Sima loyalists dangerously active, he was again accused of sedition. Although unconvinced by the weak evidence, the emperor ordered Xie Lingyun's execution.

Analysis

Early literary critics in China, particularly the sixth century Zhong Hong and Liu Xie, concerned themselves with the evolution of literary styles and forms. Their evaluations of Xie Lingyun's work therefore were concerned chiefly with placing him in the stream of literary history. According to Zhong Hong, Xie Lingyun's "talents were lofty and his diction flourishing, rich in charm and difficult to emulate," so that as "the master of the Yüan-chia period (424-453)" he transcended the literary giants who preceded him. Placing Xie Lingyun in the top rank of three categories of poets, Zhong Hong remarked that Xie Lingyun's poetry was derived from that of the politically minded Cao Zhi (192-232) and interspersed with elements of the florid Zhang Xie (flourished 295).

Early influences

By the seventeenth or eighteenth century, in spite of evidence to the contrary, Xie Lingyun was firmly ensconced in Chinese literary history as the founder of *shanshui* ("nature" or "landscape") verse. J. D. Frodsham demonstrates that landscape and nature themes were prominent from the earliest beginnings of Chinese poetry. In particular, Frodsham points out, Xie Lingyun's early landscape verse appears to have been molded by the instruction of his uncle Xie Hun. In the end, however, it matters less that Xie Lingyun was the inventor of the genre than that he was its most qualified exponent.

Among the various influences that enhanced Xie Lingyun's native literary genius were his childhood Daoist studies and his later association with the most advanced Buddhist intellectuals of his day, his personal involvement in the perilous political life of his times, and his travels in the course of official postings, exiles, and banishments in the forested mountains and rivers of South China—in the fifth century, still mostly virgin territory.

Unlike his predecessor Ruan Ji (210-263), for example, Xie Lingyun wrote very little poetry satirizing political evils. Occasionally he quotes from the Confucian canon, saying that when government is in decay, it is proper to retire. Otherwise, he criticizes his own disinterest in mundane administration, apologizing to his liege-lord and eulogizing him rather than remonstrating with him. He admits that he is idle and stupid, his administration far from ideal, quite unworthy of the honors bestowed on him. The emperor, on the other hand, is perfectly sincere and excels in the Way. Such was the accepted rhetoric of the time, and no great political or satirical construction should be placed on these worn lines.

Daoist anchorite escapism abounds in the poetry of Xie Lingyun, usually expressed in admiration for the sages of ancient tradition. Within the space of a few lines in a single poem, one reads both of his ambivalence toward an official career ("Throughout my life I'd have preferred distant solitude") and of the seductive appeal of a steady government salary. Free at last—involuntary retirement—in bucolic tranquillity, he shakes off the dust of the world of affairs and chooses the simple life, strolling about his tumbleweed dwelling. After all, not for him the fret and frustration of mortal renown. No doubt he was sincere enough, but one always bears in mind that his immense wealth and nobility afforded him the easy choices of a glamorous life at the metropolitan court or gentlemanly retirement to his vast and lavish estates.

Buddhist themes

Overt expression of Buddhist affiliation also appears frequently in Xie Lingyun's verse, although it is in his prose works that his important dissertations on controversial doctrine lie. In his poetry, Buddhist themes such as the ephemeral and insubstantial nature of the world are generally introduced into larger concerns of scene and circumstance. The brevity and lyricism of the references in their contexts preclude theological exposition, but even so, one catches glimpses of the essence of Xie Lingyun's arguments: "Seeing all this, mortal thoughts vanish, In an instant of enlightenment, one attains to abandonment." Xie Lingyun's proposition that transcendental wisdom derived from sudden enlightenment, eventually vindicated by new textual evidence arriving from the troubled North, clashed with prevailing views in the South and earned for him the enmity of court favorites who subscribed to the current ritualistic and pedantic practices of gradual accumulation of Buddhistic merit by which enlightenment was thought to be attained. (It is interesting, however, that religious persecution did not exist per se in Xie Lingyun's society; while religious conflicts may have exacerbated tensions, his rivals brought only civil charges against him.)

Growing old

Anguish over political uncertainties seems to have troubled Xie Lingyun less than his enforced partings from friends and dear relatives, his peregrinations and illnesses, and his awareness of approaching old age. "Mindful of old friends, I was loath to depart," he writes. "A wanderer come upon the eventide, I cherish old [friends]." He describes how his hair has begun to show streaks of gray in the mirror and how his girdle hangs loosely about his shrunken girth. Pursuit of pay as a bureaucrat has brought him to his sickbed in exile, and he misses his friends as time and the seasons whirl by. The most celebrated expression of these concerns occurs in the set of five stanzas he wrote in matching reply to his cousin Xie Huilian, with whom he shared some eighteen months of banishment on the family estate at Shining. Prosodically, they feature an unusually developed anadiplosis in the last line of one stanza and the first line of the next.

LANDSCAPE THEMES

While these elements certainly feature conspicuously in Xie Lingyun's verse, it is overwhelmingly his *shanshui* content, the treatment of landscape themes, for which he is renowned. Buddhist and Daoist ideas, and his own sensitive humanity and love of the wild countryside, ubiquitously inform the tumultuous scenes he observes with a more profound contemplation of humanity in the universe. Nevertheless, it is the torrential cascade of crags and crevices, ranges and ridges that block out half the sky, peaks and precipices winding circuitously to bewilder the traveler's sense of direction, torrid summer forests, sunset birds in the trees of a riverbank, flying mists in abysmal ravines, the hooked moon among the autumn stars, pale willows murmuring in a breeze, crystal eddies in a bouldered stream—these things and more—that enrapture and awe the reader. The traveler may delight in the myriad creations and transformations of scene and season, but people are travelers in time, too. They pass on, politician and poet, sorrowed by partings, wearied, sickened, and aged by the vexations of their paths.

Xie Lingyun sees in grand nature the permanence of renewal and never tires of encountering these transformations. Thrusting up and growing, new bamboo is clad in spring-green shoots; tender reeds wear their purple blossoms. Each miracle further endears his world to the poet, ever responsive as he is to the beauties he sees all about him. The grandeur of the rugged mountains of his domain, traditionally the abode of divinities and sages, was a reminder to him of the insignificance and transience of social goals. Their neutrality and silence reinforced Xie Lingyun's Buddhist and Daoist notions of relativity and quiescence. If saddened and disappointed in his political fortunes, he was able to identify his own mortality in the passing seasons and ever-changing scene and with composure await his end.

BIBLIOGRAPHY

Cai, Zong-qui, ed. *How to Read Chinese Poetry: A Guided Anthology*. New York: Columbia University Press, 2008. Contains a chapter on landscape poems that has three sections on poetry by Xie Lingyun. It takes a step-by-step approach to the poetry, explaining wording and references. Contains English translations, Chinese originals, and romanizations of the Chinese.

Chang, Kang-i Sun. *Six Dynasties Poetry*. Princeton, N.J.: Princeton University Press, 1986. The second chapter provides a scholarly discussion of Xie Lingyun's life and poems.

Cheng, Yü-yü. "Bodily Movement and Geographic Categories: Xie Lingyun's 'Rhapsody on Mountain Dwelling' and the Jin-Song Discourse on Mountains and Rivers." *American Journal of Semiotics* 23, nos. 1-4 (2007): 193-222. Examines Xie Lingyun's "Dwelling in the Mountains" and his other work and argues that the poet's landscape poetry was not a static observation of his surroundings but a bodily engagement with them, thus creating a new geographical discourse.

Feng, Youlan. *A History of Chinese Philosophy*. Translated by Derk Bodde. 2 vols. 1973. Reprint. Princeton, N.J.: Princeton University Press, 1983. Chapter 7 of the second volume of this excellent scholarly work carefully examines various aspects of Buddhism and Xie Lingyun's role and influence in its interpretations. Splendid comparative chronological tables of the period of classical learning; informative notes throughout; superb bibliography; fine index.

Frodsham, J. D. *The Murmuring Stream: The Life and Works of the Chinese Nature Poet Hsieh Ling-yun (385-433), Duke of K'ang-Lo*. 2 vols. Kuala Lumpur: University of Malaya Press, 1967. Definitive scholarly study; eminently readable. Volume 1 is largely biographical; volume 2 translates and examines Lingyun's poetry extensively. Helpful footnotes throughout. Adequate appendices and index.

Hargett, James M. "The Poetry of Xie Lingyun." In *Great Literature of the Eastern World*, edited by Ian P. McGreal. New York: HarperCollins, 1996. Guide to the themes and style of Xie Lingyun's poems. Includes both biographical and bibliographical information.

Lewis, Mark Edward. *China Between Empires: The Northern and Southern Dynasties*. Cambridge, Mass.: Harvard University Press, 2009. This cultural history discusses, among many other topics, the importance of gardens and describes Xie Lingyun's country villa as well as his poem "Dwelling in the Mountains" and its meaning.

Williams, Nicholas Morrow. "A Conversation in Poems: Xie Lingyun, Xie Huilian, and Jiang Yan." *Journal of the American Oriental Society* 127, no. 4 (October-December, 2007) 491-506. Examines poetry between Xie Lingyun and his cousin Xie Huilian as well as the poetry Jiang Yan wrote in response to the Xie cousins' work. Williams says the poems between the cousins were meant to preserve their friendship against separation. Likewise, Jiang states that poetry and language can conquer physical barriers.

Xie, Lingyun. *The Mountain Poems of Hsieh Ling-Yün*. Translated by David Hinton. New York: New Directions, 2001. A translation that includes introduction, notes, a map, a list of key terms intended to outline the poet's worldview, and a bibliography. The poems are divided into three sections, from his first exile, his time in Shining, and his final exile.

Yang, Xiaoshan. *Metamorphosis of the Private Sphere: Gardens and Objects in Tang-Song Poetry*. Cambridge, Mass.: Harvard University Press, 2003. Notes in its discussion that in his poems, Xie Lingyun included the doors and windows from which he viewed the mountains and gardens.

John Marney

INDIAN ENGLISH POETRY

Before Asian Indians could write poetry in English, two related conditions were necessary. First, the English language had to be sufficiently Indianized to be able to express the reality of the Indian situation; second, Indians had to be sufficiently Anglicized to use the English language to express themselves. The first of these two conditions, the Indianization of the English language, began much before the second, the Anglicization of Indians. Hence, though the first Indian poet to write in English was Henry Derozio, in the early nineteenth century, the Indianization of English had begun about three centuries earlier, in 1498, when Vasco da Gama, sailing from Lisbon, landed in Kerala. It was almost another century before the first Englishman came to India, but by the time Father Thomas Stephens arrived in Goa in 1579, a considerable body of Indo-Portuguese words were already being assimilated into English. Such lexical borrowing accelerated with the increasing British presence in India after 1599, when the East India Company was launched. For nearly 150 years after the charter of the East India Company, Englishmen in India wrote only travel books for the public and journals and letters in private. Nevertheless, by the end of the seventeenth century, a number of Indian words had been naturalized into English. The following is a selection from G. Subba Rao's catalog in his book *Indian Words in English* (1969):

Amuck, Arrack, Bazaar, Bandicoot, Brahmin, Bungalow, Calico, Cash, Cheroot, Chintz, Chit, Compound, Cooly, Dhobi, Divan, Dungaree, Fakir, Ghee, Guru, Gunny, Hakim, Hookah, Imam, Jaggery, Juggernaut, Maharaja, Mongoose, Nabob, Pariah, Pucka, Punch, Pundit, Shampoo, Shawl, Tank, Toddy, Yogi, Zamindar.

Because the functional and pragmatic context of the language changed in India, English began to adapt itself to its new environment. This nativization process continued as the use of English increased, as schools were established to teach it, and as the number of Indians using it increased.

More important than this large-scale lexical borrowing was the fact that, by the end of the eighteenth century, Englishmen in India had started to write poetry on local Indian subjects, whereas earlier, they had written only travelogues, journals, and letters. Of these Englishmen in India, the most important was Sir William Jones (1746-1794), one of the first British Indian (or Anglo-Indian) poets. An accomplished linguist and translator, his familiarity with Indian traditions is reflected in his eight hymns to the various Indian deities. These poems are strictly Indian in both style and theme; in writing them, Jones demonstrated for future Indian poets that the English language could be a fit vehicle for Indian subject matter. Hence, by the beginning of the nineteenth century, the prospective Indian English poet inherited not only an English whose expressive range had been enlarged by a substantial lexical borrowing of Indian words, but also an English which, as British Indian poets such as Jones had shown, was richly amenable to Indian subject matter.

The second precondition, the Anglicization of Indians, began when the British became a powerful colonial power in India. This happened more than 150 years after the East India Company was chartered. In 1757, the British won the historic Battle of Plassey, which gave them control of Bengal. In 1772, they assumed the *Diwani*, or revenue administration, of Bengal, and in 1790, they took over the administration of criminal justice. Not until the British had changed from traders to administrators did the large-scale Anglicization of India begin. This Anglicization around the turn of the eighteenth century was marked by several crucial events. First, in 1780, India's first newspaper, *Hickly's Bengal Gazette*, was published in English. Second, in 1817, Raja Rammohan Roy, a prominent social reformer, helped found the Hindu College of Calcutta, which later, as Presidency College, became the premier educational institution of Bengal. Third, and most important, by 1835, the British government had laid the foundations of the modern Indian educational system, with its decision to promote European science and literatures among Indians through the medium of the English language. The result was that English became in India, as in other British colonies, a passport to privilege and prestige.

A study of the social and cultural contexts of Indian English poetry reveals several important insights into its origin. First, Indian English poetry began in Bengal, the province in which the British first gained a foothold. In addition, Indian English poetry was an urban phenomenon centered in Calcutta. In fact, for the first fifty years, Indian English poetry was confined entirely to Bengalis who were residents of Calcutta. Then, gradually, it moved to other urban centers, such as Madras and Bombay; even today, Indian English poetry is largely urban. Finally, because English was an elite language in India, Indian English poets belonged to the upper class. Thus, in its early years, most of the practitioners of Indian English poetry came from a handful of prominent Calcutta families.

CRITICAL APPROACHES

There are basically three ways of approaching Indian English poetry: as an extension of English poetry, as a part of Commonwealth poetry, or as a part of Indian poetry. The first approach is largely outdated today, while the second, though still current, has gradually yielded to the third.

When Indians first began to write poetry in English, they were outnumbered by Eurasians and Englishmen who also wrote poetry on Indian subjects. Hence, poetry by Indians was not distinguished from poetry by non-Indians. Indeed, both types were published by the same publishers, the Indian subsidiaries of British publishers such as Longman or Heinemann, or by the English newspapers and magazines of India, which were usually owned and edited by Eurasians or Englishmen. Most Indian English poets were educated by Englishmen in Anglophone schools; like other English poets, they studied English literature. Because India was a part of the British Empire, Indian English poets did not have a strong national identity, and their early efforts were considered to be a tributary of the mainstream of English literature. Anglo-Indian literature was the term used to denote their poetry, the implication being that this was English literature with Indian themes. The term referred primarily to the literature produced by Englishmen and Eurasians in India, though it also included work by "native" Indians. The first scholarly work on Anglo-Indian literature was Edward Farley Oaten's *A Sketch of Anglo-Indian Literature* (1908), a condensed version of which was included in the *Cambridge History of English Literature* (1907-1914), edited by A. C. Ward. Oaten's primary concern was with English writers such as Jones, Sir Edwin Arnold, and Rudyard Kipling, and Oaten made only passing reference to Indian writers in English. With India's independence from Britain and the withdrawal of the British from India, Anglo-Indian literature, defined as literature written by Englishmen in India, more or less came to an end. On the other hand, literature by Indians in English increased, gradually evolving an indigenous tradition for itself. Consequently, Oaten's approach became untenable in dealing satisfactorily with Indian English literature. Nevertheless, it continues to have a few adherents—among them George Sampson, who, in *The Concise Cambridge History of English Literature* (1970), contends that Indian English literature is a tributary of mainstream English literature.

Another approach, initiated by scholars in England in the early 1960's, is to consider Indian English literature as a part of Commonwealth literature or the literature of former British colonies and dominions such as Canada, Australia, the West Indies, and countries in Africa, South Asia, and Southeast Asia. The *Journal of Commonwealth Literature*, based at the University of Leeds, has done much to foster such an approach. Later, academics in the United States attempted to see Indian English poetry as a part of a global literature in English. The journal *WLWE: World Literatures Written in English* represents this approach. These approaches are fairly useful when the focus is large and the scholar is located in the United States or the United Kingdom, but they share the problem that the literatures of the various nationalities have little in common and often belong to different traditions: for example, Nigerian English literature and Australian literature. Nor does such an approach serve very well when one literature, such as Indian English poetry, is studied in depth. It then becomes clear that labels such as "Commonwealth literature" or "world literature in English" simply help to provide a forum for these literatures in Western academia and that detailed study is still pursued by nationality.

The most widely accepted approach to Indian English poetry is to regard it as a part of Indian literature. This approach might seem the obvious one, but it took nearly a century to gain wide acceptance and is not without its problems. In the first place, there is no such thing as Indian literature per se: Indian literature is constituted of literatures in the several Indian languages, including Hindi, Tamil, Bengali, and Manathi. Most of these literatures, however, have their roots in the Sanskrit tradition of Indian literature which flourished from roughly 1500 B.C.E. to 1500 C.E. After the latter date, the regional literatures in the various Indian languages emerged. Hence, it is possible to argue that a unified tradition in Indian literatures does exist. Once that is granted, the task of the critic is to place Indian English literature into such a framework. Considering that English is not traditionally an Indian language, that is not easy, although at the time that Indian English literature began to emerge, there was a renewed efflorescence in the other regional languages of India as well. Moreover, the "renaissance" of regional literatures occurred under a stimulus similar to the one that caused the emergence of Indian English literature—namely, the impact on India of British rule, Western knowledge, and the English language. It is reasonable, then, to regard Indian English poetry as a limb of the larger body of Indian poetry, a creation of the same sensibility that has produced other regional-language poetry in India since the nineteenth century.

This approach was first propounded by Indian critics during the 1930's and 1940's, the most influential among them being K. R. Srinivasa Iyengar, whose *Indo-Anglian Literature* (1943) was the first book-length discussion of Indian English literature. Iyengar used the term "Indo-Anglian" to distinguish this literature from Anglo-Indian literature and to suggest that it was a part of Indian literature. In his introduction to *Indian Writing in English* (1982), Iyengar mentions that the phrase "Indo-Anglian" was used "as early as 1883 to describe a volume printed in Calcutta containing 'Specimen Compositions from Native Students.'" Probably, "Indo-Anglian" was merely an inversion of "Anglo-Indian," used to distinguish the poetry written by Indians from that of the Englishman. Alongside the term "Indo-Anglian," "Indo-English" was also used by critics who did not like the former. Both terms were used until the early 1970's, after which Indo-English gradually acquired greater acceptance. The term "Indian English" was used from the 1960's as synonymous with "Indo-English." It is being used increasingly in preference to other terms.

HENRY DEROZIO

Henry Derozio (1807-1831) is generally credited with being the first Indian English poet. His father was of Portuguese descent and his mother an Anglo-Indian. Derozio was Indian not only by birth but also by self-definition. This was especially remarkable because Derozio, a Christian, was reared among Eurasians and Englishmen, and many of his Hindu Bengali contemporaries strove hard to identify themselves with the British. Derozio's love for India is revealed in several of his poems. In his short life of twenty-three years, Derozio had a remarkable career as a journalist, a teacher at Hindu College, a leading intellectual of his day, and a poet. He has often been compared to John Keats.

Derozio wrote short poems for several magazines and newspapers of his day, but only one volume of his poems, *The Fakeer of Jungheera* (1828), appeared during his lifetime. A selection of his poems, published in 1923 by Oxford University Press, has subsequently been reprinted. As a poet, Derozio showed great promise, though he did not live to fulfill it. His poems reveal the great influence of the English Romantic poets, particularly Lord Byron and Sir Walter Scott. Derozio's sonnets and short poems, such as "To India My Native Land" and "The Harp of India," are his most accomplished works. His ambitious long poem *The Fakeer of Jungheera* is an interesting attempt to fuse the Byronic romance with the realities of the Indian situation. Despite the fact that Derozio's output was uneven and meager, he is counted as one of the major Indian English poets for both historical and artistic reasons.

KASIPRASAD GHOSE

A contemporary of Derozio, the Indian English poet Kasiprasad Ghose (1809-1873), published *The Shair and Other Poems* in 1830. Ghose has the distinction of being the first Hindu Bengali Indian to write English verse. He continued Derozio's efforts to deal with Indian subjects in his poems. An interesting example is his semicomic poem "To a Dead Crow," in which Ghose uses the unglamorous, common Indian crow as a subject. The persona Ghose created for himself was that of the *Shair*, or the poet in the Indian Persian tradition, indicating that although he wrote in English, his stance was that of an Indian poet.

MICHAEL MADHUSUDAN DUTT

Michael Madhusudan Dutt (1824-1873), whose long narrative poem *The Captive Ladie* (1849) was published about twenty years after Ghose's book, is an interesting figure in Indian English poetry. Dutt is remembered today not as an English poet but as the first and one of the greatest modern Bengali poets. After his failure at English verse, he turned to Bengali, his mother tongue. Dutt's case is frequently cited by those critics who believe that Indians cannot write good English poetry and should write only in their mother tongue. Since Dutt, there have been several other poets who began to write in English but turned to their native languages after being dissatisfied with their efforts in English. Dutt is also interesting because, though he acquired fame as a Bengali poet, he was extremely Anglicized. He not only converted to Christianity but also married an Englishwoman and qualified for the bar in England.

OTHER EARLY POETS

Another family of the Dutt name brought out *The Dutt Family Album* in 1870, featuring about two hundred pieces by Govin Chunder Dutt (1828-1884), his two brothers, and a nephew. Earlier, the whole family had converted to Christianity and, in 1869, had left India to live in England and other parts of Europe. The volume sheds light on the literary atmosphere prevailing in the aristocratic Dutt family, which was to produce another generation of poets in Govin's daughters Aru and Toru Dutt. Another notable poet of this time was Ram Sharma, born Nobo Kissen Ghose (1837-1918), who published three volumes of verse between 1873 and 1903. Sharma, who practiced yoga for several years, tried to bring an Indian religious dimension to Indian English poetry.

In this period, Indian English poetry moved out of Bengal for the first time with the publication of the Bombay poet B. M. Malabari's *Indian Muse in English Garb* (1876). Soon Cowasji Nowrosi Versuvala's *Counting the Muse* (1879) and A. M. Kunte's *The Risi* (1879) were published in Bombay and Poona, respectively. Though still an upper-class hobby, Indian English poetry was slowly spreading to metropolitan centers outside Bengal.

The poetry of the first fifty years of Indian English poetry (1825-1875) is generally considered imitative and derivative by critics. Certainly, the poems from this period which are usually anthologized do not show signs of very great talent. A judgment on the quality of these poets, however, must not be passed hastily, because most of their books are out of print and hence not easily available for critical scrutiny.

Toru Dutt

There is almost complete critical consensus that the talent of Toru Dutt (1856-1877) was an original one among Indian English poets. Like Derozio, she died young, and like Emily Brontë, her life has been the object of as much interest as her poetry. Toru Dutt left for Europe with her family when she was thirteen and attended a French school in Nice with her elder sister, Aru. The Dutts then moved to Cambridge, England, where Toru participated in the intellectual life of the university. Though converted to Christianity and very Anglicized, the Dutts felt alienated in England, and they returned to Calcutta four years after they had left, when Toru was seventeen. In 1874, soon after their return, Aru died. Earlier, when Toru was nine, her elder brother Abju had died. One year after her sister's death, Toru published *A Sheaf Gleaned in French Fields* (1875), which also featured eight pieces by Aru. These poems, "renderings" from the French, were enthusiastically received in India and England and soon went into three editions, the third published by Kegan Paul, London, with a foreword by Arthur Symons. In that same year, 1875, Toru took up the study of Sanskrit, and ten months later she was proficient enough in it to think of producing "A Sheaf" gleaned from Sanskrit fields. This volume was published in 1882, after her death, as *Ancient Ballads and Legends of Hindustan*, with a foreword by Edmund Gosse. Meanwhile, she had written one French novel and left incomplete an English novel, both of which were published after her death. Weakened by tuberculosis, she died in 1877 at the age of twenty-one.

The most significant aspect of Dutt's literary career was her return to her Indian heritage after her sojourn in the West. In *Ancient Ballads and Legends of Hindustan*, she converted popular myths from the *Rāmāyaṇa* (c. 500 B.C.E.; *The Ramayana*, 1870-1874), the *Mahābhārata* (c. 400 B.C.E.-200 C.E.; *The Mahabharata*, 1834), and the *Purāṇas* into English verse. In this, she pioneered a way for several later Indian English writers who had similar problems regarding their literary identity. Dutt's English versions, except in a few instances, are without condescension to the original and without authorial intrusions. In addition to longer "ballads" and "legends" from Sanskrit mythology, Dutt wrote short lyrics, odes, and sonnets. The best of these, probably her best single poem, is "Our Casuarina Tree." This poem, reminiscent in both form and content of Keats's odes, is about the beautiful Casuarina tree in the poet's garden at Baugmaree. The tree, by the end of the poem, becomes a symbol not only of the poet's joyous childhood but also, through an extension in time and space, of the poet's longing for permanence and eternity. The poem is a masterpiece of craftsmanship, a fine blending of thought, emotion, and form. Though her output as a poet was not particularly prolific, *A Sheaf Gleaned in French Fields* and *Ancient Ballads and Legends of Hindustan* show sufficient accomplishment to entitle Dutt to her place in the pantheon of Indian English poets.

SRI AUROBINDO GHOSE

Sri Aurobindo Ghose (1872-1950) probably has the best claim to be regarded as the greatest Indian English poet. In a poetic career of more than fifty-five years, his output and range were truly staggering. Sri Aurobindo wrote lyrics, sonnets, long narrative poems, poetic drama, and epics. He was fluent in a variety of conventional meters, such as iambic pentameter and hexameter, and he also experimented with quantitative meter and mantric poetry.

His reputation rests most securely on the posthumously published *Savitri* (1954), an epic of some twenty-four thousand lines. In *Savitri*, Sri Aurobindo used the story of Savitri's conquest of death in *The Mahabharata*—a story that has influenced Indians for centuries as an exposition of perfect womanhood—and expanded it to create his epic. In this epic, Savitri realizes her divine potential as a human being and, like Christ, defeats death; after her conquest of death, she returns to earth as a symbol of what humanity can achieve. A mystic and a seer, Sri Aurobindo claimed merely to have described his own, palpable experience in writing the poem. In his "Letters on *Savitri*," which are attached to the authoritative edition of the poem, Sri Aurobindo says that the work was written under the highest possible poetic inspiration, which he called "overmind poetry," a state in which there was no effort on his part and in which he was merely the scribe of a "vision" which descended, perfect and complete, upon him. *Savitri*, one of the longest poems in the English language (it is roughly twice the length of John Milton's *Paradise Lost*, 1667, 1674), is the most discussed poem in Indian English literature. It took about fifty years to finish—from the germ of the idea to the final written product—and a complete reading demands a long time; nevertheless, year after year it continues to attract and challenge critics, students, and readers.

As *Savitri* is the most discussed Indian English poetic work, Sri Aurobindo is the most discussed of the Indian English poets. His was a multifaceted personality—he was a seer, mystic, Vedantist, poet, philosopher, revolutionary political activist, literary critic, and thinker. Like many other major Indian English poets, he was born into an upper-class Anglicized family and was educated in England. Finding himself completely Westernized, he strove to find his roots, to realize himself, after returning to India. Remarkably successful in this, he is considered one of the greatest thinkers of modern India. As a poet, he was extremely well-versed in the European tradition of literature as well as the Indian tradition. Sri Aurobindo was fully conscious of what he was doing as a poet; he had a comprehensible theory of poetry and a clear view of what he sought to accomplish, both formally and thematically. His appraisal of the nature of poetry is clearly formulated in *The Future Poetry* (1953), and it is with this knowledge that his later, more difficult poetry is to be approached. Sri Aurobindo's poetry is easily available in the centenary edition of his *Complete Works* (1972).

SAROJINI NAIDU

If Sri Aurobindo is the greatest Indian English poet, Sarojini Naidu (1879-1949) is certainly the most popular, accessible, and moving—in a sense, the best Indian English poet. Naidu's poems are all songs, meant more to be heard than read. She is a lyric poet whose work shows a mastery of rhyme and meter. Her typical poem is short, usually consisting of fewer than twenty lines, although she did write some long sequences of short poems. The chief quality of her poetry is melody—the sound and sense combine to produce emotion, as in music. Within this musical, lyric paradigm, Naidu is extremely versatile. Like Rabindranath Tagore, she was a truly all-Indian poet, drawing upon the poetic traditions of several Indian languages and inspired by different regions of India and by different religious traditions.

The most remarkable feature of Naidu's poetry is its complete authenticity as Indian poetry. She achieves an Indian quality of both form and content without the slightest self-consciousness. She uses both the rhythms and the conventions of Indian folk songs as inspiration for much of her poetry. The range includes songs of professions ("Palinquin Bearers," "Wandering Singers," "Indian Weavers"), love songs ("Indian Love-Song," "Love-Song from the North," "A Rajput Love-Song"), lullabies ("Cradle-Song," "Slumber-Song for Sunalini"), seasonal songs ("The Call of Spring," "Harvest-Song," "The Coming of Spring"), and devotional songs ("Lakshmi, the Lotus-Born," "Hymn to Indra, Lord of Rain," "Songs of Kanhaya"). Naidu's imagery, too, is strikingly Indian, transferred into English from conventions in Indian poetry. In "A Rajput Love-Song," for example, she says, "O Love! were you the *keora*'s soul that haunts my silken raiment?" and "O Love! were you the scented fan that lies upon my pillow?" Both of these images are stylized and sophisticated, not naïve or simplistic. Naidu also uses discourse-types from Indian folk songs: Some of her songs are monologues, others duets, and still others are communal songs in several separate voices and in chorus. Naidu uses several Indian words as well as quotations from Indian languages to enhance the

Indian flavor of her poems. These words and quotations, however, are harmonized completely in the poem and not used indiscriminately. All in all, Naidu's attempts to locate herself in an Indian tradition of poetry were highly successful.

During Naidu's lifetime, four volumes of her poems were published: *The Golden Threshold* (1905), *The Bird of Time* (1912), *The Broken Wing* (1917), and *The Sceptered Flute* (1943), a collection of the first three books. *The Feather of the Dawn* (1961) was published by her daughter after Naidu's death. Naidu's poetry shows no major change or development from her first to her last book; although the tone becomes more somber, the metric felicity is the same. Naidu was chiefly a love poet, and her poetry explores the many facets of love as outlined in the Sanskrit tradition of love poetry: love in union, love in longing, love in separation; the pain of love, the joy of love, the sin of love, the desire of love; earthly love, divine love. Toward the end of her career, she became increasingly a *bhakti*, or devotional, poet, expressing in poem sequences her transcendent love for the Almighty. Although her work is unpopular with a number of recent Indian English poets, Naidu remains the most critically acclaimed Indian English poet after Sri Aurobindo.

RABINDRANATH TAGORE

Aside from Sri Aurobindo and Naidu, the period from the 1880's to the 1920's produced two other major poets. Chief among these is Rabindranath Tagore (1861-1941). Strictly speaking, Tagore is not considered an Indian English poet. He wrote only one long poem, *The Child* (1931), directly in English, writing all of his other works in Bengali, translating some later into English. Nevertheless, it was Tagore's 1912 English rendering of his famous Bengali poem *Gitanjali* (1910) that won for him the Nobel Prize in 1913. After that, Tagore "translated" several of his works into English, deviating considerably from the originals in the process. These renderings into English pose a unique, theoretical problem for the student of Indian English poetry: Should these works be regarded as originals or as translations? This problem has not been solved satisfactorily, but the consensus is that they are translations. Tagore, as the greatest Bengali writer, obviously belongs rightfully to Bengali; his influence on Indian English poets, however, is so great that he cannot simply be ignored in that area of study. The least that can be said is that Tagore is another example of a bilingual poet, a phenomenon not at all uncommon in the traditionally multilingual society of India.

MANMOHAN GHOSE

Another important poet of this period is Sri Aurobindo's elder brother, Manmohan Ghose (1869-1924). Some of Ghose's early poems appeared in *Primavera* (1890) while he was still in England. During his lifetime, only one volume of his verse, *Love Songs and Elegies* (1898), appeared, but when he died, he left in manuscript several volumes of poetry—short poems; two incomplete epics, *Perseus, the Conqueror* and *Adam*

Unparadised; and one long, incomplete poetic drama, *Nollo and Damayanti*. After his death, his longtime English friend Laurence Binyon published some of these lyrics as *Songs of Life and Death* (1926), prefaced by a memoir of Ghose. Recently, Calcutta University published Ghose's complete poems in five volumes, under the supervision of his daughters. Ghose's life was tragic. Returning to India after a completely English upbringing, he found himself out of place—in his own words, "de-nationalized." His wife's health had deteriorated, and she died after being paralyzed for years. Finally, the poet himself went blind. The most common criticism of his poetry is that it is totally un-Indian in form and content. This is largely true, though he did try to write his long poetic drama, *Nollo and Damayanti*, on an Indian theme. Ghose came close to being an English poet despite being Indian, but at that, too, he was doomed to fail. Today, despite his metric virtuosity, neither do his poems appeal to Indian readers nor has he found a place in the canon of English poetry. Ghose, at best, is uneasily an Indian English poet. His example, unfortunately, has not deterred other Indians from completely Westernizing themselves.

Twentieth Century: 1920's-1950's

The period from the 1920's to the 1950's was marked by a great efflorescence of Indian English poetry. It produced literally scores of poets, each with several volumes of verse to his or her credit. For the first time, a large mass of Indian English poetry was created, no longer confined to the upper class. Unfortunately, though this period produced a large quantity of poetry, it has been neglected by critics, primarily because the modernist poets of the 1950's were so united in their aversion to their predecessors.

Though this period produced a large quantity of poetry, it is the most neglected and underrated period in Indian English poetry. The chief reason for this is the severe reaction against this poetry by the post-1950's poets. Indeed, contemporary Indian English poets have been so united in this aversion that most recent anthologies totally omit the poets who came to maturity in the preceding generation. Although it is common in literature for the present generation to react against the previous generation, this reaction has reached allergic proportions in contemporary Indian English poetry. Much of the poetry of the period from the 1920's to the 1950's is becoming scarce—many of the publishers of that era are now defunct, and no serious attempt has been made to preserve these texts. Few libraries outside India possess texts from this period, and even in India, they are scattered in different places. Consequently, the poets of this period have received very little critical attention.

The best-known poet of this period is Harindranath Chattopadhyaya (1898-1990). Starting with his *Feast of Youth* (1918), he regularly published volumes of verse and poetic drama into the 1960's. He was easily one of the most prolific poets in Indian English poetry. The range of his content was very diverse, covering a whole spectrum of ideologies from extreme Aurobindonian idealism to revolutionary Marxist materialism. His formal range, however, was limited; he usually wrote rhymed, metric verse which, though competent, is sometimes predictable and cloying.

Most of the other poets of this period can be divided into three groups: the Aurobindonian and religious poets, the lyric and Romantic poets in the tradition of Naidu and Tagore, and the poets whose work reflects a transition from this Romanticism to the modernity of the post-1950's poets.

This period produced several poets who were inspired by Sri Aurobindo; they are sometimes called the Pondicherry school, because they lived in the Aurobindo ashram in Pondicherry and were disciples of Sri Aurobindo. The most famous of them are K. D. Sethna (born 1904) and Dilip Kumar Roy (1897-1980). Others, also inspired by Sri Aurobindo, are Nirodbaran (1903-2006), Nolini Kanta Gupta (1889-1983), Prithwi Singh Nahar (1898-1976), Anil Baran Roy (1901-1952), Punjalal (1901-?), and Romen Palit (born 1920). Some of their poetry has seemed obscure to readers because of its mysticism. Other religious and devotional poets are Ananda Acharya (1881-1945), T. L. Vaswani (1879-1966), and Jiddu Krishnamurti (1895-1986).

The largest number of poets in this period practiced the lyric, Romantic mode of Naidu and Tagore. It is perhaps because of these two poets that the impact of European modernism on Indian English literature was considerably delayed. Many of these neo-Romantics were professors of English in India; examples are P. Seshadri (1887-1942), N. V. Thadani, Shyam Sunder Lal Chordia, Govinda Krishna Chettur (1898-1936), Armando Menezes (1902-1983), Hymayun Kabir, V. N. Bhushan (1909-1951), and P. R. Kaikini. There are many more, and their total output is massive. Their poetry has long been out of fashion, seeming effusive and quaint, but certainly not all of it can be dismissed outright, as has often been the case.

Several poets of this period effected the transition from Romanticism to the modernism of the post-1950's poets. These transitional poets introduced concrete, commonplace imagery, irony, the language of common speech, and a personal, psychological dimension to Indian English poetry. Probably the earliest "new" poet of Indian English was Shahid Suhrawardy (1890-1965), whose *Essays in Verse* (1937) was avowedly influenced by T. S. Eliot and other modernists. Though some of his poetry seems to be merely self-conscious muttering and vague, allusive cerebration, Suhrawardy certainly brought a new tone to Indian English poetry. His work, however, was lost to most Indians after he migrated to Pakistan after the partition of India in 1947. Another poet who struck a new, realistic note was Manjeri Iswaran (1910-1968). Bharati Sarabhai created a sensation in English literary circles with her poetic drama *The Well of the People* (1943), in which she used several of Eliot's techniques.

Joseph Furtado (1872-1947) was another talented poet of this period who experimented considerably with language. Though he was predominantly a lyric poet, he brought an element of realism and rustic humor to Indian English poetry. His chief contribution was his use of Indian English pidgin and code-mixed varieties in poems such as "Lakshmi" and "The Old Irani." In these poems, Furtado not only anticipated contemporary poets such as Nissim Ezekiel, who exploit pidgin in their poetry, but also helped to bring the language of Indian English poetry closer to the language of the bilingual speech community in which English is actually used in India. What is interesting is that Furtado's use of pidgin, unlike Ezekiel's, is not parodic or condescending; whereas for Ezekiel, the joke is at the expense of an Indian variety of English, for Furtado, the comedy derives from authentic characterization.

A REVOLUTION IN TASTE

During the 1950's, the dominant tone in Indian English poetry shifted from Romanticism to irony. The revolution in taste did not occur overnight, but once established, its impact was swift and sweeping. What had been minority voices suddenly became the majority: A whole generation rejected its immediate past. This rejection is nicely voiced in Nissim Ezekiel's first book, *A Time to Change, and Other Poems* (1951).

The new poets were a vocal group and did not hesitate to denigrate openly their predecessors. P. Lal, for example, attacked Sri Aurobindo at length, though Lal retracted his strictures a few years later; dividing readers into those who could appreciate Sri Aurobindo and those who could not, Lal firmly placed himself and the poets of his generation in the latter category. This debunking of poetic ancestors continued. In the influential article "The New Poetry," published in *The Journal of Commonwealth Literature* (July, 1968), the poet Adil Jussawala required fewer than three pages to dismiss Indian English poets from Derozio to Naidu, claiming that the best Indian English poetry was being written by poets of his generation. Eight years later, R. Parthasarathy, another contemporary poet, introducing his now widely used anthology *Ten Twentieth Century Indian Poets* (1976), reiterated Jussawala's claims. Many other poets of this generation echoed the notion that theirs was the only Indian English poetry worthy of the name. However, these "new" poets soon divided into two main factions, those who practiced the dominant ironic mode and those who preferred a more traditional lyricism and Romanticism.

Besides Ezekiel, some of the poets who practice the ironic, clipped mode are Parthasarathy, A. K. Ramanujan, Gieve Patel, Shiv K. Kumar, Arun Kolatkar, and Jayanta Mahapatra. A typical poem in this mode involves an alienated speaker observing a typically Indian situation with detachment. Examples are numerous: In Keki Daruwala's "Routine," a police officer cynically regards yet another violent mob that he has to disperse. In Ezekiel's "Background, Casually," the poet assesses ironically his own lack of identity. In Kolatkar's *Jejuri* (1974, 1976), a place of pilgrimage is seen through the eyes of a detached and nonconformist visitor. Mahapatra's "The Whorehouse in Calcutta Street" shows a detached, self-critical observer recording his impressions of a brothel. In "Homecoming," Parthasarathy records his homecoming experience with self-critical irony. In "Naryal Purnima," Patel sits apart, commenting on a religious tradition from which he is alienated. In "Obituary," Ramanujan views the death of his father with ironic detachment. The same paradigm repeats itself. The situation is Indian; the observer is a self-critical, detached outsider. The poets use this mode to write both about themselves and, as in Mahapatra and Daruwala, about the external world. Often, as in Kamala Das, the early poems of A. K. Mehrotra, or in Pritish Nandy, the irony turns to anger. Most of these poets write free verse in a language that is as precise and close to "standard" English as possible. Exceptions, such as Ezekiel's poems in Indian English, are usually parodies.

There were, however, some poets who chose to write in the lyric and Romantic strain. The chief practitioners of this mode include V. K. Gokak, Keshav Malik, Karan Singh, Shankar Mokashi-Penekar, and, in their later works, Lal and Nandy.

Indian women poets

In the final years of colonial rule and even in the first decade after Independence, there were far fewer women poets in India than men. In the 1960's, Kamala Das (1934-2009) established her reputation by writing striking, confessional poems exploring female sexuality and arguing for women's sexual rights. However, it was not until the middle 1970's that works by women poets began appearing in significant numbers. *The Bird's Bright Ring: A Long Poem*, by Meena Alexander (born 1951), was published in 1976, and her collection *Without Place*, in 1978. In 1979, the Goan Eunice de Souza (born 1940) published her first volume, *Fix*. The telling portraits of de Souza's fellow Catholics made this book not only the writer's most controversial but also probably the most distinctive of her many fine works. *Fix* is also important in that it was published by Newground, a cooperative started by three poets, including Melanie Silgardo (born 1956), another of the many outstanding women writers who came to the attention of readers late in the 1970's.

It should be noted that controversial ideas and radical views were also expressed by women writing in the regional languages, such as the Bengali poet and social worker Maitreyi Devi (1914-1990), who voiced her concern for peasants and for tribal people, and Amrita Pritam (1919-2005), whose poems in Punjabi focus on the mistreatment of women after her native area of India became part of Pakistan. Pritam herself settled in India, and her experiences help to explain why there are so many more women writers in India than in Muslim Pakistan. However, in *We Sinful Women: Contemporary Urdu Feminist Poetry* (1991), seven Urdu women poets protest the ongoing repression of their gender by the religious and civil authorities of Pakistan. This collection was recognized throughout the world as an important expression of feminist feeling within the Muslim world. Wisely, the editor of this collection, Rukhsana Ahmad, had made wide circulation of the volume possible by translating all of the poems into English and printing her versions beside the Urdu originals.

Although not all of the women writers who have emerged since the 1960's are preoccupied with sexuality, feminism, or social justice, they are far more concerned with such issues than with that of language, which loomed so large in the minds of the first postcolonial generation of writers. It now seems to be generally accepted that English is no longer to be regarded as the language of an oppressor, but instead is seen as a convenience, as a common means of expression, which can be adapted to reflect everyday life on the Indian subcontinent and which will probably ensure a much wider distribution of one's work than publication in a regional language. On the other hand, those who choose to write in one or another of the regional languages are no longer faced with almost insurmountable difficulties in finding a translator. As Vinay Dharwadker comments in his preface to *The Oxford Anthology of Modern Indian Poetry* (1994), there are now a great many excellent translators actively seeking new materials for new audiences throughout the world. Whether they write in regional languages or in English, Indian poets of both genders can now aspire to international distribution.

Writers and the Wider World

If Partition displaced some writers, many more left their native areas as international travel became less costly and as opportunities for them to study and to teach abroad multiplied. Since the new multiculturalism among Western readers was creating a rapidly expanding market for works by Indian writers, whether written in English or translated into English, it was only natural that those writers would go west to meet this new and highly appreciative public, some of them to visit or to stay for a time, some of them to remain permanently.

Agha Shahid Ali

These new developments made the old nationalistic objections to writing in English seem irrelevant; now the question was whether or not the writers of the diaspora should even be classified as Indian writers. The English-language Muslim poet Agha Shahid Ali (1949-2001), for example, was born in Delhi, grew up in Kashmir, and returned to Delhi for his education before moving permanently to the United States in 1976. One might expect exile to be the theme of Ali's poems. However, he drew upon his own experiences primarily as a basis for his definition of the human condition. Wherever people live, Ali suggested, they are subject to change, and as a result they will suffer from a sense of loss and of longing for what is past.

Dom Moraes

Displacement and loss are also major themes in the poetry of Dom Moraes (Dominic Frank Moraes, 1938-2004). Born in Bombay, educated there and at Jesus College, Oxford, Moraes was a great success in England, both personally and professionally, from the time his first book of poems, *A Beginning* (1957), written when he was only nineteen, won the 1958 Hawthornden Prize. However, he did not feel at home there or in his native Bombay, where he finally settled after a journalistic career that took him all over the world. Like Ali, Moraes believed that one always feels like an exile, even if technically one is "at home."

Keki N. Daruwalla

Keki N. Daruwalla (born 1937) would agree. Although he was born and educated in India and made his home in New Delhi, Daruwalla does not feel any sense of stability. Again and again he points out in his poetry that no place on earth is exempt from change. What bothers him about history, which Daruwalla defines as no more than a record of changes, is that it records public events rather than private tragedies. In "Hawk" and "A City Falls," Daruwalla stresses his conviction that what transpires in the life of an individual, caught in cataclysmic change, is more significant than what happens to a city or even to a society.

Vikram Seth

In his revised edition of *Modern Indian Poetry in English* (1987), Bruce King credits Vikram Seth (born 1952) with altering the Western world's attitude toward Indian poetry in English, which up to that point had been classified more as a hobby for a few readers than as part of mainstream English literature. Seth's volume *The Humble Administrator's Garden* (1985) so delighted the London reading public, King explains, that critics began talking about including the title poem in future anthologies of English poetry. Their approval was due as much to Seth's evident rejection of the excesses of modernism in favor of a more polished style as to his captivating wit. Seth was soon just as popular in New York as he had become in London, and with the publication of his novel in rhymed verse titled *The Golden Gate: A Novel in Verse* (1986), he gained an international reputation.

Seth is a typical representative of the new cosmopolitanism among Indian writers. He was born in Calcutta and eventually made his home in New Delhi. However, Seth was educated at Oxford, at Nanjing University in China, and at Stanford University in California, where for several years he also was an editor for the Stanford University Press. Tibet was the setting of Seth's award-winning travel book, *From Heaven Lake: Travels Through Sinkiang and Tibet* (1983). Perhaps it was not surprising that his verse novel, which is set in San Francisco, drew criticism in India for not being "Indian" enough. These critics were happier with Seth's story of an Indian family, the best-selling novel *A Suitable Boy* (1993).

Sujata Bhatt

Wherever they live and whatever their subject matter, however, it is evident that Indian poets remain conscious of their roots. For example, Sujata Bhatt (born 1956), who was born in Ahmedabad of a family originally from Gujarat, was educated in the United

States and eventually made her home in Germany. However, not only does she translate Gujarati poetry into English, but she also uses Gujarati words and even whole lines of Gujarati in her own poems. It has been pointed out that good intentions do not necessarily make for good poetry. Often Bhatt's bilingual experiments do not work. Nevertheless, her attempts to express the multicultural experience must be noted, and some of her poems, especially those in *Brunizem* (1988) are very good indeed.

At the beginning of the twenty-first century, Indian poetry written in English, as well as regional poetry translated into English, was at last attaining the recognition it deserved. Critics were enthusiastic about the new generation of Indian writers; publishers in Great Britain and in the United States were anxious to bring out their works; and readers throughout the world were becoming familiar with poets hitherto unknown to them. In this case, at least, change was all for the better.

BIBLIOGRAPHY

Agrawal, K. A. *Toru Dutt: The Pioneer Spirit of Indian English Poetry—A Critical Study*. New Delhi: Atlantic, 2009. Analyzes the works of the Bengali woman who is often called the first Indian writer to produce English poetry of high quality. The writer concludes that Dutt not only is important historically, but also remains one of the finest Indo-Anglian poets.

De Souza, Eunice. *Talking Poems: Conversations with Poets*. New Delhi: Oxford University Press, 1999. Interviews with ten important Indian poets, conducted by a writer and editor who is herself a major poet.

_____, ed. *Early Indian Poetry in English: An Anthology, 1829-1947*. New Delhi: Oxford University Press, 2005. Includes the works of twenty poets, ranging from epics, ballads, narratives, and romantic verse to devotional poetry. Notes on each poet and an informative introduction by the editor.

_____. *Nine Indian Women Poets: An Anthology*. New Delhi: Oxford University Press, 1997. Two generations of post-Independence Indian writers, selected because their poetry is of consistently high quality, are represented in this volume. Contains biographical notes, critical commentaries, and an index of first lines.

King, Bruce. *Modern Indian Poetry in English*. Rev. ed. New Delhi: Oxford University Press, 2006. An important critical work, which first appeared in 1987. Chronology, useful appendexes, and index.

_____. *Three Indian Poets: Ezekiel, Moraes, and Ramanujan*. 2d ed. New York: Oxford University Press, 2005. Since the publication in 1991 of the first edition of this book, all three of these important modern poets have passed away. In this revised volume, the author reconsiders the total output of three distinguished but very different writers. Excellent introduction.

Naik, M. K., and Shyamala A. Narayan. *Indian English Literature, 1980-2000*. Delhi: Pencraft International, 2004. A critical survey of the fiction, poetry, drama, and nonfictional prose produced during an exceptionally active literary period. Includes a comprehensive bibliography of secondary sources.

Prasad, G. J. V. *Continuities in Indian English Poetry: Nation, Language, Form*. Delhi: Pencraft International, 1999. A new and original study of the history of Indian English poetry, discussing all the major writers and presenting new readings of many of their poems. The author considers such matters as the poets' attempts to place themselves within the context of their native country despite the fact that they are writing in a nonnative language.

Singh, Kanwar Dinesh. *Contemporary Indian English Poetry: Comparing Male and Female Voices*. New Delhi: Atlantic, 2008. Various critical approaches are used to determine the influence of gender and sexuality on the themes of poets and on their poetic practice. The works of twelve important Indian poets, five men and seven women, are discussed at length.

Thayil, Jeet, ed. *The Bloodaxe Book of Contemporary Indian Poets*. Cambridge, Mass.: Bloodaxe, 2008. An anthology covering fifty-five years of Indian poetry in English. Contains poems by seventy Indian poets, living all over the world, who nevertheless write out of shared traditions and express themselves in a common language.

Verma, K. D. *The Indian Imagination: Critical Essays on Indian Writing in English*. New York: St. Martin's Press, 2000. In addition to an introductory discussion of "Structure of Consciousness, Literary History and Critical Theory," contains chapters on Sri Aurobindo and Nissim Ezekiel. Notes and an index.

Makarand Paranjape
Updated by Rosemary M. Canfield Reisman

POSTCOLONIAL POETRY

As the British Empire spread to all corners of the world, so did the English language and literature. The empire faded after World War II, but what had become the international tongue and medium for creative writing survived and even prospered. English and its literature had long been enriched by speech and writing from Africa, the West Indies, Canada, India, Australia, and New Zealand. The dismantling of the Commonwealth neither subordinated nor silenced the distinctive voices that had arisen and that continue to arise. Traditionally, this body of fiction, drama, and poetry has been referred to as "Commonwealth literature" to distinguish it from English and American literatures. It is often still called Commonwealth literature for want of a better name, but as the old British Commonwealth recedes into history, so does a once-significant but now largely meaningless political term. These days, names such as "postcolonial literature," "world literature written in English," or "international literature in English" are more common. Some critics envision a time when all literature in English, including that of England and the United States, will blend into a single body, a time when no literary works will receive preference because of their national origins and all literature will be judged entirely on merit.

The circumstances in which poetry grew out of the one-time Commonwealth affected all aspects of the poetry's development. Such effects were felt in the poetry both of the "settler" countries—Australia, Canada, New Zealand, and South Africa—and that of the colonized areas—great parts of Africa, India, and the West Indies. The distinction between "settler" and "colonized" is simple: The settlers came to stay, taking over the land from those they considered primitives—the Aborigines in Australia, the First Nations in Canada, the Maoris in New Zealand, and the blacks in South Africa—and these peoples were variously ignored, enslaved, or exterminated. During the last few decades, the descendants of the dispossessed indigenous peoples have added their poetic voices to those of the settlers, who had through the years created their own exclusionary literature. The colonizers, on the other hand, went forth from England to rule and to exploit, not to settle; of course some did settle, but once the empire dissolved, their descendants left, unlike those in the settler countries. During the heyday of colonialism, the British set up schools for select groups of the natives they colonized; although those they educated in such places as Kenya, Nigeria, or India were intended to help rule their fellows, some became writers instead, thus giving Commonwealth poetry a third voice.

The writers in all three voices had available the centuries-old British literary tradition from which to draw forms, standards, and inspiration. Always, though, this fully developed text—a part of the colonial baggage—set up a creative tension that both benefited and hindered the poets.

Settler poets

How were the settlers in Australia, South Africa, Canada, and New Zealand to express in poetry the peculiarities of a new land and the life there? Could English poetry alone serve as a model? The emu had replaced the skylark; the flamboyant blossoms of the frangipani had dimmed the daffodil and primrose. Colonial outposts like Cape Town or Sydney bore little resemblance to London. Makeshift towns or isolated homesteads on the bleak veld of South Africa or in the vast outback of Australia contrasted starkly with the villages, meadows, copses, and moors of England. As the settlers communicated less with their former home, even their language changed: New words came into usage to describe unfamiliar things, accepted grammar fell by the wayside, and indigenous expressions crept in. Neither could the heterogeneous and structured English society survive intact among those in the isolated pockets of the Empire; no matter how hard the settlers tried to preserve their traditions, they faced lives in altered societies where rules and conduct adjusted to circumstance.

Despite their circumstances, the poetic impulse loomed strong among the early settlers. Perhaps the writing of poetry served as a comfort, as a way to overcome loneliness and isolation, a way to grasp the radical changes the settlers experienced. For example, even though Australia's convict pioneers were not literate for the most part, they were the colony's first poets. Soon after their arrival in 1788, they altered familiar English and Irish ballads to express the despair and misery that marked their lives. Like the literate free settlers who followed them to Australia and like those who went to Canada, South Africa, and New Zealand, they drew from the established text, imitating it and adding a new dimension. In 1819, an Australian judge named Barron Field (1786-1846) published two poems in a booklet, *First Fruits of Australian Poetry* (1819), in which he claimed to be the colony's first poet: "I first adventure; follow me who list/ And be Australia's second harmonist." Traditional in form, these two poems—"The Kangaroo" and "Botany Bay Flowers"—are typical of much early settler poetry. While Field finds the unfamiliar flora and fauna intriguing, he neither captures it wholly in his imitation of English verse nor refrains from recording his amusement over such oddities.

On the other hand, an anonymous Canadian settler expresses greater appreciation for his new land in "The Lairds of Esquesing," which appeared in 1826. This poem celebrates "Canada's wild woody shore" and "The Oak and the Hemlock and Pine" as the means of a better life for those who "are still coming o'er;/ In hopes of a good situation." However, pride and delight in the potential exploitation of natural resources, not in their beauty, lies at the center of the poem. These examples—like the early poetry from New Zealand and South Africa—express not a national identity but rather a colonial mentality. Such was the case with the abundant verse that continued to be written well into the twentieth century. Some was brazenly nationalistic in its celebration of the heroic pioneers, those hardy individuals who conquered the land; although the pioneers have long been admired for destroying the forests or eroding the veld and killing the indigenous peoples, later generations have questioned whether these acts deserve epic status. Some records of pioneer exploits, usually too mundane for true heroic stature, have found posterity as folk verse, such as the work of Australia's Banjo Paterson (1864-1941). Much of the poetry was far removed in spirit from the place where it originated, a pale imitation of distant literary fashions. For example, while there was no dearth of localized nature poetry, too often the poets saw the New World, the antipodes, or Africa through a Romantic sensibility they inherited from earlier English nature poetry. A true voice had not yet emerged, and for the most part, this poetry has been forgotten, deservedly so.

The established text continued both to bless and to debilitate, for that which came from England was considered the real literature and that written in the colonies a shadow of the original. Those who had never seen a daffodil or a skylark were strictly schooled in a poetry that celebrated such phenomena and were led to believe that the literature of their own country was second rate. After all, it was not until the 1950's that the national literatures entered into the school curriculum of the settler countries, which after World War II were at last breaking their ties with England. Further, as the political and economic influence of the United States spread during the postwar period, so did its literature, which had long before rebelled against the British tradition. The maturing of poetry in these countries, then, came about during the twentieth century and in particular after 1945.

Roy Campbell

One exception is Roy Campbell (1901-1957), South Africa's major English-language poet. Born in Durban, South Africa, of British descent and schooled in English literature, Campbell broke away from his heritage. Revolted by South African racial attitudes, he became one of the country's first literary exiles and spent most of his life abroad, mainly in France, Spain, and Portugal. At times, he satirized South African settler society, as in the biting wit of a poem like "The Wayzgoose," whose opening stanza contains the lines: "Where having torn the land with shot and shell/ Our sturdy pioneers as farmers dwell,/ And twixt the hours of strenuous sleep, relax/ To shear the fleeces or to fleece the blacks." Campbell experienced a divided relationship with his native land, calling it "hated and adored" in his poem "Rounding the Cape." This dichotomy continues to haunt South African writers and consequently dominates much of the country's literature. Campbell, a major lyric poet and one of the first Commonwealth writers to attain an overseas reputation, also wrote about his homeland with fervor and captured its essence in poems like "The Zebras" and "Zulu Girl."

Judith Wright

Another poet of international standing is the Australian writer Judith Wright (1915-2000), who discovered her homeland as a metaphorical entity from which she could draw meaning and through extending the metaphor express that meaning to others. For

Wright, nature serves as a bridge to universal understanding, and the landscape she explores to attain this knowledge is purely Australian; she approaches nature with a sensibility untainted by the inherited text of English literature. Her first book of poems, *The Moving Image*, appeared in 1946. One of her major themes is the relationship between humankind and nature, which led her to become a public figure fighting to protect the environment: "a landscape that the town creeps over;/ a landscape safe with bitumen and banks," she laments in one of her poems, "Country Town." Some critics have observed that Wright's later poetry suffered from her political involvement with environmental issues. However this work might be judged, Wright helped to show the generation of poets who followed how they could be Australian without being provincial, how they could express an Australian sensibility without cringing, and how they could examine the landscape honestly.

Wright is also the first poet of Anglo-Saxon origin to treat the Australian Aborigine in an understanding way. One of the best of these poems is "Bora Ring," in which she mourns the loss of the ancient rites of those who inhabited the country for forty thousand years before the white man came: "The song is gone; the dance/ is secret with the dancers in the earth,/ the ritual useless, and the tribal story/ lost in an alien tale."

A. D. HOPE

A. D. Hope (1907-2000), the third poet from a settler country who gained an international reputation, was Australian as well. However, he made no effort to explore the metaphysical dimension of his native land as a basis for poetry; instead he followed the dictates of eighteenth century neoclassicism. Damning free verse, modernism, and lyricism, Hope wrote in a highly structured, witty, cosmopolitan way. For him, the inherited text was not to be discarded but to be used and improved upon. He rarely mentioned Australia, for he felt more at home in Greece than he did in a place where, as he wrote in his poem "Australia," "second-hand Europeans pullulate/ Timidly on the edge of alien shores."

LES A. MURRAY

The Australian poet Les A. Murray (born 1938) gained recognition around the world, receiving numerous international awards and regularly publishing overseas. In 2000, a collection of his poems called *Learning Human: Selected Poems* appeared in New York. His poetry, noted for its verbal intensity and lyrical qualities, is undergirded by conservative political and religious views. A dichotomy marks his work. On one hand, it celebrates the strength and character of ordinary people and assumes an anti-intellectual pose. On the other, though, it is extremely erudite in its references and allusions.

AL PURDY AND MARGARET ATWOOD

Canada and New Zealand have strong poetic traditions, and both have many poets widely admired in their own countries, but who have not yet achieved the stature of Campbell, Wright, Hope, or Murray. Contemporary Canadian poets have moved far from the anonymous nineteenth century versifier who exulted in the pioneers' despoilment of the land. One of Canada's best-known poets, Al Purdy (1918-2000), for example, sees the necessity of reinventing a poetic tradition divorced from the colonial past, a tradition that takes into account Canada's geographical vastness, a primary theme in his own work. While Margaret Atwood (born 1939) has established a worldwide reputation as a fiction writer, her considerable achievement as a poet is little recognized outside Canada.

THREE NEW ZEALANDERS

New Zealand, too, has produced a wide array of poets, the best-known being James K. Baxter (1926-1972). An old-fashioned poet by some standards, Baxter gained his popularity and lasting fame through a rare ability to meld language and location, for his was truly a national voice that spoke apart from the established British text. The far more sophisticated work of another New Zealander, Allen Curnow (1911-2001), is also highly regarded, for both its rich language and its handling of the metaphysical aspects of the remote country; for instance, in "House and Land," he speaks of the "great gloom" that "Stands in a land of settlers/ With never a soul at home." A New Zealand poet who has received attention overseas is Bill Manhire (born 1946). His poetry is simple and direct yet sophisticated and dense in its suggestiveness. It takes varied forms, covers a wide variety of subjects, and draws its material both from his native country and from places abroad.

INDIGENOUS POETS IN SETTLER COUNTRIES

Silent, or silenced, for the two hundred or so years since whites invaded their lands, the indigenous people of the settler countries—Australia, South Africa, Canada, and New Zealand—have added their voices to Commonwealth poetry. They are the victims of a secondary colonialism, for they have long been subjected and in the past often murdered by the settlers who saw them as one more pest on the landscape. Also secondary to the indigenes is the English language and literature, which was forced onto them for survival on the fringes of the white world. Beset by a borrowed written text and an oral literature that has eroded during two centuries of assimilation, the indigenous writers face peculiar problems as they set out to create a tradition that is not a thirdhand version of the British text. They need to determine whether they should write in the conqueror's language or their own languages, which sometimes have been corrupted or lost. They must decide whether to use standard English or the creolized language that many indigenes speak as a result of poor education and segregation. Other challenges include how to incorporate the remnants of their oral traditions and how to reach the largest audience.

The question of audience often seems the most important, for much of the poetry protests the second-class citizenship to which the indigenes have been relegated. At first, the main audience for such writing was white liberals, so English became the mandatory language. In the 1970's, though, the poetry began to play a more direct role in the lives of those it talked about, as the land-rights campaigns and the consciousness movement gained momentum, inspired in part by the Civil Rights movement in the United States. Because English stood as the common language among the indigenes, most of the writing was of necessity done in the borrowed language.

KATH WALKER

One of the first such voices to be heard was that of Kath Walker (1920-1993), an Australian Aborigine later known by her tribal name, Oodgeroo Noonuccal. In 1964, she published the volume of poetry *We Are Going*, and in "Aboriginal Charter of Rights," she asked, "Must we native Old Australians/ In our own land rank as aliens?" Widely admired by black Australians as well as by their oppressed fellows in other settler countries, Oodgeroo's poetry helped awaken these long-silent people. White readers also discovered her work, which made them realize that something new was afoot. The poems in *We Are Going* now seem tame and have in later years been called too conciliatory by some activist Aborigines, who have taken a harsher stance toward the white world in their poetry. Later Aborigine poets such as Lionel Fogarty (born 1958), Archie Weller (born 1957), and Kevin Gilbert (1933-1993) take a stronger approach in taking up the Aborigine cause. In their work and that of some emerging poets, the protest rings loud and the anger erupts. Often, though, a comic strain runs through the poems and makes them even more immediate. Also, these poets tend to mix aboriginal words and slang terms with standard English, which is an effective technique.

SOUTH AFRICAN POETS

The South African poet and novelist Dennis Brutus (1924-2009) was another early and widely acclaimed writer of protest poetry. In particular, his poems from prison, *Letters to Martha* (1968), describe vividly the abuse he and other political prisoners suffered. In "This Sun on this Rubble," he writes: "Under jackboots our bones and spirits crunch/ forced into sweat-tear-sodden slush/ —now glow-lipped by this sudden touch." Other black South African poets include Oswald Mbuyiseni Mtshali (born 1940), who published *Sounds of a Cowhide Drum* in 1971, and Mongane Wally Serote (born 1944), who, in "Ofay-Watcher Looks Back," observes that "jails are becoming necessary homes for people." Although it is too soon to make judgments or to name major poets, the post-apartheid era in South Africa has unleashed a vast amount of poetry by those formerly oppressed by the political system. For one thing, publishing opportunities and financial support have become more available. This work addresses the triumph over apartheid as well as its lingering effects, taking up the challenges, problems, and disappointments facing the majority native population after a century of submission.

Maori poets

New Zealand poets Rosemary Kohu (born 1947), Robert DeRoo (born 1950), and Hone Tuwhare (1922-2008) express in their work what it is like to be a Maori among the Pakehas—the Maori word for the Anglo-Saxon settlers. In "Taken," for example, Kohu recalls how as a child she was placed in the Bethlehem Native School, which methodically stripped away her heritage so she might become a "Pakeha-thinking Maori." Between stanzas of the poem appears the refrain "'To get on in this world you must be Pakeha.'" In "Aotearoa/New Zealand/Godzone?," DeRoo speaks to the land, calling it "Aotearoa," its name before the colonial "New Zealand" and the affectionate "Godzone" were affixed. He sees history as "conquest," in which "we claw each other for rights" to the land, then concludes that as an inhabitant of Aotearoa he can claim no single piece of the land but must embrace it all, telling Aotearoa that "my mind's birth-knot ties me irrevocably to you." Another Maori, Tuwhare is one of New Zealand's most popular poets. Neither didactic nor angry, his work is full of warmth and wit. Still, he speaks strongly for his community and its marginal place in New Zealand society.

Canadian indigenous poetry

The work of the early Canadian activist-poet Duke Redbird (born 1939) condemns white society for its insensitive treatment of the indigenous peoples. "I Am the Redman," one of his best-known poems, became a rallying cry in the 1970's for the long-silent First Nations. Another native poet, Rita Joe (1932-2007), articulates her people's plight in a more conciliatory fashion—reminiscent of Oodgeroo in some ways—saying, for example, in one of her untitled poems published in *Poems of Rita Joe* (1978), "Pray/ meet me halfway—/ I am today's Indian." Other poets in this group include Chief Dan George (1899-1981), Daniel David Moses (born 1952), and George Kenny (born 1951).

Combining traditions

It would be misleading, though, to leave the impression that indigenous poetry constitutes nothing more than protest. As the years have passed, some rights have been gained and certainly consciousness has been raised, and many indigenous poets have moved toward familiar topics of poetry: love, home, nature, and spiritual quest. They have also combined with English-language forms their oral heritage, which has been retrieved through great effort. These writers are thus in the process of establishing a poetic tradition that echoes the borrowed literature and at the same time imbues it with their own ancient text.

One of the writers who has combined the two texts most impressively is the Australian poet Mudrooroo Narogin (born 1939), who published as Colin Johnson before taking a tribal name. His poetry volume *Dalwurra* (1988) records the travels of the Black Bittern, a totemic bird from Aborigine mythology. Like the poet himself, this bird sets out on a spiritual quest, visiting Singapore, India, the United Kingdom, and other parts of Asia before returning to his native Australia. In the introduction to *Dalwurra*, Mudrooroo describes the work as a way of showing how ancient Aborigine song cycles can serve as the framework for poems in English, adding that by using such traditional materials, the poet is to some degree disciplined by them.

The highly original poetry of Mudrooroo, of such Maori writers as Keri Hulme, born 1947 (who is better known abroad for her novel *The Bone People*, 1983, than for her poetry), and of emergent South African and Canadian poets promises that this new voice in Commonwealth poetry will prevail.

Colonial and postcolonial poets

The most important poet of the colonial and postcolonial poets of India, Africa, and the West Indies, Derek Walcott (born 1930), is of African descent but was born and grew up in the West Indies when his remote Caribbean island still formed part of the British Empire. In "A Far Cry from Africa," he speaks of "the English tongue I love," but then asks a question common to many postcolonial poets who are not Anglo-Saxon but whose heritage and language is largely English: "Where shall I turn, divided to the vein?" While the West Indies have produced a number of poets, Walcott overshadows the others and to a great degree represents international poetry in English at its very best. He received the Nobel Prize in Literature in 1992. Walcott has incorporated his native Caribbean into a metaphor of universal proportions. Although some of his work takes up other locales and subjects, his best poetry returns to the land of his birth, with all its seductive beauty and internal decay.

Like Walcott, many of the postcolonial writers spent their first years as colonials, then at maturity found themselves in young nations set free from the imperial fetters of the past. Were they at that point to continue writing in English, thus building a national literary tradition based on the language and text of the departed conquerors? Should they not turn their backs on the English tongue they loved and write in the native languages of, say, Kenya, Nigeria, or India? By writing in English were they not pandering to the Western world rather than speaking to their own people, thereby creating what some have called "tourist literature"? While these questions have been debated by critics and writers in the half century since the era of independence, an English-language literature has continued to develop in Africa, India, and the West Indies. "Develop" carries significance: What has emerged in all the genres is not a postcolonial facsimile but a sturdy hybrid, which grows out of what West Indian novelist Wilson Harris (born 1921) calls "the universal imagination," be its source African, ancient Greek or Roman, British, European, or American; its mythology Hindu, Buddhist, Muslim, or Christian; its forms expressionistic, romantic, neoclassic, or indigenous.

Sarojini Naidu

The first major poet from India, Sarojini Naidu (1879-1961), long preceded independence. Born into an Anglicized Indian family at the height of the British Raj and educated in England, Naidu published her first book of poems in English, *The Golden Threshold*, in London in 1905 and received immediate recognition at home and abroad. She published three more books of poems that still hold charm—and immense promise—with their curious blend of Romantic and Victorian forms with Indian imagery and subject matter. Her poetry reveals a passionate love for India along with an Eastern preoccupation with death and immortality, as in "Imperial Delhi," which celebrates the ancient city of so many past glories: "But thou dost still immutably remain/ Unbroken symbol of proud histories,/ Unageing priestess of old mysteries/ Before whose shrine the spells of Death are vain." Naidu gave up her poetic career in "the English tongue" she loved to join Mahatma Gandhi's freedom movement and became one of Gandhi's closest associates throughout India's struggle for independence, which was finally gained in 1947. Had she been born later her story might have been different.

Kamala Das

In postcolonial India, one of the major poets is also a woman, Kamala Das (1934-2009). Her work, infinitely more modern in form, sophisticated in tone, and confessional in nature, still brings to mind Naidu's poetry as it blends Indian imagery, Western forms, and the universal concerns of love, passion, alienation, spirituality, and death. Although Das wrote in both the Indian language Malayalam and in English, she describes language in her poem "An Introduction" as nothing more than a tool for expression, a way of communicating what is said in the other language of nature and experience, which she calls "the deaf blind speech/ Of trees in storm or of monsoon clouds or of rain or the/ Incoherent mutterings of the blazing/ Funeral pyre." While the imagery is purely Indian, the idea it expresses reaches far beyond its source. Das validates her use of English by divorcing language from superficial nationalism and seeing it as just one form of human expression, which she calls in the same poem "the speech of mind that is/ Here."

Nissim Ezekiel

Another important Indian poet in English, Nissim Ezekiel (1924-2004), is considered a pioneer figure who introduced European expressionistic forms into Indian poetry but at the same time diffused what he borrowed to express a purely Indian sensibility. His often-experimental work encompasses a wide range: Some of it is highly personal in its revelation of the inner experience, as in "Two Images," and some in its frank treatment of sexuality, as in "Nudes"—two of his best-known poems. In "Poster Poems," he creates collages of the subcontinent's variegated human landscape. Some Indian critics, however, have found Ezekiel's work—and that of Das as well—too Western in orientation, objecting, for instance, to the use of Christian imagery; these poets and others writing in English should, the critics say, rely more heavily on Indian mythology, history, and literature, even if their language is non-Indian.

An African approach

To a great extent, contemporary African poets have been more faithful than their sometimes all-too-literary Indian counterparts at integrating the African languages and heritage into English poetry. Many African poets write first in an African language and then render their work into English, often retaining many of the African words. Some write in pidgin to reproduce the flavor that English has acquired in Africa. Others attempt to evoke, through verbal effects, traditional drum or flute poetry, or the chanted verses that are a part of tribal ceremonies. A single poem may refer to Christian mythology alongside allusions to African religion, or may contain lines from Ezra Pound or echo the rhythms of Gerard Manley Hopkins while focusing on a purely African subject. The Western hero Odysseus might be mentioned in the same breath as Chaka, the legendary African warrior.

The colonial African poets concentrated on subject matter, often protest, and let technique take care of itself, usually adhering to the forms and diction set by the British text. In contrast, postcolonial writers have exercised admirable craft in their work; from a technical standpoint, they do not write in a vacuum but show a keen awareness of the current trends in English-language poetry. Of course, many were educated abroad, in England, Europe, or the United States. Still, they do not sacrifice their Africanness in order to be fashionable or acceptable on the international scene. Finally, African writers, whatever their genre, have never indulged in art for art's sake, but see a high seriousness and purpose in what they do. The Somali novelist Nuruddin Farah (born 1945) expresses this intent forcefully in his 1981 address "Do Fences Have Sides?": "The writer in Africa and the Third World countries is looked upon as the contributor to and/or creator/shaper of the nation's enlightened opinion . . . he is, to a great number of people, the light whose beams guide the ark to safety."

Wole Soyinka

Certainly the approach to literature espoused by the Nigerian writer Wole Soyinka (born 1934) exemplifies Farah's statement. Soyinka, who received the Nobel Prize in 1986, is better known for his poetic drama than for his separate poems, even though he has excelled in the latter form, as well as in fiction and the essay. Soyinka's work is sometimes described as creatively eclectic; a single play or poem may bring together such disparate elements as African purification ceremonies, the rhythms of Shakespearean verse, folk narrative of the Yoruba people (Soyinka's tribal identity), and the dramatic techniques of Bertolt Brecht. His work represents brilliantly the subtle interaction that takes place when a writer borrows from and responds to a wide variety of texts.

While nationalist critics and theorists in Africa and elsewhere may denounce such interdependence and call it artistic neocolonialism, the artists apparently—and fortunately—realize that they do not create within set boundaries.

CHRISTOPHER OKIGBO

Another such poet is Christopher Okigbo (1932-1967), who was born in Nigeria and was killed in the Biafran War. Lyrical, cryptic, intense, and frequently obscure, his highly personal work blends the sounds of African music and the performance of ancient ritual with Western artistic and literary elements. Okigbo is usually considered the most modern of the African poets, and the fusion of sound and symbol makes his work extremely difficult—at times incomprehensible—on an intellectual level, but it is always resonant and exciting.

OKOT P'BITEK

Okot p'Bitek (1931-1982) was born in Uganda but spent the last decade of his life in Kenya after his criticism of the Ugandan government made him persona non grata in his homeland. Trained as an anthropologist, p'Bitek received international attention when his four "Songs" were published, the first in 1961, the last in 1971. The overriding theme of the "Songs"—actually dramatic monologues in which various Africans speak—is the conflict between Western influence and African ways. For example, in the *Song of Lawino* (1966), the speaker laments her husband's desertion of her, complaining that the "manhood" of all the young African men "was finished/ In the classrooms,/ Their testicles/ Were smashed/ With large books!" Witty, at times satirical toward both African and Western ways, the "Songs" record in addition to the lament of the African woman the observations and sometimes the desperation of a Europeanized African man, a prisoner, and a prostitute. The poems serve to supplement anthropologist p'Bitek's scholarly writing on African culture.

Along with their counterparts in India and the West Indies, the Africans join the settler poets and emergent indigenous writers to lend contemporary poetry in English voices that are unmistakably international.

BIBLIOGRAPHY

Bery, Ashok. *Cultural Translation and Postcolonial Poetry*. New York: Palgrave Macmillan, 2007. Included are critical essays on Judith Wright, Les A. Murray, Louis MacNeice, Seamus Heaney, A. K. Ramanujan, and Derek Walcott.

Coplan, David B. *In the Time of Cannibals: The Word Music of South Africa's Basotho Migrants*. Chicago: University of Chicago Press, 1994. History and critical analysis of Sotho music and poetry. Bibliography and index.

Keown, Michelle. *Pacific Islands Writing: The Postcolonial Literatures of Aotearoa/ New Zealand and Oceania*. New York: Oxford University Press, 2007. The first book of its kind, this volume combines an introduction to the literatures of the region with specific analyses of major authors. Though the volume emphasizes literature in English, francophone and hispanophone writing are also discussed.

Kleinert, Sylvia, and Margo Neale, eds. *The Oxford Companion to Aboriginal Art and Culture*. New York: Oxford University Press, 2000. Contains a wealth of information, including comments on myth, ritual, and performance poetry.

Newell, Stephanie. *West African Literatures: Ways of Reading*. New York: Oxford University Press, 2006. Newell presents various approaches to literature and differing views on colonialism.

Patke, Rajeev S. *Postcolonial Poetry in English*. New York: Oxford University Press, 2006. Includes chapters on South Asia and Southeast Asia, the Caribbean, and black Africa, as well as the settler countries.

Ramazani, Jahan. *The Hybrid Muse: Postcolonial Poetry in English*. Chicago: University of Chicago Press, 2001. Discusses the cultural environment, as well as the artistry, of William Butler Yeats, Derek Walcott, A. K. Ramanujan, Louise Bennett, and Okot p'Bitek. Extensive bibliography and index.

Rymhs, Deena. *From the Iron House: Imprisonment in First Nations Writing*. Waterloo, Ont.: Wilfrid Laurier University Press, 2008. A volume in the Aboriginal Studies series. The chapter "Hated Structures and Lost Talk: Making Poetry Bear the Burden" is of particular interest.

Schürmann-Zeggel, Heinz. *Black Australian Literature: A Bibliography of Fiction, Poetry, Drama, Oral Traditions, and Non-Fiction, Including Critical Commentary, 1900-1991*. Bern, Switzerland: Peter Lang, 1997. Focuses on Australian Aborigines and Torres Strait islanders. An indispensable reference work for students of postcolonial literature.

Smith, Rowland, ed. *Postcolonizing the Commonwealth: Studies in Literature and Culture*. Waterloo, Ont.: Wilfrid Laurier University Press, 2000. Wide-ranging essays on various subjects, including J. Edward Chamberlain's "Cowboy Songs, Indian Speeches, and the Language of Poetry." Bibliographical references and index.

Robert L. Ross
Updated by Ross

AGHA SHAHID ALI

Born: New Delhi, India; February 4, 1949
Died: Amherst, Massachusetts; December 8, 2001

PRINCIPAL POETRY
Bone-Sculpture, 1972
In Memory of Begum Akhtar, 1979
The Half-Inch Himalayas, 1987
A Walk Through the Yellow Pages, 1987
A Nostalgist's Map of America, 1991
The Belovéd Witness: Selected Poems, 1992
The Country Without a Post Office, 1997
Rooms Are Never Finished, 2002
Call Me Ishmael Tonight: A Book of Ghazals, 2003
The Veiled Suite: The Collected Poems, 2009

OTHER LITERARY FORMS

Agha Shahid Ali (AH-lee) was both a poet and a scholar. In 1986, he published *T. S. Eliot as Editor*, a critical work based on his doctoral dissertation. Ali also was a translator and an editor. With the help of his mother, Sufia Agha Ashraf Ali, he translated the poems of Faiz Ahmed Faiz from Urdu into English, collecting them in *The Rebel's Silhouette: Selected Poems* (1995). In 2000, he edited *Ravishing Disunities: Real Ghazals in English*, with an afterword by Sara Suleri Goodyear.

ACHIEVEMENTS

Agha Shahid Ali won a Pushcart Prize and was a finalist for the National Book Award in 2001. A fellowship from the Ingram Merrill Foundation aided his writing of *A Nostalgist's Map of America* and his work on *The Rebel's Silhouette*. He was also awarded a fellowship from the John Simon Guggenheim Foundation and an Artist's Fellowship for Poetry from the New York Foundation for the Arts, which helped in the writing of *The Country Without a Post Office*. In addition, Ali received fellowships from the Pennsylvania Council on the Arts and the Bread Loaf Writers' Conference. Since 2003, the University of Utah Press and the University of Utah's Department of English have annually awarded the Agha Shahid Ali Prize in Poetry.

These awards are testament to Ali's tremendous contribution to poetry through his successful blending of both Western and Eastern influences in his life and in his writing. His thoughtful responses as a native in the multiracial, multicultural, multireligious, and multilingual environment of India (and Kashmir) and as an immigrant in the United

States to racial, cultural, religious, and linguistic differences are reflected throughout his poetry. Furthermore, Ali solidified the North American understanding of the verse form of the ghazal through his translation of Faiz's poetry, his anthology of North American ghazals, and his publication of his own ghazals.

Biography

Agha Shahid Ali was born into a very highly educated, multilingual, and liberal Muslim family. In his introduction to *The Rebel's Silhouette*, he recounts how his paternal grandmother quoted John Milton, William Shakespeare, John Keats, and Thomas Hardy in English; Hafiz and Jalāl al-Dīn Rūmī in Persian; Faiz in Urdu; and Habba Khatun, Mahjoor, and Zinda Kaul in Kashmiri. While he was growing up, his immediate family lived in New Delhi, India; Srinagar, Kashmir; and Muncie, Indiana, where his parents (Agha Ashraf Ali and Sufia Agha Ashraf Ali) both completed their doctorates in 1964. English, Urdu, and Kashmiri were all spoken in his home. Ali considered English to be his first language (it was the only language in which he wrote) and Urdu to be his mother tongue.

As a child, Ali was educated in Roman Catholic schools, but he attended an American high school while his parents were in graduate school. Ali earned several degrees: a B.A. from the University of Kashmir (1968), an M.A. from the University of Delhi (1970), an M.A. (1981) and a Ph.D. (1984) from Pennsylvania State University, and an M.F.A. from the University of Arizona (1985).

Ali lectured at the University of Delhi from 1970 to 1975 before moving to the United States to teach, study, and write. At Pennsylvania State University, he served as an instructor from 1976 to 1983, and at the University of Arizona, he worked as a graduate assistant from 1983 to 1985. Ali became the communications editor in the marketing department of the JNC Companies from 1985 to 1987 in Tucson, Arizona.

Ali was assistant professor of English and creative writing at Hamilton College from 1987 to 1993. Subsequently, he became an associate professor of English and director of the master of fine arts in creative writing program at the University of Massachusetts in Amherst. Ali also taught in the master of fine arts and doctoral programs at the University of Utah and the master of fine arts program at Warren Wilson College. He attained full professorship at the University of Utah in 1999. He held visiting appointments as professor or writer-in-residence at Princeton University, New York University, and the State University of New York, Binghamton.

Ali visited his parents in the summers in Srinagar, Kashmir, where they remained even after all their children had moved to the United States. However, Ali's mother, accompanied by his father, came to the United States for brain cancer treatment in 1996. She died in 1997. Ali also died of brain cancer four years later.

Analysis

Agha Shahid Ali's elegant, elegiac, expansive, and exilic voice is very clear from the beginning. He mocked it himself very early on in "Introducing" (from *In Memory of Begum Akhtar*): "Death punctuated all my poems./ I tried being clever, white-washed the day,/ exchanged it for the night,/ Bones my masks, Death/ the adolescent password." Apart from the theme of death or loss, which becomes more legitimate and literal toward the end of his career, Ali was also interested in demarcation. He resisted the title "U.S. citizen." He preferred the description "immigrant" or, better still, "exile." He accepted titles such as Kashmiri American, South Asian American, or Asian American. He considered himself conservative in poetic content, form, and technique. He adhered to strict guidelines for the ghazal. In addition, Ali's poetry is rich in allusion to and inclusion of poetic influences from mythology to the works of his contemporary poet friends and larger literary community. His poems are full of dedications to various people in his life. Finally, Ali drew from and portrayed his diverse background and environment. Although conservative in art, he was not conservative in his politics.

Ali's early poems display his most powerful literary influences: British colonization, which gave him the English language, and Eastern poetry (especially ghazals) by Mir Taqi Mir, Mirza Ghalib, and Faiz, sung by Begum Akhtar, whom Ali loved. He writes in the title poem "In Memory of Begum Akhtar," "You've finally polished catastrophe,/ the note you seasoned// with decades of Ghalib,/ Mir, Faiz:// I innovate on a note-less raga." In "dear editor," from his first poetry collection, *Bone-Sculpture*, Ali writes, "they call this my alien language// i am a dealer in words/ that mix cultures/ and leave me rootless." In "The Editor Revisited" (from *In Memory of Begum Akhtar*), he adds, "'A language must measure up to one's native dust.'// Divided between two cultures, I spoke a language/ foreign even to my ears." Later, in his introduction to *The Rebel's Silhouette*, Ali comments on "dear editor," "Rootless? Certainly not. I was merely subscribing to an inherent dominative mode that insisted one should not write in English because it was not an Indian language.... But it was mine, ours." Ali had begun to blend and own both his Eastern and Western cultural and linguistic influences.

The Half-Inch Himalayas

Exile is a powerful theme in *The Half-Inch Himalayas*, which opens with an epigraph from Virginia Woolf, "... for wherever I seat/ myself, I die in exile." This collection also includes the widely anthologized poems "Postcard from Kashmir," "Snowmen," and "The Dacca Gauzes." In "Homage to Faiz Ahmed Faiz," Ali writes, "... Your lines were measured/ so carefully to become in our veins// the blood of prisoners. In the free verse/ of another language I imprisoned// each line—but I touched my own exile." In "A Darkly Defense of Dead White Males" (from *Poet's Work, Poet's Play: Essays on the Practice and the Art*, 2007), Ali states, "A multiple exile, I celebrate myself. *Émigré* and *expatriate* describe me better." He continues, "But as an exile in my own country...

I use the word for its poetic resonance, for its metaphoric power—I must use the site for the privilege of self-reflection." Strictly speaking, Ali is not an exile because he moved voluntarily. However, as a postcolonial subject, a native of a disputed and unstable territory (Kashmir), and an immigrant, he has experienced enough loss and displacement to be able to lament after and have a desire for "home."

A Nostalgist's Map of America

Loss is a major theme in *A Nostalgist's Map of America*. "Beyond the Ash Rains" contains an epigraph from the Gilgamesh epic (c. 2000 B.C.E.; *Gilgamesh Epic*, 1917): "What have you known of loss/ That makes you different from other men?" Ali's speaker in that poem links loss and exile with this wish of not being "... singled/ out for loss in your arms, won't ever again/ be exiled, never again, from your arms." Another poem on loss is "A Rehearsal of Loss." Furthermore, loss is expressed through allusions. The title poem, "A Nostalgist's Map of America," and "In Search of Evanescence" allude to "A Route of Evanescence" by Emily Dickinson, one of Ali's favorite poets. "From Another Desert" alludes to the Arabic love story of Qais (Majnoon) and Laila. The final poem in this collection, "Snow on the Desert," closes with these lines: "a time to think of everything the earth/ and I had lost, of all// that I would lose,/ of all that I was losing."

The Country Without a Post Office

Ali's next three collections—*The Country Without a Post Office*, *Rooms Are Never Finished*, and *Call Me Ishmael Tonight*—display a profound love, sorrow, strength, and hope over the escalating conflict in Kashmir, the illness and death of Ali's mother, and the knowledge of his own imminent passing. Dedications of poems to others increase. In the prologue to *The Country Without a Post Office*, the refrain questions if the blesséd women will brush/rub the ashes together. This image portrays both destruction (ashes of the dead) and construction (making a fire for survival). The prologue is also a lament for Kashmir (the blesséd word). Unsurprisingly, Ali read widely and was widely read. An excerpt from the poem, "Farewell," is quoted in the epigraph to Salman Rushdie's novel *Shalimar the Clown* (2005), which is dedicated to Rushdie's Kashmiri grandparents.

Call Me Ishmael Tonight

Ali began to write more conventional ghazals. In *Call Me Ishmael Tonight*, the ghazal "By Exiles" (which appeared in *Rooms Are Never Finished* as "Ghazal"), Ali returned to the theme of exile. This ghazal contains an epigraph from a poem by Mahmoud Darwish, which also inspires a title of a work by Edward Said. The ghazal begins, "In Jerusalem a dead phone's dialed by exiles./ You learn your strange fate: You were exiled by exiles." The ghazal ends, "Will you, Belovéd Stranger, ever witness Shahid—/ two destinies at last reconciled by exiles?" Ali dedicates "By Exiles" to Said, a fellow exile (a dedication that did not appear in his previous collection).

OTHER MAJOR WORKS

NONFICTION: *T. S. Eliot as Editor*, 1986.

TRANSLATION: *The Rebel's Silhouette: Selected Poems*, 1995 (of Faiz Ahmed Faiz's poetry).

EDITED TEXT: *Ravishing Disunities: Real Ghazals in English*, 2000.

BIBLIOGRAPHY

Ali, Agha Shahid. "Conversation with Agha Shahid Ali." Interview by Christine Benevenuto. *Massachusetts Review* 43, no. 2 (Summer, 2002): 261-268. This interview from the late 1990's examines the poet's life and work.

_____. "A Darkly Defense of Dead White Males." In *Poet's Work, Poet's Play*, edited by Daniel Tobin and Pimone Triplett. Ann Arbor: University of Michigan Press, 2007. Ali writes about the craft of poetry and how being a multiple exile affects his work.

Chiu, Jeannie. "Melancholy and Human Rights in *A Nostalgist's Map of America* and *Midnight's Children*." *Literature Interpretation Theory* 16, no. 1 (January-March, 2005): 25-39. Provides a theoretical framework for discussing nostalgia. Examines Ali's *A Nostalgist's Map of America* and Salman Rushdie's *Midnight's Children* (1981).

Ghosh, Amitav. "The Ghat of the Only World: Agha Shahid Ali in Brooklyn." *Annual of Urdu Studies* 17 (2002): 1-19. An account of Ali's life and work written after Ali's death at his own request.

Hogan, Patrick Colm. *Empire and Poetic Voice*. Albany: State University of New York Press, 2004. Dedicated to Ali and includes an entire chapter on Ali's "From Another Desert" in *A Nostalgist's Map of America*.

Woodland, Malcolm. "Memory's Homeland: Agha Shahid Ali and the Hybrid Ghazal." *English Studies in Canada* 31, nos. 2/3 (June-September, 2005): 249-272. An excellent discussion of Ali's use of the ghazal.

Lydia Forssander-Song

VIKRAM SETH

Born: Calcutta, West Bengal, India; June 20, 1952

PRINCIPAL POETRY
Mappings, 1981
The Humble Administrator's Garden, 1985
The Golden Gate: A Novel in Verse, 1986
All You Who Sleep Tonight, 1990
Beastly Tales from Here and There, 1992
The Poems, 1981-1994, 1995

OTHER LITERARY FORMS

Vikram Seth (sayt) is best known for his novels. *A Suitable Boy* (1993), a family epic set in postcolonial India, is a monumental 1,349-page work that received mixed reviews but that became one of Seth's best-known works. *An Equal Music* (1999), set in contemporary London, is a love story about the members of a string quartet. Seth wrote a prize-winning travel book, *From Heaven Lake: Travels Through Sinkiang and Tibet*, published in 1983, and translated Chinese poetry in *Three Chinese Poets: Translations of Poems by Wang Wei, Li Bai, and Du Fu* (1992). *Arion and the Dolphin* (1995), written as the libretto for an opera, was also published as a children's book.

ACHIEVEMENTS

Vikram Seth won the Thomas Cook Travel Book Award in 1983 for *From Heaven Lake*; the Quality Paperback Book Club New Voice Award and a Gold Medal from the Commonwealth Club of California, both in 1986, for *The Golden Gate*; the W. H. Smith Award in 1994 for *A Suitable Boy*; and the Commonwealth Writer's Prize in 1994. He received an Ingram Merrill Fellowship in 1985-1986, a Guggenheim Fellowship in 1986-1987, and the Order of the British Empire in 2001. In 2005, he received India's Pravasi Bharatiya Samman award for exceptional work in literature and in 2007 received India's Padma Shri award for his contributions to education and literature.

BIOGRAPHY

Vikram Seth was born in Calcutta, India, in 1952, the oldest of three children. His father, Prem Seth, was a shoe company executive and his mother, Laila Seth, served as a judge. Seth left India to study at Oxford University in England, earning degrees in philosophy, economics, and politics. He enrolled at Stanford University in California, intending to complete a Ph.D. in economics. While at Stanford, Seth was a Wallace Stegner Fellow in creative writing. He wrote the poems collected in *Mappings* during this time. From 1980 to 1982, Seth was in China for two years of travel and economic research. While there, he studied classical Chinese poetry and language at Nanjing University. He wrote an account of a hitchhiking journey to India during this time, published as *From Heaven Lake*.

Seth's works present a variety of subjects based on his experiences and travels. The poetry collections *The Humble Administrator's Garden* and *All You Who Sleep Tonight* (1990) merge Chinese, Indian, and Californian influences; *From Heaven Lake* details the hitchhiking trip through Nepal and Tibet that Seth took while a student in China; and *The Golden Gate* is about young professionals in San Francisco, searching for love and identity.

Translation has played an important part in Seth's life, reflecting the multicultural sources of his material. His earliest book of poetry includes works translated from Chinese and Hindi. In 1992, *Three Chinese Poets* was published, illustrating again the deep understanding of Chinese culture that critics appreciated in *From Heaven Lake*. In the introduction to *Three Chinese Poets*, Seth acknowledges his debt to works in translation, particularly Russian, French, and Greek, and presents the book as an offering of thanks to other translators.

After publishing *The Golden Gate* in 1986, Seth returned to India to live with his family and work on his major epic, *A Suitable Boy*. This novel, published in 1993, propelled him into the public spotlight. The book launched Seth into a series of interviews, talk shows, and book signings. However, critical reviews were mixed, and the public and his publishers were dismayed when the book was not considered for the Booker Prize in 1993. After *A Suitable Boy*, Seth returned to London, where he was commissioned by the English National Opera to write a libretto based on the Greek legend of Arion and the dolphin. His 1999 novel, *An Equal Music*, was also set in London, and in 2001 he was awarded the Order of the British Empire for his achievements.

Analysis

Vikram Seth is a versatile writer who is at ease in a variety of genres. He is known for his clear and readable style, joyful use of language, irony, and technical mastery. He has made a place for himself as an Indian writing in the English language. Though his published works reflect his versatility, set in London, San Francisco, and China, as well as India, his best-known work is his epic of Indian culture, religion, family life, and postcolonial politics, *A Suitable Boy*.

Seth's work can be analyzed in terms of several distinctive factors. One is his multicultural identity. His books of poetry contain material influenced by his residence and familiarity with the literature of Eastern and Western countries and cultures. He is further influenced by literature in translation from Russia and Greece. This cultural diversity is reflected in the variety of his themes and material. Nevertheless, Seth remains ultimately an Indian writer.

A second distinctive factor in Seth's poetry is his technical mastery of traditional forms of rhyme and meter, unusual in a poet of the modern age. Seth has written that since his academic training was in economics rather than English, he followed his own inclinations and tastes in his own poetry. Verse "in form" is what he reads and recalls, and therefore writes.

Critics have noted the simplicity of style and unassuming tone of his poetry. The sheer joy of some of his use of language; his sense of humor, ease, and fun; his joy in small daily moments; and his strong sense of irony characterize the best of his work. While Seth's form is traditional, he is thematically a postmodernist. Coming through the irony and humor is a theme of the loneliness of late twentieth century life, the difficulty of forming relationships, the ultimate failure of love as a bond. His familiarity with contemporary idiom and culture further reflects his time and place. He has a postmodern self-consciousness as well, transparently revealing his writing technique and his presence as narrator throughout his work.

Mappings

Seth's first published book of poetry reflects mixed feelings of nostalgia for India after studying for years in England and the United States. The book includes translations of poems from Hindi, German, and Chinese. His original work expresses youthful restlessness, the sadness of unfulfilled love, and ambivalent feeling toward family. These lines from "Panipat" show the poet's sense of being caught between two cultures:

> Family, music, faces,
> Food, land, everything
> Drew me back, yet now
> To hear the koyal sing
>
> Brings notes of other birds,
> The nightingale, the wren,
> The blackbird; and my heart's
> Barometer turns down.

The Humble Administrator's Garden

This book is divided into three sections—"Wutong," "Neem," and "Live-Oak"—that identify their influences: Chinese, Indian, and Californian. As in *Mappings*, Seth reports on surfaces and the trivia of life while using the traditional forms of the sonnet, quatrain, and epigrammatic couplet. Critics liked the book for Seth's unassuming tone and technical discipline. Themes of the poems include a refusal to look inward and a celebration of the simple pleasures of life. The California poems refer to loneliness and the dangers of a superficial life. Seth sometimes uses a deceptively simple form to mock emotion, as these lines from "Love and Work": "There is so much to do/ There isn't any time for feeling blue./ There isn't any point in feeling sad./ Things could be worse. Right now they're only bad." Although some of the poems appear so offhand as to be trivial, Seth's irony, humor, and ease with language express the ethic of an unromantic and eclectic contemporary mind.

THE GOLDEN GATE

The Golden Gate, widely reviewed and critically well received, established Seth's reputation as a poet and popular writer. The "novel" is a 307-page series of nearly six hundred sonnets of iambic tetrameter. The long narrative poem is loosely modeled on Russian poet Alexander Pushkin's *Evgeny Onegin* (1825-1832, 1833; *Eugene Onegin*, 1881).

The novel is driven by the lives and entanglements of its characters John, a self-controlled white Anglo-Saxon Protestant yuppie computer designer; Phil, a sensitive Jewish intellectual; Janet, a Japanese feminist rock musician; Liz, a career-driven Italian corporate lawyer; and her brother Ed, a troubled gay Roman Catholic. Each character is a part of a subculture of San Francisco life, and through them Seth demonstrates his thorough familiarity with the setting, the coffee houses, singles bars, and bookshops of 1980's San Francisco.

As in *The Humble Administrator's Garden*, central themes are loneliness, the failure of romantic love to resolve the need for others, and the significance of ordinary life. The narrative is witty and amusing and demonstrates Seth's skill and flexibility with language and mastery of verse form. While some critics found it unusual to depict 1980's yuppies through narrative verse, many found the form's unconventionality appropriate for a work that is both lightly comic and reflective. Despite the traditional model and form, *The Golden Gate* employs techniques of postmodernism, in which the act of writing is self-consciously present, as the author comments upon himself and his technique and employs unexpected coincidences and interweaving of plots.

ALL YOU WHO SLEEP TONIGHT

The poems in this volume continue the Seth hallmarks of rhyme and traditional form. The book is divided into several distinct thematic sections, reflecting Seth's diversity of material. The section "Romantic Residues" reinforces some of the themes of *The Golden Gate*: the quality of love and the reluctance to make commitments and take risks. The second section, "In Other Voices," brings a new element of high seriousness to Seth's poetry, including poems about the Holocaust, the atomic destruction of Hiroshima, and acquired immunodeficiency syndrome (AIDS). "In Other Places" is a series of vignettes about varied places including China; "Quatrains" is a series of clever presentations of Seth's perspective on life; and the final section, "Meditations of the Heart," while also witty, presents a perspective that is saddened by death, loss, and solitude. The final section includes the title poem: "Know that you aren't alone./ The whole world shares your tears,/ Some for two nights or one,/ And some for all their years."

Beastly Tales from Here and There

This 1992 book is a collection of animal fables retold by Seth in lively tetrameter couplets. Once again Seth reveals his versatility and multicultural influences, including two tales each from India, China, Greece, and Ukraine, along with two original tales. The tales are characterized by their fluent storytelling and combination of the comic and the tragic. On one level, these are children's tales, but they are more than simple retellings, as Seth gives the fables a moral twist all his own. The reader is left with a sense of ambiguity. What is the true moral?

The final story in the volume is Seth's original "The Elephant and the Tragopan." This fable has a thoroughly contemporary feel, as its theme is the protection of the environment, and the head of the council, Bigshot, is more concerned with money and votes than with saving Bingle Vale. The resolution is left open:

> And so I'll end the story here.
> What is to come is still unclear.
> Whether the fates will smile or frown,
> And Bingle Vale survive or drown,
> I do not know and cannot say;
> Indeed, perhaps, I never may.

Other Major Works

LONG FICTION: *The Golden Gate: A Novel in Verse*, 1986; *A Suitable Boy*, 1993; *An Equal Music*, 1999.

PLAY: *Arion and the Dolphin*, pr., pb. 1994 (libretto; music by Alec Roth).

NONFICTION: *From Heaven Lake: Travels Through Sikiang and Tibet*, 1983; *Two Lives*, 2005.

TRANSLATION: *Three Chinese Poets: Translations of Poems by Wang Lei, Li Bai, and Du Fu*, 1992.

CHILDREN'S LITERATURE: *Arion and the Dolphin*, 1995.

Bibliography

Agarwalla, Shyam S. *Vikram Seth's "A Suitable Boy": Search for an Indian Identity*. New Delhi: Prestige Books, 1995. A scholarly, book-length source on Seth. Employing the techniques of literary criticism, the book includes general cultural information and discussion of Seth's role as an Indian writer.

Corey, Stephen. Review of *All You Who Sleep Tonight*. *Ohio Review*, no. 47 (1991): 132-139. Critical review of the volume. Corey's conclusion is that the poetry is often trivial, singsongy, and oversimplified.

Gopal, Priyamvada. *The Indian English Novel: Nation, History, and Narration*. New York: Oxford University Press, 2009. An introduction to the Indian novel in English, now considered "a fixture on the international literary scene." Major writers covered include Seth, Rabindranath Tagore, Salman Rushdie, and Arundhati Roy.

Mohanty, Seemita. *A Critical Analysis of Vikram Seth's Poetry and Fiction*. New Delhi: Atlantic, 2007. A thorough study of Seth's writing, including both his poetry and his fiction, and the ways he approaches the writing process. Intended for scholars and general readers alike.

Perloff, Marjorie. "Homeward Ho! Silicon Valley Pushkin." Review of *The Golden Gate*. *American Poetry Review* 15, no. 6 (November/December, 1986): 37-46. Perloff asserts that Seth's concern with rhyme weakens the novel's characterization, plot, and satirical force. A scholarly article, with detailed analysis and extensive references to poetic form and poets in history.

Perry, John Oliver. "World Literature in Review: India." Review of *All You Who Sleep Tonight*. *World Literature Today* 65, no. 3 (Summer, 1991): 549-550. Perry discusses the content and form of several specific poems and concludes, "It is a tribute to the poems . . . that often they can sound a bit like Frost or Hardy."

Seth, Vikram. Introduction and foreword to *The Poems, 1981-1994*. New York: Viking Penguin, 1995. A primary source, the poet's foreword reprinted in a volume of selected poems. Seth discusses his poetry and influences and reveals themes and insight into his priorities and thought processes.

Woodward, Richard B. "Vikram Seth's Big Book." *The New York Times Magazine* 142 (May 2, 1993): 32-36. A profile of Seth that includes biographical and background information on the author, his writing, and his career.

Susan Butterworth

RABINDRANATH TAGORE

Born: Calcutta, India; May 7, 1861
Died: Calcutta, India; August 7, 1941
Also known as: Rabindranath Thakur

PRINCIPAL POETRY
 Saisab sangit, 1881
 Sandhya sangit, 1882
 Prabhat sangit, 1883
 Chabi o gan, 1884
 Kari o komal, 1887
 Mānashi, 1890
 Sonār tari, 1893 (*The Golden Boat*, 1932)
 Chitra, 1895
 Chaitāli, 1896
 Kanika, 1899
 Kalpana, 1900
 Katha o kahini, 1900
 Kshanikā, 1900
 Naivedya, 1901
 Sisu, 1903 (*The Crescent Moon*, 1913)
 Smaran, 1903
 Utsarga, 1904
 Kheya, 1905
 Gitānjali, 1910 (*Gitanjali Song Offerings*, 1912)
 The Gardener, 1913
 Gitali, 1914
 Balāka, 1916 (*A Flight of Swans*, 1955, 1962)
 Fruit-Gathering, 1916
 Gan, 1916
 Stray Birds, 1917
 Love's Gift, and Crossing, 1918
 Palataka, 1918 (*The Fugitive*, 1921)
 Lipika, 1922
 Poems, 1922
 Sisu bholanath, 1922
 The Curse at Farewell, 1924
 Prabahini, 1925

Purabi, 1925
Fifteen Poems, 1928
Fireflies, 1928
Mahuya, 1929
Sheaves: Poems and Songs, 1929
Banabani, 1931
The Child, 1931
Parisesh, 1932
Punascha, 1932
Vicitrita, 1933
Bithika, 1935
Ses saptak, 1935
Patraput, 1936, 1938 (English translation, 1969)
Syamali, 1936 (English translation, 1955)
Khapchada, 1937
Prantik, 1938
Senjuti, 1938
Navajatak, 1940
Rogsajya, 1940
Sanai, 1940
Arogya, 1941
Janmadine, 1941
Poems, 1942
Sesh lekha, 1942
The Herald of Spring, 1957
Wings of Death: The Last Poems, 1960
Devouring Love, 1961
A Bunch of Poems, 1966
One Hundred and One, 1967
Last Poems, 1973
Later Poems, 1974
Final Poems, 2001

OTHER LITERARY FORMS

Besides more than fifty collections of poetry, Rabindranath Tagore (tuh-GOHR) wrote thirteen novels, ten collections of short stories, more than sixty plays, and numerous volumes of literary criticism, letters, translations, reminiscences, lectures, sermons, travel sketches, philosophy, religion, and politics. In addition, he translated a considerable amount of his own work from its original Bengali into English.

Tagore's drama, which generally tends to be more lyric than dramatic, is best repre-

Rabindranath Tagore
(©The Nobel Foundation)

sented by *Visarjan* (pb. 1890; *Sacrifice*, 1917), *Chitrāngadā* (pb. 1892; *Chitra*, 1913), *Prayaschitta* (pr. 1909; atonement), *Rājā* (pb. 1910; *The King of the Dark Chamber*, 1914), *Dākghar* (pb. 1912; *Post Office*, 1914), and *Raktakarabi* (pb. 1924; *Red Oleanders*, 1925). Examples of later plays—*Muktadhārā* (pb. 1922; English translation, 1950), *Natir Pujā* (pb. 1926; *Worship of the Dancing Girl*, 1950), and *Chandālikā* (pr., pb. 1933; English translation, 1938)—were translated by Marjorie Sykes in *Three Plays* (pb. 1950).

Tagore's fiction, which also reflects his lyric bent, sometimes seems to prefigure the "open form." Including some of his best work, his short stories have been compared to those of Guy de Maupassant. Some of his short stories have been translated in *The Hungry Stones, and Other Stories* (1916), *Mashi, and Other Stories* (1918), and *The Runaway, and Other Stories* (1959). *Gora* (1910; English translation, 1924) is usually considered his best novel, but others of interest are *Chokher bāli* (1902; *Binodini*, 1959), *Ghare bāire* (1916; *Home and the World*, 1919), *Chaturanga* (1916; English translation, 1963), *Jogajog* (1929; cross currents), *Shesher kabita* (1929; *Farewell My Friend*, 1946), and *Dui bon* (1933; *Two Sisters*, 1945).

Tagore's nonfictional prose, some of which was originally written as lectures in English, is represented by *Jivansmriti* (1912; *My Reminiscences*, 1917), *Personality* (1917), *Nationalism* (1919), *Creative Unity* (1922), *The Religion of Man* (1931), and *Towards Universal Man* (1961).

ACHIEVEMENTS

Few writers have achieved such fame as came to Rabindranath Tagore when he was awarded the 1913 Nobel Prize in Literature. The first Asian to receive the award, he was viewed in the West as the embodiment of Eastern mystical wisdom. Indian critics at the time, however, often attacked his work, usually for political reasons, even though he did more than any other writer to establish Bengali as a flexible literary language (he was experimenting with it to the end of his life). Perhaps needing money for the school he had established at Santiniketan, Tagore took advantage of his fame to churn out English translations. Although he admitted his limited skill in English, he was shrewd enough to satisfy the sentimental streak in his English-speaking audiences. The combination of modest skill and banality was devastating for his poetry. His so-called prose poems—usually paraphrases, though they occasionally break into Whitmanesque free verse—are noteworthy examples of what is lost in the translation of poetry. Eventually, these translations caught up with his reputation, which began sinking in the West about the time that graduates of Santiniketan began producing books on their *Gurudev*. One of these former students, Aurobindo Bose, has produced the best English translations of Tagore's poetry now available.

As Jane Addams (of Hull House) noted, Tagore was "at once a poet, a philosopher, a humanitarian, an educator," and as Hermann Hesse said, Tagore's reputation was built in part on "the rich heritage of ancient Indian philosophy." Similarly, Tagore's work reflects certain native literary traditions, such as Indian drama and the *Baul* folk songs, which are alien to the West. Finally, where his poetry is concerned, it should be borne in mind that Tagore was a songwriter (he composed about two thousand songs), that he set some of his poems to music, and that in Bengali his poetry has rich musical qualities—rhythm, rhyme, alliteration, assonance—that accompany the words, images, and ideas. All these factors must be carefully weighed in evaluating Tagore's overall achievement.

Otherwise, each individual work must be considered separately. Tagore wrote too much, so there is repetition and wide variation in quality, especially in his poetry. (Apparently he needed a critical audience off which to bounce his poems, but he found it neither in his Indian milieu nor in the adulatory West.) For example, the same period that produced *Gitanjali Song Offerings* and *A Flight of Swans* also produced the soppy poems in *The Crescent Moon*. Besides *Gitanjali Song Offerings* and *A Flight of Swans*, perhaps his finest works are the short stories translated in *The Hungry Stones, and Other*

Stories. Readers of English would also do well to rediscover his lectures, wherein Tagore speaks for peace, internationalism, and understanding—themes prominent in his literary work.

Biography

Rabindranath Tagore was born into a wealthy, influential, and culturally active Brahmin family. The name Tagore is an English corruption of the title *Thakur* (that is, Brahmin), and the name Rabindranath means "lord of the sun" (*rabi* means "the sun"). Tagore's father was Maharishi (Great Sage) Devendranath Tagore, an important religious writer and leader of Brahmo Samaj (Society of God), a new monotheistic religion founded on a return to the Upanishads and progressive political ideas. A response both to orthodox Hinduism (characterized by idolatry, the caste system, suttee, and similar oppressive practices) and to Western culture (especially Christianity), the reformist Brahmo Samaj virtually defined the development of Tagore's own thought.

Despite his apparent advantages, Tagore, the youngest of fourteen children, had a difficult childhood. His father was involved with his activities as a maharishi, and Tagore's mother was sickly (she died when he was thirteen). The infant Rabi was turned over to the care of servants, who simplified their duties by confining him within rooms and chalk circles. He did not last long in any of the several schools he attended, consequently receiving little formal education. He was saved by his father and family activities. At the age of twelve, he accompanied his father, whom he idolized, on an extended journey to Santiniketan (his father's rural retreat, about one hundred miles west of Calcutta), Amritsar, and the Himalayas, where they lived in a mountain hut and where his father instructed him. On his return to Calcutta, the young Tagore gradually became involved in family activities.

The family was ostracized by orthodox Hindus, thus leaving the Tagores free to do as they pleased. As a result, the family home, Jorasanko Palace, was the cultural center of Calcutta, buzzing with more than a hundred inhabitants as well as a steady flow of distinguished visitors—reformist religious leaders, nationalist politicians, writers, artists, and musicians. The evenings were filled with musical performances, plays, readings, and discussions that lasted far into the night. Even the women were involved, further scandalizing the neighbors, who still practiced purdah (the formal seclusion of women from public view). The lively teenage Tagore plunged into this activity, contributing songs, readings, and critical observations. When, in 1877, the family started its own monthly magazine, *Bharati*, the sixteen-year-old Tagore helped edit it and was a main contributor. What better education could one find for Tagore the writer (not to mention Tagore the singer, songwriter, actor, critic, politician, philosopher, and artist)?

One more try at formal education occurred in 1878, when Tagore was sent to Great Britain to prepare to study law, first at a school in Brighton, then at University College, London. He continued to make contributions to *Bharati*, expressing his dislike for the

British people and his love for British literature (especially William Shakespeare and the Romantics). After two years, Tagore returned home, and in 1883, a marriage was arranged for him with Mrinalini Devi (then only nine years old), whom he called Nalini. In 1891, they settled down in Shelidah, where Tagore's father assigned him to manage the family estates and where Tagore for the first time came into direct contact with the Indian countryside and peasant life. This period was an eye-opener for Tagore, providing him with some of his best material for short stories. (For example, he rescued a tenant's wife who was being swept down a flooding river, but did she thank him? No, she was trying to commit suicide.) Sympathy for the conditions of peasant life also deepened his involvement in the growing Indian Nationalist movement, for which he wrote and made speeches. When the Nationalist movement eventually became violent, however, he broke off his involvement and withdrew to Santiniketan (which, appropriately, means "abode of peace"). Later, he would come to believe that nationalism is one of the great evils of the modern world.

In 1901, Tagore began his career as an educator, starting a school at Santiniketan. It is ironic, but understandable, that the dropout should become the educator; some of his five children were of school age, and, recalling his school experience, he had his own ideas about how to teach them. These ideas he put into practice at Santiniketan. He was also responding to the conditions around him, seeking to uplift his countrymen in a way that did not involve violence. Besides, there was always something of the teacher in Tagore, as shown by his campaign to enlighten first his own countrymen and later the West. The teacher comes out frequently (though indirectly) in his poetry, in which he sometimes seems to adopt the stance of the Great Sage. Above all, Tagore was interested in seeing certain ideas prevail, as proclaimed by the motto of Santiniketan: "Santam, sivam, advaitam" (peace, good, union).

The early years at Santiniketan were marred for Tagore by great personal loss: In 1902 his wife died, in 1904 his eldest daughter, in 1905 his father, and in 1907 his youngest son. However, the deepening process of meditating on these losses produced his best poetry, *Gitanjali Song Offerings* and *A Flight of Swans*. The school was also in constant need of money, which eventually required him to make several fund-raising and lecture trips to the United States, Great Britain, and the European Continent. These journeys established him as an ambassador to the West—a role he found much easier to fill after he won the 1913 Nobel Prize in Literature. Everywhere he went, he was received as the Great Sage, and he was awarded numerous honors (such as a British knighthood in 1915). He visited the Soviet Union and Japan, both of which he admired, but he criticized Communist suppression of individual rights and the militant nationalism of the Japanese. He was especially appalled by Japanese efforts to conquer China.

Tagore's last years were spent in traveling, in expanding the Santiniketan complex, in practicing a new art (painting), and in pointing the world toward peace. In 1922, he established Sriniketan (abode of grace), an institute for agriculture and rural reconstruction, and Visva-Bharati (universal voice), an international university for bringing the message of the East to the West. His paintings were exhibited in Europe to favorable reviews. He was disappointed in his work for peace, thinking that nations that had endured one world war would not want another. The 1930's were increasingly depressing for him, and he died in 1941, just as World War II was reaching its full incarnation.

Analysis

The main theme of Rabindranath Tagore's poetry is the essential unity (or continuity) of all creation, which is also the main theme of the ancient Hindu Upanishads. Indeed, a brief summary of Hindu belief provides a useful introduction to Tagore's work. According to Hindu thought, the only absolute, unchanging, eternal thing is Brahman, the supreme being or world soul who forms the essence of everything. In living things, the essence of Brahman is known as Atman, or soul. Brahman operates through three aspects: Brahma, the creator; Siva, the destroyer; and Vishnu, the preserver or renewer. Brahma's work is finished, but Siva and Vishnu are necessary for change, and change is necessary so that living things may grow toward union with Brahman, a perfect, changeless state, nirvana. Few, if any, achieve nirvana in one lifetime, so reincarnation is necessary. In each successive incarnation, one improves one's status in the next through good karma or deeds (broadly interpreted as actions, thoughts, or faith).

The questions raised by Hindu belief may be ignored here (for example, why would Brahman create something imperfect in the first place?); so also may certain negative social implications (such as the potential for inaction, the caste system, and unconcern for the individual human life). Instead, what should be noticed is the positive emphasis of Hinduism, in contrast to Western thought as characterized by the old Germanic notion that everything is moving toward *Götterdämmerung*; the Christian emphasis on Original Sin, evil, and Hell; the masked versions of human sacrifice. It is the positive implications of Hindu belief that Tagore develops in his poetry. For example, his imagery—dwelling on sunrises and sunsets, flowers and their scents, songs and musical instruments, the beautiful deodar tree (*deodár* meaning "divine wood"), the majestic Himalayas—is a constant reminder that creation is charged with divinity: Beauty and majesty are concrete manifestations of Brahman. Change, natural disasters, and death are necessary for renewal, which will come. All people have divine souls, so they should tolerate, respect, and love one another. The advantaged should help the disadvantaged; thereby, they both rise toward Brahman. The individual should strive to live in such a way as to throw off impurities and achieve the essence of divinity within the self. The development of these and related themes can be traced throughout Tagore's oeuvre.

Gitanjali Song Offerings

Published in 1910, *Gitanjali Song Offerings* is Tagore's most popular work. The English edition, published in 1912, includes translations not only from the original

Gitānjali but also from other collections, particularly *Naivedya* (offerings). As light work to keep his mind occupied, Tagore did the translations himself while he was convalescing from an illness at Shelidah and on board a ship for Great Britain. He showed them to British friends who wanted to read his work. They in turn showed the translations to William Butler Yeats, and the result was English publication followed by the 1913 Nobel Prize in Literature. Aware of the undistinguished quality of his translations, Tagore himself could never understand why he was rash enough to do them or why they created such a sensation.

Sometimes compared to the Book of Psalms, *Gitanjali Song Offerings* explores the personal relationship between the poet and divinity. This divinity he calls Jivandevata, which he often translates as "Lord of my life" or "life of my life" but also refers to as "my God," "King," "Father," "Mother," "lover," "friend," and "innermost one." The range of terms here suggests the varied associations of Jivandevata and also the conventional metaphors Tagore generally uses to develop his relationship with Jivandevata. Perhaps the most numerous poems are those in which, like John Donne or Saint Teresa of Ávila, Tagore speaks of the deity as a lover with whom he longs to be united. In Song 60 (numbers refer to the English edition), Tagore varies the formula somewhat. He describes a woman who dwells in purdah within his heart. Many men have come asking for her, but none has seen her face, because she waits only for God. The woman represents the spark of divinity in Tagore which longs to be reunited with its source, and the purdah suggests its loneliness and purity. The divinity within inspires Tagore's songs and motivates him to lead a pure life, but he confesses that involvement in commonplace events sometimes creates a smoke screen that obscures the divinity within and without. The commonplace, however, also has its divinity. God is to be found not only in the temple but also with the workers in the fields. Because divinity runs through everything, even the metaphors that Tagore uses to describe God have an element of literal truth.

The most interesting poems in *Gitanjali Song Offerings* are a group dealing with death. Songs 86 and 87 are about a family member—probably the poet's wife—whom death has taken. Although heartbroken by her death, Tagore welcomes the visit of God's "servant" and "messenger," and seeking her in the oneness of the universe has brought Tagore closer to God. Thus reconciled, Tagore welcomes his own death as "the fulfillment of life." His dying will be like a bride meeting her bridegroom on the wedding night or like a feeding babe switching from the right breast to the left breast of its mother. Meanwhile, his soul is like "a flock of homesick cranes," on the wing day and night to reach "their mountain nests."

A FLIGHT OF SWANS

Perhaps Tagore's best work, *A Flight of Swans*, takes its title from the image on which *Gitanjali Song Offerings* ends. Thematically, *A Flight of Swans* also takes up where *Gitanjali Song Offerings* ends. Although *A Flight of Swans* continues to develop the personal relationship between the poet and divinity, there is a new emphasis on the impersonal workings of divinity throughout creation. The dual emphasis can be seen in the opening poem of the English edition, the title poem, wherein the flight of swans breaking the silence of the evening symbolizes not only the aspiration of the human soul but also the yearning of inanimate nature for "the Beyond." Even the mountains and deodar trees long to spread their wings like the "homeless bird" inside the breast of Tagore and "countless others." The images of movement and yearning here also serve to introduce the theme of change so prominent in *A Flight of Swans*.

For Tagore, the abstract notion of change is embodied in the dance of Siva, the destroyer, who is featured in several poems. Sometimes called Rudra (the terrible one), Siva brings violence, destruction, and death. To scholars of Sigmund Freud, Tagore's worship of Siva might sound like an Eastern version of the death wish, and his reveling in "the sea of pain" and "the sport of death" might repel squeamish readers. Nevertheless, there is a reason for Tagore's embrace of resounding agony. The dance of Siva purges the cosmological systems. It prevents the flow of "gross Matter" from backing up and putrefying, "renews and purifies" creation in "the bath of death," and speeds souls onward toward nirvana. The only thing which survives Siva's dance is immortal art, as represented by the Taj Mahal. Becoming Siva's partner, Tagore aligns himself with the young rather than the old, with the unknown rather than the known, with wandering rather than home, with movement rather than stagnancy.

With its focus on movement and change, on the cyclic nature of things, *A Flight of Swans* breathes the same spirit as Percy Bysshe Shelley's "Ode to the West Wind": If Siva comes, can Vishnu be far behind? Indeed, Tagore hoped that Vishnu, the preserver and renewer, would come soon. Tagore wrote *A Flight of Swans* at the outset of World War I, and the poems reflect his awareness of the war's catastrophic violence. Once the war started, he hoped that it would at least bring about some good results—that it would clean out the evils of the old world system and bring about a new order of peace and brotherhood.

PATRAPUT

Patraput means "a cup of leaves." The poems in this collection are the leaves shed by the poet's tree of life during his old age. *Patraput* is also a reminder that Tagore wrote poetry on subjects other than religion. He was a love poet, especially in his early career, a nature poet (*Banabani*) concentrating on trees and plants, and he even wrote a collection of humorous poems that he called *Khapchada* (a little offbeat). *Patraput* represents not only the mellowness of Tagore's old age but also the variety of his subjects. There are even a few love poems from the seventy-five-year-old poet.

Many of the poems in *Patraput* celebrate subtle effects. With humor and sensitivity, two poems (2 and 7) explore the idleness of holidays. At home by himself in the countryside (probably Santiniketan), the poet has trouble adjusting to doing nothing but feels himself better off than vacationers scrambling through railway stations. In the surrounding scenes of nature that Tagore pauses to observe, God provides him with a "change of air" and a visit to "the eternal ocean" for free. Meanwhile, he knows his "return ticket" will soon expire and he will have to return to the workaday world, "to return here from here itself." These two poems and others contain some attractive descriptions of nature. Another excellent example is Poem 9, which traces the coming and passing of a storm. A number of the poems also trace shifts of mood, from one season to another, from one time of day to another, from one scene to another. In some of these small effects, there are suggestions of bigger themes. For example, there are intimations of the poet's coming death ("return ticket") in the description, as though he is sinking slowly into the placid Indian countryside. The epiphany in Poem 1, where the poet climbs a mountaintop to see the sun setting on one hand and the moon rising on the other, is reminiscent of William Wordsworth's topping of Mount Snowdon in *The Prelude: Or, The Growth of a Poet's Mind* (1850).

Another interesting group of poems in *Patraput* consists of those containing social commentary. In Poem 6, Tagore urges the reader ("O thou hospitable") to invite in the destitute pilgrim so that the poor fellow can rise above his mere struggle for existence. In Poem 15, Tagore, himself ostracized when a child, identifies with the untouchables who are prohibited from entering temples, and with the itinerant *Baul* singers, who sing that God is "the Man of my heart." Like them, Tagore has no caste, no temple, no religion except the religion of Man. Poem 16 is a lament for Africa, ransacked for slaves by the purveyors of Christian "civilization." Their phony belief in religion is duplicated in the modern era by the militarists who seek Buddha's blessings for their killing (apparently a slap at Japanese aggression in Manchuria).

CRITICISM OF FORMAL RELIGION

As the unflattering references to Hindus, Christians, and Buddhists indicate, Tagore had no more enthusiasm for formal religion than he had for formal education. Nevertheless, along with such figures as Gerard Manley Hopkins and T. S. Eliot, Tagore is a leading religious poet of the modern era. The social commentary in *Patraput* marks the final stage of his spiritual journey. In *Gitanjali Song Offerings*, he is concerned with his personal fate, his individual relationship to God. In *A Flight of Swans*, he explores the impersonal workings of divinity through the terrible dance of Siva; and in *Patraput*, he shows that religious belief must ultimately be expressed through concern (and action) for one's fellow men. With his "religion of Man," Tagore ends up in a position very similar to Western Humanism, but it is a position that retains its ties to ancient religious belief, belief summed up in the teaching of the humble *Baul* singers that God is "the Man of my heart."

OTHER MAJOR WORKS

LONG FICTION: *Bau-Thakuranir Hat*, 1883; *Rajarshi*, 1887; *Chokher bāli*, 1902 (*Binodini*, 1959); *Naukadubi*, 1906 (*The Wreck*, 1921); *Gora*, 1910 (English translation, 1924); *Chaturanga*, 1916 (English translation, 1963); *Ghare bāire*, 1916 (*Home and the World*, 1919); *Jogajog*, 1929; *Shesher kabita*, 1929 (*Farewell My Friend*, 1946); *Dui bon*, 1933 (*Two Sisters*, 1945).

SHORT FICTION: *The Hungry Stones, and Other Stories*, 1916; *Mashi, and Other Stories*, 1918; *Stories from Tagore*, 1918; *Broken Ties, and Other Stories*, 1925; *The Runaway, and Other Stories*, 1959; *Selected Short Stories*, 1991 (translated with an introduction by William Radice).

PLAYS: *Prakritir Pratishodh*, pb. 1884 (verse play; *Sanyasi: Or, The Ascetic*, 1917); *Rājā o Rāni*, pb. 1889 (verse play; *The King and the Queen*, 1918); *Visarjan*, pb. 1890 (verse play; based on his novel *Rajarshi; Sacrifice*, 1917); *Chitrāngadā*, pb. 1892 (verse play; *Chitra*, 1913); *Prayaschitta*, pr. 1909 (based on his novel *Bau-Thakuranir Hat*); *Rājā*, pb. 1910 (*The King of the Dark Chamber*, 1914); *Dākghar*, pb. 1912 (*The Post Office*, 1914); *Phālguni*, pb. 1916 (*The Cycle of Spring*, 1917); *Arupratan*, pb. 1920 (revision of his play *Rājā*); *Muktadhārā*, pb. 1922 (English translation, 1950); *Raktakarabi*, pb. 1924 (*Red Oleanders*, 1925); *Chirakumār Sabhā*, pb. 1926; *Natir Pujā*, pb. 1926 (*Worship of the Dancing Girl*, 1950); *Sesh Rakshā*, pb. 1928; *Paritrān*, pb. 1929 (revision of *Prayaschitta*); *Tapati*, pb. 1929 (revision of *Rājā o Rāni*); *Bānsari*, pb. 1933; *Chandālikā*, pr., pb. 1933 (English translation, 1938); *Nritya-natya Chitrāngadā*, pb. 1936 (revision of his play *Chitrāngadā*); *Nritya-natya Chandālikā*, pb. 1938 (revision of his play *Chandālikā*); *Three Plays*, 1950.

NONFICTION: *Jivansmriti*, 1912 (*My Reminiscences*, 1917); *Sadhana: The Realisation of Life*, 1913; *Nationalism*, 1917; *Personality*, 1917; *Glimpses of Bengal*, 1921; *Greater India*, 1921; *Creative Unity*, 1922; *Talks in China*, 1925; *Lectures and Addresses*, 1928; *Letters to a Friend*, 1928; *The Religion of Man*, 1931; *Mahatmaji and the Depressed Humanity*, 1932; *The Religion of an Artist*, 1933; *Man*, 1937; *Chhelebela*, 1940 (*My Boyhood Days*, 1940); *Sabhyatar Samkat*, 1941 (*Crisis in Civilization*, 1941); *Towards Universal Man*, 1961.

MISCELLANEOUS: *Collected Poems and Plays*, 1936; *A Tagore Reader*, 1961.

BIBLIOGRAPHY

Das Gupta, Uma. *Rabindranath Tagore: A Biography*. New York: Oxford University Press, 2004. A biography of Tagore, based largely on his letters, that reveals him as a poet and writer with a social conscience.

_____, ed. *The Oxford India Tagore: Selected Writings on Education and Nationalism*. New York: Oxford University Press, 2009. An examination of Tagore's views on education and nationalism and his relationship with Oxford.

Dutta Gupta, Reeta. *Rabindranath Tagore: The Poet Sublime*. New Delhi: Rupa, 2002.

A biography that examines the life and works of Tagore, with emphasis on his poetry.

Ghosh, Dipali, comp. *Bengali Works of Rabindranath Tagore into English: A Bibliography*. Calcutta: Firma KLM, 2008. A bibliography of the works written by Tagore in Bengali and translated into English.

Ivbulis, Viktors. *Tagore: East and West Cultural Unity*. Calcutta: Rabindra Bharati University, 1999. The author looks at the influence of both the West and the East in Tagore's work. Bibliography.

Nandi, Sudhirakumara. *Art and Aesthetics of Rabindra Nath Tagore*. Calcutta: Asiatic Society, 1999. Nandi analyzes the Tagore's aesthetics as expressed in his writings. Bibliography and index.

Nandy, Ashis. *The Illegitimacy of Nationalism: Rabindranath Tagore and the Politics of Self*. New York: Oxford University Press, 1994. This study focuses on the political and social views of Tagore as demonstrated by his life and writings. Bibliography and index.

_____. *Return from Exile*. New York: Oxford University Press, 1998. An analysis of Tagore's political writing which puts him in the context of India's move in the 1920's toward nationalism. This, in turn, illuminates some of the philosophy and themes in his other writing.

Saha, Panchanan. *Tagore and USA*. Calcutta: Biswabiksha, 2009. An account of Tagore's life that focuses on his travels in the United States and relations with Americans.

Sen Gupta, Kalyan. *The Philosophy of Rabindranath Tagore*. Burlington, Vt.: Ashgate, 2005. A comprehensive introduction to Tagore's poetry and essays and the way they relate to his philosophy, politics and religion.

Harold Branam

VĀLMĪKI

Born: Ayodhya(?), India; fl. c. 500 B.C.E.
Died: India; fl. c. 500 B.C.E.

PRINCIPAL POETRY
Rāmāyaṇa, c. 500 B.C.E. (*The Ramayana*, 1870-1874)
Yoga Vāsiṣṭha, c. 500 B.C.E. (*The Supreme Yoga: A New Translation of the Yoga Vasistha*, 1976, two volumes)

OTHER LITERARY FORMS

Vālmīki (vol-MEE-kee) is not known for anything other than his poetry.

ACHIEVEMENTS

Indian tradition credits Vālmīki with having invented poetry. Particularly in the Punjab section of India, the Vālmīki sect of Hinduism worships him as divine and considers his writings to be scriptures; he is, at minimum, revered throughout the Indian community. *The Ramayana* has been extraordinarily popular for millennia, helping to establish cultural ideals. Its stories have been staples of Southeast Asian dance, drama, and painting. Adaptations of it in the major languages of Southeast Asia, such as Thailand's *Ramakien*, have themselves become influential classics. *Ramayan* (1987-1988), a television series based on *The Ramayana* and produced by Ramanand Sagar, was the most-watched series in Indian history. American adaptations of *The Ramayana* include Virgin Comics' *Ramayan 3392 a.d.* (2006), written by the best-selling author Deepak Chopra and the filmmaker Shekhar Kapur. *The Ramayana* has inspired video games, action figures, and such animated films as the Indo-Japanese anime *Ramayana: The Legend of Prince Rama* (1992). Among the classics of Yoga and Advaita Vedanta (monistic Hindu philosophy), Vālmīki's *The Supreme Yoga* is the longest and possibly the most prestigious.

BIOGRAPHY

According to one Hindu tradition, Vālmīki was an incarnate god who wrote in 867,000 B.C.E. Western scholarship argues that if a person named Vālmīki actually existed, he probably lived around 500 B.C.E. In the first century C.E., the Buddhist author Ashvagosha praised Vālmīki in a manner that establishes that some portion of *The Ramayana* had already been written. There are, however, many passages in *The Ramayana* that were composed in the very elaborate *kāvya* style, of which Ashvagosha's writings are the first known example. Therefore, the *kāvya* passages in *The Ramayana* most likely were composed in the first century C.E. or later. The standard version of *The Ramayana* states that Vālmīki is its author, although these attributions are made in sections written in third person that appear to be later additions and not written by Vālmīki himself. Similarly, in its standard version, *The Supreme Yoga* has a third-person account that attributes its writing to Vālmīki, but attempted reconstructions of the original text presume that it (and its use of characters from *The Ramayana*) come from the first century C.E. or later, when *The Ramayana* perhaps was adapted to changes in Indian religion and literary taste.

According to the *Adhyatma Rāmāyaṇa* (c. fourteenth century C.E.; *The Adhyatma Ramayana*, 1913), Vālmīki supported his family through highway robbery, but when his family members were asked whether they were willing to share his karmic sufferings for his sins, they declined. Shocked by this, Vālmīki sought salvation. Repeating the sacred syllables *ma* and *rā*, he remained immobile for years until termites formed a nest around him (the name Vālmīki being derived from the Sanskrit word for these insects). Eventually, he achieved a total reformation. Because *The Adhyatma Ramayana* emphasizes the divinity of Rāma (the protagonist of *The Ramayana*), it shows that even a thief can rise to holiness and eminence by repeating the name Rāma. However, devotees of Vālmīki, who see him as divine, consider this story slanderous.

The Ramayana begins with the sage Vālmīki complaining that the period in which he lives lacks an exemplar of morality. To contradict him, his companion Nārada (possibly a personification of the music associated with poetry) summarizes the story of Rāma. Subsequently, Vālmīki sees two cranes mating. A hunter kills the male of the pair, and Vālmīki curses the hunter. Vālmīki's words spontaneously assume a metric form—the first poem. The god Brahmā appears to Vālmīki and suggests that he compose an epic life of Rāma, following the meter of that curse. In the poem that Vālmīki then writes, however, he relates that he had already met Rāma and helped to raise the latter's twin sons. This contradiction—Vālmīki's apparent lack of knowledge about Rāma in the introductory section and his mention of an encounter with Rāma in the poem written after the crane's death—may indicate that these sections were written by different authors. Indeed, *The Ramayana*'s earliest written version may not have been the work of a single poet, but rather an accumulation of lines recited by oral bards over centuries.

Analysis

Underlying the poems ascribed to Vālmīki is the idea of poetry as magic. Verse began as Vālmīki's curse, which shortened the hunter's life. Both *The Ramayana* and *The Supreme Yoga* mention numerous effective spells. For example, both poems allude to a myth about the chief god Indra, who commits adultery with the wife of a holy man and is castrated by the man's words, then healed by another ritual. A major portion of the narratives in each of the poems concerns the characters' efficacious prayers, liturgies, chanting of mantras (magical words), and incantations. Near the conclusion of *The Ramayana*, the chief sacrifice (that of a horse) is part of a ceremony in which Rāma's two sons recite the entire Ramayana from memory—24,000 verses of thirty-two syllables each. The performance lasts for twenty-five days. The enormous length of the work suggests that memorizing (or even sitting through it all) involves an act of *tapas*: psychic energy obtained in altered states of consciousness induced, for example, by prolonged immobilization while magic words are spoken. The experience is associated even more closely with the supernatural, when Rāma and the rest of the audience hear their listening to it described in that epic and their future predicted. Vālmīki's style (in both poems) subtly contributes to this eeriness by depending less on detailed description than on metaphor. In classical Greek poetry, detail makes a narrated setting seem more solid and real, but Vālmīki's metaphors tend to compare the human world to mythological exemplars, increasing fantasy. Rāma's royal father, for example, is habitually likened to Indra, ruler of the gods.

THE RAMAYANA

Although shorter than the other great Indian epic (*Mahābhārata*, c. 400 B.C.E.-200 C.E.; *The Mahabharata*, 1834), *The Ramayana* may contain sections that predate it, if one judges by depiction of social customs. It has seven *kandas* (books), yet Western scholars tend to consider the first and last *kandas* to be later additions. The first book, for example, makes Rāma an incarnation of the god Vishnu—an identification not mentioned in the passages deemed oldest (since devotion to Vishnu grew in Hinduism).

The basic plot is a love story, albeit one that runs quite counter to modern Western notions of romance. Rāma wins his wife Sītā by drawing a great bow no one else can string, comparable to Odysseus in Homer's *Odyssey* (c. 725 B.C.E.; English translation, 1614). Whereas Odysseus's abilities, however, only slightly exaggerate human possibility, Rāma is a more extreme (and stranger) idealization, from his blue skin to his superhuman feats of strength, moving mountains and forests. His father, King Daśaratha, decides to abdicate in his favor, but owes two favors to Kaikeyī (one of the king's three queens). She insists that Rāma be banished and that her son, his half-brother Bharata, rule in his place for fourteen years. Daśaratha cannot take back the words he has spoken to Kaikeyī. While Rāma is in the forest, his father's old enemy, the demon king Rāvaṇa kidnaps Sītā. With the aid of the talking monkey Hanumān, Rāma rescues her, but false rumors that the demon seduced her cause her to prove her innocence through a trial by fire. The rumors, nonetheless, persist. Since, in this epic, words have a supernatural power that cannot be ignored, Rāma banishes her. She kills herself, and he is inconsolable.

Some Western interpretations have presumed that the story is an allegory of the conquest of India by Aryans, with Rāma personifying them, the monkeys being their racist depiction of southern Indians, and the demons being their equally racist portrait of Sri Lankans. In its present form, though, the allegory is less political than cultural, characterized by extreme stereotypes. Kaikeyī, being royal, would not have thought on her own of any scheme so evil as exiling Rāma, so she is persuaded by a hunchbacked maid. No clear motivation beyond the latter's being hunchbacked is needed. If her body is crooked, then she must be so in character, as Rāma's physically embodying the Indian ideal signifies his absolute virtue. In *The Ramayana*, evil tends to have a female origin, for example, the maid, or a female demon who arranges for Sītā's kidnapping, or Sītā's own complicity in it by greedily insisting that Rāma leave her to bring her a pet deer. This stereotyping, however, is consistent with a magical conception of language as embodying eternal archetypes—mythic patterns that give it power and conserve a static social structure.

THE SUPREME YOGA

For more than a decade, the Moksopaya Project Research Group led by Walter Slaje has been arguing that a brief Kashmir version of *The Supreme Yoga* is much closer to the original than the longer one, previously considered standard. Whereas the longer version is a series of parables told to Rāma to enlighten him, the shorter one (the *Moksopaya*) is a lecture delivered to an audience. Slaje's group tends to prefer the Kashmir version. Even if his historical argument is correct, however, one might praise the longer version as vastly enriched with stories within stories, connecting it to *The Ramayana* as well as to the growing worship of Vishnu.

Less sexist than *The Ramayana*, the longer *The Supreme Yoga* contains such charming tales as that of Queen Cūḍālā. Being enlightened herself, she tries to counsel her foolish husband against seeking enlightenment in the forest, when he could better attain it at home. While he is wasting his time in the wild, she rules. She visits him in male guise, eventually managing to enlighten him. He learns from her what each of the stories within *The Supreme Yoga* repeat: that the world is an illusion, the dream of the divine Brahman, the one reality. Suffering comes from having forgotten this primal unity. Enlightenment is best achieved by combining this knowledge with an active life rather than (like the foolish king) abandoning one's duties for *tapas* in the wilderness. This belief that Brahman alone exists is also the argument of those Hindu scriptures the Upanishads, some of which contain sections from the longer *The Supreme Yoga*. Ironically, if this doctrine is correct, then Vālmīki indeed is merely a fiction, since the whole world is.

BIBLIOGRAPHY

Bose, Mandakranta, ed. *"The Ramayana" Revisited.* New York: Oxford University Press, 2004. This collection of essays both documents and engages in many facets of the reinterpretation of *The Ramayana* throughout Southeast Asia, particularly concerning the epic's attitudes toward gender and caste.

Chatterjee, Asim Kuma. *A Historical Introduction to the Critical Edition of the Rāmāyaṇa.* Calcutta: Rajyashree Bhattacharya, 2007. This valuable supplement to the 1960-1973 critical edition not only examines the historical context of *The Ramayana*, but also the history of its influence.

Khan, Benjamin. *The Concept of Dharma in Valmiki Ramayana*. Delhi: Munshi Ram Manohar, 1965. In addition to its main subject (the epic's presentation of ethics), Khan also summarizes considerable scholarship on Vālmīki and the epic.

Leslie, Julia. *Authority and Meaning in Indian Religions: Hinduism and the Case of Valmiki*. Burlington, Vt.: Ashgate, 2003. Beginning with a twenty-first century controversy in the United Kingdom between Hindu worshipers of Vālmīki and Hindus criticizing him, Leslie searches for roots of the conflict through an analysis of works traditionally attributed to Vālmīki and their historical development.

Sena, Nabanītā Deba. *Alternative Interpretations of the Rāmāyaṇa: Views from Below*. New Delhi: Centre for Women's Development Studies, 2001. Part of the J. P. Naik Memorial Lecture Series, this volume exemplifies a feminist approach to *The Ramayana* in modern India.

Vālmīki. *The Rāmāyaṇa of Vālmīki*. 6 vols. Princeton, N.J.: Princeton University Press, 1990-2009. A multivolume translation of most of the epic. Contains background information, scholarly introductions, and copious notes. Translators and editors include R. P. Goldman, S. S. Goldman, R. Lefeber, S. I. Pollock, and B. A. van Nooten.

Yardi, M. R. *"The Rāmāyaṇa," Its Origin and Growth: A Statistical Study*. Poona, India: Bhandarkar Oriental Research Institute, 1994. This examination of changes in the writing style comes to similar (but slightly more conservative) conclusions than the consensus view of *The Ramayana*'s textural history. For example, Yardi considers part of the first book to have been written by someone other than the poet who wrote the epic's earliest version.

James Whitlark

JAPANESE POETRY TO 1800

The history of Japanese poetry begins indisputably with the eighth century anthology *Manyōshū* (mid-eighth century; *The Collections of Ten Thousand Leaves*; also as *The Ten Thousand Leaves*, pb. 1981, and as *The Manyoshu*, 1940) although the earlier historical chronicles *Kojiki* (c. 712 C.E.; *Records of Ancient Matters*, 1883) and *Nihon shoki* (c. 720; *Nihongi: Chronicles of Japan from the Earliest Times to A.D. 697*, 1896), as well as a few stone inscriptions, also preserve scattered early poems and sacred songs. The significance of *The Manyoshu* is manifold. As the most literal translation of its title, "collection of myriad leaves," suggests, it is a work of imposing bulk; containing more than 4,500 poems, it is by virtue of its age and size simply not to be ignored. Another interpretation of its title, "collection of (or for) myriad generations," hints at the importance accorded poetry in eighth century Japan.

THE MANYOSHU

The Manyoshu was assembled at a stage of Japanese cultural development roughly comparable to that of northern and western Europe at the close of the Dark Ages. In both cases, literacy was confined to very small groups, elite islands of advanced culture in a sea of what was by comparison barbarism. In the European case, literacy was a legacy of the Roman conquests, held in trust by the Roman Catholic Church until an ebbing in the tide of barbarian invasion allowed it to infiltrate secular courts. Literacy was in a sense indigenous, a skill that, from the viewpoint of the early Middle Ages, had been known (although not widely practiced) from time immemorial. The written word came to Japan, however, as the central monument of a flourishing, contemporary foreign civilization, embodied in the energetic culture of the Sui (581-618) and Tang (618-907) Dynasties. Chinese culture and the idea of literacy did not come with a conquering army but rather, it appears, by choice. The future imperial court, having consolidated its sway over competing tribal or regional groups, began in perhaps the fifth century to maintain what seems to have been fairly regular intercourse with China by way of the land route up the Korean peninsula. It was at this time, most agree, that written records began to be kept in Japan, but they were in Chinese, the work of Chinese and Korean scribes imported by the court.

The rich sophistication of Chinese culture in comparison with that of Japan, Korea, and Vietnam must have been almost absurdly evident to the first generations of Japanese who set themselves the task of learning Chinese and its complex writing system, through which medium the entirety of more than a thousand years of literary culture was suddenly visible in an undigested mass. In addition to the native Chinese classics, there was a huge body of Buddhist texts in Chinese to contemplate. By the end of the seventh century, however, the emerging Japanese state, headed by an aristocratic court, had accomplished much by way of assimilating the new culture. Governmental forms and court rites were modeled on Tang examples, and alongside the native animist religion, Shintō, Chinese Buddhism was officially established and encouraged, for the power of Tang in China—where Buddhism was enjoying a short-lived ascendancy—was thought to rest in part on the magical efficacy of Buddhist ritual. Under such circumstances, where political power was legitimized by Chinese precedent and the spiritual realm was increasingly dominated by a complex Indian faith that the Japanese could approach only in Chinese, the dominance of Chinese in the field of letters is no surprise. The true cause for wonder is that *The Manyoshu* testifies to a vigorous parallel tradition of sophisticated literary activity in Japanese—a tradition that was a century and more old by the time the collection was compiled.

The poetry of *The Manyoshu* dates largely from the first half of the eighth century, but a significant portion of it was composed in the preceding century, and a small number of verses seem to be authentic survivals, if perhaps retouched by later hands, from even earlier. The poetry of *The Manyoshu* and the history of the *Records of Ancient Matters* are written with Chinese characters, but because the Chinese ideographs are used for their phonetic values, these texts may be read as pure Japanese. However absorbed they may have been, therefore, in making Chinese culture their own, the Japanese were occupied as well with the difficult task of adapting the new tool of writing to record in their own language what they most valued in the native tradition, at a very early time in comparison with other East Asian societies.

The Manyoshu and the *Records of Ancient Matters* thus may be viewed as evidence of a persistent Japanese determination to maintain a significant degree of independence from foreign cultural influence, but their existence also ironically underlines the power of Chinese example, for poetry and historiography occupied the vital center of the Chinese literary canon as it reached the Japanese. These works can thus also be thought of as part of a broader enterprise on the part of the Japanese aristocracy to equip itself with all the trappings of a modern Asian state in the age of the Tang. That *The Manyoshu* exists at all is symbolic of the ambitions of the imperial court, an assertion of cultural equality with China, the emulation of which was not simply a matter of fashion but a conscious policy designed to enhance the power and dignity of the state.

It would be a mistake, however, to dismiss *The Manyoshu* as nothing more than an exercise in imitation, for it contains some of the most technically sophisticated, imaginative, and emotionally satisfying poetry in the entire Japanese canon. It does show a great deal of Chinese influence, as in its "songs of the East" and "songs of the border guards," the inclusion of which may echo one of the supposed functions of the *Shijing* (traditionally fifth century B.C.E.; *The Book of Songs*, 1937), the oldest Chinese anthology of verse—namely, the gathering of intelligence about the temper of the people of the realm. More broadly, the poetry in *The Manyoshu* in general is strongly colored by Chinese poetic practice, and some individual verses can be shown to have been based on specific Chinese sources. Nevertheless, this is genuinely Japanese poetry in its language and special emphases. *The Manyoshu* is also an anthology that can give considerable pleasure to modern readers, for its poets possess, to a surprising degree, individuality of voice.

KAKINOMOTO HITOMARO

Manyoshu poet Kakinomoto Hitomaro (fl. 680-700) is usually accorded primacy of place as the earliest master of poetry in Japanese. He wrote in both of the dominant verse forms of the period, the *tanka*, or short poem, and *chōka*, or long poem. The *tanka* was short indeed, fixed at a length of thirty-one syllables which were distributed in five lines or, more properly, in units of five, seven, five, seven, and seven syllables. This would become the standard form of Japanese poetry in succeeding centuries—so dominant, in fact, that another name for it would be *waka*, simply "Japanese verse," as opposed to *kanshi*, Japanese poetry written in the Chinese language. The *chōka*, despite its name, was long only in comparison with the *tanka*; the longest example in *The Manyoshu* occupies only four pages in an English translation with generous margins, hardly an extended composition by the standards of other literary cultures. The *chōka* was of indeterminate length, a formally simple sequence of alternating five- and seven-syllable phrases ending in a couplet of seven-syllable lines. The *chōka* was usually followed by one or more verses in standard *tanka* form that were called *hanka* (envois or responses). Hitomaro originated neither of these forms, but his consummate mastery of both helped to establish them at the core of the Japanese poetic tradition.

Rhyme schemes and metrical feet play no part in the formal apparatus of Hitomaro's poetry, for they are simply meaningless in Japanese. Rhyme is more or less trivial, because every syllable in Japanese ends in a vowel or *n*, and there are only five vowels in the language, meaning that rhyme occurs randomly and frequently without poetic intercession. All syllables in Japanese are stressed so nearly equally that metric patterns based on alternation of stress are impossible. Nor does assonance or alliteration play any role in the formal rules of composition, again because of the simplicity of the sound system. Thus the prominence of syllable count in Japanese poetic structure: It is virtually all that is left by way of effects based on sound alone. Why units of five and seven syllables have proved so congenial to Japanese poets is unknown, but Hitomaro's importance lies in part in his success in demonstrating the ample sufficiency of this simple scheme, which has prevailed until the present alongside blank-verse forms introduced in the nineteenth century. In Hitomaro's verse, these small building blocks are built into phrases and sentences of great length and complexity; some entire *chōka* can be construed as consisting grammatically of single extended sentences with a complicated structure of parallel independent and dependent clauses rolling forward in rhythmic cadence to a final predication in the concluding couplet. Hitomaro showed the way for later poets, developing in both the expansive *chōka* and the terse *tanka* an armory of techniques to bridge the natural pauses at the end of metric units with the momentum of syntax or imagistic association.

Little is known of Hitomaro's life, but it appears that he may have functioned at least quasi-officially as a poet laureate, for many of his poems were occasioned by events important in the life of the court or nation—elegies on the death or interment of royal personages, for example, and celebrations of more auspicious events. These public poems are suffused with a sense of the awesome, even divine dignity of the sovereign and his or her (women could still occupy the throne in Hitomaro's day) immediate family. This sense of immanent divinity extended to the land itself. Place-names, for example, figure prominently in Hitomaro's poetry, recalling other *Manyoshu* poems that are actually attributed to emperors themselves, rulers of generations even earlier than that of Hitomaro, whose compositions seem sometimes to be little more than ritual incantations of the names of the mountains and plains of Yamato, the region south of modern Kyoto from which the imperial clan ruled early Japan. Hitomaro reinforced this invocation of place-names, originally no doubt a way of claiming hegemony by "naming" the bounds and features of the realm, through the use of *makurakotoba* (pillow words), which were either epithets traditionally coupled with certain place-names (or other parts of speech) or similar attributive phrases coined by Hitomaro himself on traditional models. Thus, epithets such as "Izumo of the eight-fold clouds," "Yamato which fills the skies," and "Sanuki of gemlike seagrass" make the earthly landscape glow with hints of the heavenly connections of high places and the mysteries of the depths. Such poems have as their purpose the exaltation of imperial rule, but they succeed as art because of Hitomaro's mastery of language and a particular gift for personalizing verse on even the most public occasions by relating them to the individualizd human emotions they evoke in their participants.

The elegance and grandeur of Hitomaro's public commemorations are complemented in a body of highly personal verse of great emotional power, the most impressive of which is a sequence of *chōka* laments honoring his love for his wife (or wives—his biography is unclear) at partings in this life and at the final, awful parting of death. These poems share with his public verse a nice manipulation of *makurakotoba* epithets (such as "seagrass-lithe and bending girl"), which serve here not to add mythic significance to the landscape, but rather to relate the emotional substance of the poem to the phenomena of the natural world, a technique that gives this poetry a universality that transcends its intimate particularity.

The balance of majesty and individuality in Hitomaro's poetry moves both his public and nominally private verse toward a tonal middle ground precisely suited to poems composed for public recitation—which, authorities agree, was probably their original mode of presentation. Hitomaro was not, however, the last bard of a preliterate tradition, despite his use of the *makurakotoba* technique, which is obviously related to similar phenomena in indisputably oral traditions. The public recitation of poetry would continue to be a formal part of court life for centuries, making that aspect of his practice doubtful proof that Hitomaro was a late survivor of a diminished breed of oral poets. There is, moreover, substantial evidence of Chinese influence in Hitomaro's choice of imagery and subject matter and in the strong parallelism that structures his longer pieces. Finally, there is in his verse an idealization of a simpler past close to nature that can best be called pastoralism, clearly the product of a poet who still had access to the oral past but could speak in a complex and sophisticated voice trained in the methods and attitudes of a foreign, written literature.

OTHER EARLY POETS

Poets of the generation immediately following Hitomaro's wrote in an idiom even more clearly shaped by contact with Chinese poetry. Yamanoe Okura (c. 660-733), for example, is represented in *The Manyoshu* by a group of *chōka* on such subjects as poverty, destitution, and old age that can be read almost as a translated pastiche of Chinese poetic statements on the same themes, although his masterly use of Japanese has made them an admired (if rarely emulated) part of the native canon. Ōtomo Tabito (665-731), a close associate of Okura, left a series of *tanka* on the virtues of rice wine in which his adopted persona, that of the talented literary bureaucrat languishing in an enforced retirement, is as Chinese as anything by Okura, though Tabito's poetry is in a Japanese quite free of Chinese linguistic influence and in a form quintessentially Japanese. Both men were members of what was probably one of the earliest generations thoroughly at home in the world of Chinese letters, and their poetry may be read both as an homage to Chinese verse and as an intelligent experiment with expanding the range of Japanese poetic expression. They represent an extreme, however, for few later poets went as far as they did toward a Sinification of Japanese poetry, perhaps because the pessimism and intellectuality of their verse was believed to be simply too Chinese, too much a violation of the sunnier precedents of Japanese poetry.

Tabito's son, Ōtomo Yakamochi (718-785), may safely be called the most important and influential of the final generation of *Manyoshu* poets, both because of the quality of his verse and because he appears to have taken the leading role in the compilation of the anthology itself. Yakamochi's poetry marks him genuinely as a transitional figure. He is among the last masters of the *chōka*, which seems to have fallen from fashion rather soon after *The Manyoshu* was put together; at the same time, his work foreshadows what would become the dominant traditions of Japanese poetry for centuries to come.

There is a strong element of nostalgia in Yakamochi's poetry, most especially a longing for a glorious martial past, because the Ōtomo were a warrior clan. Later poets would not focus on this particular past—too redolent of violence for courtly tastes—preferring a more generalized evocation of antique timelessness; still, the stance toward the present, which is somehow drab, pedestrian, and ephemeral, is much the same as Yakamochi's, and quite different from Hitomaro's pastoralism. In Yakamochi's time, too, poetry moves indoors, or at least into the urban nobleman's garden; gone are the grand vistas of mountain and plain, replaced by the singularities of garden plantings viewed close up over a balcony rail. Here Yakamochi was following one strand of Chinese verse, but he was also writing poetry germane to his time and place, since his was the first poetic generation to know the distinctive qualities of settled urban life; until 710, when a permanent capital city modeled on the Chinese metropolis was laid out on the site of modern Nara, the capital of Japan was wherever the emperor's court happened to be, and the court was mobile, for in accordance with Shintō belief, death rendered the sovereign's palace irremediably unclean, unfit for the sacral duties of the throne.

Kokinshū

The next great landmark in Japanese poetry after *The Manyoshu* is another anthology, the *Kokinshū* (905; *Kokinshu: A Collection of Poems Ancient and Modern*, 1984), which is dated to 905 by its introduction. The *Kokinshu* marks the maturation of a tradition that has become known in English as court poetry. It is significant that it is once again an anthology that Japanese literary historiography singles out as important rather than, say, the achievements of a single poet or innovative poetic school, and doubly significant that this collection should bear the title it does—together these facts attest a conception of poetry as a collective cultural endeavor to which tradition and precedent are as important as innovation. Important also is the fact that the *Kokinshu* was an imperially commissioned collection, the first in a series of twenty-one that would appear at irregular intervals until 1433, and thus an early symbolic declaration of how important a part of court life poetry was and would be thereafter.

The scope and variety of the poetry of the *Kokinshu* are much constricted in comparison with *The Manyoshu*. The collection is smaller—it contains only some eleven hundred poems—and the overwhelming majority of the verses in it are *tanka*. There is little doubt, moreover, that this was a highly selective anthology. The *Kokinshu* was not meant as a representative sampler of the best of Japanese poetry, but rather, it appears, as a normative guide to what its compilers thought poetry should be. Principal among the compilers was Ki no Tsurayuki (884-946), whose introduction to the collection, the earliest extant piece of literary criticism in Japanese, would stand for centuries as the definitive statement of the proper concerns of the poet. Tsurayuki's most famous dictum is his metaphoric definition of Japanese poetry, which "takes as its seed the heart of man, and flourishes in the countless leaves of words." Emotion and its direct expression, he is saying, are what poetry is all about; in short, lyricism is at the core of Japanese poetry, and from Tsurayuki forward it would not be displaced. The classical Japanese canon would simply never admit the more expansive and multidimensional allegories, ballads, epics, and poetical discourses on religion, philosophy, and even politics that constitute so much of the high classical tradition of Western verse.

The *Kokinshu* is for the most part arranged topically, grouping together in the first books of the collection, for example, poems with seasonal subjects, season by season. Within each of these books, the poems are arranged roughly according to the order in which their dominant natural images occur as the seasons progress, so that in the first spring book, the flowering plum precedes the cherry. Love poems are arranged in like manner, to echo in the aggregate the pattern of a love affair, from initial infatuation through tentative courtship and passion to the inevitable abandonment. Not all topics allow this kind of mimetic organization—the books of celebratory poems, poems on parting, and poems based on wordplay are instances—but nowhere do Tsurayuki and his colleagues seem to have in mind the usual literary-historical objectives of Western anthologizers, grouping poems by author or in some way chronologically, to show stylistic changes over time.

The *Kokinshu*, it appears, was assembled not as a work of scholarship or preservation, but rather for the use of practicing poets, to whose needs its finely tuned topical organization was ideally suited. Despite Tsurayuki's insistence that poetry be an expression in "the leaves of words" of the movements of the heart, all the evidence—fiction, diaries, annotations to private and official anthologies—argues that poets in the age of the *Kokinshu* composed for specific occasions, not when seized by a lyric impulse. In this context, the *Kokinshu* and subsequent anthologies look very much like handbooks that were assembled as authoritative guides to the sort of poetry sanctioned by tradition and contemporary taste as appropriate to any number of clearly defined circumstances. As works such as the eleventh century novel *Genji monogatari* (c. 1004; *The Tale of Genji*, 1925-1933) illustrate so well, court poetry was a social art practiced either in full public view—at poetry contests, on flower-viewing expeditions, at banquets—or, if in private, as a form of communication between friends or lovers; any courtier or lady of the court with pretensions to social grace had to be ready to produce passable verse whenever called upon. The *Kokinshu* and other anthologies were organized to allow quick consultation for an appropriate model or for a poem that could be alluded to in one's own composition.

Within the narrowed confines of the poetry of the *Kokinshu*, there is still much to be admired, for its special province, the human heart, is after all not an easily exhausted subject. Poetry of love and courtship is not surprisingly one of the long suits of the collection. Particularly engaging is the work of such ninth century poets as Ariwara no Narihira (825-880), a courtier who quickly became a model of the ideal courtly lover, and the court lady Ono no Komachi (834-880), whose passionate verse threatened to escape the bounds of seemly reserve that most other poets were at pains to observe. Narihira's is a poetry of great wit and elegance, but it is colored also by a much-admired Buddhist awareness of the inconstancy of the temporal world and the deceptiveness of the emotions. Komachi, on the other hand, is a very subjective poet whose immersion in her own sometimes violent emotional states cost her admirers in a world that valued the

163

pose, at least, of detachment more than direct cries from the heart. She and Narihira stand at the head of a long line of poets, male and female, whose *Kokinshu* verses established love poetry as one of the honored genres of court poetry.

By the time the *Kokinshu* was compiled, Buddhism had become a powerful force in shaping the Japanese poetic sensibility, which it entered indirectly through the influence of Chinese verse and directly as it became more and more a part of Japanese life. It did not, however, result in the development of an explicitly religious or devotional poetry. Rather, it provided a fundamental point of view for the poet in its insistence on a radical conception of phenomenal reality as a slippery, ever-changing flux given an illusory substance and stability by fallible human perception and rationalization. Impermanence and the unreliability of subjective observation are seldom spoken of explicitly in *Kokinshu* verse, which like all premodern Japanese poetry shies away from abstract nouns and overt philosophizing, but an acceptance of them as fundamental truths underlies much of the literature of the time.

There is a dark quality of resignation in the Buddhist conception of human experience that seems to be at odds with the more life-affirming, unreflective vision of humans and their world that characterizes Shintō animism, but in fact court poetry frequently manages a resolution of the conflict by finding a paradoxical comfort in the wholly reliable way the natural world eternally reaffirms the truth of universal flux; nature continues to be invested with meaning, but the meaning changes. Viewed in this way, nature is a rich repository of metaphor directly relevant to the human condition, which is why natural imagery comes to play such a large role in the lyric poetry of the Japanese court, particularly imagery that underlines change as a constant in nature and in human affairs. The beauty of spring blossoms is less interesting to the poet than the fact that they will fall or that fallible human eyes mistake them for a late spring snow.

Several techniques peculiar to Japanese poetry were exploited to their fullest for the first time by *Kokinshu* poets. The first is the *kakekotoba*, or pivot word, which takes advantage of both the special features of Japanese syntax and the existence in the language of a large number of homophones in what amounts to a highly refined form of wordplay. In the phrase *ko no me no haru ni*, for example, the word *haru* carries two distinct meanings. As a verb, it means "to swell," and with *ko no me*, "tree buds," and the subject-marking particle *no*, it produces the phrase, "tree buds swell." As a noun, however, *haru* means "spring," the season, and with the locative *ni* it makes an adverb of time, "in spring." Here, *haru* is therefore a *kakekotoba*, a word that "pivots" between two overlapping phrases that together mean something like, "in spring, when tree buds swell." The effect in Japanese is far less contrived than it would be in English, as in a phrase such as "in the grass spring blossoms forth," where "spring" and "blossoms" could be called pivot words of an awkward sort. In the Japanese example, as in the English, the *kakekotoba* consists of two superimposed homophones of different meaning and grammatical function. In other cases, the meaning of the pivot word is unchanged, but its syntactic function is different in the two phrases it links. In practiced hands, the *kakekotoba* technique—whose compact "punch" can almost never be translated adequately—is an effective method not only of adding a few precious syllables of meaning to the *tanka*, but also of greatly enriching the texture of a poem by involving the reader (or listener) in unraveling its overlapping meanings and functions.

A second device frequently exploited by *Kokinshu* poets is the *jokotoba* or *joshi*, a "preface" of one or more lines that forms part of the poem proper but is not directly related to its primary statement, to which it is most often linked by a pivot word. The *jokotoba* preface is similar to the *makurakotoba* epithet, but it is more complex, usually longer, rarely conventional, and more likely to be used consciously by the poet to establish a metaphoric relationship between two otherwise unrelated images. The *jokotoba* virtually disappears in translation, where it becomes simply a simile or metaphor, but it is a distinctive feature of classical *tanka* in Japanese.

A third technique polished in the *Kokinshu* and often used in conjunction with both *jokotoba* and *kakekotoba* to enrich the *tanka* is *engo* (related words). The *engo* technique is a refinement of diction in which the poet chooses his or her words in such a way that they both carry the intended meaning of the poem and at the same time relate to one other semantically or by sound alone in ways quite unrelated to the primary content of the poem. "Giving her a frosty glance, he leaves; from crimsoned lips fall raging storms of words" will have to serve as an English illustration of the principle of *engo*. The Japanese classical poet would recognize two parallel statements here—a surface description of an angry lovers' parting and an embedded evocation of late autumn in the sequence of related words: frosty-leaves-crimsoned-fall-raging-storms. Once again, the English example is labored because the technique is alien, but the conception is not inappropriate, since autumn in Japanese poetry is the season to reflect on the transience of life and love. In its native environment, when the *engo* technique is used in conjunction with other devices, the result is poetry of great complexity that can carry two or more serious messages simultaneously—no small feat in the compass of thirty-one syllables.

These techniques clearly functioned to allow far more to be said in the scant confines of a *tanka* than would otherwise have been the case, and it is probably no accident that they came into use at a time when the conventions of the form were becoming ever more clearly defined and restrictive. As previously noted, certain sorts of discourse and subject matter were felt to be more properly the province of Chinese poetry than Japanese, but diction itself was regulated as well. Loan words from Chinese, for example, were out of bounds to the *tanka* poet, even though by the time of the *Kokinshu* they had begun to enter everyday language in considerable numbers; no doubt they were prohibited in part because of their phonetic inelegance, but there may well have been an element of linguistic chauvinism at work as well. In any case, from the *Kokinshu* forward, poetic language would necessarily move further and further from the spoken language, which continued quite naturally to assimilate a great deal of Chinese vocabulary.

Perhaps even more important, the poetic consensus seems to have been that entire categories of imagery and native Japanese vocabulary were simply unpoetical. Bodily functions, for example, are almost entirely absent from classical Japanese poetry, even as metaphor—no poet would seriously "drink in" the beauty of a landscape or even "breathe" the fragrance of a blossom, much less "hunger" for a lover's "touch." Given the strong Buddhist influence in poetry of the classical period, it is perhaps a little surprising that even birth and death and any words clearly associated with them have no place, except by the most oblique sort of reference. This particular taboo probably had something to do with the preoccupation of Shintō ritual with cleanliness and purification, but more generally, it appears that there was an unspoken agreement among poets that poetic language simply did not admit of reference to the grosser stuff of human existence, not out of prudery but rather in the spirit of what is best called courtliness, a set of attitudes that valued above all else stylization, refinement, restraint, cultivation, and a disdain for the pedestrian and coarse in all aspects of behavior.

Shinkokinshū

The courtly pose could and did sometimes result in a facile and shallow poetry in a world where versification was widely practiced as a social art, but it is a tribute to the high seriousness of purpose of the court poets that it did not produce, on the whole, a mannered and precious body of poetry. In the centuries following the appearance of the *Kokinshu*, the ever-growing canon of court verse took on the status almost of secular scripture, a collaborative text to be elaborated by each succeeding generation of poets. The culmination of this process is aptly symbolized in another great anthology, the *Shinkokinshū* (new *Kokinshu*), which appeared as the eighth in the series of imperial collections about 1206. The title was more than a token homage to the *Kokinshu*: It was a declaration affirming the primacy of tradition in the world of court poetry. The intervening anthologies had all, in a general way, taken the *Kokinshu* as their model of organization, but the *Shinkokinshū* makes constant reference to the earlier collection in ways alternately explicit and extremely subtle.

To explain the complex relationship between the "new *Kokinshu*" and its antecedent requires an acquaintance with the poetic technique known as *honkadori*—literally, "taking from a source verse," or incorporating into a new verse recognizable elements of an older poem in the canon. *Honkadori* is nothing more than a specialized variety of allusion requiring a clear quotation from an earlier poem, but that does not begin to explain its significance, for in many ways it is a key to understanding how poetry developed after the *Kokinshu*.

First, *honkadori* gave the poet another escape route from the confines of the classical *tanka*. The canon of "quotable" poetry was relatively manageable, being limited to the imperial anthologies and a small number of widely circulated private collections and prose works, such as *The Tale of Genji*, that contained poetry; this meant that in the elite subculture of the court, a poet could be confident of having an audience that would recognize his allusions. A poem using a *honkadori* allusion, therefore, expanded in the minds of its readers or listeners to include the entirety of the excerpted source poem. Thus, for example, a *Shinkokinshū* verse describing the desolation of a deserted village in autumn gains significant depth because the village, identified by name, is described with words borrowed from a pair of *Kokinshu* love poems, set in the same place, which dwelt on the sorrows of parting.

Beyond their effects within individual poems, *honkadori* allusions had a second important role to play in court poetry—namely, their function in tying new poems into an expanding canon that was not merely an accumulation of successively newer strata of poetry, but a complex fabric of allusion, cross-reference, and echo that worked continuously to revivify old poems while at the same time adding depth and the authority of tradition to new ones. The process was supported by the remarkable conservatism of poetic language, which came to be defined as the language of the *Kokinshu*. Because the language of the new poems was essentially of the same age as that of the source poems, it was possible to weave words and phrases from poems centuries old into original compositions with virtually no seams showing. The difficulty of composing poetry in antique language was mitigated for the poets of the *Shinkokinshū* and later periods by their intense absorption in the poetic canon, whose language became a natural mode of expression, neither dead nor artificial.

The loyalty of the compilers of the *Shinkokinshū* to the idea of precedent in poetry is most strikingly revealed at a number of places in the collection where entire sequences of poems, a dozen or more at a time, are selected and arranged so that they allude individually and collectively to precisely parallel sequences in the *Kokinshu*. Such feats of creative editorship required not only erudition and artistic sensitivity but also painstaking care on the part of the poets who assembled the anthology, a group led by Fujiwara Teika (1162-1241) under the active, involved sponsorship of the retired poet-emperor Gotoba (1180-1239). At a distance of eight centuries, it is possible only to speculate about what motivated such labors. One cause may have been simply the sheer intellectual and aesthetic pleasure of this complex interplay of old and new, a pleasure denied the modern reader but no doubt quite unaffected among poets to whom the *Kokinshu* was an old friend and who were thoroughly accustomed to the effects of *honkadori*. Their purpose may have been also in part didactic, insofar as the elaborate juxtaposition of modern poems to their *Kokinshu* analogues illustrated what was meant by the contemporary injunction to "old words, new heart" in the writing of poetry—that is, to compositions that obeyed the iron rules of diction but were informed by contemporary sensibilities that saved them from a sterile antiquarianism.

The "new heart" of *Shinkokinshū* poetry is often defined with reference to an elusive aesthetic concept known as *yūgen*, whose definitions include allusiveness, evocativeness, "dark mystery," "mysterious vagueness," "mysterious depth," and even, simply, "elegance." A poem embodying *yūgen* points to a world beyond words whose outlines a true artist can evoke in the inner eye of his or her audience. *Yūgen* is in a way a specialized instance of the more general Buddhist philosophical preoccupation with the problematic relationship between perception and reality. The primary concern of the poet remained the authentic expression of emotion, but the true poet was moved by what a refined sensibility could see behind superficial reality—not by beauty, but by its transience, not by love, but by the inevitability of its loss. The characteristic mood of the *Shinkokinshū* is therefore emphatically not a sunny one but rather thoughtful and somber. That it is so clearly defined is remarkable, for this is a poetry that leaves much unspoken, the truths with which it concerns itself being of a sort that cannot be explained directly in the limited vocabulary of the court poet, from which all of the immense Chinese philosophical lexicon was banned. *Shinkokinshū* poets relied instead on highly concrete language and objective description devised to evoke in the reader, without intermediation, the same subtle vision that inspired the poetic act in the first place.

The tendency of *Shinkokinshū* poetry to reveal its "heart," its real meaning, not in its words but rather in the spaces between them, as it were, or in the history behind them, bespeaks a highly sophisticated understanding that "poetry" is not merely words on a page but the result of a very complex interactive process involving poet, ideas, words, and the reader. That this understanding was not subliminal but fully conscious is borne out by the evidence of modern Japanese scholarship.

As noted above, the *Shinkokinshū* closely follows the lead of the *Kokinshu* in its organization. Like the *Kokinshu*, the *Shinkokinshū* arranges poems so that they mimic natural progressions in the real world, be they those of the seasons or that of a love affair. Konishi Jin'ichi and other scholars have discovered that such sequences in the later collection were also ordered, however, in accordance with certain rules quite independent of the natural progressions they follow. Specifically, each poem in a sequence seems to have been chosen not only to forward the movement in question but also with a clear awareness of how it "fit" with the poems before and after it. Each successive, overlapping pair of verses must therefore be in harmony, sharing a common or closely similar tone, image, or point of view. A sequence of early-spring poems might thus begin with a verse containing the image of scattered patches of snow in a garden where flowering plums have begun to bloom; the next verse might then mention water trickling out from under melting snow, to be followed in its turn by one describing a swollen hillside freshet; the scene might then shift to a mountain village still snowbound but wreathed in wisps of springlike haze.

The reader supplies continuity to such a series by sensing, perhaps not always even consciously, that there is a logic operating in multiple dimensions here which makes for a natural movement from poem to poem. The location, for example, gradually shifts upward in space from garden to hillside (linked by the common image or implied image of melting snow) to mountain village, while at the same time the successive scenes are rendered from an increasingly distant point of view. The mood changes from the domesticity of a garden to the daunting isolation of the mountains, but the changes come slowly and naturally, thanks to the intervening verses. The sequence in effect reverses the natural progress of spring by beginning with blossoms and ending with a snowbound village, but the geographical shift up into the mountains explains the retrogression, which itself has the secondary effect of reaffirming the larger framework of early spring, always a time of false starts and late snows.

How aware any given reader might have been of this complex manipulation of images and associations is problematic, but it seems quite undeniable that the compilers themselves were fully conscious of the effects they created. Nothing else can really account for what is otherwise a puzzling randomness in the order of the verses when they are considered from the point of view of age or authorship, or for the inclusion of a surprising number of verses that by any standard are not the best the age produced, but that turn out to be precisely what is needed to effect transitions between pairs of clearly superior poems which carry associations that would otherwise clash or at least not dovetail neatly.

Haiku and renga

While the *Shinkokinshū* marks a high point in the classical poetic tradition, it by no means marks its end, which in a sense has come only in the past century with the decay of the custom of rote memorization of the poetic canon (or at least large parts of it)—a custom that was integral both to the appreciation and to the practice of court poetry. Indeed, until the first decades of the twentieth century, *tanka* in the court style, still subject to the ancient rules of diction and style, were a natural part of the repertoire of the literary-minded elite, and they are still far more a part of the popular conception of what poetry is than any specific poetic form of comparable age in the West.

This survival is all the more remarkable in view of the fact that the classical tradition itself engendered an entirely new world of poetic practice as early as the fifteenth century, culminating in the haiku, the only form of Japanese poetry generally known in the West and the only serious challenge in Japanese literary history to the preeminence of *tanka*. The seventeen-syllable haiku is a direct descendant of a form of poetry known as *renga* (linked verse), which in its origins was both an elaboration of and a challenge to the attitudes that shaped the poetry of the *Shinkokinshū* and the late classical age.

Renga developed originally as a pastime among court poets, a formalization of poetic games that included "verse-capping," in which contestants had to supply the second half—the seven/seven-syllable "lower verse"—of either a well-known *tanka* or an opponent's original composition, and *utaawase* poetry competitions, in which teams of poets publicly composed poems on a series of set themes. The term *renga* refers specifically to a sequence of alternating five/seven/five- and seven/seven-syllable units, each verse except the first being written in response to the verse preceding it. Each pair of verses, written by two different poets, was expected to be able to stand alone as a coherent *tanka*, even though every second pair necessarily inverted the upper and lower verses of the standard *tanka* form. The resulting chain, usually of thirty-six or one hundred links, was in effect a single poetic composition by multiple authors (most commonly three) who took turns supplying each successive verse. There was, however, no requirement that the *renga* sequence be restricted to a single theme. In fact, as it developed, one of the requirements of *renga* was that the subject matter of the verses in a sequence be varied to include as many of the traditional topics—seasons, love, grievance, and so on—as possible. There was therefore no overall unity to a *renga* chain, only the serial unity within each overlapping pair of verses. That late-classical poetics favored concrete imagery and objectivity aided the *renga* poet, because verses with those qualities were subject to multiple interpretations. A verse centering on the image "dew at daybreak," for example, could function nicely as a companion to a spring poem before it, and equally well as a lead-in to a verse describing a lover stealing away after a nighttime tryst.

Renga began as a light entertainment but soon began to be taken seriously as a poetic form of great potential. By the fifteenth century, two varieties of *renga* were being practiced, a light or comic form labeled *mushin* (frivolous, or lacking heart) and a serious form called *ushin*. In the hands of its most accomplished practitioners, such as the poet-priest Sōgi (1421-1502), serious *ushin renga* became what some regard as the supreme achievement of Japanese classical poetry. *Renga* was not, however, a form of poetry whose practice or appreciation could ever be widespread, since it required skills and erudition not to be found outside a small population of dedicated practitioners. As an outgrowth of classical *tanka*, serious *renga* conformed to all the rules of the court tradition within its constituent verses; in addition, it developed a detailed, elaborate set of conventions governing the poetics of the sequence as a whole.

A typical *renga* chain shares a number of characteristics with the carefully constructed *Shinkokinshū* sequences described above, but there are also major differences. In both cases, adjacent verses are linked on any of several levels—imagery, subject, point of view, and so on; *renga* sequences also often contain very complex links formed on the basis of *honkadori* in which a source poem called to mind by an allusion in one verse supplies materials that inspire the next. Both kinds of sequence depend for their coherence on manipulation not only of poetic materials but also of the actual experience of reading or hearing each verse as it is added to the chain, for it is the totality of all the associations a verse evokes in the mind's eye with which the compiler or poet works in building links from verse to verse.

The *renga* chain differs fundamentally from *Shinkokinshū* precedents, however, in two vital ways. First, it is an original composition, not compiled from existing materials; second, there is no external framework corresponding to the progression of a season or a love affair as is seen in the *Shinkokinshū*. The formal rules of *renga* composition no doubt developed as a strategy for averting the shapelessness that these characteristics made likely. The rules sometimes seem to have been needlessly minute and almost arbitrary in their specifications—as of exactly which verses in a sequence could and must contain the word "moon"—but their effect was to establish a tension between imagination and tight control that in the best surviving sequences results in a very pleasing rhythm of excitement and relaxation as the poets deal, verse by verse, with the difficulty of submitting inspiration and free association to discipline.

The sheer difficulty of serious *renga* made it the province of a small elite of professional poets, often Buddhist priests or laymen who adopted a priestly lifestyle to free themselves of ordinary social concerns. *Renga* poets were no longer courtiers for whom poetry was a polite art, but full-time artists who subsisted either on inherited means or the largesse of patrons. The imperial court itself, for so long the locus of poetic activity, had ceased to be an institution of any but symbolic political significance by the time *renga* became an important poetic mode. Patronage had therefore passed into the hands of a new class, the military leaders who gradually assumed control of the country as power slipped away from the court, beginning as early as the twelfth century. The old court culture enjoyed a brief resuscitation under the hereditary military dictators or shoguns of the Ashikaga clan, whose power base was the old imperial capital of Kyoto, but by the first decades of the fifteenth century, real power began to pass into the hands of local magnates known as *daimyō* or "great names," petty warlords who maintained their own courts and, as their means permitted and their tastes inclined them, extended patronage to poets and other artists. The stable, refined world that had nurtured the genteel ideal of the courtly poet, however, was gone forever. It is little wonder that the *renga* poets, men of immense learning and sensitivity surrounded by people who in an earlier age would have been thought unimaginably coarse, produced a poetry whose predominant moods were melancholy and nostalgia.

Sixteenth and seventeenth centuries

The sixteenth century brought change and upheaval on a scale that had not been seen since the earliest years of imperial expansion and the importation of Chinese culture nearly a thousand years before. Civil war touched all corners of the country, its destructiveness magnified by the use of firearms, which were introduced by Portuguese traders when they reached Japan in the middle of the century. Except in this one respect, the West would not have a profound effect upon Japan for another three centuries, but until Japan was officially cut off almost completely from foreign contacts in the seventeenth century, a small but steady stream of Portuguese, Spanish, Dutch, and English missionaries and traders destroyed forever the complacent Japanese view of civilization as something coterminous with the self-contained Chinese cultural sphere. The nearly total collapse of the old order—one famous story has a sixteenth century emperor peddling samples of his calligraphy to make ends meet—raised men to power who had only the most tenuous of connections with the courtly values of the past, and it was inevitable that when peace finally came again at the end of the century, the art of poetry would emerge no less profoundly changed than any other sphere of Japanese life.

The year 1600 (or, by some reckonings, 1603) marks the beginning of a dynamic new era known to Japanese historians either as the Tokugawa period, after the dynasty of shoguns founded by Tokugawa Ieyasu, or the Edo period, after the city that was the seat of Tokugawa rule, modern Tokyo. Through a combination of political negotiation and brute force, Ieyasu brought the civil wars to an end after more than a century, and peace was soon followed by unprecedented prosperity. The democratization of formerly elite kinds of artistic endeavor that this new prosperity fostered would prove to be the most dramatic cultural development of the new era.

The activities of Matsunaga Teitoku (1571-1653) illustrate how profoundly poetry in particular was affected by these changes in the larger cultural environment. Teitoku was trained in the ancient traditions of classical *tanka*, which by his day were treated as a hermetic body of secret lore by the remaining court poets in Kyoto. He shared with his teachers the Confucian attitude that the practice of literature was an essential element in the cultivation of moral rectitude, but he saw that literature could never be accessible to the greater mass of the population, among whom literacy was spreading rapidly, if it continued to be treated as the private property of a hereditary poetic priesthood. He therefore undertook a career as a popularizer, giving public lectures on the classics in direct defiance of his mentors and—most important for the development of Japanese poetry—promoting a new style of linked verse that met what he believed were the needs of the time for a form of literature that could be practiced by the educated common man but that at the same time was not vulgar. Teitoku's chosen vehicle of literary instruction was *haikai*, more formally *haikai no renga*, or "comic *renga*," a descendant of the *mushin* mode in linked verse.

Before Teitoku, *haikai* was most decidedly a comic poetry of dubious morals. Its humor came in part from wordplay, parody, scatology, and other obvious comic effects, but also in considerable measure from the deliberate violation of the rules of serious *renga*, particularly those regarding diction—there was humor, for example, in the mere presence of as innocent a word as "nose" in a verse that otherwise followed thousand-year-old conventions of decorum. Teitoku lamented the unabashed vulgarity of *haikai* but recognized certain virtues in it. The proficient *haikai* poet still honored, if in a backhanded way, the principle that poetry was a matter of precedent and convention, without which much of the humor of *haikai* was meaningless, and *haikai* also admitted the use of colloquial language, which meant that it could become a poetry accessible to people who lacked a thoroughgoing education in the classical idiom.

Teitoku did not single-handedly make *haikai* the characteristic verse form of the Edo period, but his tireless promotion of it, aided by the beginnings of a printing industry, was certainly important in its spread. His attitude was condescending and didactic, but he attracted a great number of literary disciples from classes previously uninvolved in literary activity, particularly the middle and lower ranks of the samurai military caste and newly wealthy urban merchants. There quickly arose, however, a reaction against the uneasy compromise between vulgarity and traditional belletrism that characterized *haikai* of Teitoku's school. It is significant that the reaction came not, as might be supposed, from poets who protested against Teitoku's vulgarization of the high classical tradition, but rather from those who believed he was destroying the straightforward, comic irreverence of *haikai* by trying to turn it into an ersatz "serious" poetry for the masses.

The fight against what they considered to be the pretentious stuffiness of the Teitoku school was led by a group known as the Danrin school of *haikai*, disciples of Nishiyama Sōin (1605-1682), a traditional *renga* poet turned *haikai* partisan. Danrin *haikai* was a short-lived phenomenon, defeated by its excesses in combat with the Teitoku school in the first public literary feud Japan had seen. The Danrin poets steadfastly refused to credit the Teitoku school's insistence that *haikai*, if only it would accept the discipline of serious *renga* while changing with the times to allow everyday language and subject matter, could become a form of poetry with real depth and dignity.

There is an element suggestive of Dadaism in Danrin-school reactions against the Teitoku-school attitude toward *haikai*, best illustrated, perhaps, by the brief poetic career of Ihara Saikaku (1642-1693), better known as a fiction writer who was the first to chronicle the new, vigorous life of the urban middle classes. Saikaku's claim to fame as a poet comes from his practice of the extemporaneous solo composition of *haikai* sequences in public. His first great success came in 1675, when he produced a thousand verses at a single sitting. He finally retired from competition—actually, there was no competition—in 1684, after composing a record 23,500 linked verses in the space of a day and night, a tour de force that earned for him the sobriquet Niman'ō, "Old Man Twenty Thousand." (No record of the poems survives, since Saikaku produced them orally faster than a scribe could follow.)

MATSUO BASHŌ

Haikai survived and flourished, despite the guerrilla tactics of Sōin's Danrin-school followers and the excesses of Teitoku didacticism, thanks largely to the artistry of Matsuo Bashō (1644-1694), who is probably the only poet of the premodern period whose name is known to practically every Japanese person and whose poetry, rightly or wrongly, has come in the minds of Western readers to represent Japanese poetry in general. Bashō's early training in *haikai* was in the Teitoku school, favored in the conservative rural samurai milieu of his youth. After moving to Edo to pursue a career as a poet and teacher in 1672, however, he came under the influence of the Danrin poets, who found the openness of the shogun capital, still something of a boomtown, more congenial than the tradition-bound atmosphere of Kyoto.

Bashō did not join in the Teitoku-Danrin conflict; instead, he borrowed elements of both styles to produce his own, distinctive poetry in what came to be known as *shōfū*, the Bashō manner. In Teitoku *haikai*, Bashō found a commitment to discipline, polish, and technical skill essential to any real poetry. From the Danrin school, Bashō learned the importance of direct observation and objective description of the world of the senses, unmediated by artificial ideas of what was and was not "poetic." To this synthesis, he added a certain philosophical depth derived from his study of Chinese poetry and Zen Buddhism. His poetry, quickly disseminated in printed form, struck such a responsive chord that even by the time of his death, Bashō had become a national institution; some two thousand poets all over Japan claimed personal discipleship.

Interestingly, the immense popularity of Bashō's poetry played no small part in the demise of the *haikai* form, for the haunting beauty and technical sparkle of his individual verses overshadowed their role in linked-verse sequences. Bashō himself almost always composed in a group linked-verse setting, and much of his critical writing concerns itself with the paramount importance of keeping the linking process foremost in mind when writing *haikai*. Poetic practice and the spread of publishing, however, were at work even in his day to put greater emphasis on the individual units of the *haikai* chain, particularly the *hokku*, the first verse in a sequence. The *hokku* was of great importance in *haikai*, as it had always been in *renga*. First, it was the only verse in a sequence that was specifically required to have reference to anything outside the other poems in the chain—the rules dictated that it specify as clearly as possible the setting, circumstances, and season in which the poets were gathered. Further, the *hokku* was by tradition the responsibility of the most accomplished poet present, who was by convention, if not in actuality, treated as an honored guest. The *hokku*, therefore, could be and often was composed beforehand; its distinctive status encouraged its author to take special pains.

The great majority of the verses by which Bashō's poetry came to be known in Japan were originally composed as *hokku*, whose distinctive qualities and special status made them attractive candidates for inclusion in published handbooks of *haikai* practice. Furthermore, one important means by which Bashō's work was disseminated was his published travel diaries, which recorded a number of poetic pilgrimages he took late in life, visiting sites important in the classical tradition. Bashō was by that time a literary celebrity, and so at nearly every stop on these journeys he was put up by local poets, in return for whose hospitality he participated in *haikai* sessions. As a guest, he invariably had responsibility for the *hokku*, and naturally enough it was his *hokku* that he chose to preserve in his diaries, for they alone were uniquely tied to the places he visited.

These circumstances conspired to help make the seventeen-syllable *hokku* an independent verse form, called haiku, which is nothing more than a *hokku* composed with no thought of its being part of a *haikai* sequence. Linked verse in the modern *haikai* style continued to be practiced, but poets after Bashō tended increasingly to concentrate on single haiku, which proved to be highly satisfying vehicles for poetic expression, insofar as they partook of the special qualities of the *hokku*—the polish that was possible in a verse that need not be an impromptu public performance, for example, and the way in which it took much of its inspiration from the immediate surroundings of the poet.

Eighteenth century

Bashō was followed by a legion of notable *haikai* (or haiku—the terms were for some time interchangeable) poets, among whom might be singled out Takarai (or Enomoto) Kikaku (1661-1707), who added the kaleidoscope of city life to the poet's palette, restoring something of the earthiness that Bashō's otherworldliness had temporarily banished from *haikai*; Kikaku's poetry was not, however, any less touched with meaning than that of Bashō. Another poet deserving special note is Yosa Buson (1716-1783), whose verse is very elegant and at the same time sentimental. It is difficult to generalize about haiku. One of its chief virtues, fostered by Bashō's insistence on combining craftsmanship with authenticity of observation and emotional content, is that it allowed the expression of greater individuality than any poetic form that had preceded it, save perhaps the *chōka* a thousand years earlier.

The revolution that the haiku brought to Japanese poetry by disencumbering it of the most stifling aspects of classicism is characteristic of the diverse, iconoclastic creativity of Edo-period culture—a culture that flourished in spite of its near-total isolation from the currents of social and economic change that were reshaping other traditional cultures elsewhere in the world. Some of the important innovations of Edo literary culture lie beyond the scope of this essay, but the eighteenth century was not lacking in significant developments. Even the *tanka*, so long the embodiment of traditionalism, began to change as haiku poets redefined the purposes of poetry; *tanka* admitted colloquial language and prosaic subject matter and generated its own lively comic derivative, the *kyōka* ("mad verse"), which was wildly popular in the 1780's among a slightly jaded coterie of avant-garde intellectuals in Edo. Nativist scholars such as Kamo Mabuchi (1697-1769) and Motoori Norinaga (1730-1801) experimented with revivals of *chōka* and *tanka* in the style of *The Manyoshu* with a decidedly chauvinistic, anti-Chinese coloration. At the same time, however, the intense involvement of many eighteenth century intellectuals in the study of Chinese literature also produced much verse written in Chinese, some of it of remarkable quality. Together, these trends foreshadowed the explosion of creativity in all fields of literature that would occur when Japan once more opened its doors to outside influence in the nineteenth century.

Bibliography

Bownas, Geoffrey, and Anthony Thwaite, eds. and trans. *The Penguin Book of Japanese Verse*. Rev. ed. London: Penguin Books, 2009. A volume in the UNESCO Collection of Representative Works, Japanese series. A collection of Japanese verse from its beginnings through the Edo period. Introductions by the editor-translators, both of them distinguished scholars, noted for their expertise in Japanese culture.

Brower, Robert, and Earl Miner. *Japanese Court Poetry*. 1961. Reprint. Stanford, Calif.: Stanford University Press, 1988. Still the standard history of the development of the standard thirty-one-syllable *waka*, from its beginnings through the medieval period.

Carter, Steven D. *Waiting for the Wind: Thirty-six Poets of Japan's Late Medieval Age*. Reprint. New York: Columbia University Press, 1994. Part of the Asian Classics series. Presents more than four hundred poems by a range of poets from Japan's late medieval age (1250-1500), along with biographical sketches and critical evaluations of each.

_____, comp. and trans. *Traditional Japanese Poetry: An Anthology*. Stanford, Calif.: Stanford University Press, 1991. A collection of more than eleven hundred poems dating from the earliest times to the twentieth century. Though emphasis is placed on poets of literary or historical importance, there are also examples of such genres as poetic diaries, linked verse, and comic verse. Illustrations and maps. Bibliographical references and indexes.

Keene, Donald. *Seeds of the Heart*. 1993. Reprint. New York: Columbia University Press, 1999. The definitive account of the development of Japanese literature from the beginnings through the late sixteenth century. A good deal of space is dedicated to the development of Japanese poetry in all forms.

_____. *World Within Walls*. 1976. Reprint. New York: Columbia University Press, 1999. A continuation of Keene's history of Japanese literature until 1867. Provides useful analyses of poets and poetry in all styles.

Miner, Earl. *Japanese Linked Poetry*. Princeton, N.J.: Princeton University Press, 1979. A detailed history of medieval linked verse, or *renga*, with copious translations.

Ooka, Makoto. *The Poetry and Poetics of Ancient Japan*. Translated by Thomas Fitzsimmons. Santa Fe, N.Mex.: Katydid Books, 1997. Explores the great library of poetry anthologies compiled by the Imperial order. Re-creates in detail the social, political, and cultural realities surrounding the development of Japanese poetry from ancient until modern times.

Sato, Hiroaki. *One Hundred Frogs: From Renga, to Haiku, to English*. 1983. Reprint. New York: Weatherhill, 1995. Provides definitions, history, the forms, and the rules of these poems, with many useful insights into the techniques of translating Japanese poems, and adds many examples of poems and translations.

Shirane, Haruo. *Traces of Dreams*. Stanford, Calif.: Stanford University Press, 1998. A history of the development of haiku, concentrating on the career and accomplishments of Matsuo Bashō.

_____. *Traditional Japanese Literature: An Anthology, Beginnings to 1600*. Rev. ed. Translated by Sonja Arntzen et al. New York: Columbia University Press, 2007. A comprehensive anthology, containing a wide variety of texts, representing both elite and popular cultures. Introductions to the works provide information on historical and cultural contexts. Illustrations and maps. Extensive bibliographies. Index.

_____, ed. *Early Modern Japanese Literature: An Anthology, 1600-1900*. Translated by James Brandon et al. New York: Columbia University Press, 2002. Of special interest to students of Japanese poetry is the section in this massive book devoted to the prose and poetry of Matsuo Bashō. Another section deals with comic and satiric poetry. Introductions and commentary by Shirane. Illustrations and maps. English-language bibliography. Index.

Robert W. Leutner
Updated by J. Thomas Rimer

JAPANESE POETRY SINCE 1800

At the beginning of the nineteenth century, the long and powerful tradition of Japanese poetry continued to make possible the production of accomplished and moving poems in the great forms that had developed during various periods in the past: the thirty-one-syllable *waka* (also known as *tanka*, the name by which the form is familiar to many Western readers), the seventeen-syllable haiku, and the more philosophical medium of *kanshi*, or poetry in Chinese, which permitted both greater length and the kind of philosophical abstraction that had long been deemed unsuitable for the shorter forms of classical Japanese verse. These traditions might well have ossified but for the spread of literacy and learning and the inspiration of Chinese poetry available from the continent, which made it possible to achieve new variations within old forms. For example, Kobayashi Yatarō, known as Issa (1763-1827), a farmer from the mountainous countryside, had been able to create a style of haiku that could capture both the joys and the anguish of the plebeian world in which he lived, while Ōkuma Kotomichi (1798-1868) extended the boundaries of *waka* to include an interest in human personality and psychology that gave his poems a strikingly modern flavor. Rai Sanyō (1780-1832), writing in Chinese, dealt with extremely diverse subject matter—including the presence of the Dutch in Nagasaki—in his lengthy and sometimes polemical poetry. The traditions of Japanese poetry, then, were by no means moribund.

On the other hand, Japan's self-imposed seclusion from other nations, dating from the early 1600's, had denied its poets the opportunity to gain any real perspective on their own traditions, as they had always done before, through an exposure to literary traditions from other cultures. Thus, in the closing decades of the nineteenth century, when young Japanese finally were permitted to go abroad, an awakening interest among them in European literature brought about a profound change in the development of the Japanese poetic sensibility. Native traditions were continued, although much expanded in range of subject matter and vocabulary permitted, but a whole new form of poetry, based on Western models and usually referred to as *shintaishi* ("new style verse" or "free-style verse"), developed into the standard vehicle for modern Japanese poetry. Both the traditional forms and the new forms grew and developed in response to the profound interest taken by Japanese poets in Western verse, which led to their attempts to understand, translate, and make use of those forms themselves.

First experiments

Before it became possible to write effective poetry in the new forms, a period of experimentation was required. These experiments were undertaken by a variety of gifted poets and usually involved their attempts to translate Western poems into Japanese (a language itself moving quickly, under the influence of Western example, toward a closer alignment between the written and spoken forms than had ever before seemed possible). Their various enthusiasms assured that, by the first decade of the twentieth century, there would be examples in good modern Japanese of some of the finest examples of European and American poetry from all periods. These translated poems, in turn, inspired an efflorescence of high poetic accomplishment in the Japanese language that continues unabated today.

The first significant contribution to the acculturation of Japanese poetry appeared in 1882, when three Tokyo University professors, two of whom had studied in the United States, produced a series of fourteen translations and five poems of their own based on Western models. This small collection, the *Shintaishisho* (selection of new style verse), included a number of poems quite popular with nineteenth century English and American readers, including Alfred, Lord Tennyson's "The Charge of the Light Brigade" and "The Captain," Thomas Gray's "Elegy Written in a Country Churchyard," and Henry Wadsworth Longfellow's "A Psalm of Life," as well as a few bits and pieces of William Shakespeare, including Hamlet's famous soliloquy, "To be or not to be." In presenting these works in translation, the authors stressed their conviction that such poems could well serve as models for the future, since both *waka* and haiku were too short to express any sustained mood or argument and too bound by traditional vocabulary and subject matter. This small collection remained very influential with young writers, and the interest it generated was reinforced by the publication, in 1889, of *Omokage* (vestiges). This collection of translations included selections from the German Romantic poets, Johann Wolfgang von Goethe, Heinrich Heine, Nikolaus Lenau, and E. T. A. Hoffmann; the volume also included selections from Shakespeare by way of the German translation of Friedrich von Schlegel and from Lord Byron by way of Heine's German version. The translations were prepared by Mori Ōgai (1862-1922), one of the foremost novelists of early modern Japan, who had lived in Germany from 1884 to 1888 and had learned to appreciate the great German poets in the original. He prepared his translations with a group of colleagues, sometimes attempting a literal rendering, sometimes developing forms that captured the content but strove to achieve a more natural expression in Japanese.

These widely read translations brought Japan closer to a truly modern poetry, but the most influential models were those provided by Ueda Bin (1874-1916) in his 1905 collection *Kaichōon* (the sound of the tide), which brought the first adequate versions of Symbolist poetry to Japan. Through these elegant and still widely appreciated translations, Japanese readers were first able to read important poems by Charles Baudelaire, Paul Verlaine, Stéphane Mallarmé, Gabriele D'Annunzio, Christina Rossetti, Dante Gabriel Rossetti, and Émile Verhaeren. Response to these poems suggested a certain congruence between European Symbolist values, with their suggestion of an unspoken and mysterious beauty, and the traditional values of Japanese poetry, with its emphasis on such qualities as the hidden depths of beauty captured in the courtly ideal of *yūgen*. Indeed, for several decades, the influence of French poetry was to remain paramount in

Japan, and it was very much under the French influence that the first great collection of modern Japanese poetry, Hagiwara Sakutarō's *Tsuki ni hoeru* (*Howling at the Moon*, 1969), appeared in 1917.

Changes in traditional forms

The same influences that were to create the new forms in Japanese poetry also helped bring about enormous changes in the traditional forms. In fact, four of the most important poets of the modern period continued to write in the traditional modes, using the possibilities of personal involvement and fresh vocabulary that had opened up to them by the turn of the century. The first of these was the poet Masaoka Shiki (1867-1902), who wrote both haiku and *waka* and did much to introduce the element of real and observed life into these forms. For Masaoka, the composition of poetry involved going out into nature to record what the poet himself could observe, and his principle of *shasei*, or "sketching from life," brought new vigor and reality to traditional forms that had tended to be restricted to a fixed vocabulary and a narrow range of emotional attitudes. Yosano Akiko (1878-1942), a poet whose vibrancy recalls the women writers of the early classical period such as the *waka* poet Ono no Komachi (834-880), instead plumbed the depths of her own emotional responses to life in order to produce *waka* full of emotional force and sensual consciousness. In a somewhat similar vein, Ishikawa Takuboku (1886-1912) wrote *waka* that told unsparingly of himself, his moods, and his defeats. Toward the end of his short career, Takuboku also began to introduce an element of political consciousness into his poetry that gave him another important role in the development of the modern poetic consciousness.

Saitō Mokichi (1882-1953) began his career as a doctor and studied neuropsychiatry in Vienna, yet he continued to make use of the *waka* form to record his intimate feelings and responses to the emotional complexities of his experiences. In the work of all of these writers, poetry became in a highly significant way an extension of their own personalities, permitting new possibilities for the *waka* and haiku forms. Thus, the democratization of poetry that began with Matsuo Bashō (1644-1694) and the Tokugawa (1579-1632) haiku has continued into the contemporary scene, where collections by dozens of poets provide for the continuity of a now comfortable tradition, which, while no longer at the cutting edge of modern poetry, still serves an honorable purpose in Japanese letters.

Other poets experimented with the older forms to make them as spare and flexible as possible. Several of the finest haiku poets of the period withdrew from conventional society and dedicated themselves to the service of Buddhism and the pilgrimage ideal. Their poetry thus shows powerful ties with the past wedded to complex contemporary sensibility. Ozaki Hōsai (1885-1926) was an insurance executive who after a period of instability abandoned his employment to serve as a Buddhist sexton in a small temple, where he wrote most of his remarkable free-style haiku. Taneda Santōka (1882-1940) led a dissolute life until becoming a mendicant monk; in the style of his great predecessor, Ryōkan (1758-1831), Taneda walked through the countryside, seeking salvation and writing down his trenchant and striking responses to the lonely life that he led. Ogiwara Seisensui (1884-1976) also did much to develop the style of free-form haiku and so make the tradition more available to modern writers and readers as a mechanism for expressing genuine contemporary concerns. Indeed, the work of these three men revealed the enormous range of which the venerable seventeen-syllable form was capable.

Kanshi also remained a possibility for those Japanese writers in the late nineteenth and early twentieth centuries who had been educated in classical Chinese, although, by the turn of the century, German, English, and French had replaced Chinese as the most important foreign languages to be studied in Japan, and as a result interest and skill in composing traditional Chinese verse waned. Perhaps the finest *kanshi* poet in the early years of the twentieth century, and indeed perhaps the greatest in the history of Chinese poetry written in Japan, was the novelist Natsume Sōseki (1867-1916), one of the pivotal figures in modern Japanese culture. Educated in English literature and the author of the most sophisticated psychological novels of his time, Sōseki nevertheless summoned up his classical training to write down his private thoughts in a series of Chinese poems that tell more about his aspirations, disappointments, and spiritual life than most of his other, more accessible works. By Sōseki's time, very few Japanese were capable of reading, let alone appreciating, such poetry; perhaps it was precisely Sōseki's realization that he was writing in what was destined even in his time to become a kind of private code that made it possible for him to be so open about himself in this most ancient form.

JAPAN AND THE EUROPEAN AVANT-GARDE

Japanese free-style verse came of age with the publication of Hagiwara's *Howling at the Moon*, a short book of poems, which, despite its debts to European Symbolism, revealed a mastery of colloquial language in the service of an authentic rendering of Hagiwara's inner world—troubled, ironic, and highly colored. Hagiwara himself had never been abroad ("I thought I'd like to go to France," he wrote in one of his poems; "France is too far away"). *Howling at the Moon* and the collections that followed contained poems filled with images that served as objective correlatives to elements in Hagiwara's own neurotic sensibility. Some of these are drawn from nature ("blurred bamboo roots spreading"), some from his own imagination. The most famous poem in *Howling at the Moon* begins: "At the bottom of the ground a face emerging,/ a lonely invalid's face emerging."

Reading Hagiwara's poetry while living in Europe, Nishiwaki Junsaburō (1894-1982) realized that it might be possible after all to write poetry in Japanese rather than in English or French. Nishiwaki, who once described himself as a "beggar for Europe," had decided that to participate in the creation of modern poetry, he would have to leave his homeland in order to shake off the weight of old traditions. Nishiwaki met Ezra

Pound and T. S. Eliot (he was later to become the definitive translator of Eliot's works into Japanese) and began to publish in little magazines in London, but his encounter with Hagiwara's revolutionary volume of poems brought him back to Japan and the beginnings of a genuine avant-garde movement there. Nishiwaki had become interested in Surrealism while in Europe and found a means to adapt for his own work that method of piercing through everyday reality ("like looking at a hole in a hedge into eternity," he wrote). Nishiwaki's difficult verse, filled with references to Blaise Pascal, Rainer Maria Rilke, Pablo Picasso, and other figures of European culture, represents the high tide of Japanese poetry in the international style. Nishiwaki's high accomplishments seem to owe relatively little to the Japanese tradition and set him apart from his more conservative contemporaries in somewhat the same way that Pound's work constituted a break with the conservative traditions of English poetry. Both are eclectic, highly committed, and utterly individual, and both, in a special way, represent the literary ideals of the period in which they lived. Translations of a wide variety of Nishiwaki's best work can be found in Hosea Hirata's *The Poetry and Poetics of Nishiwaki Junzaburō: Modernism in Translation* (1993).

Other poets traveled to Europe but remained more within the developing traditions of modern Japanese poetry. Takamura Kōtarō (1883-1956) went to France, where he studied sculpture with Auguste Rodin, and returned to become one of the major lyric voices of his day. His poems were modern in style and spirit, but not aggressively so, and his best-known poems deal with the growing madness and death of his wife, Chieko, who haunts the pages of these remarkable lyrics like the ghost in a traditional Nō play. Extensive translations can be found in Hiroaki Sato's *A Brief History of Imbecility: Poetry and Prose of Takamura Kōtarō* (1992). Others, such as Kitahara Hakushū (1885-1942), Kaneko Mitsuharu (1895-1975), and Miyoshi Tatsuji (1900-1964), added other elements from European and American poetry to the expanding vocabulary of techniques available to modern Japanese poets and left behind important collections that are still widely appreciated.

While it may be correct to say that European models suggested possibilities for modern Japanese poetry, it would be wrong indeed to hold that the poetry produced was merely derivative. The work of Nishiwaki and the others described above is, as is clear even when read in translation, distinctly individual. In terms of authenticity of voice, no modern Japanese poet is more appreciated than Miyazawa Kenji, or Kenji Miyazawa (1896-1933), as he is known in the West. Miyazawa was a devout Buddhist. After training at an agricultural college, he taught poor farmers in Iwate Prefecture, far to the north of Tokyo, how to better their lives. Miyazawa was little read during his lifetime, but later he became a powerful presence in modern Japanese poetry, even a cult figure. His remarkable verse, which owes more to Buddhist sutras than it does to European models, develops its metaphysical stance with an almost hallucinatory force. Miyazawa's work first became known to English-speaking readers through a series of translations by the

American poet Gary Snyder, included in his collection *The Back Country* (1968); Sato produced a much more extensive collection of translations in *Miyazawa Kenji: Selections* (2007). In addition, Miyazawa's *Haru to shura* (1924) appeared in translation as *Spring and Asura* in 1973. As a result, Miyazawa's utterly individual voice is widely appreciated in translation. The best of his work is a rich and dazzling mixture of language and imagery that stretches modern Japanese to its limits and reveals possibilities of the congruence of sound and meaning unexplored in Japanese poetry before or since.

War and postwar years

The rich and sophisticated mix of poetry produced in the 1920's and early 1930's came to an end with the dark days leading up to World War II. Some poets, such as Hagiwara, retreated to the use of traditional forms; some, such as Takamura, wrote patriotic poetry. Cut off from European developments and beleaguered at home by a repressive government and the difficulties of everyday living, Japanese poets seemed to turn inward. It was not until the end of the war that new trends could develop. When they did, it was perhaps not surprising that, in the wake of the war and the destruction that it had caused, younger poets came to distrust their own cultural past, which in their view had permitted a complicity with Japanese war aims. For them, the Japanese past seemed tainted, and beginning in the 1950's, poets looked again to Europe for their inspiration. In a sense, then, the war could be looked upon as an interruption in the internationalization of Japanese literature that had begun by the 1920's. In the postwar period, however, the break with the past became more definite and often assumed political significance.

Two trends in particular characterized the immediate postwar years. Following the example of Nishiwaki, who remained an immensely powerful figure in literary circles, a number of younger poets drew on European poetry in their effort to create a new tradition for themselves out of the ruins of the past. Considering that time of despair, it is perhaps not so surprising that in 1947, Ayukawa Nobuo (1920-1986) and his colleagues formed a group they called Arechi (the wasteland), suggesting both the impact of Eliot and their own sense of destruction and hopelessness. Others, such as Yoshioka Minoru (born 1919), continued to develop highly idiosyncratic symbolism and poetic forms that call to mind the commitment to the expanding mechanisms of language first undertaken by Nishiwaki. In the work of writers such as these, the legacy of European experimentation was still predominant.

A second trend placed a number of poets in the role of social critics who used the insights of the lyric mode to deepen and intensify their critique of postwar society. In this position, they had a powerful predecessor in the figure of Takuboku, who toward the end of his life had become increasingly wary of what he took to be reactionary trends in the development of the Japanese government and had begun to write poems that expressed his interest in socialism, even anarchism. Among the postwar poets who wanted to put society and its concerns back into the scope of their poetic vision, some were humanists horrified by the war, by the way in which human character had been degraded by destruction on the battlefield, and by the destruction caused by the atomic bomb. A few were Marxists. Little of this poetry has been studied or translated by Western scholars, but the work of early figures such as Oguma Hideo (1901-1940) certainly deserves proper study. Poets such as Ando Tsuguo (born 1919), most of whose work has been written in the postwar period, perhaps capture best this need of a generation to look back in an attempt to understand—emotionally, intellectually, and politically—what has happened to them. A reader who encounters their work in English may find it difficult to appreciate. A wider understanding of, say, Bertolt Brecht's poetry in England and the United States has now made it possible to write ironically in English on political issues, but the lyric thrust of the Japanese tradition applied to the war brings an overloading of images that may remain difficult for a reader from the Western tradition to encompass. Still, a search for authenticity in the early postwar period doubtless required this kind of linguistic travail, and the best of the works produced have a somber power that cannot be denied.

As the United States became involved in the Cold War and the Korean War as well, Japanese intellectuals began to react to what seemed to them a usurpation of their own sovereignty by the collusion of the Japanese and American authorities. Thus, there was a strain of contemporary Japanese poetry that, paralleling political movements, was largely reactive, particularly against the American involvement in Vietnam. Some of this political poetry had a satiric bite that was undeniably as effective as it was bitter.

A still later generation of poets, those who now have pride of place in Japanese literary circles, were born too late to have any direct experience of the war. These writers reached their maturity at a time when powerful changes had been wrought upon the fabric of Japanese society, where the processes of democratization and equalization of social class begun by the American occupation after World War II had altered the language as well as the society. Accordingly, Japanese poetry has tended to become increasingly colloquial, emphasizing the interior life of the poet, oppressed by the flatness, emptiness, and arbitrariness of modern life. As in English and American poetry, the grand gesture has been reduced to the ironic shrug, the powerful spiritual insight transformed into a wry and temporary awakening of sensibility. With the commercialization of communication, poets have found themselves more popular, and more vulnerable, than ever before. The work of Tamura Ryūichi (1923-1998), who owes something of his development to the Arechi school, has moments of a certain somber grandeur, but Tanikawa Shuntarō (born 1931) writes of the small disappointments and pleasures of his private world in a fashion that recalls the horizons, if not the style, of John Updike. His poetry is extremely popular in Japan and widely translated; the authenticity of his stance, which accurately reflects the spiritual condition of men and women in so many countries of the world, seems unquestioned.

Other writers among the postwar poets have attempted to strike out against this lassitude—some highly sophisticated, such as Anzai Hitoshi (1919-1994), whose work is characterized by brilliant language and a suggestive and ironic treatment of the Japanese past, and others, aggressively plainspoken, such as Ishigaki Rin (1920-2004), who used her experience as a working woman as the basis for moving and often wryly humorous verses.

LATE TWENTIETH CENTURY ONWARD

In more recent decades, it has become more difficult to make any definitive generalizations about poetic practice, as the quantity and diversity of poetry published, both in traditional and contemporary forms, remain enormous. It is perhaps too early for the reputations of younger writers to be settled in the minds of the multitude of readers attracted to poetry. In the midst of such continuing vitality, the increasing prominence of women poets, among them Tada Chimako (1930-2003), Shinkawa Kazue (born 1929), and Yoshihara Sachiko (born 1932) is an important and welcome development. A range of new themes have also become possible, as the high reputation of Takahashi Mutsuo (born 1937), a poet dealing extensively with homosexuality, makes evident.

Tanka (*waka*), the thirty-one-syllable form that goes back more than one thousand years, are still being composed. Certain poets have declared themselves as avant-garde poets in the genre and are anxious to set aside much of the traditional vocabulary in order to work towards what they consider a more unsentimental style. In any case, the form can still remain widely attractive. Indeed Tawara Machi (born 1962) achieved an international best seller in her fresh and often piquant collection of *tanka* titled *Salada kinenbi* (1987; *Salad Anniversary*, 1989).

Haiku, the seventeen-syllable form, also continues to attract a wide variety of poets, both professional and amateur. The kinds of expanded subject matter and fresh uses of the form which helped set the trends for more recent generations can be found in the seminal work of Saitō Sanki (1900-1962), with some of his best translated in *The Kobe Hotel* (1993).

Modern forms of verse, not surprisingly, retain pride of place as a privileged means of poetic expression. At least three larger trends might be noted here. The first involves the continued influence of French poetry and poetics in Japan. In those terms, such French poets as Baudelaire, Arthur Rimbaud, Paul Éluard, Mallarmé, André Breton, and Paul Valéry remain important; indeed, many contemporary Japanese poets who work and teach in university circles have done academic research on the French school and incorporate many of those principles into their own poetics. The resulting poetry is the most international in style of that composed in Japan at the end of the twentieth and beginning of the twenty-first centuries. More often than not, poems are produced that are about words or the nature of language itself. Such work is particularly difficult to translate, since the subject matter itself involves the nature of the Japanese language. Some poets, such as the popular and highly respected Ōoka Makoto, (born 1931) can sometimes link their work to the classical language of the traditional *tanka*, while the use of patterns and sounds is important in the work of such prominent "intellectual" poets as Hiraide Takashi (born 1950) and Asabuki Ryōji (born 1952).

In contradistinction to these kinds of verse, which overtly aim at the status of high art, a more popular kind of verse has also emerged, also often international in atmosphere, but one which makes use of elements in popular culture, such as the rhythms of jazz, and seeks to move poetry closer to a living oral culture. These poets in particular have revived the custom of poetry readings, long a feature in classical times, and come closer to expressing in their work an overt expression of political and social concerns. The best-known poet working in this vein, and arguably the best-known Japanese poet outside the country is Shiraishi Kazuko (born 1931), whose wit, feminist point of view, and antiestablishment stance have won her many friends and admirers around the world.

A third trend is the emergence of important longer poems and poetry sequences. Such efforts go back to the prewar generation of Nishiwaki, but more and more of these extended efforts have captured and sustained public interest. Here, three widely appreciated poets might be noted. Gōzō Yoshimasu (born 1939), who at one point studied in the United States, has expressed his admiration for Rimbaud. For many of his readers, he seems uniquely successful in capturing a certain sense of the emptiness and vacuum he finds in contemporary Japanese life. His poetry has sometimes been characterized as a series of voyages away from that felt sense of futility. Soh Sakon (born 1919) belongs to an earlier generation but began writing poetry after World War II, inspired by his reading of Rimbaud and Valéry. His book-length poem *Moeru haha* (mother burning), published in 1967, now a classic of modern Japanese poetry, deals with the death of his mother in a 1942 fire bombing. Hara Shirō (born 1924), like other contemporary Japanese poets, is widely traveled and has been especially attracted to France. His highly regarded 1985 book-length poem *Ishi no fu* (*Ode to Stone*, 1990), uses as its links a series of stones, which serve as narrators from a variety of cultures and historical periods. These sections are interspersed with a continuing focus on a famous stone bridge in the southern city of Nagasaki, the town where Hara was raised.

Whatever the experimental nature of the language employed by all these poets, the very length of their work puts a necessary emphasis on larger themes, rather than merely a focus on the words themselves. This scale of verbal architecture creates a larger and more unified scale impossible to achieve in the shorter forms of poetry written in the Japanese classical and modern traditions.

Poetry has always been a highly respected form of artistic practice in Japan, and that pattern persists today. Most Japanese with a high school diploma can make an educated stab at writing haiku, perhaps even *waka*, and the relative evenness of vowel and consonant patterns in the Japanese language makes the composition of free verse relatively easy in a technical sense. Poetry magazines abound, and many accomplished writers compose for a circle of friends rather than for a national audience; indeed, some critics would maintain that this personal interchange between poets and their friends, so much a part of the Japanese poetic tradition since its beginnings in the *Manyoshuōshū* (mid-eighth century; *The Collections of Ten Thousand Leaves*; also as *The Ten Thousand Leaves*, pb. 1981, and as *The Manyoshu*, 1940) and the *Kokinshū* (905; *Kokinshu: A Collection of Poems Ancient and Modern*, 1984), helps explain why so many achieve some real sense of craft and why the best of the poets have become supreme manipulators of the language. The popularity and acceptance of poetry in Japanese life may debase it on the lower end of the scale, where businessmen without sensibility scribble down haiku, the imagery of which is worn clear of genuine meaning. However, on the other end of that scale, those who write and rewrite for their poetic colleagues have achieved a level of accomplishment that is remarkably high.

Translation of any language is slippery enough, and good translations of poetry are particularly difficult to achieve; certainly, the barrier of the difficult Japanese language prevents most Western readers from discovering one of the most active poetic traditions in the world today. It may well be, however, that in the generations to come, the increasing number of good translations of contemporary Japanese poetry will create and sustain the same kind of excitement among readers and writers of poetry in English that European artists felt one hundred years ago when they first saw woodblock prints imported from Japan.

BIBLIOGRAPHY

Beichman, Janine. *Embracing the Firebird: Yosano Akiko and the Birth of the Female Voice in Modern Japanese Poetry*. Illustrated edition. Honolulu: University of Hawaii Press, 2002. A study of the early life and work of Yosano Akiko, whose first book, *Midaregami* (1901; *Tangled Hair*, 1935, 1971), radically changed *tanka* poetry and became a modern classic. The author has included her own masterful translations of poems by Yosano and her contemporaries. Bibliographical references and index.

Bownas, Geoffrey, and Anthony Thwaite, eds. and trans. *The Penguin Book of Japanese Verse*. Rev. ed. London: Penguin Books, 2009. A volume in the UNESCO Collection of Representative Works, Japanese series. Poetry of the Edo period is included in this anthology, followed by selections from the works of modern poets such as Tamura Ryūichi and Tanikawa Shuntarō. Bibliographical references and index.

Carter, Steven D., comp. and trans. *Traditional Japanese Poetry: An Anthology*. Stanford, Calif.: Stanford University Press, 1991. A collection of more than eleven hundred poems in traditional genres by poets selected for their merit or their historical significance. Illustrations and maps. Bibliographical references and indexes.

Heinrich, Amy. *Fragments of Rainbows: The Life and Poetry of Saitō Mokichi, 1882-1953*. New York: Columbia University Press, 1983. A useful account of developments in the use of classical forms in the modern period, centering on the work of Saitō Mokichi.

Keene, Donald, ed. *Modern Japanese Literature: From 1868 to the Present Day*. 1956. Reprint. New York: Grove Press, 1994. Contains historical introduction by the editor, as well as brief introductions to the writers. Selected bibliographical references. A landmark work.

Koriyama, Naoshi, and Edward Lueders, eds. and trans. *Like Underground Water: Poetry of Mid-Twentieth Century Japan*. 1995. Reprint. Port Townsend, Wash.: Copper Canyon Press, 2000. Presents 240 poems by eighty poets, each of whom is introduced in a brief biographical headnote. Poetic styles range from conventional lyricism to surrealism, symbolism, anarchism, and nihilism. Excellent introduction.

Morton, Leith. *Modernism in Practice: An Introduction to Postwar Japanese Poetry*. Honolulu: University of Hawaii Press, 2004. This long-overdue study traces the modernist movement in Japan from its prewar origins to its emergence in the works of seven outstanding poets, presented in flawless translations and analyzed in detail. Other topics discussed at length are poetry by women and poetry from Okinawa.

Rimer, J. Thomas, and Van C. Gessel, eds. *The Columbia Anthology of Modern Japanese Literature*. 2 vols. New York: Columbia University Press, 2005-2007. The first volume of what has been called a "monumental" collection covers the years 1868-1945, the second, from 1945 to the present. Part of the Modern Asian Literature series. Includes fiction, poems, plays, and essays, organized both chronologically and by genre.

Sato, Hiroaki, ed. and trans. *Japanese Women Poets: An Anthology*. Armonk, N.Y.: M. E. Sharpe, 2007. Selections from the works of more than one hundred Japanese women poets in a broad range of genres, from ancient folk songs to court poetry, from *chōka* to free verse. Explanatory headnotes precede each section. Glossary, chronology, and bibliography.

Shirane, Haruo, ed. *Early Modern Japanese Literature: An Anthology, 1600-1900*. Translated by James Brandon et al. New York: Columbia University Press, 2002. One section of this book focuses specifically on haiku of the early nineteenth century. Introductions and commentary by Shirane. Illustrations and maps. English-language bibliography. Index.

Solt, John. *Shredding the Tapestry of Meaning*. Cambridge, Mass.: Harvard University Press, 1999. An account of the rise of avant-garde poetry in Japan, centering on the career and work of Kitasono Katsue.

Ueda, Makoto. *Modern Japanese Tanka: An Anthology*. New York: Columbia University Press, 1996. The poems of twenty writers appear in this collection. Each writer's work is preceded by a biographical and critical introduction. Selected bibliography.

J. Thomas Rimer
Updated by Rimer

ISSA
Kobayashi Yataro

Born: Kashiwabara, Japan; June 15, 1763
Died: Kashiwabara, Japan; January 5, 1827

PRINCIPAL POETRY
Kansei kuchō, 1794
Kansei kikō, 1795
Kyōwa kuchō, 1803
Bunka kuchō, 1804-1808
Shichiban nikki, 1810-1818
Hachiban nikki, 1819-1821
Kuban nikki, 1822-1824
The Autumn Wind, 1957
A Few Flies and I, 1969
The Spring of My Life, and Selected Haiku, 1997

OTHER LITERARY FORMS

Although Issa (ee-sah) is known primarily as one of the three great haiku poets, he also wrote prose—in *Chichi no shūen nikki* (1801; *Diary of My Father's Death*, 1992), a response to his father's death—and mixed prose and verse, or *haibun*, in *Oragu haru* (1819; *The Year of My Life*, 1960), an autobiographical account of his most memorable year.

ACHIEVEMENTS

Ezra Pound's recognition of the power of a single image that concentrates poetic attention with enormous force and his examination of the complexity of the Japanese written character led to an increasing awareness of the possibilities of haiku poetry for Western readers in the early part of the twentieth century. Combined with a growing interest in Asian studies and philosophy, haiku offered an entrance into Japanese concepts of existence concerning the relationship of humans and the natural world. Because the brevity of haiku is in such contrast to conventional ideas of a complete poem in the Western tradition, however, only the most accomplished haiku poets have been able to reach beyond the boundaries of their culture.

The most prominent among these are Matsuo Bashō (1644-1694), Yosa Buson (1715-1783), and Issa. As William Cohen describes him, "in humor and sympathy for all that lives, Issa is unsurpassed in the history of Japanese literature and perhaps even in world literature." A perpetual underdog who employed humor as an instrument of endurance, who was exceptionally sensitive to the infinite subtlety of the natural world, and who was incapable of acting with anything but extraordinary decency, Issa wrote poetry that moves across the barriers of language and time to capture the "wordless moment" when revelation is imminent. More accessible than the magisterial Buson, less confident than the brilliant Bashō, Issa expresses in his work the genius that is often hidden in the commonplace. The definition of haiku as "simply what is happening in this place at this moment" is an apt emblem for a poet who saw humans forever poised between the timely and the timeless.

Biography

The poet known as Issa was born Kobayashi Yatarō in 1763 in the village of Kashiwabara, a settlement of approximately one hundred houses in the highlands of the province of Shinano. The rugged beauty of the region, especially the gemlike Lake Nojiri two miles east of the town, led to the development of a tourist community in the twentieth century, but the harsh winter climate, with snowdrifts of more than ten feet not uncommon, restricted growth in Issa's time. The area was still moderately prosperous, however, because there was a central post office on the main highway from the northwestern provinces to the capital city of Edo (now Tokyo). The lord of the powerful Kaga clan maintained an official residence that he used on his semiannual visits to the shogun in Edo, and a cultural center developed around a theater that featured dramatic performances, wrestling exhibitions, and poetry readings.

Issa was the son of a fairly prosperous farmer who supplemented his income by providing packhorse transportation for passengers and freight. His composition of a "death-verse" suggests a high degree of literary awareness. In the first of a series of domestic tragedies, Issa's mother died when he was three, but his grandmother reared him with deep affection until Issa's father remarried. Although his stepmother treated him well for two years, on the birth of her first child, she relegated Issa to a role as a subordinate. When she suggested that a farmer's son did not need formal schooling, Issa was forced to discontinue his study of reading and writing under a local master. When her baby cried, she accused Issa of causing its pain and beat him so that he was frequently marked with bruises.

According to legend, these unhappy circumstances inspired Issa's first poem. At the age of nine or so, Issa was unable to join the local children at a village festival because he did not have the new clothes the occasion required. Playing by himself, he noticed a fledgling sparrow fallen from its nest. Observing it with what would become a characteristic sympathy for nature's outcasts, he declared:

> Come and play,
> little orphan sparrow—
> play with me!

The poem was probably written years later in reflection on the incident, but Issa displayed enough literary ability in his youth to attract the attention of the proprietor of the lord's residence, a man skilled in calligraphy and haiku poetry, who believed that Issa would be a good companion for his own son. He invited Issa to attend a school he operated in partnership with a scholar in Chinese studies who was also a haiku poet. Issa could attend the school only at night and on holidays—sometimes carrying his stepbrother on his back—when he was not compelled to assist with farm chores, but this did not prevent him from cultivating his literary inclinations. On one of the occasions when he was assisting his father by leading a passenger on a packhorse, the traveler ruminated on the name of a mountain that they were passing. "Black Princess! O Black Princess!" he repeated, looking at the snow-topped peak of Mount Kurohime. When Issa asked the man what he was doing, he replied that he was trying to compose an appropriate haiku for the setting. To the astonishment of the traveler, Issa proclaimed: "Black Princess is a bride—/ see her veiled in white."

Issa's studies were completely terminated when his grandmother died in 1776. At his stepmother's urging, Issa was sent to Edo, thrown into a kind of exile in which he was expected to survive on his own. His life in the capital in his teenage years is a mystery, but in 1790, he was elected to a position at an academy of poetics, the Katsushika school. The school had been founded by a friend and admirer of Bashō who named it for Bashō's home, and although Issa undoubtedly had the ability to fulfill the expectations of his appointment, his innovative instincts clashed with the more traditional curriculum already in place at the school. In 1792, Issa voluntarily withdrew from the school, proclaiming himself Haikaiji Issa in a declaration of poetic independence. His literary signature literally translates as "Haikai Temple One-Tea." The title "Haikai Temple" signifies that he was a priest of haiku poetry (anticipating Allen Ginsberg's assertion "Poet is Priest!"), and as he wrote, "In as much as life is empty as a bubble which vanishes instantly, I will henceforth call myself *Issa*, or One Tea." In this way, he was likening his existence to the bubbles rising in a cup of tea—an appropriate image, considering the importance of the tea ceremony in Japanese cultural life.

During the next ten years, Issa traveled extensively, making pilgrimages to famous religious sites and prominent artistic seminars, staying with friends who shared his interest in poetry. His primary residence was in Fukagawa, where he earned a modest living by giving lessons in haikai, possibly assisted by enlightened patrons who appreciated his abilities. By the turn of the century, he had begun to establish a wider reputation and his prospects for artistic recognition were improving, but his father's final illness drew him home to offer comfort and support. His father died in 1801 and divided his estate equally between Issa and his half brother. When his stepmother contested the will, Issa was obliged to leave once again, and he spent the next thirteen years living in Edo while he attempted to convince the local authorities to carry out the provisions of his father's legacy. His frustrations are reflected in a poem he wrote during this time: "My old village calls—/ each time I come near,/ thorns in the blossom."

Finally, in 1813, Issa was able to take possession of his half of the property, and in April, 1814, he married a twenty-eight-year-old woman named Kiku, the daughter of a farmer in a neighboring village. Completely white-haired and nearly toothless, he still proclaimed that he "became a new man" in his fifties, and during the next few years, his wife gave birth to five children. Unfortunately, all of them died while still quite young. Using a familiar line of scripture that compares the evanescence of life to the morning dew as a point of origin, Issa expressed his sense of loss in one of his most famous and least translatable poems:

> This dewdrop world—
> yet for dew drops
> still, a dewdrop world

In May, 1823, Issa's wife died, but he remarried almost immediately. This marriage was not harmonious, and when the woman returned to her parent's home, Issa sent her a humorous verse as a declaration of divorce and as a statement of forgiveness. Perhaps for purposes of continuing his family, Issa married one more time in 1825, his bride this time a forty-six-year-old farmer's daughter. His wife was pregnant when Issa died in the autumn of 1828, and his only surviving child, Yata, was born after his death. Her survival enabled Issa's descendants to retain the property in his home village for which he had struggled during many of the years of his life.

In his last years, while he was settled in his old home, he achieved national fame as a haikai poet. His thoughts as a master were valued, and he held readings and seminars with pupils and colleagues. After recovering from a fairly serious illness in 1820, he adopted the additional title Soseibo, or "Revived Priest," indicating not only his position of respect as an artist and seer but also his resiliency and somewhat sardonic optimism. As a kind of summary of his career, he wrote a poem that legend attributes to his deathbed but that was probably given to a student to be published after his death. It describes the journey of a man from the washing bowl in which a new baby is cleansed to the ritual bath in which the body is prepared for burial: "Slippery words/ from bathtub to bathtub—/ just slippery words." The last poem Issa actually wrote was found under the pillow on the bed where he died. After his house had burned down in 1827, he and his wife lived in an adjoining storehouse with no windows and a leaky roof: "Gratitude for the snow/ on the bed quilt—/ it too is from Heaven." Issa used the word *jōdo* (Pure Land) for Heaven, a term that describes the Heaven of the Buddha Amida. Issa was a member of the largest Pure Land sect, Jōdo Shinshū, and he shared the sect's faith in the boundless love of Amida to redeem a world in which suffering and pain are frequent. His final poem is an assertion of that faith in typically bleak circumstances, and a final declaration of his capacity for finding beauty in the most unlikely situations.

Analysis

The haiku is a part of Japanese cultural life, aesthetic experience, and philosophical expression. As Lafcadio Hearn noted, "Poetry in Japan is universal as air. It is felt by everybody." The haiku poem traditionally consists of three lines, arranged so that there are five, seven, and five syllables in the triplet. Although the "rules" governing its construction are not absolute, it has many conventions that contribute to its effectiveness. Generally, it has a central image, often from the natural world, frequently expressed as a part of a seasonal reference, and a "cutting word," or exclamation that states or implies the poet's reaction to what he sees. It is the ultimate compression of poetic energy and often draws its strength from the unusual juxtaposition of image and idea.

It is very difficult to translate haiku into English without losing or distorting some of the qualities that make it so uniquely interesting. English syllables are longer than Japanese *jion* (symbol sounds); some Japanese characters have no English equivalent, particularly since each separate "syllable" of a Japanese "word" may have additional levels of meaning; a literal rendering may miss the point while a more creative one may remake the poem so that the translator is a traitor to the original. As an example of the problems involved, one might consider the haiku Issa wrote about the temptations and disappointments of his visits to his hometown. The Japanese characters can be literally transcribed as follows:

Furosato ya
yoru mo sawaru mo
bara-no-hana

Old village:
come-near also touch also
thorn's-flowers

The poem has been translated in at least four versions:

At my home everything
I touch is a bramble. (*Asataro Miyamori*)

Everything I touch
with tenderness alas
pricks like a bramble. (*Peter Beilenson*)

The place where I was born:
all I come to—all I touch—
blossoms of the thorn. (*Harold Henderson*)

My old village calls—
each time I come near,
thorns in the blossom. (*Leon Lewis*)

Bashō's almost prophetic power and Buson's exceptional craftsmanship may be captured fairly effectively in English, but it is Issa's attitude toward his own life and the world that makes him perhaps the most completely understandable of the great Japanese poets. His rueful, gentle irony, turning on his own experiences, is his vehicle for conveying a warmly human outlook that is no less profound for its inclusive humor. Like his fellow masters of the haiku form, Issa was very closely attuned to the natural world, but for him, it had an immediacy and familiarity that balanced the cosmic dimensions of the universal phenomena that he observed. Recognizing human fragility, he developed a strong sense of identification with the smaller, weaker creatures of the world. His sympathetic response is combined with a sharp eye for their individual attributes and for subtle demonstrations of virtue and strength amid trying circumstances. Although Issa was interested in most of the standard measures of social success (family, property, recognition), his inability to accept dogma (religious or philosophical) or to overlook economic inequity led him to a position as a semipermanent outsider no matter how successful he might be.

OBSERVER OF NATURAL PHENOMENA

Typically, Issa depicts himself as an observer in the midst of an extraordinary field of natural phenomena. Like the Western Romantic poets of the nineteenth century, he uses his own reactions as a measuring device and records the instinctive responses of his poetic sensibility. There is a fusion of stance and subject, and the world of business and commerce occurs only as an intrusion, spoiling the landscape. What matters is an eternal realm of continuing artistic revelation, the permanent focus of humankind's contemplation: "From my tiny roof/ smooth . . . soft . . ./ still-white snow/ melts in melody." The poet is involved in the natural world through the action of a poetic intelligence that re-creates the world in words and images and, more concretely, through the direct action of his participation in its substance and shape: "Sun-melted snow . . ./ with my stick I guide/ this great dangerous river." Here, the perspective ranges from the local and the minimal to the massively consequential, but in his usual fashion, Issa's wry overestimation of his actions serves to illustrate his realization of their limits. Similarly, he notes the magnified ambition of another tiny figure: "An April shower . . ./ see that thirsty mouse/ lapping river Sumida." Amid the vast universe, humans are much like a slight animal. This perception is no cause for despair, though. An acceptance of limitations with characteristic humor enables him to enjoy his minuscule place among the infinities: "Now take this flea:/ He simply cannot jump . . ./ and I love him for it."

Because he is aware of how insignificant and vulnerable all living creatures are, Issa is able to invest their apparently comic antics with dignity: "The night was hot . . ./ stripped to the waist/ the snail enjoyed the moonlight." The strength of Issa's identification of the correspondence between the actions of human beings and animals enables him to use familiar images of animal behavior to comment on the pomposity and vanity of much human behavior. In this fashion, his poems have some of the satirical edge of eighteenth century wit, but Issa is much more amused than angry: "Elegant singer/ would you further favor us/ with a dance, O Frog?" Or if anger is suggested, it is a sham to feign control over something, because the underlying idea is essentially one of delighted acceptance of common concerns: "Listen, all you fleas . . ./ you can come on pilgrimage, o.k. . . ./ but then, off you git!" Beyond mock anger and low comedy, Issa's poems about his participation in the way of the world often express a spirit of contemplation leading to a feeling of awe. Even if the workings of the natural world remain elusive, defying all real comprehension, there is still a fascination in considering its mysterious complexity: "Rainy afternoon . . ./ little daughter you will/ never teach that cat to dance."

Forbidding nature

At other times, however, the landscape is more forbidding, devoid of the comfort provided by other creatures. Issa knew so many moments of disappointment that he could not restrain a projection of his sadness into the world: "Poor thin crescent/ shivering and twisted high/ in the bitter dark." For a man so closely attuned to nature's nuances, it is not surprising that nature would appear to echo his own concerns. When Issa felt the harsh facts of existence bearing heavily on him, he might have found some solace in seeing a reflection of his pain in the sky: "A three-day-old moon/ already warped and twisted/ by the bitter cold." Images of winter are frequent in Issa's poetry, an outgrowth of the geographical reality of his homeland but also an indication of his continuing consciousness of loss and discouragement. Without the abundant growth of the summer to provide pleasant if temporary distraction, the poet cannot escape from his condition: "In winter moonlight/ a clear look/ at my old hut . . . dilapidated." The view may be depressing but the "clear look" afforded by the light is valuable and, in some ways, reassuringly familiar, reminding the poet of his real legacy: "My old father too/ looked long on these white mountains/ through lonely winters."

Home and family

Issa spent much time trying to establish a true home in the land in which he was born because he had a strong sense of the importance of family continuity. He regarded the family as a source of strength in a contentious and competitive environment and wrote many poems about the misfortune of his own family situation. Some of his poems on this subject tend to be extremely sentimental, lacking his characteristic comic stance. The depth of his emotional involvement is emphasized by the stark pronouncement of his query: "Wild geese O wild geese/ were you little fellows too . . ./ when you flew from home?" These poems, however, are balanced by Issa's capacity for finding some unexpected reassurance that the struggle to be "home" is worthwhile: "Home again! What's this?/ My hesitant cherry tree/ deciding to bloom?" Although nothing spectacular happens, on his home ground, even the apparently mundane is dressed in glory: "In my native place/ there's this plant:/ As plain as grass but blooms like heaven." In an understated plea for placing something where it belongs, recalling his ten-year struggle to win a share of his father's property, he declares how he would dispense justice: "Hereby I assign in perpetuity to wit:/ To this wren/ this fence." For Issa, the natural order of things is superior to that of society.

The uncertainty of his position with respect to his family (and his ancestors) made the concept of home ground especially important for Issa as a fixed coordinate in a chaotic universe. His early rejection by his stepmother was an important event in the development of an outlook that counted uncertainty as a given, but his sense of the transitory nature of existence is a part of a very basic strain of Japanese philosophy. The tangible intermixed with the intangible is the subject of many of his poems: "The first firefly . . ./ but he got away and I—/ air in my fingers." A small airborne creature, a figure for both light and flight, is glimpsed but not caught and held. What is seen, discernible, is rarely seen for long and never permanently fixed. The person who reaches for the elusive particle of energy is like the artist who reaches for the stuff of inspiration, like any person trying to grasp the animating fire of the cosmos. The discrepancy between the immutable facts of existence and the momentary, incredible beauty of life at its most moving is a familiar feature of Issa's work: "Autumn breezes shake/ the scarlet flowers my poor child/ could not wait to pick." Issa's famous "Dewdrop" haiku was also the result of the loss of one of his children, but in this poem too, it is the moment of special feeling that is as celebrated—a mixture of sadness and extraordinary perception.

Spiritualism and faith

The consolation of poetry could not be entirely sufficient to compensate for the terrible sense of loss in Issa's life, but he could not accept standard religious precepts easily either. He was drawn to the fundamental philosophical positions of Buddhist thought, but his natural skepticism and clear eye for sham prevented him from entering into any dogma without reservation. Typically, he tried to undermine the pomposity of religious institutions while combining the simplicity of understated spiritualism with his usual humor to express reverence for what he found genuinely sacred: "Chanting at the altar/ of the inner sanctuary . . ./ a cricket priest." Insisting on a personal relationship with everything, Issa venerated what he saw as the true manifestation of the great spirits of the universe: "Ah sacred swallow . . ./ twittering out from your nest in/ Great Buddha's nostril." The humanity of his position, paradoxically, is much more like real religious consciousness than the chanting of orthodox believers who mouth mindless slogans although unable to understand anything of Amida Buddha's message to humankind: "For each single fly/ that's swatted, 'Namu Amida/ Butsu' is the cry." Above all, Issa was able to keep his priorities clear. One is reminded of the famous Zen description of the universe, "No holiness, vast emptiness," by Issa's determination to keep Buddha from freezing into an icon: "Polishing the Buddha . . ./ and why not my pipe as well/ for the holidays?" As translator Henderson points out, "the boundless love attributed to Amida Buddha coalesced with his own tenderness toward all weak things—children and animals and insects." Even in those poems of a religious nature that do not have a humorous slant there is a feeling of humility that is piety's best side: "Before the sacred/ mountain shrine of Kamiji . . ./ my head bent itself." In this poem, too, there is an instinctive response that does not depend on a considered position or careful analysis, thus paralleling Issa's reacion to the phenomena of the natural world, the true focus of his worship.

While most of Issa's haiku are like the *satori* of Zen awareness, a moment of sudden enlightenment expressed in a "charged image," Issa's "voice" also has a reflective quality that develops from a rueful realization of the profound sadness of existence. What makes Issa's voice so appealing in his more thoughtful poems is his expression of a kind of faith in the value of enduring. He can begin the new year by saying: "Felicitations!/ Still . . . I guess this year too/ will prove only so-so." Or he can draw satisfaction from triumphs of a very small scale: "Congratulations Issa!/ You have survived to feed/ this year's mosquitos." The loss of five children and his wife's early death somehow did not lead to paralysis by depression: "If my grumbling wife/ were still alive I just/ might enjoy tonight's moon." When his life seemed to be reduced almost to a kind of existential nothingness, he could see its apparent futility and still find a way to feel some amusement: "One man and one fly/ buzzing together in one/ big bare empty room." Or he could calculate the rewards of trying to act charitably, his humor mocking his efforts but not obscuring the fact that the real reward he obtained was in his singular way of seeing: "Yes . . . the young sparrows/ if you treat them tenderly—/ thank you with droppings."

SOMBER POEMS

There were moments when the sadness became more than his humor could bear. How close to tragic pessimism is this poem, for example: "The people we know . . ./ but these days even scarecrows/ do not stand upright." How close to despair is this heartfelt lament: "Mother lost, long gone . . ./ at the deep dark sea I stare—/ at the deep dark sea." Issa is one of those artists whose work must be viewed as a connected body of creation with reciprocal elements. Poems such as these somber ones must be seen as dark seasoning, for the defining credo at the crux of his work is that his effort has been worthwhile. In another attempt at a death song, Issa declared: "Full-moon and flowers/ solacing my forty-nine/ foolish years of song." Since death was regarded as another transitory stage in a larger vision of existence, Issa could dream of a less troubled life in which his true nature emerged: "Gay . . . affectionate . . ./ when I'm reborn I pray to be/ a white-wing butterfly." He, knew, however, that this was wishful thinking. In his poetry, he was already a "white-wing butterfly," and the tension between the man and the poem, between the tenuousness of life and the eternity of art, energized his soul. As he put it himself, summarizing his life and art: "Floating butterfly/ when you dance before my eyes . . ./ Issa, man of mud."

OTHER MAJOR WORKS
NONFICTION: *Chichi no shūen nikki*, 1803 (*Diary of My Father's Death*, 1992).
MISCELLANEOUS: *Oragu haru*, 1819 (*The Year of My Life*, 1960); *Issa zenshū*, 1929; *Issa zenshū*, 1979 (9 volumes).

BIBLIOGRAPHY
Blyth, R. H. *Eastern Culture*. Vol. 1 in *Haiku*. 4th ed. Tokyo: Hokuseido Press, 1990. Discusses Issa in the context of the spiritual origins of haiku in Zen Buddhism and other Eastern spiritual traditions. Sees Issa as the poet of destiny, who saw his own tragic experiences as part of the larger motions of fate. Also interprets him both as a poet within Japanese culture and as a poet of universal appeal.

_____. *From the Beginnings Up to Issa*. Vol. 1 in *A History of Haiku*. 1963. Reprint. Tokyo: Hokuseido Press, 1973. Devotes four chapters to Issa, presenting Issa's work in chronological order, ending in the haiku of Issa's old age. Includes interpretations of Issa's work plus examples of his portrayals of plants and the small creatures of the earth and of meaningful personal incidents, such as the deaths of his wife and children. Compares and contrasts him with the great haiku poet Bashō.

Issa. *Autumn Wind Haiku: Selected Poems by Kobayashi Issa*. Translated by Lewis Mackenzie. New York: Kodansha International, 1999. This volume was originally published as *Autumn Wind* in 1957. The translator provides an informative introduction to a selection of Issa's haiku. Mackenzie assesses Issa's contributions to the haiku form, includes a detailed narrative of Issa's often troubled life, and comments on individual haiku. Includes both English translations of the poems and phonetic Japanese versions.

Kato, Shūichi. *A History of Japanese Literature: The Modern Years*. Vol. 3. Translated by Don Sanderson. New York: Kodansha International, 1990. Includes a short chapter on Issa as a realistic, down-to-earth poet of everyday life and in the context of the Japanese society of the time.

Ueda, Makoto. *Dew on the Grass: The Life and Poetry of Kobayashi Issa*. Boston: Brill, 2004. A biography of Issa that incorporates his poetry and modern Japanese scholarship. In the preface, Ueda notes that Issa has had a marked influence on Japanese poets and novelists but is viewed as less skilled than Buson and Bashō by Japanese scholars.

Yasuda, Kenneth. *Japanese Haiku: Its Essential Nature, History, and Possibilities in English, with Selected Examples*. Rutland, Vt.: Charles E. Tuttle, 1994. References to Issa and samples of his work in the context of a thorough analysis of the theory and practice of haiku.

Leon Lewis

MATSUO BASHŌ

Born: Ueno, Iga Province, Japan; 1644
Died: Ōsaka, Japan; October 12, 1694
Also known as: Matsuo Kinsaku

PRINCIPAL POETRY
Sarumino, 1691 (*Monkey's Raincoat*, 1973)
Bashō's Haiku: Selected Poems by Matsuo Bashō, 2004
Haikai shichibu-shū, n.d.

OTHER LITERARY FORMS

The literary works of Matsuo Bashō (mah-tsew-oh bah-shoh) are difficult to classify, even for those acquainted with Japanese literary history. Bashō is popularly known as the greatest of all haiku poets, although the literary form was not defined and named until two hundred years after his death. Modern collections labeled "Bashō's *haiku*" are generally bits and pieces taken from his travel journals and *renku* (linked poems). In a sense, all Bashō's literary works are broader and more complex than the seventeen-syllable haiku for which he is remembered. The seven major anthologies of his school, listed above, contain *hokku* (opening verses) and *renku* composed by Bashō and his disciples, as well as an occasional prose piece. Besides *hokku* and *renku*, Bashō is known for his *haibun*, a combination of terse prose and seventeen-syllable *hokku* generally describing his pilgrimages to famous sites in Japan. His best-known travel journals include *Nozarashi kikō* (1687; *The Records of a Weather-Exposed Skeleton*, 1966), *Oku no hosomichi* (1694; *The Narrow Road to the Deep North*, 1933), *Oi no kobumi* (1709; *The Records of a Travel-Worn Satchel*, 1966), and *Sarashina kikō* (1704; *A Visit to Sarashina Village*, 1957). Bashō's conversations on poetry were preserved by disciples, and his surviving letters, numbering more than a hundred, are treasured today.

ACHIEVEMENTS

Matsuo Bashō is the favorite poet of Japan and one of the only poets of Asia whose verses are known popularly in the West. It is paradoxical that this complex poet whose profundity continues to tease the minds of Japan's greatest literary critics is read and recited by schoolchildren in many lands. Although technically he never wrote a haiku, Bashō serves as a model for many children, East and West, writing their first verses as haiku. The wedding of simplicity and profundity that characterizes Bashō's work provides a true measure of his stature as a poet.

The continuing popularity of Bashō in his homeland, a country where laymen pride themselves on being aesthetic critics, is itself an extraordinary tribute to his work. Japanese still make pilgrimages to the stone monuments marking the stopping places on his journeys. Many recite his verses when they hear a frog splash, smell plum blossoms on a mountain trail, or hear a cicada's shrill voice. Thanks in no small part to his work, many average citizens of Japan still write poetry, hang scrolls containing verse, and read the poetry column in Japan's daily newspapers.

In an age when aristocrats were the arbiters of taste, setting the complex rules for the writing of *waka* and *renga*, the chief poetic forms of Japan, Bashō devoted himself to *haikai*, an informal style of poetry celebrating the seasons of nature and the round of ordinary life among peasants and merchants. Without Bashō, *haikai* was in danger of sliding into slavish imitation of aristocratic canons or of degenerating into a display of vulgarity, coarse humor, and puns. Bashō democratized literature in Japan, and through literature, he helped democratize Japanese aesthetics. Bringing to bear his own sensitivity to the nature mysticism of Chinese Daoism and the radical sacramentalization of the ordinary in Zen Buddhism, he created a poetry of breadth and depth for the Japanese populace. As he observes in one of his *hokku*: "The beginning of art:/ Songs sung by those planting rice/ In the back country."

More specifically, Bashō's achievements in literature led to the maturing of three forms: the *hokku*, the *haikai no renga* (informal linked verse), and the *haibun*. Devoting a lifetime of effort to *hokku*, those seventeen-syllable verses intended as openings for linked poems, Bashō prepared the form for its modern independence as haiku. Working tirelessly with disciples in Japan's cities and countryside, Bashō infused a sense of the shared spirit of poetry that led to Japan's greatest *renku*, perhaps the high point of *za no geijutsu* (group art) in the history of world literature. Finally, his mastery of the combination of prose and poetry in travel journals set a new standard for the form the Japanese call *haibun*.

Describing himself in one of his *haibun*, *The Records of a Travel-Worn Satchel*, Bashō suggested a further unity, the unity of all arts when sounded to their depths, and the unity of art with nature, a philosophy that has given Japan its unique character:

> Finally, this poet, incapable as he is, has bound himself to the thin line of poetry. One and the same thread runs through the *waka* of Saigyō, *renga* of Sōgi, paintings of Sesshū, and tea ceremony of Riky. What the arts hold in common is a devotion to nature and companionship with the four seasons.

Biography

Centuries of warfare among the lords and samurai of Japan's chief clans came to an end when Tokugawa Ieyasu established a military dictatorship, the Shogunate, about 1600. With a Tokugawa shogun established in the thriving merchant city of Edo (modern-day Tokyo) and a ceremonial imperial court in ancient Kyoto, Japan officially closed its doors to the outside world in 1638. Such was the setting in which Matsuo

Bashō was born as Matsuo Munefusa in 1644 at Ueno in Iga province, only thirty miles from the imperial palace in Kyoto and two hundred miles from the powerful shogun in Edo.

Bashō was one of several children born to Matsuo Yozaemon, a minor samurai nominally in the service of the Tōdō family that ruled the Ueno area. Bashō's father had limited means and probably provided for his family by farming and giving lessons in calligraphy. At about age twelve, perhaps the year his father died, Bashō entered the service of the Tōdō family as a study companion to one of the Tōdō heirs, Yoshitada, a youth two years his senior with a bent toward poetry. A genuine friendship with Yoshitada encouraged young Bashō in the study of poetry and gave him access to one of the leading teachers of the day, Kitamura Kigin (1624-1705). When Yoshitada died suddenly in 1666, Bashō, only twenty-two years of age, lost both a friend and a patron. He apparently remained in the area of Ueno and Kyoto, devoting himself to poetry in the *haikai* style of the Teitoku school favored by his teacher Kigin. Pursuing a career as a poet, by 1672, he had published at his own expense *Kai-ōi* (seashell game), a collection of humorous verses by local poets that he matched and commented upon as poet-teacher. Some scholars believe that during this period, Bashō entered a relationship with a woman later known by her religious name, Jutei, and perhaps fathered children by her, but other scholars have dismissed this as pure speculation.

In 1672, at age twenty-eight, Bashō established himself in the bustling city of Edo, where his reputation as *haikai* poet and teacher increased. In 1680, he published *Tōsei montei dokugin nijū kasen* (twenty *kasen* by Tōsei's pupils), a collection of thirty-six-link *renku*. That year, he settled in a hut on the outskirts of Edo, next to which one of his disciples planted a *bashō*. In time, the poet's residence became known as the *Bashō-an* (banana-plant hut), and his students began to address him as "Master Bashō." Thus was born the nickname by which he was known for the rest of his life.

Bashō's early poetry was influenced by the Teitoku or Teimon style of *haikai*, using clever literary allusions and wordplay. In Edo, he came under the influence of the Danrin school, which explored greater freedom in theme and diction and demonstrated genuine interest in the life of the merchants and laborers of Edo. By about 1681, his own style, called *shōfū*, had begun to emerge, as evidenced in his *hokku* describing a crow on a withered branch in autumn twilight. Bashō also began practicing meditation under the direction of a Zen priest, Butchō (1642-1715).

In the fall of 1684, Bashō put on the robes of a Buddhist priest and began a series of pilgrimages over the roads and rugged mountain trails of Japan to perfect the new ideal of his art, *sabi* (solitariness). The final twelve years of his life were given largely to strenuous travel, the perfecting of the *haibun*-style travel journal, and sessions with disciples along the way who responded to his teaching and joined him in the art of *haikai no renga*, the linking of verses to produce *renku*. By 1686, he had written his most famous verse, describing the contrast of an old pond and a frog's splash, and by 1689, he had taken the difficult inland journey that led to the height of *haibun* art, *The Narrow Road to the Deep North*. Near the end of his life, to the chagrin of some of his disciples, Bashō had begun to advocate a new principle for the writing of *haikai*: *karumi* (lightness), a focus on the ordinary and unadorned.

During a final trip to Ueno and Ōsaka to preach *karumi* and to patch up a quarrel among his disciples, Bashō's strength failed and an old illness flared up; he dictated a final verse from his deathbed: "Ill on the journey/ My dreams going round and round/ Over withered fields."

Analysis

At a time when many *haikai* poets wrote hundreds of verses during a single night's linked-poetry session, Matsuo Bashō's lifetime accumulation of barely a thousand seventeen-syllable *hokku* is indicative of the seriousness with which he took his art. Constantly struggling with each of these verses, Bashō established a standard of craftsmanship and profundity that would later lead to *hokku*'s independent status as haiku.

The *hokku* often singled out as Bashō's first masterpiece is his crow verse of 1681: "On a withered branch/ A crow settles itself down—/ Autumn evening." The stark tableau of a black branch against the darkened sky is broken by the sudden movement of a crow alighting. Here, timelessness and the momentary meet, and as they merge, the wider and deeper cycle of nature's seasonal pattern is revealed. The darkness of branch, crow, and autumn nightfall interpenetrate, suggesting the Japanese aesthetic qualities called *wabi* (poverty) and *sabi* (solitude).

Themes

What the poet has not said is as significant as his choice of theme. The traditional aristocratic themes of Japanese court poetry, the scented love notes, koto music, and tear-drenched sleeves of *waka* are absent. Bashō reaches back to the themes and cadences of the great Tang Dynasty poets of China, Du Fu and Li Bo, to lend universality to his verse. The monochromes of the great Chan masters are suggested by the black branch and crow, and perhaps the *hokku* itself suggests the Chinese poetic topic, "shivering crow in leafless tree." The merging of all in the mystery of darkness suggests Bashō's reading preferences: Daoism's Zhuangzi (Chuang-tzu) and Japan's poet-priests Saigyō and Sōgi. The rhythm and repetition of sounds, lost in English translation, witness Bashō's careful craftsmanship in the crow verse: *kare* (withered), *karasu* (crow), *aki no kure* (autumn evening).

Frog verses

One of Bashō's Edo disciples, Senka, compiled a *haikai* matching of verses on the subject "frog" in 1686, *Kawazu awase* (frog contest). Bashō provided the opening verse, or *hokku*, the most famous of all his works: "An age-old pond—/ A frog leaps into it/ Splash goes the water." The presence of *kawazu* (frog), a *kigo* (season word), tells the reader that it is spring. The poet sees the still surface of a murky pond, probably an ancient pond edged by rocks and reeds designed centuries earlier by some Zen priest as a setting for a temple. A sudden splash shatters the stillness of the pond, and in that disruption a new awareness of the eternal is sealed on the consciousness. Asian philosophy's yin-yang complementarity is revealed in the relation of stillness to sound, and the Daoist theme of a void from which momentary forms of life emerge and to which they return is celebrated. The consummate demonstration of just how much can be suggested in a few words constitutes Bashō's principal contribution to the *hokku* and suggests the Asian "one-corner philosophy": Sensitivity to the smallest creature or the briefest moment within the cycle of nature provides a gateway to the motion and meaning of the entire universe. In the words of Zen Buddhism, "The mountains, trees, and grasses are the Buddha."

ZEN AND DAOISM

Bashō's training in Zen Buddhist meditation and his donning the robes of a Buddhist priest for his travels might suggest that the key concept of Buddhism, *sunyata* (emptiness), would find expression in his verses. It is significant that many of Bashō's *hokku* focus not on a presence but rather on an "absence," a creative emptiness that suggests "pure potentiality." He writes of a skylark "clinging to nothing at all," of Mount Fuji "disappearing in mist," of flowers "without names," and of "a road empty of travelers." The Daoist void and Buddhist emptiness are expressed in the aesthetic quality Japanese call *yūgen* (mysterious vagueness), a quality of the *hokku* akin to the vacant spaces in a Zen scroll painting.

KARUMI

In 1693, just a year before his death, Bashō "shut his gate" for a time, refusing all visitors. When he opened the gate again to his disciples, he began teaching a further development of *haikai* poetry, the principle of *karumi* (lightness). Even close disciples had misgivings and uncertainties about this principle to which the poet devoted his final year. Moving beyond *wabi, sabi,* and *yūgen,* Bashō sought a return to some primal simplicity in the ordinariness of life, simplicity beyond both technical excellence and poetic response to the past. He wrote of a "sick wild duck/ falling in the cold of night," of "salted fish" in a street market, of a "white-haired/ graveyard visit," a "motionless cloud," and "autumn chill." The experience of eternity was no longer simply intensified by the momentary; for Bashō, it had become incarnate in the unadorned ordinariness of life.

THE ART OF HAIKAI

Modern interest in Bashō's art has generally focused on the *hokku*. Bashō himself, however, believed the art of *haikai* was to be found less in isolated verses than in cooperative effort of a like-minded school of poets involved in "sequence composition," and apparently he felt his greatest achievements occurred in this area: "Among my disciples many are as gifted as I am in writing *hokku*. But this old man knows the true spirit of *haikai*." The art of *haikai*, or *haikai no renga*, is so foreign to Western experience that appreciation of its merits and of Bashō's contribution is especially difficult.

The *waka* was the chief poetic form of the Japanese from prehistory through the thirteenth century. The special possession of the aristocracy at court, short *waka* called *tanka* were sometimes created by two persons, one composing the upper seventeen syllables and another responding with the lower fourteen. When *tanka* rules became too confining, some poets began to compose *renga* (linked verses) of a *haikai* (informal) or *mushin* (frivolous) sort. *Renga* soon became adopted by the court and developed its own *ushin* (serious) rules, and so by the sixteenth century a *haikai no renga* movement sought to democratize the form again.

Bashō, an artist of *haikai no renga*, sought to keep the form open to creative contact with everyday life, yet sought also to transcend common wordplay and vulgarities. His cooperative poetic efforts with four Nagoya merchants in *Fuyu no hi* (a winter's day) and with sixteen disciples in a hundred-verse sequence called *Hatsu kaishi* (*First Manuscript Page*), culminating in a series of thirty-six-link *renku* collected in *Monkey's Raincoat*. Using the rules regarding season sequences and moon and flower verses with freedom yet sensitivity, he advocated linking alternate seventeen-syllable and fourteen-syllable verses through the principle of *nioi* (fragrance), a vague but effective sense of atmosphere and mood conveyed by one poet and verse to another.

"IN THE CITY"

A *renku* in thirty-six verses titled "Ichinaka wa" ("In the City") appears in *Monkey's Raincoat*. Its opening verse (*hokku*) is by the poet Bonchō, who introduces the "heavy odor of things" in the city and uses the seasonal words "summer moon." Bashō responds with the answering verse (*waki*), describing voices in the night at "gate after gate." They repeat, "It is hot, so hot." From there, a third poet shifts the scene to a rice paddy, Bonchō continues with a verse describing a farmer's "smoked sardine" meal, and Bashō adds a link that pictures himself as a visitor to this poor farm neighborhood, where "they don't even recognize money." Within the next half dozen verses, a young girl's religious experience is described, the season shifts to winter, and Bashō introduces an aged peasant who "can only suck the bones of fish." Sounds and word associations linking one verse to another are so subtle that even experienced *haikai* poets disagree in their analysis, though not in their high evaluation of the *renku*.

Perhaps the greatest facet of Bashō's art, linked poetry written cooperatively through a shared "fragrance," is largely closed to the Western reader, though a good *renku* translation and commentary may be of some aid. Those familiar with Western chamber music may detect similarities, as themes pass from one player to another, exciting changes in tempo and mood are introduced, and one instrument modulates to support the contribution of another.

THE NARROW ROAD TO THE DEEP NORTH

Finally, it should be noted that some critics view neither the *hokku* nor the *haikai no renga* as the height of Bashō's art. They would view his travel journals, culminating in *The Narrow Road to the Deep North*, as the epitome of his creative efforts.

In *The Narrow Road to the Deep North*, widely regarded as one of the finest works in all Japanese literature, the pilgrim-poet seeks to mature his art by hiking to those sites of beauty and history that inspired Saigyō and other poet-priests of the past. Taking arduous trails both to the inner country of Japan and the inner reaches of his own art, Bashō weaves prose and poetry into a record of a pilgrimage of the Japanese spirit as it responds to the history and beauty of the homeland. The famous opening declares that "moon and sun are eternal travelers," and bids the reader to join in the journey. Bashō describes famous sites and views at Matsushima, Hiraizumi, and Kisagata, pausing to muse over ruined castles and ancient battlefields:

> The summer grasses—
> For courageous warriors
> The aftermath of dreams.

In a land ruled by powerful military shoguns who had closed Japan to all outside contacts, such musings in the spirit of the great T'ang poets of China made this travel journal an act of courage and a proclamation that art cannot be confined by political borders. Allusions to Chinese poetry and philosophy, Japanese history and aesthetics, are woven together in such a complex tapestry that, once again, the Western reader is in need of a superior translation and a helpful commentary, but the treasures to be discovered are worth the effort.

Bashō, the poet whose verses are loved by children yet challenge the best efforts of mature scholars, spent his life in pilgrimage for his art and died on the road. In *The Narrow Road to the Deep North*, he sums up the relevance of his wanderings in a few simple words, identifying his readers as pilgrims, too: "For each day is a journey, and the journey itself is home."

OTHER MAJOR WORKS

NONFICTION: *Nozarashi kikō*, 1687 (travel; *The Records of a Weather-Exposed Skeleton*, 1966); *Oku no hosomichi*, 1694 (travel; *The Narrow Road to the Deep North*, 1933); *Sarashina kikō*, 1704 (travel; *A Visit to Sarashina Village*, 1966); *Oi no kobumi*, 1709 (travel; *The Records of a Travel-Worn Satchel*, 1966).

MISCELLANEOUS: *The Essential Bashō*, 1999.

Bibliography

Aitken, Robert. *A Zen Wave: Bashō's Haiku and Zen*. New York: Weatherhill, 1978. One of the few studies of Bashō by a Western roshi, or master teacher of Zen. This overview evaluates the poet's work in the context of Zen philosophy, offering the claim that Bashō's haiku transcend mere nature poetry and instead serve as a way of presenting fundamental religious truths about mind, nature, and cosmos.

Caws, Mary Ann, ed. *Textual Analysis: Some Readers Reading*. New York: Modern Language Association of America, 1986. Earl Miner's chapter on Bashō has as its main thesis that Bashō has not been known in the West as he would have wished to be known. The focus of his discussion is the fact that the Western concept of mimesis, what is real and what is fiction, differs from its Eastern counterpart, opening the way to misunderstanding.

Hamill, Sam, trans. *The Essential Bashō*. Boston: Shambhala, 1999. The introduction to this work represents Bashō as a consummate writer. In this work, religious issues are significantly downplayed. Instead Hamill presents his subject as a poetic and philosophical wanderer: someone engaged in a lifelong process of literary experimentation and discovery. Particularly fascinating is the overview of Bashō's transformation from a highly derivative stylist to a powerfully original poet.

Qiu, Peipei. *Basho and the Dao: The Zhuangzi and the Transformation of Haikai*. Honolulu: University of Hawaii Press, 2005. Examines the relationship between Daoism and Bashō's poetry. Contains considerable discussion of themes and influences.

Shirane, Haruo. *Traces of Dreams: Landscape, Cultural Memory, and the Poetry of Bashō*. Stanford, Calif.: Stanford University Press, 1998. This work puts the poet in the position of cultural conservationist, arguing that Bashō's poems drew on deeply held concepts of nature.

Ueda, Makoto. *Matsuo Bashō*. New York: Twayne, 1970. This study offers a brief biography as well as general perspectives on the author's major works. In addition to the expected focus on haiku, it treats Bashō's *renku* (long, collaboratively written poems) and prose works.

_____, ed. *Bashō and His Interpreters: Selected Hokku with Commentary*. Stanford, Calif.: Stanford University Press, 1992. This work is a chronologically organized anthology of Bashō's poems, each accompanied by the original Japanese text (transliterated into Western characters) and literal translations. Although this anthology offers little new insight into Bashō's life or interpretations of his work, this volume does demonstrate the tremendous influence of translation on the written word.

Cliff Edwards

KENJI MIYAZAWA

Born: Hanamaki, Japan; August 27, 1896
Died: Hanamaki, Japan; September 21, 1933

PRINCIPAL POETRY
Haru to shura, 1924 (*Spring and Asura*, 1973)
The Back Country, 1957
Miyazawa Kenji: Selections, 2007 (Hiroaki Sato, translator)
Strong in the Rain: Selected Poems, 2007 (Roger Pulvers, translator)

OTHER LITERARY FORMS

In addition to a substantial body of free verse and many *tanka* (the *tanka* is a fixed form of thirty-one syllables in five lines), Kenji Miyazawa (mee-yah-zah-wah) wrote children's stories, often in a fantastic vein. He also wrote a limited number of essays, the most important one of which outlines his ideas for an agrarian art. The children's stories have proved popular in Japan, and some of them are available along with the major poems in English translation. It should also be noted that Miyazawa drafted and reworked his poems in a series of workbooks over the course of his creative life; while the notebooks are not publications in a formal sense, they might be considered part of the Miyazawa canon. In any case, they are commonly utilized by scholars investigating the sources of the poet's art.

ACHIEVEMENTS

A poet of unique gifts, Kenji Miyazawa spent his relatively brief life in almost total obscurity. Living in a primitive rural area, writing virtually as a form of religious practice, Miyazawa published only one volume of stories and one of poetry during his life. Neither work attracted attention at the time of its publication.

Shortly after Miyazawa's death, however, his work began to be noticed. His utilization of scientific, religious, and foreign terms became familiar, and the striking images and energy of his verses seemed exciting alongside the generally restrained modes of Japanese poetic expression.

Most surprising of all, Miyazawa started to attain the prominence and affection he still enjoys among the general public. Almost any literate Japanese would know one poem that he jotted down in his notebook late in life. Sketching the portrait of Miyazawa's ideal selfless person, the poem begins with the lines, "Neither to wind yielding/ Nor to rain."

Miyazawa began composing *tanka* poems while still a middle school student. His principal works are in free verse, however, and these he composed mostly during the decade of the 1920's. Throughout these years, various forms of modernism—Futurism and Surrealism, for example—were being introduced to Japan, and certain native poets experimented with these new styles of writing. Miyazawa, however, worked in total isolation from such developments. This is not to say that his work is sui generis in any absolute sense. Assuredly a religious poet, Miyazawa worked out a cosmology for certain of his poems that, according to one Western scholar, resembles in a general way the private cosmologies of such poets as William Blake and William Butler Yeats.

Biography

Kenji Miyazawa was born on August 27, 1896, in the town of Hanamaki in the northern prefecture of Iwate. Iwate has a cool climate, and the farmers of the region led a precarious existence. Miyazawa's father ran a pawnshop, a business that prospered in part because of the poverty of the local farmers.

As the oldest son, Miyazawa would normally have succeeded his father as head of the family business. Uneasy at the thought of living off the poverty of others, however, Miyazawa neglected the task of preparing himself to succeed his father in the family business. Instead, he immersed himself in the study of philosophy and religion. An exemplary student in grade school, Miyazawa's record became worse from year to year in middle school as he pursued his own intellectual interests. Some of this independence is also discernible in occasional escapades during his youth, one of which led to his expulsion from the school dormitory.

By 1915, Miyazawa had decided to find work outside the family business. In this year, he entered the Morioka College of Agriculture and Forestry. Along with his studies in such areas as chemistry and soils, Miyazawa formulated various plans for his future, plans whereby he could utilize his knowledge to contribute to the amelioration of the harsh conditions of rural life. For a time, he even hoped to turn the resources of the family business to some new venture that might be of general economic benefit—producing industrial chemicals from the soil of the area, for example.

A new dimension was added to Miyazawa's differences with his father during these years. Initially he had followed his father's religious preference as a believer in the Jōdo Shin sect of Buddhism. Eventually, however, Miyazawa decided that ultimate truth resided in the militant Nichiren sect, especially in its intense devotion to the Lotus Sutra. In January, 1921, he took the extraordinary step of fleeing the family home in Hanamaki to join a Buddhist organization in Tokyo known as the State Pillar Society. Miyazawa returned home late that same year, partly because of the serious illness of his younger sister Toshiko and partly to take a teaching position at the two-year Hienuki Agricultural School.

Toshiko died in November, 1922, an event that the poet commemorated in a number of impressive elegies. Miyazawa continued to teach until March, 1926. In his spare time, he took his students for long treks in the countryside, writing incessantly in the notebooks that he took on these excursions. The poet made his first and only attempt at publishing his work in 1924. In addition to a volume of children's stories, he brought out at his own expense a volume of sketches in free verse, *Spring and Asura*.

Miyazawa gave up teaching from a sense of guilt. How could he accept a regular wage, no matter how small, when the average farmer was often destitute? Miyazawa decided, therefore, to become a farmer himself. A bachelor his entire life, he lived by himself raising vegetables for his own table and several small cash crops. Using the knowledge he had acquired over the years, he attempted to serve as an informal adviser to the farm community. In addition, he tried to instill in the rural populace a desire for culture.

Miyazawa had never possessed a strong constitution. He was ill on a number of occasions, and around 1928, unmistakable signs of tuberculosis began to appear. During the final years of his life, Miyazawa seems to have lost his creative urge—or, perhaps, sensing the imminence of death, he simply tried to rework the poems he had already written. The poet spent his last two years, from 1931 to 1933, as an invalid at the family home in Hanamaki. He and his father put aside their religious differences as death came closer for the son. Just before he died, on September 21, 1933, Miyazawa pointed toward a bookshelf and remarked that his unpublished manuscripts lying there had been produced out of a delusion.

Analysis

Like the American poet and physician William Carlos Williams, Kenji Miyazawa absorbed himself in ceaseless service to other people, whether his students or the local farmers. Like the American, Miyazawa, too, would jot down poems in the spare moments available to him. Unlike Williams, however, Miyazawa never seems to have considered a poem finished. With only one volume of poems published in his lifetime, Miyazawa worked steadily at revising and reworking his drafts. Three different sets of poems are titled *Spring and Asura*, a fact that suggests a common ground for a number of seemingly disparate works.

Spring and Asura

The first volume of *Spring and Asura* contains the title poem, a crucial poem that describes the poet caught up in intense visions of his own making. The persona narrates the vision from the viewpoint of an asura, that is, a being that ranks between humans and beasts in the six realms of existence in the Buddhist cosmology. (The six realms are devas, humans, asuras or demons, beasts, hungry ghosts, and dwellers in hell.) Despite the Buddhist references, the world of this asura is one of the poet's own making. A close study of Miyazawa's visionary poems by the American scholar Sarah Strong has uncovered a structure of levels—from a kind of Vacuum at the highest level (with the possibility of other worlds beyond) to the realm of the Western Marshes at the lowest. In between are various levels, with the Radiant Sea of Sky being the most complicated. The asura of Miyazawa's poems rushes about in this universe, finding "ecstasy" and "brightness" at the upper levels while encountering "unpleasantness" and "darkness" toward the bottom. This "structure," it must be noted, is not an immediately obvious feature of the poem. Indeed, to the untutored reader, many of Miyazawa's poems will seem mystifying and kaleidoscopic. For many, the effect of reading such works will surely be dizzying.

Miyazawa's visionary poems are difficult, but the poet has inserted passages that point the way to understanding. Preceding the Japanese text of "Spring and Asura," for example, he has entered these words in English that indicate the nature of the work to follow: "mental sketch modified." The initial volume of *Spring and Asura* also has an introductory poem or "Proem" preceding the title poem of the collection. In "Proem," Miyazawa includes lines and phrases that appear to point quite definitely at his intentions. For example, the poet says that the sketch to follow represents the workings of his imagination over the past twenty-two months. His way of putting the matter may be unusual (each piece on paper is a "chain of shadow and light," linked together "with mineral ink"), but the difficulty is more with the oddity of expression than with the meaning.

ELEGIES FOR TOSHIKO

Another set of poems by Miyazawa, the famous elegies composed upon the death of his sister Toshiko, also shows the imaginative energy of the poet. In this instance, however, the persona tends to stay within the normal and identifiable bounds of nature. The poet races outdoors to collect snow for comforting his dying sister or, after her death, wanders far beyond the region of the home in search of her whereabouts. The reader, however, knows exactly where the action is occurring. Bound to a specific and easily identifiable situation, these works seem more accessible than the aforementioned works from *Spring and Asura*.

Miyazawa's elegies on Toshiko exhibit an idiosyncrasy of vocabulary and image equal to that of "Spring and Asura." In contrast to the thematic uniqueness of this visionary poem, however, the elegies actually fit into a venerable tradition of Japanese poetry. Indeed, the elegy goes back to almost the beginnings of Japanese poetry in the *Manyōshū* (mid-eighth century; *The Collections of Ten Thousand Leaves*; also as *The Ten Thousand Leaves*, pb. 1981, and as *The Manyoshu*, 1940). Admittedly, the grief expressed by Miyazawa over the death of his sister seems more private and concentrated than the emotion found in certain of *The Manyoshu* elegies—in the partly ritualistic works by Kakinomoto no Hitomaro, which mourn the deaths of the high nobility, to mention a celebrated example. At the same time, Miyazawa follows Hitomaro and other elegists of *The Manyoshu* in his search for a trace of the deceased in nature and in his refusal to be satisfied with encountering anything less than the actual person.

DIDACTIC POEMS

If Miyazawa had written only visionary and elegiac poems, he probably would not have attained popularity except as a writer of children's tales. At the very least, his frequent use of foreign terms, whether Chinese or Sanskrit, German or Esperanto, would have made the poetry difficult for the average reader. Aside from the poems in which Miyazawa addresses his private concerns, however, certain works reflect the desire to instruct the common people. In the most celebrated of these didactic works—invariably printed as recorded in a notebook, that is, in the *katakana* syllabary understandable even to a beginning schoolchild—the poet sketches a portrait of the ideal person he wishes to be. That person lives a life of extreme frugality and of selfless devotion to others. Like the Bodhisattva of Buddhist doctrine, Miyazawa's ideal person is totally compassionate—caring for the sick, alleviating hunger, patching up quarrels, and carrying out other works of charity.

"DROUGHT AND ZAZEN"

Miyazawa was very much involved in the everyday life of the common people. This, in conjunction with his high ideals, occasionally elicited from him at least a partly satiric response. A work in this vein, titled "Kanbatsu to zazen" ("Drought and Zazen"), seems to belittle the Zen practice of meditation (zazen)—either for ignoring a pressing practical problem or for deluding its adherents into a false sense of religion's sphere of efficacy. The poem begins by describing some frogs as a Zen chorus anxiously trying to solve those perplexing puzzles known as koans. After this comic opening, Miyazawa depicts himself intently calculating the sequential phases through which the rice seedlings must pass before ripening. The contrast between religious petition on one hand and this primitive sort of scientific calculation on the other is striking.

LIGHTER POEMS

To claim that Miyazawa is satirizing Zen or meditation in this poem might well be an overstatement. If satire is at work, it is certainly good-humored. In fact, the lighthearted side of the poet needs special emphasis in view of the fact that his central works, especially a poem such as "Spring and Asura" and the elegies on Toshiko, are so somber and brooding.

On occasion, the poet will enjoy a lighter moment by himself—when, for example, in a poem titled "Shigoto" ("Work") he momentarily worries about the manure he threw from a cart and left on a hillside. More often, he will jest with the farmers and peasants of the region. In one poem, he pokes fun at a farmer named Hosuke for getting upset when a manure-carrying horse proves unruly; in another instance, he counsels a hardworking farmer to leave off bundling rice at midnight for the sake of the weary wife who is doing her best to assist him. In most of these works, the poet seems a carefree observer and counselor. Since Miyazawa is normally a somber poet, though, and the farmers, even in his lighthearted poems, are always hard at work, one might surmise that the poet regarded humor principally as a way for the farmer to cope with his burdens.

In any event, this playful side of Miyazawa is present in many different poems. Sometimes, the poet simply observes an appealing scene. His poem on an Ayrshire bull is a good example. The animal, seen at night against the light of a pulp factory, enjoys itself by rubbing its horns in the grass and butting a fence. At other times, Miyazawa seems to play with language in an extravagant manner. A certain horse in another poem is said to "rot like a potato" and "feel the bright sun's juice." A second horse meets a dire fate by running into a high-voltage wire in its stable, the funeral taking place with the human mourners shedding "clods of tears" upon the "lolling head" of the dead animal. Hosuke's manure horse engages in some impressive acrobatics, rearing up with "scarlet eyes" on one occasion as if to "rake in blue velvet, the spring sky."

The poem on the Ayrshire bull depicts a casual encounter, the sort of event that happens often in Miyazawa's playful poems about people. Running into an acquaintance, the poet engages this other in a little drama. These poems, most of them brief, present simple emotions and often contain some deft humor. Certain works employ the same techniques but pursue more ambitious aims. Among them is a fascinating piece titled "Shita de wakareta sakki no hito" ("The Man I Parted from, Below"). The man in question is a somewhat disembodied image that remains in the memory of the poet after the meeting to which the title alludes has taken place. Defined mainly as a smoker, the man has been leading a horse somewhere, possibly to another group of horses visible in the distance. At least this thought occurs to the poet as he surveys the scene before him and composes his appreciation of it. Certain of Miyazawa's typical concerns manifest themselves in the course of the work—the identification and naming of places, for example, or the sense of things happening in a kind of space-time continuum. Occasionally, an odd turn of phrase, too, reminds the reader of the poet's identity—the "aquamarine legs of winds," for example, or the highlands spread out "like ten or more playing cards." The horses on those highlands originally looked to the poet like "shining red ants." Such language, hardly startling to the Miyazawa aficionado, helps to elevate parts of the poem above mere plain description.

Indeed, "The Man I Parted from, Below" might seem tame alongside the coruscating images of "Spring and Asura" and the vibrating language of "Proem." The poem has certain compensations, however, even as a somewhat atypical work of Miyazawa. It shows that the poet could be at home in the calmer modes of Japanese lyricism and could deftly lay out a pattern of relationships involving himself, nature, and his fellow men.

Having parted from the poet, the smoker is now observed together with his horse moving off toward the distant herd. Though abandoned by the smoker as surely as he had once been by Toshiko, Miyazawa does not seem bereft in this poem. All about him are the familiar mountains and valleys for which, at this moment, he feels an "oddly helpless love." All the men in the poem—the keeper of the distant herd, the man with his sole horse, and the poet, too—seem related to one another, and to the animals as well, by their mere presence in the scene. Slightly idiosyncratic, moderately optimistic, entirely understandable, "The Man I Parted from, Below" shows the poet submitting his vision to the requirements of realism on a human scale.

OTHER MAJOR WORKS

SHORT FICTION: *Ginga tetsudo no yoru*, 1922 (*Night of the Milky Way Railway*, 1991); *Chūmon no ōi ryōriten*, 1924 (*The Restaurant of Many Orders, and Other Stories*, 2001); *Winds and Wildcat Places*, 1967; *Night Train to the Stars, and Other Stories*, 1987; *Once and Forever: The Tales of Kenji Miyazawa*, 1993.

MISCELLANEOUS: *Miyazawa Kenji zenshū*, 1967-1968 (12 volumes); *Kohon Miyazawa Kenji zenshū*, 1973-1977 (15 volumes); *A Future of Ice: Poems and Stories of a Japanese Buddhist*, 1989.

BIBLIOGRAPHY

Bester, John. Foreword to *Once and Forever: The Tales of Kenji Miyazawa*. Tokyo: Kodansha International, 1993. The preeminent translator of Miyazawa provides insights into the poet and his poetics.

Miyazawa, Kenji. *Miyazawa Kenji: Selections*. Edited by Hiroaki Sato. Berkeley: University of California Press, 2007. This collection of Miyazawa's poetry includes an introduction by the editor that examines the poet's significance and legacy and his place in Japanese literature. Includes several other essays on the poet.

Mori, Masaki. *Epic Grandeur: Toward a Comparative Poetics of the Epic*. Albany: State University of New York Press, 1997. Argues that the epic genre can be discerned in the twentieth century in works promoting peace as opposed to war. Considers Miyazawa's *Night of the Milky Way Railway* as a "transitional epic."

Pulvers, Roger. "Miyazawa Kenji, Rebel with a Cause." *Japan Quarterly* 43, no. 4 (October-December, 1996): 30-42. Pulvers, who published a translation of Miyazawa's poetry in 2007, describes the life and works of Miyazawa, noting his respect for nature. He discusses the poet's surge in popularity in the mid-1990's.

Ueda, Makoto. *Modern Japanese Poets and the Nature of Literature*. Stanford, Calif.: Stanford University Press, 1983. Summaries of modern Japanese poets, including Miyazawa.

Watson, Burton. Introduction to *Spring and Asura*. Chicago: Chicago Review Press, 1973. An overview of Miyazawa's work.

James O'Brien

MITSUYE YAMADA

Born: Fukuoka, Kyushu, Japan; July 5, 1923

PRINCIPAL POETRY
Camp Notes, and Other Poems, 1976

OTHER LITERARY FORMS

Mitsuye Yamada (yah-mah-dah) published two short stories in *Desert Run: Poems and Stories* and, in addition to producing her own work, has collaborated with others in editing poetry collections. Her essays on literature, personal history, and human rights have appeared in anthologies and periodicals, and she compiled a teachers' guide for Amnesty International. In 1981, the Public Broadcasting Service aired a documentary, *Mitsuye and Nellie: Two Asian-American Poets*, featuring Yamada and Chinese American writer Nellie Wong.

ACHIEVEMENTS

Mitsuye Yamada is one of the first writers to publish a personal account of the United States' internment of citizens of Japanese descent. Publication of the "Camp Notes" poems also marked an important event in the resurgence of feminist literature in the 1970's. Yamada has served on the national board of Amnesty International on the organization's Committee on International Development. She has received numerous awards for her writing, teaching, and human rights work.

BIOGRAPHY

Mitsuye May Yamada was born in Fukuoka, Kyushu, Japan, the third child and only daughter of Jack Yasutake and Hide Yasutake. She was brought to the United States at age three. At the age of nine, she went to Japan to live with her father's family for eighteen months. She lived with her parents and three brothers in Seattle until she was nineteen. Her high school education was curtailed in 1941 when her father, a translator for the United States Immigration Service, was imprisoned as an enemy alien. Mitsuye, her mother, and her brothers were later removed to internment camps in Puyallup, Washington, and Minidoka, Idaho. She spent eighteen months in the camps, finally leaving to work and study at the University of Cincinnati. She completed her bachelor's degree at New York University and a master of arts degree in English literature at the University of Chicago.

She was able to become a naturalized American citizen following passage of the McCarran-Walter Immigration Act and received citizenship in 1955. In 1950, she married chemist Yoshikazu Yamada (becoming Mitsuye Yasutake Yamada). They lived in

New York, where their four children were born, until the early 1960's, when the family moved to Southern California. In 1966, she began teaching in community colleges and was professor of English at Cypress Community College from 1968 until her retirement in 1989. Following publication of *Camp Notes, and Other Poems*, she held many university appointments as visiting professor, artist-in-residence, and consultant.

A lifelong commitment to human rights emerged as Yamada's response to her incarceration, and she has related her sense of urgency on the subject to years of living with a diagnosis of incurable emphysema when her children were very young. She was an early member of Amnesty International and has served on the executive board and national committees in that organization. Her poetry was published by feminist presses; she organized a multicultural women writers group and has participated in numerous projects addressed to the concerns of women, ethnic groups, and environmental awareness.

Analysis

Originally published by Shameless Hussy, a struggling feminist press, Mitsuye Yamada's *Camp Notes, and Other Poems* is a personal volume involving family participation. The cover illustration, by the author's older daughter, Jeni Yamada, is a line drawing of a female figure in three stages: a shy little girl, an older girl walking forward, and a striding woman carrying either a briefcase or suitcase. The ambiguity of the last figure can refer to the camp experience, where internees were able to bring only what they could carry, or to the author's professional life as writer, teacher, and activist. The author's husband contributed the book's calligraphy, and the volume is dedicated to Yamada's parents, husband, two daughters, and two sons. The actual "Camp Notes" poems center the volume and are bracketed by an opening section on the author's parents and a closing series of poems looking to the present and future.

The seven poems in the section "My Issei Parents, Twice Pioneers, Now I Hear Them" were written after the central "camp notes" set, and they look back to parents, grandparents, and great-grandparents. The section opens with a folk saying: "What your Mother tells you now/ in time/ you will come to know." The text appears first in brush-stroke ideograms, then in transliterated Japanese, and finally in the author's translation. The theme permeates the author's work, which engages with the ways that origins—"the mother"—shape a person, through both acceptance and resistance.

The next poem offers a portrait of "Great Grandma" figured in her orderly collection of ordinary objects: "colored stones," "parched persimmons," "powdery green tea." Great Grandma's static world and calm acceptance of fate stand in contrast to the turmoil, pain, and conflict documented in much of Yamada's work.

"Marriage Was a Foreign Country" and "Homecoming" are narrated in the voice of the persona's mother; they tell stories of pain and difficulty of life as a Japanese immigrant woman in a country both alien and hostile. Following these poems are two poems relating to the speaker's father. Contrasting the mother's monologues, these dialogues comment on traditional Japanese wisdom that the father is attempting to impart.

The section titled "Camp Notes" highlights poems composed while Yamada was imprisoned with her mother and brothers in the Minidoka camp. Thirty years later, the poems were culled from their early inscription in a large writing tablet, one of the few possessions the author could take with her to the camp. The section opens with another line drawing by Jeni Yamada, picturing a small child clutching a stuffed animal and seated amid piles of luggage. The first poems tally the upheaval of the removal experience with titles such as "Evacuation," "Curfew," and "On the Bus." The title of "Harmony at the Fair Grounds" reflects the irony in many of these brief, acrid poems: The "grounds" on which the Japanese Americans were imprisoned were anything but "fair." The last lines offer a stark picture of concentration camp life: "Lines formed for food/ lines for showers/ lines for the john/ lines for shots."

A secondary subheading, "Relocation," designates poems about life in the Minidoka camp. The author continues to document the grim, degrading aspects of prison life, where monotony and uncertainty intensified the physical stresses of primitive, cramped quarters and the denial of amenities such as radios and cameras. Even more demoralizing are the irrationality, stupidity, and lies of the bureaucratic internment system. As the family huddles under bedclothes to survive a "Desert Storm," the speaker observes

>   This was not
>   im
>   prison
>   ment.
>   This was
>   re
>   location.

Likewise, the opening of "Block 4 Barrack 4 'Apt' C" demolishes the excuse that relocation benefited the imprisoned, noting that barbed wire protected the inmates from "wildly twisted/ sagebrush." In two poems, the persona notes the paradox of guards locked inside their watchtowers. Hedi Yamada, the author's younger daughter, illustrated "The Watchtower" with a silhouette drawing of an adult holding a child's hand and gazing at such a tower; it is impossible to tell whether they are looking out of or into the prison area. The double bind of Nisei (second-generation Japanese American) citizens emerges in the protest to the "Recruiting Team":

>   Why should I volunteer!
>   I'm an American
>   I have a right to be
>   drafted.

As the persona notes in "The Trick Was," notwithstanding propaganda or disinformation, "the mind was not fooled."

Several poems return with poignancy to the theme of family. The author translates two *senryu* poems (three-line unrhymed Japanese poems) written by her father, at that time incarcerated at a camp in New Mexico. "The Night Before Good-Bye" pictures the mother performing the intimately caring task of mending her daughter's clothes. "Cincinnati," written after the actual camp experience, comes to terms with a racist assault, in which the speaker loses a lace handkerchief given her by her mother.

The remaining poems in this volume reflect the author's life from the end of the war through the 1950's and 1960's and introduce themes of personal challenge, illness, raising children, education, and activism. The section opens with another drawing by Jeni Yamada, suggesting a serene Japanese village scene of a cove surrounded by woods and mountains with small boats at anchor and a line of houses on the beach. The past is still important: The author recollects, in the twinned poems "Here" and "There," being taunted as an "outsider" by classmates in both Japan and the United States. "Freedom in Manhattan" opens particularly feminist concerns, depicting police officers' indifference to attempted rape.

Desert Run

The professional production of Yamada's second collection, published by Kitchen Table: Women of Color Press, testifies to recognition of the author and establishment of ethnic and women's cultural institutions in the twelve years after the appearance of *Camp Notes, and Other Poems*. The later volume is professionally typeset, pages are numbered, and a single thematic illustration—a calligraphy of the author's name—appears on the cover, section divisions, and end of each poem. The author's husband again contributed the calligraphy, and the book is dedicated to her three brothers.

The poems in *Desert Run* extend themes introduced in *Camp Notes, and Other Poems*, now developed in more discursive, meditative modes. The initial set, headed "Where I Stay," is a sequence completed after a camping trip in the Southern California desert. The experience was unique: Part of an experimental college course co-taught with a biologist to connect creative writing and natural science, it marked for the author a reexamination of the "desert" experience of internment. The title poem, "Desert Run," meditates on the fragility, power, and beauty of the desert ecology, the author's contrast of her present interest in the desert with the earlier rancor and hatred of the apparently barren landscape and her continuing sense of the irreparable injustice of arbitrary imprisonment. The address of this poem—the author's longest—embodies the speaker's difficult ruminations as she speaks sometimes as a meditative "I" and at other times addresses a "you" that appears in other poems and that implies the "other," the "dominant" or "mainstream" or "official" American perspective. In this section, "Lichens" and "Desert Under Glass" are also notable close observations of nature.

Titles of the three remaining sections—"Returning," "Resisting," and "Connecting"—express the author's continuing project of synthesizing the disparate elements of her life. The poems and short story in "Returning" revisit experience and heritage in Japan. The grandmother's ambivalent pride and resentment over the emigration of the author's father emerges in "American Son," which with "Obon: Festival of the Dead" recollects the months Yamada spent as a child being tutored in Japanese language and culture.

A thread of women's stories and women's plight runs through the "Resisting" section. Two poems are framed in the personas of other women. "Jeni's Complaint," presented as in the voice of the author's daughter, captures the chaos of a multigeneration, multicultural family celebration. "I Learned to Sew" tells, in the Japanese Hawaiian cadence of the author's mother-in-law, a story of immigration, hardship, endurance, and survival; this poem contains a brief retelling of the Japanese folktale of Urashima Taro. The short story "Mrs. Higashi Is Dead" elaborates the anecdote briefly referred to in the poem "Homecoming" in *Camp Notes, and Other Poems*.

The "Connecting" section of *Desert Run* contains half the poems in the volume and recapitulates the major themes: nature, human dignity, family, and roots. Several poems in this section are voiced by "fictional" personas, notably "The Club," a woman's narration of her husband's abuse. "Connecting" also refers to the links between the author's personal experience of injustice with those of others: a Holocaust survivor, a battered wife, even animals sacrificed for fur.

CAMP NOTES, AND OTHER WRITINGS

Camp Notes, and Other Writings (1998) continues a canonization process. The volume reprints both *Camp Notes, and Other Poems* and *Desert Run*. Although it contains no previously unpublished work, the poems and dedication of *Camp Notes, and Other Writings* have been professionally typeset; also, the order of the poems has been substantially altered and the illustrations eliminated. One important addition is the cover illustration. A photograph taken around 1908 of Yamada's mother as a child, it commemorates a grade-school dramatization of the legend of Urashima Taro with Yamada's mother in the title role. (In the legend, Urashima Taro is rewarded for saving a turtle by a visit to the underseas palace of the Dragon King, where he spends a few days in the company of a beautiful princess. The young man returns home to see his parents, but the few days underseas were hundreds of years in his village, and everyone he knew is gone and everything has changed.) A historical and documentary return to the author's origins, complementing anecdotal and personal connections, the photograph also serves as a return and gloss to the translation of the mother's folk saying that opens *Camp Notes, and Other Writings*.

OTHER MAJOR WORKS

EDITED TEXTS: *The Webs We Weave: Orange County Poetry Anthology*, 1986 (with others); *Sowing Ti Leaves: Writings by Multi-Cultural Women*, 1990 (with Sarie Sachie Hylkema).

MISCELLANEOUS: *Desert Run: Poems and Stories*, 1988; *Camp Notes, and Other Writings*, 1998 (includes *Camp Notes, and Other Poems* and *Desert Run*).

BIBLIOGRAPHY

Cheng, Scarlet. "Foreign All Your Life." Review of *Desert Run*, by Mitsuye Yamada, and *Seventeen Syllables*, by Hisaye Yamamoto DeSoto. *Belles Lettres* 4, no. 2 (Winter, 1989). The reviewer finds Yamada's poetry nostalgic and filled with lyricism but notes the way in which poems consistently confront pain and alienation.

Harth, Erika. *Last Witnesses: Reflections on the Wartime Internment of Japanese Americans*. New York: Palgrave/St. Martin's Press, 2001. Contains "Legacy of Silence I," by Yamada, which gives *gaman*, the virtue of endurance, as a cultural reason for why the Japanese Americans are not more vocal about their experiences, and "Legacy of Silence II," by Jeni Yamada, in which she explains how her marriage to a Jew exposed her to a group that is not as reluctant to speak about past injustices.

Patterson, Anita Haya. "Resistance to Images of the Internment: Mitsuye Yamada's *Camp Notes*." *MELUS* 23, no. 3 (Fall, 1998): 103-128. Examines poems in *Camp Notes, and Other Writings* in light of the concept of "obligation" and the problematic issue of the seeming nonresistance by Americans of Japanese ancestry to unconstitutional imprisonment in concentration camps. The essay contains photographs from newspapers and other sources to illustrate images of Japanese Americans as visualized in American popular culture during and after World War II.

Schweik, Susan. "A Needle with Mama's Voice: Mitsuye Yamada's *Camp Notes* and the American Canon of War Poetry." In *Arms and the Woman: War, Gender, and Literary Representation*, edited by Helen M. Cooper, Adrienne Auslande Munich, and Susan Merrill Squier. Chapel Hill: University of North Carolina Press, 1989. Examination of Yamada's poems in the context of war poetry by women. The author considers the silencing of Yamada's voice between the writing of the "camp notes" poems and their publication thirty years later and maintains that such silence was brought about by the unique situation of Japanese American women—especially Issei women—who were considered "enemy aliens." The discussion compares mother-daughter and father-daughter expressions in the difference between retelling of transmitted oral tales versus translation of the father's poems.

Srikanth, Rajini, and Esther Y. Inwanaga, eds. *Bold Words: A Century of Asian American Writing*. New Brunswick, N.J.: Rutgers University Press, 2001. This anthology contains several poems by Yamada. The introduction to the poetry section provides context for understanding Yamada.

Woolley, Lisa. "Racial and Ethnic Semiosis in Mitsuye Yamada's 'Mrs. Higashi Is Dead.'" *MELUS* 24, no. 4 (Winter, 1999): 77-92. Using poems from *Camp Notes, and Other Poems*, the author analyzes Yamada's short story "Mrs. Higashi Is Dead" according to a theory called ethnic semiosis. The theory postulates that Americans realize "ethnicity" through performance in instances of contact between individuals from different ethnic backgrounds; these relational moments both define and contest characteristics considered as belonging to particular ethnicities. The analysis of Yamada's story examines how it reflects "ethnic semiosis" in the different ways that a mother and daughter interpret a request from a woman of a different ethnicity.

Yamada, Mitsuye. "A *MELUS* Interview: Mitsuye Yamada." Interview by Helen Jaskoski. *MELUS* 15, no. 1 (Spring, 1988): 97-108. The poet reflects on family influences in her writing (her father founded a society devoted to the Japanese *senryu* poem) and the impact of the concentration camp experience on her life and work. Also mentioned are women's writing, human rights activism, political persecution of poets, and formal aspects of poetry.

Helen Jaskoski

YOSANO AKIKO

Born: Sakai, Japan; December 7, 1878
Died: Tokyo, Japan; May 29, 1942

PRINCIPAL POETRY
Dokusō, 1901
Midaregami, 1901 (*Tangled Hair*, 1935, 1971)
Koōgi, 1904
Koi goromo, 1905
Mai hime, 1906
Yume-no-hana, 1906
Hakkō, 1908
Tokonatsu, 1908
Sabo hime, 1911
Shundeishū, 1911
Seikainami, 1912
Pari yori, 1913
Sakura Sō, 1915
Maigoromo, 1916
Shubashū, 1916
Myōjōshū, 1918
Wakakiotome, 1918
Hinotori, 1919
Tabi-no-uta, 1921
Taiyō-to-bara, 1921
Kusa-no-yume, 1922
Nagareboshi-no-michi, 1924
Ningen ōrai, 1925
Ruriko, 1925
Kokoro no enkei, 1928
Shiro zakura, 1942
The Poetry of Yosano Akiko, 1957
Tangled Hair: Selected Tanka from "Midaregami," 1971
Akiko shukasen, 1996
River of Stars: Selected Poems of Yosano Akiko, 1996

OTHER LITERARY FORMS

Although the married name of Yosano Akiko (yoh-sah-noh ah-kee-koh) was Yosano (placed before her personal name, in the normal Japanese order), she is commonly called Akiko, which is her "elegant name." Among her many translations and modernizations, the most enduringly popular is her modern Japanese version of the greatest Japanese novel, *Genji monogatari* (early eleventh century; *The Tale of Genji*, 1881), written by Murasaki Shikibu. Akiko's version was published in 1912 and 1939. This monumental work revived general interest in Murasaki and other classical authors; it is included with Akiko's autobiography, novels, fairy tales, children's stories, essays, and original and translated poetry in the standard Japanese edition of her works, *Yosano Akiko zenshū* (1972).

Achievements

Yosano Akiko is generally admired as the greatest female poet and *tanka* poet of modern Japan, as an influential critic and educator, and as the grand embodiment of Romanticism, feminism, pacifism, and social reform in the first three decades of the twentieth century. She has been called a princess, queen, and goddess of poetry. In fact, Japanese Romanticism in the early twentieth century has been called the age of Akiko. She also influenced feminist writers internationally. She infused erotic and imaginative passion into the traditional *tanka* form (a poem of five lines containing five, seven, five, seven, and seven syllables respectively) at a time when it had grown lifelessly conventional, having lost the personal vitality of ancient times; in the same way, she revived certain classical qualities of the *Manyōshū* (mid-eighth century; *The Collections of Ten Thousand Leaves*; also as *The Ten Thousand Leaves*, 1981, and as *The Manyoshu*, 1940) and other ancient collections, while introducing stunning innovations of style. Projecting her own life and spirit into the form, she insisted that every word be charged with emotion. Such intensity is rarely transmitted through English translations, but Kenneth Rexroth's translations are fine poems in their own right as well as the most expressive renditions of Akiko's strong but subtle art.

Akiko's first book, *Tangled Hair*, was an immediate success and remains her most popular collection. It contains 399 *tanka* about her tempestuous love for the man who became her husband, Yosano Hiroshi (known as Tekkan). Her sequence of poems dramatically reveals the agonizing and sometimes ecstatic interactions among Akiko; Tekkan, his second wife (whom he was divorcing), and Yamakawa Tomiko. Tomiko, a beautiful poet beloved by both Tekkan and Akiko, was the leader of Shinshisha (the new poetry society) and edited its journal, *Myōjō* (the morning star), the chief organ of Japanese Romanticism.

Altogether, Akiko published seventy-five books, of which more than twenty are collections of original poetry. She wrote approximately seventeen thousand *tanka* as well as five hundred poems in free verse, which she devoted primarily to social issues such as pacifism and feminism. One of her outstanding poems of this kind, "Kimi shinitamō koto nakare" ("Never Let Them Kill You, Brother!"), was addressed to her own brother, who participated in the attack on Port Arthur in 1904 during the Russo-Japanese War.

Akiko disliked war, observing that it brought nothing but suffering and death. Her rhetorical question—How can the emperor, who does not fight, allow his subjects to die like beasts?—was so outrageously subversive at the time that people stoned her house. It was, in fact, the first criticism of the emperor, aside from political prose, that had been published. She was defended by Mori Ōgai and other writers, and this most famous of all Japanese antiwar poems has been revived periodically by antimilitarists. Akiko also courageously defended radicals who were executed in 1912.

Another often-quoted poem in free verse, "Yama no ugoku hi kitaru" ("The Day When Mountains Move"), was one of twelve of her poems to appear in *Seitō* (bluestocking) when that feminist journal was founded in 1916, establishing Akiko as the leading poet of women's consciousness in Japan. In 1921, with Tekkan, Akiko founded the Bunka Gakuin (culture school) for girls, where she worked as a teacher and dean, while also advancing the cause of women's education and social emancipation in essays in *Taiyō* and other journals. Between 1925 and 1931, with Tekkan and a third editor, she edited and published an authoritative fifty-volume set of Japanese classics, a work that helped to democratize the study of literature and gave her and her husband financial security. Her literary and financial success never interfered with her struggle for justice, which in her view was inseparable from literature. In "Kogan no shi" ("Death of Rosy-Cheeked Youth"), for example, she mourned the slaughter of Chinese boy-soldiers by the Japanese in Shanghai.

Some conservative critics ruthlessly denounced both Akiko and Tekkan for their scandalous lives and writings, which violated so many conventions, both literary and social. Undeterred by such attacks, Akiko struggled ceaselessly against prejudice and abuse to attain a high place among major Japanese poets of all eras.

Biography

Yosano Akiko was born in Sakai, Japan, December 7, 1878. Her father, Hō Sōshichi, owned a confectionery shop in Sakai, a suburb of Osaka. Both Akiko's father and her mother imposed traditional constraints on her, but she soon developed precocious literary enthusiasms and talents, thanks to the libraries of her great-grandparents; her great-grandfather was called the "master's master" of the town because of his knowledge of Chinese literature and his skilled composition of haiku. Akiko read all the literature that she could find from France and England, as well as from ancient and modern Japan—especially such classics as *The Manyoshu*, Sei Shōnagon's *Makura-no-sōshi* (early eleventh century; *Pillow Book*, 1928), and *The Tale of Genji* (which Akiko eventually translated from the archaic style into modern Japanese).

At age nineteen, Akiko published her first poem in a local journal, and within three years, she became prominent in Kansai-area literary activities. In 1900, Tekkan, the poet-leader of the new Romanticism, discovered Akiko's genius, began teaching her literature, brought her into his Shinshisha in Tokyo, and had her work published in the journal *Myōjō*; Akiko helped to edit the journal from 1901 until its demise in 1908, and again during its revival from 1921 to 1927. In 1901, Tekkan also edited and arranged publication for Akiko's first book, *Tangled Hair*. Her immediate success ensured her impact as a feminist and a pacifist, as well as the popularity of her many other books of poetry and prose, the royalties from which helped to finance Tekkan's three-year trip to France. Akiko was able to join him for six months in 1912, also visiting Germany, Holland, England, and Manchuria. She was inspired by European writers and artists, especially Auguste Rodin. She was also intrigued by the relative freedom of European women, and her tour strengthened her determination to change Japanese life through the power of the creative word. Her husband died in 1935, and two years later, she began working on a collection of others' poetry, *Shin Manyōshū* (1937-1939). In addition to her vigorous cultural activities, she gave birth to thirteen children, rearing eleven of them to adulthood. She died in 1942, of a stroke.

Analysis

Not even the finest translations can fully convey the subtle nuances of tone, the delicacy of imagery, and the great suggestiveness and complex allusiveness of Yosano Akiko's poetry—or indeed of most Japanese literature; English simply does not have the "feel" of Japanese, in sound, diction, grammar, or prosody. For example, there are no English equivalents for poignant sighs at the ends of many poems, or exclamations such as *ya!* and *kana!*

Fortunately, Rexroth's masterful renditions reveal Akiko's sensibility, passion, and imagination in English poems that are themselves enduring works of art. In the selections from her work included in his *One Hundred More Poems from the Japanese* (1974)—in which each English version is followed by the poem in romanized Japanese—Rexroth captures the erotic intensity that shocked Akiko's first readers. Other poems in this selection poignantly foreshadow separation—as a man fondles his lover in the autumn, as lovers gaze at each other without speaking or thinking of the future, or as a woman smells her lover's clothes in the darkness as he says good-bye. In others, the poet remembers writing a poem with her lover before separating from him, looks back on her passion like a blind man unafraid of the dark, contemplates sorrow as if it were hail or feathers falling, and watches cherry blossoms fall as stars go out in a false dawn. Such poems suggest the intricate, heartbreaking love story that comes alive, as in a novel, in hundreds of Akiko's original poems, many of them arranged to be read in a kind of narrative sequence. Most of them, however, are still unavailable in English.

Akiko also wrote many poems that calmly contemplate nature—poems in which, for example, snow and stars shine on her disheveled hair; an old boat reflects the autumn sky; ginkgo leaves scatter in the sunset; the nightingale sleeps with doubled-up jeweled claws; a white bird flying over the breakers becomes an obsessive dream; and cranes fly crying across Waka Bay to the other shore (an image traditionally suggesting Nirvana).

In his 1977 anthology, *The Burning Heart: Women Poets of Japan*, Rexroth included additional translations of Akiko's poetry. This collection illustrates how Akiko's influence has enabled women poets to speak out in a country whose literary tradition has been dominated by men. Some of Akiko's *tanka* included in the volume concern the love triangle in which Tomiko—Akiko's friend and her husband's lover—appears as a lily or queen in summer fields; Akiko's heart is envisioned as the sun drowned in darkness and rain. One of Akiko's poems in free verse, "Labor Pains," is also included; in it, the birth of her baby is likened to truth pushing outward from inwardness.

Rexroth usually renders Akiko's *tanka* in five lines, and he often approximates the normal syllable count without distorting sound or sense; his cadences, as well as his melodies and imagery, evoke the tone of the Japanese much more reliably than does H. H. Honda's rhymed quatrains, which seem more akin to A. E. Housman's verse than to Akiko's. Honda's *The Poetry of Yosano Akiko* is useful, however, for readers with even an elementary knowledge of Japanese, for the original poem is given in Japanese script as well as in romanized Japanese under each translation; Honda's selections from nineteen of Akiko's books are arranged so the reader can follow the overall development of the poet's work and her growing consciousness of aging, of her children, and of her place in society and in the universe. Although he bypasses the explicitly erotic passages that attracted Rexroth, Honda does convey something of Akiko's sensuousness in poems that show her cherishing her five-foot-long hair after a bath or rain, gazing at herself in a mirror for an hour, caressing herself, and floating like a serene lily in a pond. Some of Honda's best renditions are "The Cherries and the Moon," a snow scene in Kyoto; "Upon the Bridge of Shijo," where twilight hail falls on the brow of a dancer; "Down in the Ocean of My Mind," where fish wave jewel-colored fins; "Like Open-Eyed Fish," in which the fish are compared to the poet, who is unable to sleep; "There Side by Side," about being a slave to love; and the satirical poems "O That I Could," a defiance of Japanese conventionality, and "Naught Knowing the Blissful Touch," in which Akiko teases a youthful Buddhist monk.

Akiko's poetry is characterized by lyric, rhetorical, dramatic, and narrative strength. Each poem expresses an intense feeling of a particular moment in the poet's life, a feeling that is often too subtle, complex, or ambiguous to be fully comprehended by Westerners unfamiliar with the nuances of Japanese sensibility. The rhetorical thrust of many of Akiko's poems can readily be understood, however, especially in those poems concerned with dramatic conflicts between lovers, with the plight of women generally, and with protests against social conventions. The drama of Akiko's stormy life, concentrated in the *tanka*, reveals the intricate story of her romance, marriage, and literary career; thus, a study of her collections as unified works is usually more fruitful than formal analysis of individual poems. The narrative dimension of her work does not unfold chronologically, as a rule, but evolves cyclically from poem to poem, as she returns periodically to the dominant images and themes of her life. Indeed, the details of her life are inseparable from her poems, which require far more biographical knowledge on the part of the reader than is usually required for Western poetry. Such themes as love, jealousy, fear, loneliness, rebellion against oppression, and death are, however, universal, and may be directly and deeply appreciated by any reader.

TANGLED HAIR

The best English translations of Akiko's work, besides Rexroth's, are those by Sanford Goldstein and Shinoda Seishi. Their 1971 translation of *Tangled Hair* (which includes 165 of the 399 *tanka* in the collection, along with the Japanese originals) is supplemented by an excellent biographical introduction and useful notes based in part on the pioneering commentaries by Satake Kazuhiko. Goldstein and Shinoda's free-verse translations (usually in five lines, but without the conventional syllable count) are sensitive, vivid, and faithful to the meaning and feeling of the original, though not as intense. In "Yawahada no" ("You Have Yet to Touch"), the translators convey Akiko's seductive, sarcastic, teasing tone, as she asks an "Expounder of the Way" if he is not lonely for her blood and flesh. Satake's commentary on this poem identifies the "Expounder" as Tekkan; in Satake's reading, the poem reflects Akiko's impatience with Tekkan before he divorced his second wife and married her. Satake disagreed with Akiko's own interpretation of the poem as a generalized polemic against society, but its attack on hypocritical moralizing is surely as universal as it is personal. Akiko's rival Tomiko also figures in many poems in *Tangled Hair*. In "Sono namida" ("Tears in Your Eyes"), Akiko turns away unsympathetically from Tomiko's tears and gazes at the waning moon (always an image of sadness) reflected in a lake. The poignancy is heightened by knowledge that Akiko has just discovered that Tekkan still loves Tomiko, although he intends to marry Akiko.

Other poems evolve from customs such as the Dolls' Day celebration in "Hitotsu hako ni" ("Laying"), in which Akiko, in adolescence, sighs with some strange sexual awareness after putting the emperor and empress dolls together in a box; in an amazing image, she is afraid of her sigh being heard by peach blossoms. Sometimes Akiko identifies herself with women in ancient times, such as courtesans. In "Nakade isoge" ("Complain Not"), she tells a man to hurry on his way to other women who will undress him. Buddhism enters many of her poems in original ways. In "Wakaki ko no" ("Only the Sculptor's Fame"), she writes that she was attracted to the artist (probably Tekkan) because of his reputation when he was young, but now she is drawn to the face of the Buddha that he has carved (perhaps Tekkan's Buddha nature).

Sakanishi Shio's *Tangled Hair* (1935) includes translations not only from Akiko's first book but from eleven others as well, along with an informative introduction and a sketch of Akiko that might be compared to the photograph in Honda's volume. Sakanishi's versions are much more aesthetically subtle than Honda's and deserve close attention for their suggestively vivid imagery, natural speech rhythms, and artfully controlled syntax, all of which help to convey Akiko's tone. The sensuous and psychological implications of her hair are spun out in a variety of startling images. Her hair, for example, sweeps the strings of her koto, and its breaking strands recall the sound of the koto's strings; elsewhere, nightingales sing in a nest made from her fallen hair. Her discontent with traditional religions is manifest in her turning from the gods toward natural beauties, from the sutras to her own song, to the attractive flesh of a young monk, or to her loving husband. At other times, she prays to bodhisattvas while cherry blossoms fall on them and returns to sutras in bewilderment and despair, or sees the Buddha in the rising sun—a traditional image of Shingon Buddhism. Many of Akiko's poems included in Sakanishi's selection explicitly detail her life with Tekkan—her ambivalence about their original romance, resentful memories, ecstasies, the sadness of separation during his years in France, reunions, the agony of childbirth as three hearts beat in her body and one twin dies there, despair, children burning in volcanic eruptions, and renewed joy in rearing her children, to whom she gives her great-grandmother's prayer beads.

Thus, while the nuances of Akiko's verse remain resistant to translation, much of her artistry is accessible to English-speaking readers, who are now able to appreciate her significant contribution to the development of modern poetry in Japan.

OTHER MAJOR WORKS
LONG FICTION: *Genji monogatari*, 1912, 1939 (modern version); *Akarumi e*, 1913.
NONFICTION: *Nyonin sōzō*, 1920 (essays); *Yushosha to nare*, 1934; *Uta no tsukuriyō*, 1948; *Gekido no naka o yuku*, 1991; *Ai resei oyobi yuki*, 1993; *Travels in Manchuria and Mongolia: A Feminist Poet from Japan Encounters Prewar China*, 2001.
CHILDREN'S LITERATURE: *Watakushi no oitachi*, 1915.
MISCELLANEOUS: *Yosano Akiko zenshū*, 1972.

BIBLIOGRAPHY
Beichman, Janine. *Embracing the Firebird: Yosano Akiko and the Birth of the Female Voice in Modern Japanese Poetry*. Honolulu: University of Hawaii Press, 2002. This book-length biography of Akiko analyzes her poetry at length, especially *Tangled Hair*. Contains an appendix with the poems in the original Japanese.
Morton, Leith. *The Alien Within: Representations of the Exotic in Twentieth-Century Japanese Literature*. Honolulu: University of Hawaii Press, 2009. Contains two chapters on Akiko: One argues that Akiko adapted ideas drawn from translations of Western poetry in revitalizing the *tanka* form, the other discusses Akiko's descriptions of childbirth in her poems, a subject not previously used in poetry.
_____. "The Birth of the Modern: Yosano Akiko and Tekkan's Verse Revolution." In *Modernism in Practice: An Introduction to Postwar Japanese Poetry*. Honolulu: University of Hawaii Press, 2004. Describes how Akiko and Tekkan helped modernize Japanese poetry.

Okada, Sumie. "The Visit by Hiroshi (1873-1935) and Akiko Yosano (1878-1942) to France and England in 1912." In *Japanese Writers and the West*. New York: Palgrave Macmillan, 2003. Discusses Akiko's impressions of French women and her resulting belief that Japanese women could have a more independent existence.

Rowley, Gillian Gaye. *Yosano Akiko and "The Tale of Genji."* Ann Arbor: University of Michigan Press, 2000. A critical analysis of Akiko's modern Japanese version of *The Tale of Genji*. Includes bibliographical references and index.

Takeda, Noriko. "The Japanese Reformation of Poetic Language: Yosano Akiko's *Tangled Hair* as Avant-Garde Centrality." In *A Flowering Word: The Modernist Expression in Stéphane Mallarmé, T. S. Eliot, and Yosano Akiko*. New York: Peter Lang, 2000. This comparative study of modernism examines Akiko's most famous work for its poetic language.

Morgan Gibson and Keiko Matsui Gibson

CHECKLIST FOR EXPLICATING A POEM

I. The Initial Readings

A. Before reading the poem, the reader should:
 1. Notice its form and length.
 2. Consider the title, determining, if possible, whether it might function as an allusion, symbol, or poetic image.
 3. Notice the date of composition or publication, and identify the general era of the poet.

B. The poem should be read intuitively and emotionally and be allowed to "happen" as much as possible.

C. In order to establish the rhythmic flow, the poem should be reread. A note should be made as to where the irregular spots (if any) are located.

II. Explicating the Poem

A. *Dramatic situation.* Studying the poem line by line helps the reader discover the dramatic situation. All elements of the dramatic situation are interrelated and should be viewed as reflecting and affecting one another. The dramatic situation serves a particular function in the poem, adding realism, surrealism, or absurdity; drawing attention to certain parts of the poem; and changing to reinforce other aspects of the poem. All points should be considered. The following questions are particularly helpful to ask in determining dramatic situation:
 1. What, if any, is the narrative action in the poem?
 2. How many personae appear in the poem? What part do they take in the action?
 3. What is the relationship between characters?
 4. What is the setting (time and location) of the poem?

B. *Point of view.* An understanding of the poem's point of view is a major step toward comprehending the poet's intended meaning. The reader should ask:
 1. Who is the speaker? Is he or she addressing someone else or the reader?
 2. Is the narrator able to understand or see everything happening to him or her, or does the reader know things that the narrator does not?
 3. Is the narrator reliable?
 4. Do point of view and dramatic situation seem consistent? If not, the inconsistencies may provide clues to the poem's meaning.

C. *Images and metaphors*. Images and metaphors are often the most intricately crafted vehicles of the poem for relaying the poet's message. Realizing that the images and metaphors work in harmony with the dramatic situation and point of view will help the reader to see the poem as a whole, rather than as disassociated elements.
   1. The reader should identify the concrete images (that is, those that are formed from objects that can be touched, smelled, seen, felt, or tasted). Is the image projected by the poet consistent with the physical object?
   2. If the image is abstract, or so different from natural imagery that it cannot be associated with a real object, then what are the properties of the image?
   3. To what extent is the reader asked to form his or her own images?
   4. Is any image repeated in the poem? If so, how has it been changed? Is there a controlling image?
   5. Are any images compared to each other? Do they reinforce one another?
   6. Is there any difference between the way the reader perceives the image and the way the narrator sees it?
   7. What seems to be the narrator's or persona's attitude toward the image?

D. *Words*. Every substantial word in a poem may have more than one intended meaning, as used by the author. Because of this, the reader should look up many of these words in the dictionary and:
   1. Note all definitions that have the slightest connection with the poem.
   2. Note any changes in syntactical patterns in the poem.
   3. In particular, note those words that could possibly function as symbols or allusions, and refer to any appropriate sources for further information.

E. *Meter, rhyme, structure, and tone*. In scanning the poem, all elements of prosody should be noted by the reader. These elements are often used by a poet to manipulate the reader's emotions, and therefore they should be examined closely to arrive at the poet's specific intention.
   1. Does the basic meter follow a traditional pattern such as those found in nursery rhymes or folk songs?
   2. Are there any variations in the base meter? Such changes or substitutions are important thematically and should be identified.
   3. Are the rhyme schemes traditional or innovative, and what might their form mean to the poem?
   4. What devices has the poet used to create sound patterns (such as assonance and alliteration)?
   5. Is the stanza form a traditional or innovative one?
   6. If the poem is composed of verse paragraphs rather than stanzas, how do they affect the progression of the poem?

7. After examining the above elements, is the resultant tone of the poem casual or formal, pleasant, harsh, emotional, authoritative?

F. *Historical context.* The reader should attempt to place the poem into historical context, checking on events at the time of composition. Archaic language, expressions, images, or symbols should also be looked up.

G. *Themes and motifs.* By seeing the poem as a composite of emotion, intellect, craftsmanship, and tradition, the reader should be able to determine the themes and motifs (smaller recurring ideas) presented in the work. He or she should ask the following questions to help pinpoint these main ideas:
   1. Is the poet trying to advocate social, moral, or religious change?
   2. Does the poet seem sure of his or her position?
   3. Does the poem appeal primarily to the emotions, to the intellect, or to both?
   4. Is the poem relying on any particular devices for effect (such as imagery, allusion, paradox, hyperbole, or irony)?

BIBLIOGRAPHY

GENERAL REFERENCE SOURCES

BIOGRAPHICAL SOURCES

Colby, Vineta, ed. *World Authors, 1975-1980*. Wilson Authors Series. New York: H. W. Wilson, 1985.

_____. *World Authors, 1980-1985*. Wilson Authors Series. New York: H. W. Wilson, 1991.

_____. *World Authors, 1985-1990*. Wilson Authors Series. New York: H. W. Wilson, 1995.

Cyclopedia of World Authors. 4th Rev. ed. 5 vols. Pasadena, Calif.: Salem Press, 2003.

Dictionary of Literary Biography. 254 vols. Detroit: Gale Research, 1978- .

International Who's Who in Poetry and Poets' Encyclopaedia. Cambridge, England: International Biographical Centre, 1993.

Serafin, Steven R. *Encyclopedia of World Literature in the Twentieth Century*. 3d ed. 4 vols. Detroit: St. James Press, 1999.

Seymour-Smith, Martin, and Andrew C. Kimmens, eds. *World Authors, 1900-1950*. Wilson Authors Series. 4 vols. New York: H. W. Wilson, 1996.

Thompson, Clifford, ed. *World Authors, 1990-1995*. Wilson Authors Series. New York: H. W. Wilson, 1999.

Wakeman, John, ed. *World Authors, 1950-1970*. New York: H. W. Wilson, 1975.

_____. *World Authors, 1970-1975*. Wilson Authors Series. New York: H. W. Wilson, 1991.

Willhardt, Mark, and Alan Michael Parker, eds. *Who's Who in Twentieth Century World Poetry*. New York: Routledge, 2000.

CRITICISM

Brooks, Cleanth, and Robert Penn Warren. *Understanding Poetry*. 4th ed. Reprint. Fort Worth, Tex.: Heinle & Heinle, 2003.

Classical and Medieval Literature Criticism. Detroit: Gale Research, 1988- .

Contemporary Literary Criticism. Detroit: Gale Research, 1973- .

Day, Gary. *Literary Criticism: A New History*. Edinburgh, Scotland: Edinburgh University Press, 2008.

Draper, James P., ed. *World Literature Criticism 1500 to the Present: A Selection of Major Authors from Gale's Literary Criticism Series*. 6 vols. Detroit: Gale Research, 1992.

Habib, M. A. R. *A History of Literary Criticism: From Plato to the Present*. Malden, Mass.: Wiley-Blackwell, 2005.

Jason, Philip K., ed. *Masterplots II: Poetry Series, Revised Edition.* 8 vols. Pasadena, Calif.: Salem Press, 2002.
Lodge, David, and Nigel Wood. *Modern Criticism and Theory.* 3d ed. New York: Longman, 2008.
Magill, Frank N., ed. *Magill's Bibliography of Literary Criticism.* 4 vols. Englewood Cliffs, N.J.: Salem Press, 1979.
MLA International Bibliography. New York: Modern Language Association of America, 1922- .
Nineteenth-Century Literature Criticism. Detroit: Gale Research, 1981- .
Twentieth-Century Literary Criticism. Detroit: Gale Research, 1978- .
Vedder, Polly, ed. *World Literature Criticism Supplement: A Selection of Major Authors from Gale's Literary Criticism Series.* 2 vols. Detroit: Gale Research, 1997.
The Year's Work in Modern Language Studies. London: Oxford University Press, 1931. Annual review of scholarship.
Young, Robyn V., ed. *Poetry Criticism: Excerpts from Criticism of the Works of the Most Significant and Widely Studied Poets of World Literature.* 29 vols. Detroit: Gale Research, 1991.

DICTIONARIES, HISTORIES, AND HANDBOOKS

Carey, Gary, and Mary Ellen Snodgrass. *A Multicultural Dictionary of Literary Terms.* Jefferson, N.C.: McFarland, 1999.
Deutsch, Babette. *Poetry Handbook: A Dictionary of Terms.* 4th ed. New York: Funk & Wagnalls, 1974.
Drury, John. *The Poetry Dictionary.* Cincinnati, Ohio: Story Press, 1995.
France, Peter, ed. *The Oxford Guide to Literature in English Translation.* New York: Oxford University Press, 2000.
Henderson, Lesley, ed. *Reference Guide to World Literature.* 2d ed. 2 vols. New York: St. James Press, 1995.
Kinzie, Mary. *A Poet's Guide to Poetry.* Chicago: University of Chicago Press, 1999.
Lennard, John. *The Poetry Handbook: A Guide to Reading Poetry for Pleasure and Practical Criticism.* New York: Oxford University Press, 1996.
Matterson, Stephen, and Darryl Jones. *Studying Poetry.* New York: Oxford University Press, 2000.
Ostle, Robin, ed. *Modern Literature in the Near and Middle East, 1850-1970.* Routledge/SOAS Contemporary Politics and Culture in the Middle East Series. New York: Routledge, 1991.
Packard, William. *The Poet's Dictionary: A Handbook of Prosody and Poetic Devices.* New York: Harper & Row, 1989.
Preminger, Alex, et al., eds. *The New Princeton Encyclopedia of Poetry and Poetics.* 3d rev. ed. Princeton, N.J.: Princeton University Press, 1993.

Prusek, Jaroslav, ed. *Dictionary of Oriental Literatures*. 3 vols. Vol. 1, *East Asia*, edited by Z. Shupski; Vol. 2, *South and South-East Asia*, edited by D. Zbavitel; Vol. 3, *West Asia and North Africa*, edited by J. Becka. New York: Basic Books, 1974.

Shipley, Joseph Twadell, ed. *Dictionary of World Literary Terms, Forms, Technique, Criticism*. Rev. ed. Boston: Writer, 1970.

INDEXES OF PRIMARY WORKS

Frankovich, Nicholas, ed. *The Columbia Granger's Index to Poetry in Anthologies*. 11th ed. New York: Columbia University Press, 1997.

_____. *The Columbia Granger's Index to Poetry in Collected and Selected Works*. New York: Columbia University Press, 1997.

Guy, Patricia. *A Women's Poetry Index*. Phoenix, Ariz.: Oryx Press, 1985. Covers poetry in anthologies.

Hazen, Edith P., ed. *Columbia Granger's Index to Poetry*. 10th ed. New York: Columbia University Press, 1994.

Hoffman, Herbert H., and Rita Ludwig Hoffman, comps. *International Index to Recorded Poetry*. New York: H. W. Wilson, 1983.

Kline, Victoria. *Last Lines: An Index to the Last Lines of Poetry*. 2 vols. Vol. 1, *Last Line Index, Title Index*; Vol. 2, *Author Index, Keyword Index*. New York: Facts On File, 1991. Coverage through 1987.

Marcan, Peter. *Poetry Themes: A Bibliographical Index to Subject Anthologies and Related Criticisms in the English Language, 1875-1975*. Hamden, Conn.: Linnet Books, 1977.

Poem Finder. Great Neck, N.Y.: Roth, 2000.

POETICS, POETIC FORMS, AND GENRES

Attridge, Derek. *Poetic Rhythm: An Introduction*. New York: Cambridge University Press, 1995.

Brogan, T. V. F. *Verseform: A Comparative Bibliography*. Baltimore: Johns Hopkins University Press, 1989.

Fussell, Paul. *Poetic Meter and Poetic Form*. Rev. ed. New York: McGraw-Hill, 1979.

Jackson, Guida M. *Traditional Epics: A Literary Companion*. New York: Oxford University Press, 1995.

Hollander, John. *Rhyme's Reason*. 3d ed. New Haven: Yale University Press, 2001.

Padgett, Ron, ed. *The Teachers and Writers Handbook of Poetic Forms*. 2d ed. New York: Teachers & Writers Collaborative, 2000.

Pinsky, Robert. *The Sounds of Poetry: A Brief Guide*. New York: Farrar, Straus and Giroux, 1998.

Preminger, Alex, and T. V. F. Brogan, ed. *New Princeton Encyclopedia of Poetry and Poetics*. 3d ed. Princeton, N.J.: Princeton University Press, 1993.

Turco, Lewis. *The New Book of Forms: A Handbook of Poetics*. Hanover: University Press of New England, 1986.

Williams, Miller. *Patterns of Poetry: An Encyclopedia of Forms*. Baton Rouge: Louisiana State University Press, 1986.

Wimsatt, William K., ed. *Versification: Major Language Types: Sixteen Essays*. New York: Modern Language Association, 1972.

POSTCOLONIAL POETRY

Benson, Eugene, and L. W. Connolly. *Encyclopedia of Post-Colonial Literatures in English*. 2 vols. London: Routledge, 1994.

Bery, Ashok. *Cultural Translation and Postcolonial Poetry*. New York: Palgrave Macmillan, 2007.

Lawson, Alan, et al. *Post-Colonial Literatures in English: General, Theoretical, and Comparative, 1970-1993*. A Reference Publication in Literature. New York: G. K. Hall, 1997.

Mohanram, Radhika, and Gita Rajan, eds. *English Postcoloniality: Literatures from Around the World*. Contributions to the Study of World Literature 66. Westport, Conn.: Greenwood Press, 1996.

Parekh, Pushpa Naidu, and Siga Fatima Jagne. *Postcolonial African Writers: A Bio-Bibliographical Critical Sourcebook*. Westport, Conn.: Greenwood Press, 1998.

Patke, Rajeev S. *Postcolonial Poetry in English*. New York: Oxford University Press, 2006.

Ramazani, Jahan. *The Hybrid Muse: Postcolonial Poetry in English*. Chicago: University of Chicago Press, 2001.

Williams, Mark. *Post-Colonial Literatures in English: Southeast Asia, New Zealand, and the Pacific, 1970-1992*. Reference Publications in Literature. New York: G. K. Hall, 1996.

HISTORY OF WORLD POETRY

ANCIENT TO EIGHTEENTH CENTURY

Carter, Steven D., ed. *Medieval Japanese Writers*. Dictionary of Literary Biography 203. Detroit: Gale Group, 1999.

_____. *Waiting for the Wind: Thirty-six Poets of Japan's Late Medieval Age*. Reprint. New York: Columbia University Press, 1994.

Husain, Iqbal. *The Early Persian Poets of India (A.H. 421-670)*. Patna: Patna University, 1937.

Jackson, A. V. Williams. *Early Persian Poetry, from the Beginnings Down to the Time of Firdausi*. New York: Macmillan, 1920.

Lienhard, Siegfried. *A History of Classical Poetry: Sanskrit, Pali, Prakrit.* Wiesbaden: Harrassowitz, 1984.

Meisami, Julie Scott. *Medieval Persian Court Poetry.* Princeton, N.J.: Princeton University Press, 1987.

Ooka, Makoto. *The Poetry and Poetics of Ancient Japan.* Translated by Thomas Fitzsimmons. Santa Fe, N.Mex.: Katydid Books, 1997.

Owen, Stephen. *The Making of Early Chinese Classical Poetry.* Cambridge, Mass.: Harvard University Asia Center, 2006.

Shirane, Haruo. *Traditional Japanese Literature: An Anthology, Beginnings to 1600.* Rev. ed. Translated by Sonja Arntzen et al. New York: Columbia University Press, 2007.

_____, ed. *Early Modern Japanese Literature: An Anthology, 1600-1900.* Translated by James Brandon et al. New York: Columbia University Press, 2002.

Thông, Huynh Sanh, ed. and trans. *An Anthology of Vietnamese Poems: From the Eleventh Through the Twentieth Centuries.* New Haven, Conn.: Yale University Press, 1996.

NINETEENTH CENTURY

De Souza, Eunice, ed. *Early Indian Poetry in English: An Anthology, 1829-1947.* New Delhi: Oxford University Press, 2005.

Shirane, Haruo, ed. *Early Modern Japanese Literature: An Anthology, 1600-1900.* Translated by James Brandon et al. New York: Columbia University Press, 2002.

Singh, Amritjit, Rajiav Verma, and Irene M. Johsi. *Indian Literature in English, 1827-1979: A Guide to Information Sources.* American Literature, English Literature, and World Literatures in English: An Information Guide Series 36. Detroit: Gale Research, 1981.

Thông, Huynh Sanh, ed. and trans. *An Anthology of Vietnamese Poems: From the Eleventh Through the Twentieth Centuries.* New Haven, Conn.: Yale University Press, 1996.

TWENTIETH CENTURY AND CONTEMPORARY

De Souza, Eunice, ed. *Early Indian Poetry in English: An Anthology, 1829-1947.* New Delhi: Oxford University Press, 2005.

Haft, Lloyd, ed. *The Poem.* Vol. 3 in *A Selective Guide to Chinese Literature, 1900-1949.* New York: E. J. Brill, 1989.

Kim, Jaihiun. *Traditional Korean Verse Since the 1900's.* Seoul, Korea: Hanshin, 1991.

Lin, Julia C., trans. and ed. *Twentieth-Century Chinese Women's Poetry: An Anthology.* Armonk, N.Y.: M. E. Sharpe, 2009.

Morton, Leith. *Modernism in Practice: An Introduction to Postwar Japanese Poetry.* Honolulu: University of Hawaii Press, 2004.

Natarajan, Nalini, ed. *Handbook of Twentieth-Century Literatures of India*. Westport, Conn.: Greenwood Press, 1996.

Singh, Amritjit, Rajiav Verma, and Irene M. Johsi. *Indian Literature in English, 1827-1979: A Guide to Information Sources*. American Literature, English Literature, and World Literatures in English: An Information Guide Series 36. Detroit: Gale Research, 1981.

Thông, Huynh Sanh, ed. and trans. *An Anthology of Vietnamese Poems: From the Eleventh Through the Twentieth Centuries*. New Haven, Conn.: Yale University Press, 1996.

ASIAN POETRY

CHINA

Barnstone, Tony, and Chou Ping, eds. *The Anchor Book of Chinese Poetry: From Ancient to Contemporary, The Full Three-thousand Year Tradition*. New York: Anchor Books, 2004.

Cai, Zong-qi, ed. *How to Read Chinese Poetry: A Guided Anthology*. Bilingual ed. New York: Columbia University Press, 2007.

Chang, Kang-i Sun, and Haun Saussy, eds. *Women Writers of Traditional China: An Anthology of Poetry and Criticism*. Stanford, Calif.: Stanford University Press, c. 1999.

Haft, Lloyd, ed. *The Poem*. Vol. 3 in *A Selective Guide to Chinese Literature, 1900-1949*. New York: E. J. Brill, 1989.

Lin, Julia C., trans. and ed. *Twentieth-Century Chinese Women's Poetry: An Anthology*. Armonk, N.Y.: M. E. Sharpe, 2009.

Lynn, Richard John. *Guide to Chinese Poetry and Drama*. 2d ed. Boston, Mass.: G. K. Hall, 1984.

Lupke, Christopher, ed. *New Perspectives on Contemporary Chinese Poetry*. New York: Palgrave Macmillan, 2008.

Nienhauser, William, Jr., ed. *The Indiana Companion to Traditional Chinese Literature*. Bloomington: Indiana University Press, 1986.

Owen, Stephen. *The Making of Early Chinese Classical Poetry*. Cambridge, Mass.: Harvard University Asia Center, 2006.

Wu-chi, Liu. *An Introduction to Chinese Literature*. Bloomington: Indiana University Press, 1966.

Yip, Wai-lim, ed. and trans. *Chinese Poetry: An Anthology of Major Modes and Genres*. 2d ed. Durham, N.C.: Duke University Press, 1997.

India and South Asia

Agrawal, K. A. *Toru Dutt: The Pioneer Spirit of Indian English Poetry—A Critical Study*. New Delhi: Atlantic, 2009.

De Souza, Eunice, ed. *Early Indian Poetry in English: An Anthology, 1829-1947*. New Delhi: Oxford University Press, 2005.

Dimock, Edward C., Jr., et al. *The Literatures of India: An Introduction*. Chicago: University of Chicago Press, 1974.

Gerow, Edwin. *Indian Poetics*. Wiesbaden: Harrassowitz, 1977.

King, Bruce. *Modern Indian Poetry in English*. Rev. ed. New Delhi: Oxford University Press, 2001.

Lienhard, Siegfried. *A History of Classical Poetry: Sanskrit, Pali, Prakrit*. Wiesbaden: Harrassowitz, 1984.

Mahmud, Shabana. *Urdu Language and Literature: A Bibliography of Sources in European Languages*. New York: Mansell, 1992.

Naik, M. K. *A History of Indian English Literature*. New Delhi: Sahitya Akademi, 1989.

Natarajan, Nalini, ed. *Handbook of Twentieth-Century Literatures of India*. Westport, Conn.: Greenwood Press, 1996.

Rajan, P. K., and Swapna Daniel, eds. *Indian Poetics and Modern Texts: Essays in Criticism*. New Delhi: S. Chand, 1998.

Rama, Atma. *Indian Poetry and Fiction in English*. New Delhi: Bahri Publications, 1991.

Sadiq, Mohammed. *A History of Urdu Literature*. Delhi: Oxford, 1984.

Saran, Saraswiti. *The Development of Urdu Poetry*. New Delhi: Discovery Publishing House, 1990.

Singh, Amritjit, Rajiav Verma, and Irene M. Johsi. *Indian Literature in English, 1827-1979: A Guide to Information Sources*. American Literature, English Literature, and World Literatures in English: An Information Guide Series 36. Detroit: Gale Research, 1981.

Singh, Kanwar Dinesh. *Contemporary Indian English Poetry: Comparing Male and Female Voices*. New Delhi: Atlantic, 2008.

Sinha, R. P. N. *Indo-Anglican Poetry: Its Birth and Growth*. New Delhi: Reliance Publishing House, 1987.

Thayil, Jeet, ed. *The Bloodaxe Book of Contemporary Indian Poets*. Cambridge, Mass.: Bloodaxe, 2008.

Japan

Bownas, Geoffrey, and Anthony Thwaite, eds. and trans. *The Penguin Book of Japanese Verse*. Rev. ed. London: Penguin Books, 2009.

Brower, Robert, and Earl Miner. *Japanese Court Poetry*. 1961. Reprint. Stanford, Calif.: Stanford University Press, 1988.

Carter, Steven D., ed. *Medieval Japanese Writers*. Dictionary of Literary Biography 203. Detroit: Gale Group, 1999.

_____. *Waiting for the Wind: Thirty-six Poets of Japan's Late Medieval Age*. Reprint. New York: Columbia University Press, 1994.

_____, comp. and trans. *Traditional Japanese Poetry: An Anthology*. Stanford, Calif.: Stanford University Press, 1991.

Hisamatsu, Sen'ichi, ed. *Biographical Dictionary of Japanese Literature*. New York: Harper & Row, 1976.

Miner, Earl Roy, Hiroko Odagiri, and Robert E. Morrell. *The Princeton Companion to Classical Japanese Literature*. Princeton, N.J.: Princeton University Press, 1985.

Morton, Leith. *Modernism in Practice: An Introduction to Postwar Japanese Poetry*. Honolulu: University of Hawaii Press, 2004.

Ooka, Makoto. *The Poetry and Poetics of Ancient Japan*. Translated by Thomas Fitzsimmons. Santa Fe, N.Mex.: Katydid Books, 1997.

Rimer, J. Thomas. *A Reader's Guide to Japanese Literature*. 2d ed. New York: Kodansha International, 1999.

Rimer, J. Thomas, and Van C. Gessel, eds. *The Columbia Anthology of Modern Japanese Literature*. 2 vols. New York: Columbia University Press, 2005-2007.

Rimer, J. Thomas, and Robert E. Morrell. *Guide to Japanese Poetry*. Asian Literature Bibliography Series. 2d ed. Boston, Mass.: G. K. Hall, 1984.

Sato, Hiroaki, ed. and trans. *Japanese Women Poets: An Anthology*. Armonk, N.Y.: M. E. Sharpe, 2007.

Shirane, Haruo. *Traditional Japanese Literature: An Anthology, Beginnings to 1600*. Rev. ed. Translated by Sonja Arntzen et al. New York: Columbia University Press, 2007.

_____, ed. *Early Modern Japanese Literature: An Anthology, 1600-1900*. Translated by James Brandon et al. New York: Columbia University Press, 2002.

Korea

Kim, Jaihiun. *Modern Korean Poetry*. Fremont, Calif.: Asian Humanities Press, 1994.

_____. *Traditional Korean Verse Since the 1900's*. Seoul, Korea: Hanshin, 1991.

Korean Poetry: An Anthology with Critical Essays. Seoul: Korean Culture & Arts Foundation, 1984.

Lee, Young-gul. *The Classical Poetry of Korea*. Seoul, Korea: Korean Culture and Arts Foundation, 1981.

McCann, David R. *Form and Freedom in Korean Poetry*. New York: Brill, 1988.

Who's Who in Korean Literature. Korean Culture & Arts Foundation. Elizabeth, N.J.: Hollym, 1996.

TIBET

Cabezon, Jose I., and Roger R. Jackson. *Tibetan Literature: Studies in Genre*. Ithaca, N.Y.: Snow Lion, 1995.

Hartley, Lauran R., and Patricia Schiaffini-Vedani, eds. *Modern Tibetan Literature and Social Change*. Durham, N.C.: Duke University Press, 2008.

Jinpa, Thupten, and Jas Elsner. *Songs of Spiritual Experience: Tibetan Buddhist Poems of Insight and Awakening*. Boston: Shambhala, 2000.

VIETNAM

Thông, Huynh Sanh, ed. and trans. *An Anthology of Vietnamese Poems: From the Eleventh Through the Twentieth Centuries*. New Haven, Conn.: Yale University Press, 1996.

Vietnamese Poetry and History. In *Crossroads: An Interdisciplinary Journal of Southeast Asian Studies* 7, no. 2. DeKalb, Ill.: Center for Southeast Asian Studies, Northern Illinois University, 1992.

GUIDE TO ONLINE RESOURCES

Web Sites

The following sites were visited by the editors of Salem Press in 2010. Because URLs frequently change, the accuracy of these addresses cannot be guaranteed; however, long-standing sites, such as those of colleges and universities, national organizations, and government agencies, generally maintain links when their sites are moved.

A Celebration of Women Writers
http://digital.library.upenn.edu/women

This site is an extensive compendium on the contributions of women writers throughout history. The "Local Editions by Authors" and "Local Editions by Category" pages include access to electronic texts of the works of numerous writers. Users can also access biographical and bibliographical information by browsing lists arranged by writers' names, countries of origin, ethnicities, and the centuries in which they lived.

The Modern Word: Authors of the Libyrinth
http://www.themodernword.com/authors.html

The Modern Word site, although somewhat haphazard in its organization, provides a great deal of critical information about writers. The "Authors of the Libyrinth" page is very useful, linking author names to essays about them and other resources. The section of the page headed "The Scriptorium" presents "an index of pages featuring writers who have pushed the edges of their medium, combining literary talent with a sense of experimentation to produce some remarkable works of modern literature."

LitWeb
http://litweb.net

LitWeb provides biographies of hundreds of world authors throughout history that can be accessed through an alphabetical listing. The pages about each writer contain a list of his or her works, suggestions for further reading, and illustrations. The site also offers information about past and present winners of major literary prizes.

Poetry in Translation
http://poetryintranslation.com

This independent resource provides modern translations of classic texts by famous poets and also provides original poetry and critical works. Visitors can choose from several languages, including English, Spanish, Chinese, Russian, Italian, and Greek. Original text available as well. Also includes links to further literary resources.

Poetry International Web
http://international.poetryinternationalweb.org

Poetry International Web features information on poets from countries such as Indonesia, Zimbabwe, Iceland, India, Slovenia, Morocco, Albania, Afghanistan, Russia, and Brazil. The site offers news, essays, interviews and discussion, and hundreds of poems, both in their original languages and in English translation.

Poet's Corner
http://theotherpages.org/poems

The Poet's Corner, one of the oldest text resources on the Web, provides access to about seven thousand works of poetry by several hundred different poets from around the world. Indexes are arranged and searchable by title, name of poet, or subject. The site also offers its own resources, including Faces of the Poets—a gallery of portraits—and Lives of the Poets—a growing collection of biographies.

Voices from the Gaps
http://voices.cla.umn.edu/

Voices from the Gaps is a site of the English Department at the University of Minnesota, dedicated to providing resources on the study of women artists of color, including writers. The site features a comprehensive index searchable by name, and provides biographical information on each writer or artist and other resources for further study.

ELECTRONIC DATABASES

Electronic databases usually do not have their own URLs. Instead, public, college, and university libraries subscribe to these databases, provide links to them on their Web sites, and make them available to library card holders or other specified patrons. Readers can visit library Web sites or ask reference librarians to check on availability.

Literary Reference Center

EBSCO's Literary Reference Center (LRC) is a comprehensive full-text database designed primarily to help high school and undergraduate students in English and the humanities with homework and research assignments about literature. The database contains massive amounts of information from reference works, books, literary journals, and other materials, including more than 31,000 plot summaries, synopses, and overviews of literary works; almost 100,000 essays and articles of literary criticism; about 140,000 author biographies; more than 605,000 book reviews; and more than 5,200 author interviews. It also contains the entire contents of Salem Press's MagillOnLiterature Plus. Users can retrieve information by browsing a list of authors' names or titles of literary works; they can also use an advanced search engine to access information by numerous categories, including author name, gender, cultural identity, national identity, and the years in which he or she lived, or by literary title, character, locale, genre, and publication date. The Literary Reference Center also features a literary-historical time line, an encyclopedia of literature, and a glossary of literary terms.

MagillOnLiterature Plus

MagillOnLiterature Plus is a comprehensive, integrated literature database produced by Salem Press and available on the EBSCOhost platform. The database contains the full text of essays in Salem's many literature-related reference works, including *Masterplots*, *Cyclopedia of World Authors*, *Cyclopedia of Literary Characters*, *Cyclopedia of Literary Places*, *Critical Survey of Poetry*, *Critical Survey of Long Fiction*, *Critical Survey of Short Fiction*, *World Philosophers and Their Works*, *Magill's Literary Annual*, and *Magill's Book Reviews*. Among its contents are articles on more than 35,000 literary works and more than 8,500 poets, writers, dramatists, essayists, and philosophers; more than 1,000 images; and a glossary of more than 1,300 literary terms. The biographical essays include lists of authors' works and secondary bibliographies, and hundreds of overview essays examine and discuss literary genres, time periods, and national literatures.

Rebecca Kuzins; updated by Desiree Dreeuws

GEOGRAPHICAL INDEX

AFRICA
    Postcolonial Poetry, 117
AUSTRALIA
    Postcolonial Poetry, 117

CANADA
    Postcolonial Poetry, 117
CHINA
    Chinese Poetry, 1
    Du Fu, 36
    Li Bo, 43
    Li Qingzhao, 53
    Meng Haoran, 61
    Ruan Ji, 66
    Tao Qian, 74
    Tibetan Poetry, 25
    Wang Wei, 83
    Xie Lingyun, 93

INDIA
    Ali, Agha Shahid, 129
    Indian English Poetry, 100
    Postcolonial Poetry, 117
    Seth, Vikram, 134
    Tagore, Rabindranath, 140
    Vālmīki, 152

JAPAN
    Issa, 189
    Japanese Poetry Since 1800, 178
    Japanese Poetry to 1800, 157
    Matsuo Bashō, 199
    Miyazawa, Kenji, 207
    Yamada, Mitsuye, 214
    Yosano Akiko, 221

TIBET
    Tibetan Poetry, 25

UNITED STATES
    Ali, Agha Shahid, 129
    Yamada, Mitsuye, 214

WEST INDIES
    Postcolonial Poetry, 117

CATEGORY INDEX

ASIAN AMERICAN CULTURE
    Ali, Agha Shahid, 129
    Yamada, Mitsuye, 214

CHILDREN'S/YOUNG ADULT POETRY
    Miyazawa, Kenji, 207

CLASSICAL PERIOD, CHINA
    Du Fu, 36
    Li Bo, 43
    Li Qingzhao, 53
    Meng Haoran, 61
    Ruan Ji, 66
    Tao Qian, 74
    Wang Wei, 83
    Xie Lingyun, 93

ELEGIES
    Ali, Agha Shahid, 129
    Miyazawa Kenji, 207

EPICS
    Miyazawa, Kenji, 207
    Seth, Vikram, 134
    Vālmīki, 152

FEMINIST POETS
    Yamada, Mitsuye, 214
    Yosano Akiko, 221

GHAZALS
    Ali, Agha Shahid, 129

HAIKU
    Issa, 189
    Matsuo Bashō, 199

LOVE POETRY
    Li Qingzhao, 53
    Yosano Akiko, 221

LYRIC POETRY
    Du Fu, 36
    Li Bo, 43
    Li Qingzhao, 53
    Xie Lingyun, 93

NATURE POETRY
    Du Fu, 36
    Matsuo Bashō, 199
    Meng Haoran, 61
    Tagore, Rabindranath, 140
    Tao Qian, 74
    Wang Wei, 83
    Xie Lingyun, 93

NEW FORMALISM
    Seth, Vikram, 134

OCCASIONAL VERSE
    Du Fu, 36

POLITICAL POETS
    Du Fu, 36
    Li Qingzhao, 53
    Ruan Ji, 66
    Yamada, Mitsuye, 214
    Yosano Akiko, 221

POSTMODERNISM
    Seth, Vikram, 134

PROSE POETRY
    Tagore, Rabindranath, 140

RELIGIOUS POETRY
    Miyazawa, Kenji, 207
    Ruan Ji, 66
    Tagore, Rabindranath, 140
    Vālmīki, 152
    Wang Wei, 83

ROMANTICISM
Yosano Akiko, 221

SONGS
Tagore, Rabindranath, 140
Xie Lingyun, 93

SONNETS
Seth, Vikram, 134

WOMEN POETS
Li Qingzhao, 53
Yamada, Mitsuye, 214
Yosano Akiko, 221

SUBJECT INDEX

"Aboriginal Charter of Rights" (Walker), 122
Aboriginal poetry, Australia, 122
African poetry, 126
Ali, Agha Shahid, 113, 129-133
    Call Me Ishmael Tonight, 132
    The Country Without a Post Office, 132
    The Half-Inch Himalayas, 131
    A Nostalgist's Map of America, 132
All You Who Sleep Tonight (Seth), 137
Ariwara no Narihira, 163
Atwood, Margaret, 121
Australian poetry, 118
Avant-garde poets, Japan, 181

Bai hua (Chinese vernacular), 3
Bashō. See Matsuo Bashō
Beastly Tales from Here and There (Seth), 138
Bei Dao, 21
Bhatt, Sujata, 114
Biography (Milarepa), 32
Bo Juyi, 13
Book of Songs, The (anthology), 4

Cai Yan, 8
Call Me Ishmael Tonight (Ali), 132
Camp Notes, and Other Writings (Yamada), 218
Campbell, Roy, 119
Canadian poetry, 118
Cao Zhi, 9
Chattopadhyaya, Harindranath, 109
Chinese poetry, 1-24
Chōka, 159
Chu ci (poetic form), 7
Classical period, China, 3

"Climbing the Peak of Mount Taibo" (Li Bo), 47
Colonialism, British, 117
Commonwealth literature, defined, 117
Country Without a Post Office, The (Ali), 132

Dalai Lama, Sixth, 33
Danrin school, 173
Daruwalla, Keki N., 114
Das, Kamala, 112, 125
"Deer Park" (Wang Wei), 87
Derozio, Henry, 103
Desert Run (Yamada), 217
De Souza, Goan Eunice, 112
"Doves, The" (Ruan Ji), 70
"Drinking Alone in the Moonlight" (Li Bo), 49
"Drought and Zazen" (Miyazawa), 211
Du Fu, 12, 36-42
    "Moonlit Night," 40
    "The River by Our Village," 41
    "The Winding River," 41
Du Mu, 13
Dutt, Michael Madhusudan, 104
Dutt, Toru, 105

Elegies for Toshiko (Miyazawa), 210
Engo (poetic technique), 165
Epics, Tibet, 30
Ezekiel, Nissim, 111, 125

Feminist poets, India, 112
"Finding Fault with My Sons" (Tao Qian), 77
Flight of Swans, A (Tagore), 147
Folk poetry; China, 4; India, 107; Tibet, 31
Fu (poetic form), 8

Fu, Du. *See* Du Fu
Fujiwara Teika, 167
Furtado, Joseph, 110

"Gazing at Yellow Crane Mountain" (Li Bo), 49
Ge-sar epic, 30
Ghose, Sri Aurobindo, 106
Ghose, Kasiprasad, 104
Ghose, Manmohan, 108
Gitanjali Song Offerings (Tagore), 146
Glu (poetic form), 31
Golden age, China, 10
Golden Gate, The (Seth), 137
Gushi (poetic form), 9

Hagiwara Sakutarō, 181
Haikai no renga (poetic form), 172
Haiku (poetic form), 169, 178
Half-Inch Himalayas, The (Ali), 131
Han Yu, 13
Haoran, Meng. *See* Meng Haoran
Hara Shirō, 186
Hokku (poetic form), 174
Honkadori (poetic technique), 166
Hope, A. D., 120
Howling at the Moon (Hagiwara), 181
Hsieh K'ang-lo. *See* Xie Lingyun
Humble Administrator's Garden, The (Seth), 136
Hundred-Thousand Songs (Milarepa), 32

Ihara Saikaku, 173
Impermanence, 164
"In the City" (Matsuo Bashō), 204
"In the Mountains" (Li Bo), 48
Indian poetry, English language, 100-116, 125
Indigenous poetry
    Canada, 123
    Commonwealth, 121

Ishikawa Takuboku, 180
Issa, 189-198
Iyengar, K. R. Srinivasa, 103

Japanese poetry
    origins to nineteenth century, 157-177
    nineteenth century to present, 178-188
Ji, Ruan. *See* Ruan Ji
Jigme, Hortsang, 34
Jokotoba (poetic technique), 165
Jones, Sir William, 100
Juan Chi. *See* Ruan Ji
Jueju (poetic form), 11

Ka-bzhas (poetic form), 33
Kaichōon, 179
Kakekotoba (poetic technique), 164
Kakinomoto Hitomaro, 159
Kanshi (poetic form), 181
Ki no Tsurayuki, 162
Kobayashi Yatarō. *See* Issa
Kokinshū (anthology), 162

"Lady Xi" (Wang Wei), 86
Lde'u, 29
Li Bo, 11, 43-52
    "Climbing the Peak of Mount Taibo," 47
    "Drinking Alone in the Moonlight," 49
    "Gazing at Yellow Crane Mountain," 49
    "In the Mountains," 48
    "The Road to Shu Is Hard," 50
    "Wandering About Mount Tai," 47
Li Ch'ing-chao. *See* Li Qingzhao
Li Pai. *See* Li Bo
Li Po. *See* Li Bo
Li Qingzhao, 15, 53-60
    "To the Tune," 57
    "Tune," 56
Li Sao, The (Qu Yuan), 7
Li Shangyin, 13

Li Taibo. *See* Li Bo
Li T'ai-pai. *See* Li Bo
Li T'ai-po. *See* Li Bo
"Love Songs of the Sixth Dalai Lama," 33
Lu You, 15
Lushi (poetic form), 11
Lyric poetry, Indian, 110

Makurakotoba (poetic technique), 160
Manyoshu, The (anthology), 157
Maoist poetry, 20
Maori poets, 123
Mappings (Seth), 136
Masaoka Shiki, 180
Matsunaga Teitoku, 172
Matsuo Bashō, 173, 199-206
    "In the City," 204
    The Narrow Road to the Deep North, 205
Meng Hao-jan (Meng Haoran), 63
Meng Haoran, 61-65
    Meng Hao-jan, 63
    The Mountain Poems of Meng Hao-jan, 64
Mgur (poetic form), 31
Milarepa, 32
Minjian poets, 22
Misty poetry, 21
Miyazawa Kenji, 182, 207-213
    "Drought and Zazen," 211
    Elegies for Toshiko, 210
    "Shigoto," 211
    Spring and Asura, 209
Modernism, 110
"Monkey" (Ruan Ji), 70
"Moonlit Night" (Du Fu), 40
Moraes, Dom, 113
Mori Ōgai, 179
Mountain Poems of Meng Hao-jan, The (Meng Haoran), 64
Murray, Les A., 120

Naidu, Sarojini, 107, 125
Narogin, Mudrooroo, 123
Narrow Road to the Deep North, The (Matsuo Bashō), 205
Natsume Sōseki, 181
New Zealand poetry, 121
Nishiwaki Junsaburō, 181
Nishiyama Sōin, 173
Nostalgist's Map of America, A (Ali), 132

Oaten, Edward Farley, 102
Okigbo, Christopher, 127
Ono no Komachi, 163
Ōtomo Tabito, 161
Ōtomo Yakamochi, 161
Ouyang Xiu, 14

Padmasambhava, 27
Patraput (Tagore), 148
"Peach Blossom Spring" (Tao Qian), 80
Pian wen (poetic form), 10
Political poetry
    China, 5
    postwar Japan, 183
Pondicherry school, 110
Postcolonial poetry, 117-128
Purdy, Al, 121

Qu Yuan, 7

Ramayana, The (Vālmīki), 154
Renga (poetic form), 169
"River by Our Village, The" (Du Fu), 41
"Road to Shu Is Hard, The" (Li Bo), 50
Ruan Ji, 9, 66-73
    "The Doves," 70
    "Monkey," 70

Saitō Mokichi, 180
Sanqu (poetic form), 17
Sa-skya Pandita, 31

Scar literature (China), 20
Seth, Vikram, 114, 134-139
    All You Who Sleep Tonight, 137
    Beastly Tales from Here and There, 138
    The Golden Gate, 137
    The Humble Administrator's Garden, 136
    Mappings, 136
Settler poets, 118
Sgrung, 29
Shi (poetic form), 9
"Shigoto" (Miyazawa), 211
Shinkokinshū (anthology), 166
Shintaisho (anthology), 179
Shiraishi Kazuko, 186
Shōfū, 174
Sima Xiangru, 8
Sishui (Wen Yidou), 19
Social Realism, China, 20
Sōgi, 170
Song ci (poetic form), 8
South African poetry, 122
Soyinka, Wole, 126
Spring and Asura (Miyazawa), 209
Su Dongpo, 14
Subhasitaratnanidhi (Sa-skya Pandita), 31
Suhrawardy, Shahid, 110
Supreme Yoga, The (Vālmīki), 155

Tagore, Rabindranath, 108, 140-151
    A Flight of Swans, 147
    Gitanjali Song Offerings, 146
    Patraput, 148
Takamura Kōtarō, 182
Tangled Hair (Yosano Akiko), 226
Tanikawa Shuntarō, 184
Tanka, 159
Tantric songs, 31
Tao Qian, 10, 74-82
    "Finding Fault with My Sons," 77
    "Peach Blossom Spring," 80

Thakur, Rabindranath. *See* Tagore, Rabindranath
Tibetan Book of the Dead, The (Padmasambhava), 27
Tibetan poetry, 25-35
"To the Tune" (Li Qingzhao), 57
Translation
    Indian English poetry, 105
Tu Fu. *See* Du Fu
"Tune" (Li Qingzhao), 56

Ueda Bin, 179

Vālmīki, 152-156
    The Ramayana, 154
    The Supreme Yoga, 155
"Visiting the Temple of Gathered Fragrance" (Wang Wei), 88

Walcott, Derek, 124
Walker, Kath, 122
"Wandering About Mount Tai" (Li Bo), 47
Wang Anshi, 14
Wang Wei, 10, 13, 83-92
    "Deer Park," 87
    "Lady Xi," 86
    "Visiting the Temple of Gathered Fragrance," 88
Wen Yiduo, 19
Wenli (classical Chinese writing), 3
Wenyan (literary Chinese writing), 3
"Winding River, The" (Du Fu), 41
Women poets, India, 112
Wright, Judith, 119

Xie Lingyun, 93-99
Xin yuefu (poetic form), 13

Yamada, Mitsuye, 214-220
    Camp Notes, and Other Writings, 218
    Desert Run, 217

Yamanoe Okura, 161
Yonghuai shi (poetic form), 9
Yosano Akiko, 180, 221-228
   Tangled Hair, 226

Yuan Zhen, 13
Yuefu (poetic form), 8
Yūgen, 167